SUCCESS WITH

Windows® 95

by KRIS JAMSA Ph.D.
and NABA BARKAKATI Ph.D.

JAMSA PRESS
...a computer user's best friend®

SUCCESS WITH WINDOWS® 95

Published by
Jamsa Press
2975 S. Rainbow, Suite I
Las Vegas, NV 89102
U.S.A.

For information about the translation or distribution of any Jamsa Press book, please write to Jamsa Press at the address listed above.

Success with Windows 95

Copyright © 1996 by Jamsa Press. All rights reserved. Except as permitted under the Copyright Act of 1976, no part of this publication may be reproduced or distributed in any format or by any means, or stored in a database or retrieval system, without the prior written permission of Jamsa Press.

Printed in the United States of America.
98765432

ISBN 1-884133-16-9

Publisher	*Technical Advisor*	*Cover Design*
Debbie Jamsa	Phil Schmauder	Marianne Helm
Publisher's Assistant	*Cover Photograph*	*Proofers*
Janet Lawrie	O'Gara/Bissell	Rosemary Pasco
		Jeanne Smith
		Tammy Funk
Indexer	*Copy Editors*	
Linda Linssen	Tammy Funk	
	Heather Grigg	
	Rosemary Pasco	

This book identifies product names and services known to be trademarks or registered trademarks of their respective companies. They are used throughout this book in an editorial fashion only. In addition, terms suspected of being trademarks or service marks have been appropriately capitalized. Jamsa Press cannot attest to the accuracy of this information. Use of a term in this book should not be regarded as affecting the validity of any trademark or service mark.

The information and material contained in this book are provided "as is," without warranty of any kind, express or implied, including without limitation any warranty concerning the accuracy, adequacy, or completeness of such information or material or the results to be obtained from using such information or material. Neither Jamsa Press nor the author shall be responsible for any claims attributable to errors, omissions, or other inaccuracies in the information or material contained in this book, and in no event shall Jamsa Press or the author be liable for direct, indirect, special, incidental, or consequential damages arising out of the use of such information or material.

This publication is designed to provide accurate and authoritative information in regard to the subject matter covered. It is sold with the understanding that the publisher is not engaged in rendering professional service or endorsing particular products or services. If legal advice or other expert assistance is required, the services of a competent professional should be sought.

Contents

Chapter 1 Windows 95 in Fifteen Minutes 1

INSTALLING WINDOWS 95 1
STARTING WINDOWS 95 2
USING A MOUSE 3
FINDING OUT WHAT'S NEW 3
ALWAYS READ THE WELCOME WINDOW TIP 3
WHAT'S NEW IN WINDOWS 95? 5
RUNNING PROGRAMS FROM THE START BUTTON 5
    THE START MENU 6
    RUNNING A SINGLE APPLICATION 7
        EXPLORING A WINDOWS 95 WINDOW 7
        DISPLAYING A WINDOW"S CONTENTS FULL SCREEN 8
        MINIMIZING A WINDOW 9
USING WINDOWS 95 TITLE-BAR BUTTONS 9
    RUNNING MULTIPLE PROGRAMS AT THE SAME TIME 10
USING TOOLBAR BUTTONS 11
    SWITCHING BETWEEN PROGRAMS 11
    MOVING A WINDOW 12
    RESIZING A WINDOW 12
    CLOSING A WINDOW 12
USING THE RIGHT-MOUSE BUTTON 12
RIGHT-CLICKING ON DESKTOP OBJECTS 14
EXPLORING YOUR COMPUTER 14
    EXPLORING YOUR SYSTEM'S HARD DISK 15
    STARTING PROGRAMS FROM FOLDERS 16
    OPENING A DOCUMENT 16
    HOW TO TELL AN ICON'S TYPE 17
RIGHT-CLICKING TO IDENTIFY AN ICON 18
    EASY ACCESS TO A PROGRAM OR A DOCUMENT 18
SHORTCUT ICONS FOR DOCUMENTS 19
GETTING HELP 19
SHEETS IN WINDOWS 95 20
    BROWSING THROUGH HELP TOPICS 20
    CHECKING OUT THE INDEX 21
    SEARCHING FOR A KEYWORD 22
ENDING YOUR WINDOWS 95 SESSION 24
KEYS TO SUCCESS 24

Chapter 2 Working with Windows in Windows 95 25

- A Typical Window 25
  - Title Bar 26
  - Menu Bar 26
  - Toolbars 26
- Using Tool Tips 27
  - Status Bar 27
  - Work Area 27
  - Control Menu Icon 27
  - Buttons on the Title Bar 28
    - Minimize Button 28
    - Maximize Button 28
    - Close Button 29
- Running Programs Using the Start Menu 30
  - Using the Start Menu 30
- Starting Programs from the Start Menu 31
  - Running Multiple Programs 32
  - Moving Windows 33
  - Pile of Windows 34
  - Resizing Windows 34
  - Quickly Rearranging the Windows 35
  - Minimizing a Window 36
- Cleaning the Desktop Quickly 36
  - Maximizing a Window 37
- Switching between Programs 37
  - Switching with the Taskbar 37
  - Switching with the Keyboard 37
- Three Ways to Switch between Programs 38
- Working with Menus 38
  - Types of Menus 38
    - Pull-down Menu 39
    - Pop-up Menu 39
    - Submenu 40
  - Some Important Menu Facts 40
  - Using Menus with the Keyboard 41
- Working with Dialog Boxes 42
  - Properties Sheets in Windows 95 42
- Sheets: A Brief History Lesson 43
  - Pages in Properties Sheets 43
- Some Important Properties Sheets 43
- Using Sheets 44
  - Display Properties 44
  - Taskbar Properties 44
- Keys to Success 45

Chapter 3 Customizing the Taskbar and Start Menu 47

PURPOSE OF THE TASKBAR 47
    PARTS OF THE TASKBAR 47
    USING THE VOLUME CONTROL 48
        ADJUSTING VOLUME 49
        MORE VOLUME CONTROLS 49
PLAYING AUDIO CDS ON YOUR SYSTEM 49
        SETTING AUDIO PROPERTIES 50
SILENCING YOUR SYSTEM 51
    ADJUSTING THE DATE-AND-TIME 51
    STARTING PROGRAMS 52
    RUNNING MULTIPLE PROGRAMS 52
    USING THE START MENU RUN OPTION 53
    SWITCHING BETWEEN PROGRAMS 54
CHANGING THE TASKBAR'S LOCATION AND SIZE 55
    MOVING THE TASKBAR 55
    CHANGING THE TASKBAR'S WIDTH 56
MAKING THE TASKBAR "FIT" YOUR NEEDS 56
CHANGING THE TASKBAR PROPERTIES 57
FINDING AND HIDING THE TASKBAR 58
CUSTOMIZING THE START MENU 59
    ADDING A PROGRAM TO THE START MENU 59
    ADDING A PROGRAM USING DRAG AND DROP 62
    REMOVING A PROGRAM FROM THE START MENU 62
KEYS TO SUCCESS 64

Chapter 4 Using Online Help 65

ABOUT ONLINE HELP 65
ALL WINDOWS 95 HELP SYSTEMS ARE THE SAME 66
    HELP AT YOUR FINGERTIPS 66
    STARTING HELP FROM THE START MENU 67
STARTING HELP IN A WINDOWS 95 APPLICATION 67
HELP ON THE HELP TOPICS SHEET 67
USING THE HELP BUTTON 68
BROWSING THE CONTENTS 69
USING THE BACK AND HELP TOPICS BUTTONS 70
USING THE INDEX 70
SEARCHING FOR A WORD 72
PRINTING A TOPIC 74
COPYING A HELP TOPIC TO THE WINDOWS CLIPBOARD 75
COPYING HELP TOPICS 76
ADDING YOUR OWN NOTES TO A TOPIC 76
USING ONLINE HELP IN A PROGRAM 78

Jump Buttons in Windows 95 Online Help	78
Using Jump Buttons	80
Conversation Buttons	80
Keys to Success	82

Chapter 5 Customizing Common Hardware 83

Exploring the Control Panel	83
Accessing the Control Panel	86
Setting the Date-and-Time	86
Setting the Date	87
Setting the Time	87
Setting the Time Zone	88
Customizing the Display	89
Understanding Pixels	90
Selecting a Background Pattern and Wallpaper	91
Trying Out Background Patterns	91
Trying Out Wallpapers	92
Adding Wallpapers to Windows 95	93
Turning On the Screen Saver	93
Selecting a Screen Saver	94
Password Protection in Windows 95	94
Options for the Energy Saving Features	95
Customizing the Desktop's Appearance	96
Using an Appearance Scheme	96
Altering a Scheme	98
Changing the Display Settings	99
Saving Your Appearance Schemes	99
Setting Colors and Desktop Area	100
Scaling Fonts	100
Selecting a Display Adapter and Monitor	101
Controlling the Keyboard	102
Making the Keyboard Match Your Typing Skills	104
Customizing the Mouse	104
Managing the Buttons	105
Creating a Left-Handed Mouse	105
Selecting Pointer Shapes	106
Controlling Pointer Motion	107
Setting Up Your Modem	108
Understanding Modem Speeds	108
Adding a New Modem	109
Understanding Your System's Serial and Parallel Ports	109
Wizards in Windows 95	110
Specifying a Generic Modem	111
Inspecting Properties of a Modem	112

Setting the Dialing Properties	113
Modem Diagnostics	114
Working with Your Printer	115
Installing a Printer	115
Controlling a Printer	118
Pausing or Stopping a Print Job	119
Assigning System Sounds	119
Keys to Success	120

Chapter 6 Customizing Advanced System Settings 121

Adding New Hardware	121
Using the Add New Hardware Wizard	122
Typical Hardware Additions	123
Why Windows 95 Needs to Detect Hardware	123
What to Do When Your System Locks	124
Installing Hardware with a Vendor-Supplied Disk	126
Adding and Removing Programs	127
Installing New Windows 95 Programs	128
Adding Windows 95 Components	128
Removing a Windows 95 Component	133
Choosing Windows 95 Components Effectively	133
Creating a Startup Disk	133
Working with Fonts	134
Viewing a Font	135
Installing a New Font	136
Customizing a Joystick	137
Using ODBC (Open Database Connectivity Software)	139
ODBC Overview	139
Setting up ODBC	140
Installing ODBC Drivers	140
Adding ODBC Data Sources	141
Preparing Your Windows 95 System to Use ODBC Applications	143
Setting Passwords	143
Changing Your Windows 95 Password	144
Specifying a New Password	145
Setting User Profile Options	145
Making Windows 95 Please Everyone	146
Customizing International Settings	146
Other Control Panel Items	147
Multimedia	147
Network	147
Mail and Fax	148
Microsoft Mail Post Office	148
System	148
Keys to Success	148

Chapter 7 Working with Files and Folders 149

UNDERSTANDING THE WINDOWS 95 FILE SYSTEM 149
A FOLDER IS A DIRECTORY 150
NAMING DRIVES, FOLDERS, AND FILES.. 150
    DRIVE LETTERS 151
    UNDERSTANDING ROOT DIRECTORIES 151
    DIRECTORY NAMES AND FILENAMES UNDER MS-DOS 151
UNDERSTANDING EXTENSIONS 152
    PATHNAMES IN MS-DOS 153
    LONG FILENAMES IN WINDOWS 95 154
UNDERSTANDING LONG FILENAMES 154
    USING WINDOWS 95 FILES IN MS-DOS AND WINDOWS 3.1 155
UNDERSTANDING THE 8.3 ALIAS 155
BROWSING YOUR SYSTEM'S DRIVES AND DIRECTORIES 155
    LOOKING AT THE FOLDERS IN YOUR SYSTEM'S HARD DRIVE 155
LEARNING MORE ABOUT A FILE ICON 158
    BROWSING FOLDERS THE SMART WAY 158
    USING THE TOOLBAR IN A FOLDER WINDOW 159
    VIEWING THE FULL MS-DOS NAMES 162
USING OPEN AND SAVE AS DIALOG BOXES 162
RECOGNIZING WINDOWS 3.1 AND WINDOWS 95 DIALOG BOXES 163
CREATING A NEW FOLDER FROM THE SAVE AS DIALOG BOX 165
KEYS TO SUCCESS 166

Chapter 8 Using the Microsoft Network (MSN) 167

MSN—AN ONLINE SERVICE 167
    WHAT IS AN ONLINE SERVICE 168
    MECHANICS OF GETTING ONLINE 168
        MODEMS AND PHONE LINES 169
        SOFTWARE 169
        CREDIT CARD 169
SIGNING UP FOR MSN 169
WHAT DOES MSN COST 173
A GUIDED TOUR OF MSN 173
    STARTING MSN 174
    MSN TODAY 174
UNDERSTANDING HOW MSN DRAWS IMAGES 175
    TAKING ADVANTAGE OF MEMBER ASSISTANCE 176
MSN IS LIKE A FANCY HOTEL 177
        ONLINE HELP IN MSN 177
    E-MAIL 178
    SENDING AN E-MAIL MESSAGE 180
BROWSING MSN AREAS THE SMART WAY 181

Saving an Area in the Favorite Places 181
Visiting a Chat Area 182
Understanding the Conversational Dynamics of an Online Chat 182
Using a Bulletin Board 184
Favorite Places 186
Categories 186
Browsing Down a Hierarchy of Folders 187
Access to Internet Newsgroups 188
Keys to Success 190

Chapter 9 Windows 95 Multimedia 191

What is Multimedia? 191
Taking Windows 95 Multimedia for a Test Drive 192
Improved Multimedia Support in Windows 95 193
Understanding Plug and Play 194
Using the Media Player 194
Playing Sound Files 195
Controlling Multimedia Volume 197
Playing Audio CDs 197
Customizing an Audio CD 198
Recording Information About an Audio CD 198
Removing One or More Tracks From the Play List 199
Adding Tracks to Play List 199
Naming a CD Track 199
Defining the Track Playback Order 199
Controlling CD Player Preferences 200
Controlling How the CD Player Uses Your Play List 200
Using the Sound Recorder 201
Recording a Sound 201
Recording a New Sound 202
Using the Position Bar 202
Editing your Sound File 202
Inserting or Appending a Second Sound File 202
Mixing an Existing Sound 203
Discarding Your Changes 203
Deleting Part of Your Recording 203
Applying Special Effects to Your Recording 203
Controlling Sound File Formats 204
Changing the Sound Quality 204
Multimedia Controls 205
Controlling Audio Devices 206
Controlling Video Playback 206
Controlling Audio CD Playback 207
Controlling MIDI Playback 207

ADVANCED MULTIMEDIA SETTINGS	208
VOLUME CONTROLS	209
VIEWING INFORMATION ABOUT A MULTIMEDIA FILE	210
KEYS TO SUCCESS	211

Chapter 10 Connecting Windows 95 to the Internet and the World Wide Web 213

THE INTERNET IS A WORLDWIDE NETWORK OF NETWORKS	213
THE INTERNET PAYS FOR ITSELF	214
CONNECTING TO THE INTERNET USING AN ONLINE SERVICE	214
YOUR PROVIDER COSTS ARE THE ONLY COSTS YOU WILL PAY	215
WHERE THE WORLD WIDE WEB FITS IN	215
UNDERSTANDING HOMEPAGES	217
HOW THE WEB SIMPLIFIES INFORMATION RETRIEVAL	217
IMPORTANT INFORMATION YOU MUST GET FROM YOUR INTERNET PROVIDER	217
UNDERSTANDING INTERNET ADDRESSES AND HOSTNAMES	217
SETTING UP WINDOWS 95 TO USE DIAL-UP TCP/IP NETWORKING	218
CONFIGURING YOUR TCP/IP SETTINGS	220
ESTABLISHING A DIAL-UP CONNECTION	220
CONNECTING TO YOUR PROVIDER	223
WINDOWS 95 INTERNET-BASED SOFTWARE	224
TESTING A REMOTE COMPUTER USING PING	224
USING TELNET TO CONNECT TO A REMOTE COMPUTER	225
TRANSFERRING FILES FROM A REMOTE COMPUTER	226
USING THE FTP COMMAND TO DOWNLOAD A WEB BROWSER	227
SURFING THE WORLD WIDE WEB	228
KEYS TO SUCCESS	228

Chapter 11 Using Windows 95 on Your Notebook PC 229

NOTEBOOK PCS AND WINDOWS 95	230
INSTALLING THE WINDOWS 95 PORTABLE PC CONFIGURATION	230
CONNECTING YOUR NOTEBOOK PC TO YOUR DESKTOP PC	231
NETWORK	231
LEARNING A NETWORK COMPUTER'S NAME	233
UNDERSTANDING SHARED FOLDERS	233
DOCKING BAY	233
DIRECT CABLE CONNECTION	234
THE BRIEFCASE	236
CREATING A BRIEFCASE	236
USING THE BRIEFCASE	236
UPDATING DOCUMENTS WITH THE BRIEFCASE	237
OVERRIDING THE SUGGESTED UPDATE ACTION	239
SPLITTING A DOCUMENT	240

Using the Briefcase with a Floppy Disk	241
Using Windows 95 Power Management	242
Suspending Your Notebook PC	243
Using PCMCIA Cards	243
Keys to Success	244

Chapter 12 Using Tried and True Windows 3.1 Accessories 245

Running an Accessory Program	245
Using the Calculator Accessory	246
Performing a Simple Arithmetic Operation	247
Understanding Standard Calculator Buttons	247
Using the Scientific Calculator	248
Performing Statistical Operations	249
Using the Character Map Accessory	250
Using the Clipboard Viewer Accessory	251
Using the Notepad Accessory	252
Notepad is Not a Word Processor	252
Creating a Notepad Document	253
Controlling Your Document's Page Settings	253
Opening an Existing Notepad Document	253
Performing Cut-and-Paste Operations in Notepad	254
Creating a Log File within Notepad	254
Searching Your Notepad Document for Text	255
Using Notepad to Edit ASCII Files	255
Using the Cardfile Accessory	255
Adding a Card to Your Deck	256
Saving Your Card Deck to a File	257
Opening an Existing Card Deck File	257
Moving through Your Card Deck	257
Deleting a Card from Your Deck	257
Changing a Card's Contents	258
Printing Your Card Deck	258
Controlling Your Card Deck's Display	258
Searching for a Specific Card	258
Using Cardfile to Autodial	259
Setting Up Cardfile to Autodial	259
Tracking Your Appointments with Windows Calendar	259
Cutting and Pasting an Appointment	261
Saving Your Appointments to a File	261
Printing Your Appointments	261
Displaying the Appointments for a Specific Date	262
Setting Alarms within Calendar	262
Drawing Simple Illustrations in Windows Paint	263
Using Paint to Save Screen Captures	265

TAKE ADVANTAGE OF CLIPART AND PHOTO IMAGES	266
SAVING YOUR PAINT IMAGE	268
PRINTING YOUR PAINT IMAGE	268
CUTTING OR COPYING AN IMAGE TO THE CLIPBOARD	268
KEYS TO SUCCESS	268

Chapter 13 Using the Windows 95 Accessory Programs 269

USING THE WINDOWS 95 SYSTEM TOOLS	269
BACKING UP YOUR FILES AND FOLDERS	270
BUY A TAPE DRIVE	270
UNDERSTANDING BACKUP OPERATIONS	271
UNDERSTANDING BACKUP-FILE SETS	271
STARTING THE BACKUP ACCESSORY	271
PERFORMING A FULL-DISK BACKUP OPERATION	272
CREATING YOUR OWN BACKUP-FILE SET	273
SELECTING YOUR TARGET DEVICE AND SAVING YOUR BACKUP-FILE SET	274
USING YOUR BACKUP-FILE SET	275
RESTORING YOUR BACKUP FILES	275
LEARNING MORE ABOUT BACKUP	276
CHECKING YOUR DISKS, FOLDERS, AND FILES FOR ERRORS	277
PERFORMING SCANDISK'S STANDARD TEST	277
PERFORM SCANDISK'S STANDARD TEST ONCE A WEEK	278
PERFORMING SCANDISK'S THOROUGH TEST	278
CONTROLLING SCANDISK THOROUGH TEST OPTIONS	279
EXAMINE SCANDISK'S LOG FILE	279
CONTROLLING SCANDISK'S ADVANCED OPTIONS	279
DOUBLING YOUR DISK'S STORAGE CAPACITY	280
BACKUP YOUR DISKS BEFORE YOU COMPRESS THEIR CONTENTS	280
COMPRESSING A DISK	281
UNDERSTANDING HOST AND COMPRESSED DRIVES	281
COMPRESSING A FLOPPY DISK IS CONVENIENT	282
UNCOMPRESSING A DRIVE	282
LEARNING MORE ABOUT DRIVESPACE	283
SPEED DIALING USING THE PHONE DIALER ACCESSORY	283
USING THE PHONE DIALER TO PLACE A CALL	283
USING PHONE DIALER TO SPEED DIAL	284
CHANGING A SPEED DIAL ENTRY	284
UNDERSTANDING PHONE DIALER PROPERTIES	285
CONNECTING TO A REMOTE COMPUTER USING HYPERTERMINAL	285
DOWNLOADING A FILE	288
ENDING YOUR HYPERTERMINAL SESSION	288
LEARNING MORE ABOUT HYPERTERMINAL	288
USING THE WORDPAD WORD PROCESSOR	289
PRINTING YOUR WORDPAD DOCUMENT	290

SAVING YOUR WORDPAD DOCUMENT	290
TYPING WITHIN WORDPAD	290
ENDING YOUR WORDPAD SESSION	290
OPENING A WORDPAD DOCUMENT FROM A FILE ON DISK	290
CONTROLLING YOUR PARAGRAPH ALIGNMENT	291
CONTROLLING FONTS WITHIN WORDPAD	291
SEARCHING YOUR WORDPAD DOCUMENT FOR SPECIFIC TEXT	292
CUSTOMIZING YOUR PAGE SETTINGS	293
REPLACING TEXT WITHIN YOUR DOCUMENT	293
MOVING TEXT USING A CUT-AND-PASTE OPERATION	294
CUSTOMIZING WORDPAD OPTIONS	294
KEYS TO SUCCESS	295

Chapter 14 Using the Windows 95 Explorer 297

STARTING THE WINDOWS 95 EXPLORER	297
EXPLORER DISPLAYS YOUR DISK'S DIRECTORY STRUCTURE	299
CHANGING THE EXPLORER'S DISPLAY	299
CONTROLLING THE ORDER IN WHICH DOCUMENTS APPEAR WITHIN THE FILES AND FOLDERS LIST	300
EXPANDING AND COLLAPSING EXPLORER FOLDERS	300
CREATING YOUR OWN FOLDERS	301
RENAMING FILES AND FOLDERS	302
UNDERSTANDING EXPLORER UNDO OPERATIONS	302
DELETING A FILE OR FOLDER	302
UNDERSTANDING THE RECYCLE BIN	303
VIEWING YOUR DOCUMENT TYPES	303
REGISTERING (ASSOCIATING) A FILE TYPE WITH A PROGRAM	304
COPYING A FILE OR FOLDER	306
COPYING A FILE OR FOLDER USING CUT-AND-PASTE OPERATIONS	306
UNDERSTANDING PASTE AND PASTE SHORTCUT	307
COPYING FILES AND FOLDERS USING DRAG-AND-DROP OPERATIONS	307
MOVING A FILE OR FOLDER	308
RUNNING PROGRAMS WITHIN THE EXPLORER	308
WORKING WITH MULTIPLE FILES	308
RECOGNIZING COMMON FILE ICONS	309
INVERTING A FILE SELECTION	310
WORKING WITH TWO EXPLORER WINDOWS	310
DISPLAYING ALL THE FILES IN A FOLDER	311
USING THE STATUS BAR	312
VIEWING A FILE'S CONTENTS USING QUICK VIEW	312
UNDERSTANDING THE EXPLORER'S SEND TO OPTION	313
DISPLAYING A FILE'S COMPLETE PATHNAME WITHIN THE TITLE BAR	313
DISPLAYING AND CHANGING FILE PROPERTIES WITHIN THE EXPLORER	314
UNDERSTANDING AND USING FILE ATTRIBUTES	314
UNDERSTANDING THE READ-ONLY PROPERTY	314

UNDERSTANDING THE ARCHIVE PROPERTY 315
UNDERSTANDING THE HIDDEN PROPERTY 315
UNDERSTANDING THE SYSTEM PROPERTY 315
SETTING OR CLEARING PROPERTIES FOR MULTIPLE FILES IN ONE OPERATION 315
UNDERSTANDING THE EXPLORER TOOLBAR 315
FINDING A FILE ON YOUR DISK 316
   FINDING A FILE OR FOLDER BY NAME 316
   FINDING A FILE OR FOLDER BY DATE 317
   USING ADVANCED FILE SEARCH OPTIONS 317
KEYS TO SUCCESS 318

Chapter 15 Revisiting My Computer and the Recycle Bin 319

REVISITING MY COMPUTER 319
CONTROLLING MY COMPUTER WINDOWS 320
RUNNING PROGRAMS FROM WITHIN MY COMPUTER 321
ARRANGING ICONS WITHIN THE MY COMPUTER WINDOW 321
PERFORMING FILE MOVE AND COPY OPERATIONS 321
CHANGING MY COMPUTER'S APPEARANCE 322
USING THE RECYCLE BIN 322
CHANGING THE RECYCLE BIN'S APPEARANCE 324
KEYS TO SUCCESS 324

Chapter 16 Using the Windows 95 Registry 325

UNDERSTANDING THE WINDOWS 95 REGISTRY 325
OPENING AND CLOSING REGISTRY BRANCHES 327
CHANGING A REGISTRY ENTRY 327
DO NOT CHANGE A REGISTRY ENTRY'S VALUE FOR AN ENTRY YOU DON'T UNDERSTAND 328
CREATE A REGISTRY EDITOR SHORTCUT 328
PRINTING YOUR REGISTRY DATABASE 329
WHERE WINDOWS 95 STORES THE REGISTRY DATA 329
WINDOWS 95 STILL SUPPORTS WINDOWS 3.1 INI FILES 330
USE SYSEDIT TO EDIT YOUR INI FILES 330
FINDING A REGISTRY ENTRY 331
RENAMING OR DELETING A REGISTRY ENTRY 331
RENAME AN ENTRY BEFORE YOU DELETE IT 332
USING AN EXPORT OPERATION TO BACKUP YOUR REGISTRY ENTRIES 332
   EXPORTING A REGISTRY BRANCH 333
EXPORT A BACKUP COPY OF THE REGISTRY DATABASE 333
IMPORTING A REGISTRY FILE 333
ADDING A REGISTRY ENTRY 334
EXPLOITING THE WINDOWS 95 REGISTRY 335
ACCESSING ANOTHER USER'S REGISTRY DATABASE 335
KEYS TO SUCCESS 336

Chapter 17 Using Exchange for Faxes and E-Mail 337

SENDING AND RECEIVING FAXES 337
      SENDING A FAX 338
CUSTOMIZING FAX SETTINGS 338
RETRYING AN UNSUCCESSFUL FAX TRANSMISSION 340
SENDING A FAX FROM WITHIN A PROGRAM 340
DRAG-AND-DROP FAXING 341
REQUESTING A FAX-ON-DEMAND MESSAGE 341
CREATING A FAX COVER SHEET 341
GETTING STARTED WITH MICROSOFT EXCHANGE 342
      PREPARING TO USE MICROSOFT FAX 343
      PREPARING TO USE MICROSOFT MAIL 344
      PREPARING TO USE MICROSOFT NETWORK 345
      ADDING EXCHANGE TO THE STARTUP GROUP 346
      STARTING EXCHANGE 346
      EXCHANGE USES EXPLORER-LIKE FOLDERS 348
      SENDING A MAIL MESSAGE FROM WITHIN EXCHANGE 348
ATTACHING A FILE TO YOUR MESSAGE 349
      COMPOSING A FAX WITHIN EXCHANGE 349
RECEIVING MAIL FROM YOUR INTERNET-BASED ACCOUNT 349
LEARNING MORE ABOUT EXCHANGE 349
UNDERSTANDING AND USING YOUR ADDRESS BOOK 350
MANAGING YOUR PERSONAL ADDRESS-BOOK ENTRIES 352
      ADDING A NEW ADDRESS-BOOK ENTRY 352
      DELETING AN ADDRESS-BOOK ENTRY 352
      UPDATING AN ADDRESS-BOOK ENTRY 352
USING A PERSONAL DISTRIBUTION-LIST 353
KEYS TO SUCCESS 354

Chapter 18 Windows 95 Networking Operations 355

SHARING RESOURCES ON A LOCAL-AREA NETWORK 355
GETTING AROUND YOUR NETWORK 355
      USING A REMOTE PRINTER 356
MAPPING TO A NETWORK DRIVE 356
      DISCONNECTING FROM A MAPPED DRIVE 357
ALLOWING REMOTE USERS TO ACCESS YOUR FOLDERS AND PRINTERS 358
      SHARING A FOLDER 358
      TURNING OFF A FOLDER'S SHARED ACCESS 359
      SHARING A PRINTER 359
      TURNING OFF PRINTER SHARING 360
      USING WINDOWS 95 DIAL-UP NETWORKING 361
MONITORING YOUR PC'S NETWORK USE 363
KEYS TO SUCCESS 364

XIII

Chapter 19 Managing Low-Level Hardware Operations 365

UNDERSTANDING HOW HARDWARE CONFLICTS OCCUR 365
    SPECIFYING A DEVICE'S INTERRUPT REQUEST LINE 366
    PLUG-AND-PLAY SIMPLIFIES THE INSTALLATION PROCESS 366
USING THE WINDOWS 95 DEVICE MANAGER TO TROUBLESHOOT HARDWARE CONFLICTS 367
PRINTING YOUR DEVICE SETTINGS 368
    UNDERSTANDING BASE MEMORY ADDRESSES 369
USING THE DEVICE MANAGER TO RECOGNIZE HARDWARE CONFLICTS 369
    USING THE DEVICE MANAGER TO SPECIFY NEW DEVICE SETTINGS 369
    CHANGING DEVICE SETTINGS 371
    REMOVING A DEVICE 371
KEYS TO SUCCESS 371

Chapter 20 Windows 95 and DOS 373

RUNNING A DOS-BASED PROGRAM 373
HELPING WINDOWS 95 LOCATE YOUR PROGRAM FILES 374
    CLOSING A DOS-BASED PROGRAM WINDOW 374
USE ALT-ESC TO EXPAND A DOS-BASED PROGRAM TO FULL SCREEN 375
ACCESSING THE DOS COMMAND LINE 375
STARTING PROGRAMS FROM A COMMAND PROMPT 376
WHERE WINDOWS 95 STORES YOUR DOS COMMANDS 376
A QUICK WAY TO CHANGE DIRECTORIES WITHIN WINDOWS 95 376
HOW WINDOWS 95 USES CONFIG.SYS AND AUTOEXEC.BAT 377
STARTING YOUR SYSTEM IN DOS MODE 377
UNDERSTANDING DOS MODE 378
STARTING YOUR SYSTEM IN DOS MODE 378
UNDERSTANDING SAFE MODE 378
USING THE DOS WINDOW TOOLBAR 379
CHANGING THE WINDOW'S FONT 380
    PERFORMING CUT-AND-PASTE OPERATIONS 381
HAVING A LITTLE CUT-AND-PASTE FUN 382
UNDERSTANDING BACKGROUND PROCESSING 382
    CONTROLLING PROGRAM PROPERTIES 382
WINDOWS 95 REPLACES THE PIF EDITOR WITH THE PROPERTIES DIALOG BOX 383
    ACCESSING PROGRAM SETTINGS 383
    CONTROLLING ADVANCED PROGRAM SETTINGS 384
    FURTHER REFINING A PROGRAM'S CONFIGURATION 385
    CONTROLLING PROGRAM FONTS 385
    CONTROLLING A PROGRAM'S MEMORY USE 385
    CONTROLLING THE PROGRAM'S SCREEN DISPLAY 386
    CONTROLLING OTHER PROGRAM SETTINGS 387
KEYS TO SUCCESS 389

Chapter 21 Improving Windows 95 Performance 391

UNDERSTANDING SYSTEM BOTTLENECKS 391
UNDERSTANDING HERTZ AND MEGAHERTZ (MHZ) 392
MEASURING YOUR SYSTEM BOTTLENECKS 392
REMOVING AN ITEM FROM YOUR MONITOR LIST 394
CUSTOMIZING A MONITORED ITEM 394
UNDERSTANDING THE NUMBERS 395
CHANGING THE SYSTEM MONITOR'S CHART DISPLAY 395
CUSTOMIZING THE SYSTEM MONITOR'S CHARTING INTERVAL 396
USING THE SYSTEM MONITOR TOOLBAR 396
MONITORING A REMOTE COMPUTER 397
UNDERSTANDING THE WINDOWS 95 KERNEL 397
UNDERSTANDING THE WINDOWS 95 FILE SYSTEM 398
UNDERSTANDING WINDOWS 95 MEMORY MANAGEMENT 401
USING THE RESOURCE METER 402
DEFRAGMENT YOUR DISK ON A REGULAR BASIS 402
RUNNING THE RESOURCE METER EACH TIME YOU START WINDOWS 95 403
KEYS TO SUCCESS 404

Chapter 1
Windows 95 in Fifteen Minutes

For one reason or another, you have decided to use Windows 95. Perhaps your PC came with Windows 95 already installed. Or maybe you are the adventurous type—you already use Windows 3.1, and now you are upgrading to Windows 95. No matter what your reason, you may be apprehensive because you don't know what Windows 95 has to offer. After all, using a new operating system like Windows 95 is somewhat like visiting a new city—a mysterious place with unfamiliar street names and landmarks where you might easily lose your way. Fortunately, in the new city that is Windows 95, you are not alone. You have this book, *Success with Windows 95*, as your personal guide.

Just as a good tour guide takes you to fine restaurants, famous museums, critically-acclaimed shows, and popular attractions, the 21 chapters of this book will show you how to use the key features of Windows 95. First, you will learn how to navigate and customize Windows 95. Later, you will explore Windows 95's exciting capabilities, such as accessing the Internet and the World Wide Web. As you explore, *Success with Windows 95* will help you avoid difficult operations that require a better understanding of Windows 95, just as a good tour guide makes sure you avoid the bad parts of a new city.

As with any computer program, the best way to learn to use Windows 95 is to start using it. As such, this chapter teaches you how to perform simple yet key tasks with Windows 95. In later chapters, you will learn how to use Windows 95's more advanced features. As you go through this chapter, keep in mind that this is only your first look at Windows 95—a 15-minute, hands-on tour of the new operating system. This chapter will simply introduce you to topics that the rest of *Success with Windows 95* will describe in great detail. By the time you finish this chapter, you will understand the following key concepts:

- After you install Windows 95, you start it by simply turning on your computer.
- To run your programs under Windows 95, you click your mouse on the Start button and then choose your program from a menu.
- Windows 95 runs all programs within a window. Using your mouse, you can move, resize, and close a program window.
- Windows 95 provides a powerful program called the Explorer, with which you explore your disks, folders (directories), and files.
- To answer your questions and walk you through common operations, Windows 95 provides an extensive online Help system.
- To end your Windows 95 session, you select the Start menu Shutdown option. Never turn off your PC without first shutting down Windows 95.

INSTALLING WINDOWS 95

In this chapter, you will begin your tour of Windows 95. If your PC already has Windows 95 installed, you are ready to take Windows 95 for a test drive. If your PC does not yet have Windows 95, perform these steps:

1. To install Windows 95 from the Windows 95 CD, insert the CD into your PC's CD-ROM drive. If you are installing from floppy disks, insert Disk 1 into the appropriate floppy drive.
2. Select the Program Manager File menu and choose Run. Windows 3.1, in turn, will display the Run dialog box.

3. Within the Run dialog box command field, enter the letter of the drive that contains the Windows 95 disk or CD, followed by a colon, a backslash, and the **SETUP** command. For example, if you have Disk 1 in floppy drive A, enter **A:\SETUP** as the command line.

4. Click your mouse on the OK button or press ENTER. The Windows 95 Setup program, in turn, will run and guide you through the installation process.

STARTING WINDOWS 95

To start Windows 95, all you need to do is turn on your computer. Windows 95, in turn, will display its initial screen, which Microsoft calls the Desktop. Figure 1.1 shows an example of the Windows 95 Desktop.

Figure 1.1 Windows 95 display at startup.

At the center of the Desktop, Windows 95 displays the Welcome window. Each time your system starts, Windows 95 uses the Welcome window to display helpful tips. Take a look at the rest of the Desktop as it appears in Figure 1.1. As you can see, Windows 95 places graphical *icons* on the Desktop that correspond to specific programs. The following bulleted list describes several key Desktop items:

- The *Taskbar* normally appears along the bottom edge of the Desktop. The most important item on the Taskbar is the Start button, which appears at the Taskbar's leftmost edge. You will use the Start button to run programs, access the Windows 95 online Help system, and display a variety of menus and submenus.

- Each time you open a new window, Windows 95 places a button on the Taskbar that contains the window's name (which normally corresponds to the program name). You use such *Taskbar buttons* to switch between windows open on the Desktop. For example, the Desktop in Figure 1.1 shows a Taskbar button that corresponds to the Welcome window.

- The Taskbar's rightmost edge shows the current time and may have an icon of a speaker. You will use the speaker icon to access the Windows 95 volume controls. Using these controls, you can set the volume at which Windows 95 and the programs you run play sounds.

- A number of *icons*—small pictures with labels—appear along the Desktop's left edge. The My Computer icon represents your computer. As you will learn, you can use this icon to explore the documents, programs, and devices on your system. Likewise, you can use the Network Neighborhood icon to explore any network to which your computer is connected. The Recycle Bin icon lets you throw away documents you no longer need. You can retrieve such discarded documents as long as you have not emptied the bin.

Now that you have examined the Windows 95 Desktop, the next step of your Windows 95 tour is to check out the Welcome window and to learn how to remove it from your display. To explore the Welcome window, you will need to perform mouse operations. If you are not familiar with the mouse (or if you are not sure about the terms this book uses to describe various mouse operations), consult the Success Hint, "Using a Mouse."

USING A MOUSE

The *mouse* is a small, hand-held device that you move around on your desk, usually on a mousepad. When you move the mouse across your desk, a pointer moves on the screen. This mouse pointer tracks the movement of the mouse. A mouse makes it easy for you to point at objects on the screen—an operation that you cannot do easily with a keyboard. Using a mouse, you can quickly select different screen objects, such as icons or menus. Also, it is much easier to draw with a mouse than with a keyboard.

To perform a mouse operation, you move the mouse so that the pointer rests on a specific object within a window or on the Desktop. Then, you usually perform some action with the mouse buttons. Although a mouse typically has one to three buttons, two-button mice are the most common. Most of the time, you will use only the left-mouse button. However, as you will learn, Windows 95 does use the right-mouse button as well.

Using the mouse buttons, you can perform six basic actions: you can press and release a mouse button; click or double-click a mouse button; and move or drag the mouse pointer. To *press* a mouse button, hold the button down without moving your mouse. To initiate an action, *release* the mouse button that you had previously held down. To *click* a mouse button, quickly press and release the button without moving the mouse. To *double-click* a mouse button, click twice in rapid succession without moving the mouse. (Often, this book will instruct you to double-click on objects, but not specify which mouse button you should use. On such occasions, double-click your left-mouse button.)

To *move* the pointer, move the mouse across your desk without pressing any button. To *drag* the mouse pointer, position the pointer over an object, such as a window or an icon, that you wish to move. Then, press the left-mouse button and hold it down as you move your mouse. As long as you hold down the left-mouse button, the object moves with your pointer. When you release the button, you essentially *drop* the object into its new position. Thus, most Windows users refer to this object-moving procedure as a *drag-and-drop* operation.

FINDING OUT WHAT'S NEW

As briefly discussed, each time your system starts, Windows 95 displays a Welcome window, similar to that shown in Figure 1.1, which contains a helpful tip for working with Windows 95. Usually, the tip, which changes each time you start your system, provides some information on how to perform a specific task in Windows 95.

ALWAYS READ THE WELCOME WINDOW TIP

After you have used Windows 95 for awhile, you might feel tempted to ignore the Welcome window tip and move immediately to other tasks. However, you may want to pause for a second and read the tip anyway. The small piece of information the tip contains may solve some problem that's been plaguing you for months. Likewise, you may learn something from the tip that helps you avoid future problems and thus use Windows 95 more effectively.

In addition to displaying a tip, the Welcome window lets you jump right into a Windows Help window that highlights the new elements of Windows 95. The word *new* in "new elements" refers to features that were not in the earlier version of Windows—Windows 3.1. To open the Windows Help window, click your mouse on the What's New button. Windows 95, in turn, will display the Windows Help window, shown in Figure 1.2.

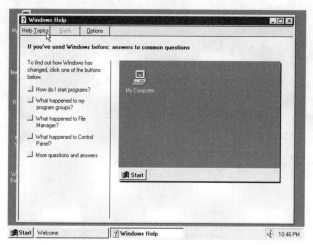

Figure 1.2 Windows 95 Help window with information on what's new.

Look at the small buttons along the left edge of the window. Notice that each button precedes a question. If you click your mouse on a button, the right side of the window shows the answer to the corresponding question. Go ahead—click on the button labeled "How do I start programs?" (because that is what you will do soon—start programs). As you can see in Figure 1.3, the left side of the Windows Help window now shows information about starting programs. If you want answers to the other questions in the Windows Help window, take a minute or two to click on each button and look at the Help information that Windows 95 displays. When you are satisfied, click your mouse on the small button in the upper-right corner of the window—the button with an "X" on it. Windows 95, in turn, will close the Windows Help window and redisplay the Welcome window on the Desktop.

Note: Microsoft calls the button with an "X" on it the **Close button**. Every window in Windows 95 includes a Close button in its upper-right corner.

In the Welcome window, notice the Online Registration button. You can use the Online Registration button to register your copy of Windows 95 over the phone (provided you have a modem installed in your system). Later in this book, you will learn how to do so. For now, click on the Close button. Windows 95, in turn, will close the Welcome window.

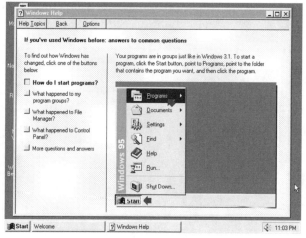

Figure 1.3 Help information on starting a program in Windows 95.

1: Windows 95 in Fifteen Minutes

What's New in Windows 95?

If you have used Windows 3.1, you may have noticed that Windows 95 looks quite a bit different from Windows 3.1. Here is a short list of Windows 95's new features:

- The Start button takes the place of the Program Manager. You now run programs from the Start menu, which appears after you click on the Start button.

- The Windows Explorer (you will learn more about this program in Chapter 16, "Using the Windows 95 Explorer") replaces the Windows 3.1 File Manager. The Explorer lets you look at documents and programs on your system's disk drives.

- In addition to the Windows Explorer, you can use the My Computer icon to view the contents of all the storage devices in your computer.

- The window frames in Windows 95 look different from their Windows 3.1 counterparts. For example, Windows 95 window frames have different title-bar buttons. In particular, you can use the new Close button (the title-bar button with an "X" on it) to close a window with a single mouse click.

- You can use as many characters as necessary (up to 255) to give your documents descriptive names. Furthermore, Windows 95 does not prohibit you from using spaces in filenames.

- Windows 95 groups documents and programs into *folders*. Windows 95 folders serve the same function as Windows 3.1 directories.

- Windows 95 displays a pop-up menu when you click your right-mouse button on any object, such as a document, program, folder, disk drive, or printer. You can then click on the pop-up menu's Properties option to view or change the object's characteristics.

- Windows 95 has built-in support for a wide variety of network protocols. Network protocols, such as TCP/IP, are important if you want to connect your computer to the Internet.

Running Programs from the Start Button

With the Welcome window out of the way, the Desktop looks sparse. As Figure 1.4 shows, the Desktop contains only the Taskbar and a handful of icons. However, as you will learn in this section and throughout *Success with Windows 95*, the Taskbar and icons let you easily access every program, document, and device on your system.

Figure 1.4 A sparse, but functional, Desktop in Windows 95.

THE START MENU

A main function of the Taskbar, or more specifically, the Start button, is to start programs. To start a program, click your mouse on the Start button. Windows 95, in turn, will display the Start menu, as shown in Figure 1.5.

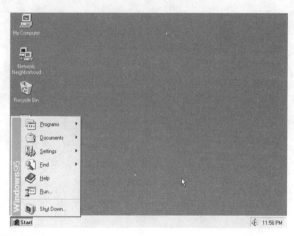

Figure 1.5 The Start menu in Windows 95.

After the Start menu pops up, move your mouse pointer on to the Desktop. Notice that the Start menu stays up even though you've released your mouse button and moved your mouse pointer away from the menu. To minimize the number of actions you have to perform to select menu options, Microsoft designed the Start menu, and all other Windows 95 pop-up menus, to stay up until you click at another location on the Desktop.

Note that each of the first four Start menu options has a right-pointing triangle at the right end of its label. When you move your mouse pointer over a menu option that precedes such a triangle, Windows 95 will display a *submenu*. To see a submenu appear, move your mouse pointer on to the Start menu Programs option. Windows 95 will display the Programs submenu, as shown in Figure 1.6.

The Programs menu, in turn, contains options (such as Accessories) that have their own submenus. Move your mouse pointer on to the Accessories option to see that submenu. Now, move your mouse pointer to the Accessories menu Paint option. Windows 95, in turn, will highlight the Paint option's label, as shown in Figure 1.7.

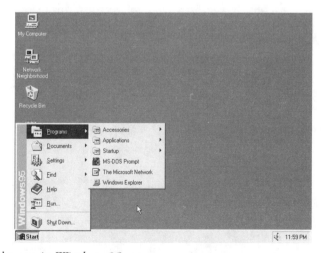

Figure 1.6 The Programs submenu in Windows 95.

1: WINDOWS 95 IN FIFTEEN MINUTES

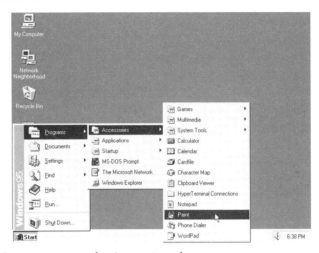

Figure 1.7 *Highlighting the Paint option on the Accessories submenu.*

RUNNING A SINGLE APPLICATION

In the previous section, you used the Start button to tell Windows 95 to display a collection of menu options. Then, you used your mouse pointer to reach a specific submenu (Accessories) and highlight the option label for Windows 95's Paint program. In this section, you will learn how to run a program (in this case, Paint) using the Windows 95 operating system. The Accessories menu Paint option refers to the Paint program that comes with Windows 95. To start the Paint program, click your mouse on the Paint option. Windows 95, in turn, will open the Paint window, as shown in Figure 1.8. As you can see, to start a program in Windows 95, all you have to do is click on the program's Start menu option.

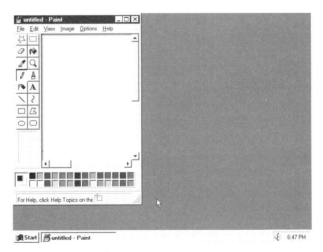

Figure 1.8 *Running the Paint program in Windows 95.*

EXPLORING A WINDOWS 95 WINDOW

The purpose of this section is not to show you how to use the Paint program. Rather, this section uses the Paint program to show you some characteristics that all Windows 95 windows share, as well as to demonstrate operations you can perform with windows. (You will learn more about the Paint program in Chapter 12.) Before you examine the Paint window, notice that the Taskbar contains a new button. This new Taskbar button has an icon and the label "untitled - Paint," which tells you that the Paint program is running with a document named "untitled." As previously mentioned, you can use the Taskbar buttons to switch between programs (when you run more than one program at the same time). Later in the chapter, you will learn exactly how to use Taskbar buttons to do so. At the top of the Paint window, you see the window's title bar, which shows an icon and the label "untitled - Paint." Move your mouse pointer to the title-bar icon and click your *left*-mouse button. Paint, in turn, will display a *pull-down menu*, as shown in Figure 1.9. The pull-down menu gets its name from the fact that it drops down when you click on the menu icon. You will find this particular pull-down menu, called the *Control menu*, on every window in Windows 95. Notice the last menu option, Close. If you click on the Close option, the Paint window will close, and Paint will stop running.

[RIGHT]

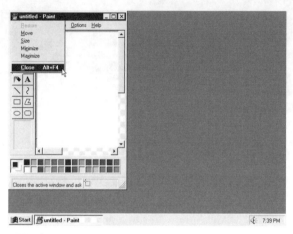

Figure 1.9 The Control menu in Windows 95.

Look at the three small buttons on the right side of the Paint window's title bar. As previously mentioned, the rightmost button lets you close a window with a single mouse click. In the next section, you will learn how to use the other two buttons to change a window's size.

Displaying a Window's Contents Full Screen

To perform certain tasks in Windows 95, you will need a lot of screen space. For example, when you use the Paint program to create illustrations, you'll likely want the program window to occupy the entire screen so you can closely inspect and, if necessary, correct your pencil marks and brush strokes. To expand or maximize the Paint window to fill the entire screen, click on the second button from the right (the one with a rectangle etched on it) on the Paint window's title bar. Paint, in turn, will expand the window so that it fills the entire screen and provides you with a large work area, as shown in Figure 1.10.

Figure 1.10 The Paint window after you maximize it.

Look at the button you clicked to maximize the Paint window. Notice that the button now shows a different picture (a pair of overlapping rectangles). If you click on that button again, the Paint window will revert back to its original shape, as in Figure 1.8.

MINIMIZING A WINDOW

As you have learned, each time you start a program, Windows 95 opens a window and adds a Taskbar button. As such, if you have several programs running at the same time (you will soon learn how to run multiple programs concurrently), your Desktop may become too cluttered with program windows for you to use it effectively. One way to clean up the Desktop is simply to close all windows (and thus exit all programs) you're not using.

However, there may be times when you won't want to close any window on the Desktop. For example, you may be working on a project that requires you to use many programs and switch frequently between them. In such a situation, continually exiting and restarting programs just to keep your Desktop clean is not a practical option. Fortunately, in Windows 95, you don't need to exit a program to remove its window from the Desktop. Instead, you can use the window's Minimize button (the title-bar button with an underscore etched on it) to stow the window on the Taskbar without exiting the corresponding program or closing any document the window may display. To see how this window-stowing feature works, click on the Paint window's Minimize button. The Paint window, in turn, will appear to shrink down into the Taskbar. Windows users refer to this window-stowing process as *minimizing* a window. As Figure 1.11 shows, when you minimize the Paint window, the Taskbar displays the Paint program's Taskbar button in a raised position.

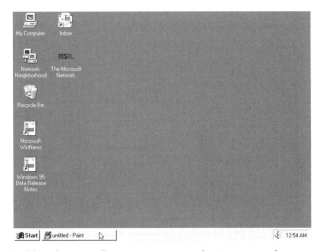

Figure 1.11 Paint program's Taskbar button after you minimize the Paint window.

To return the Paint window to normal size, simply click on the Paint program's Taskbar button. The Paint window, in turn, will appear exactly as it did before you minimized it.

USING WINDOWS 95 TITLE-BAR BUTTONS

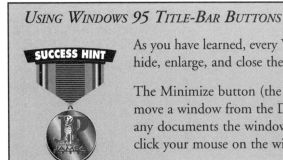

As you have learned, every Windows 95 window contains title-bar buttons you can use to hide, enlarge, and close the window.

The Minimize button (the title-bar button with an underscore etched on it) lets you remove a window from the Desktop without exiting the corresponding program or closing any documents the window contains. To redisplay the window on the Desktop, simply click your mouse on the window's Taskbar button.

> The Maximize button (the title-bar button with a rectangle etched on it) lets you expand a window until it fills your entire Desktop and provides you with the largest possible work area. After Windows 95 expands a window, Windows 95 replaces the Maximize button with the Restore button (the button with a pair of overlapping rectangles), which you click on to return the window to its normal size and shape.
>
> The Close button (the title-bar button with an "X" on it) lets you close a window, and exit the corresponding program, with a single mouse click.

RUNNING MULTIPLE PROGRAMS AT THE SAME TIME

As you work with your computer, there will be times when you need to run two or more programs at the same time. For example, you might need to run Microsoft Word (a word-processing program) so you can work on a report. In addition, you frequently may need to switch to a Microsoft Excel (a spreadsheet program) window to copy data you want to include in your report. At the same time, you might want to have a Mail window open so you can periodically check your incoming messages. In this section, you will learn how to run several programs concurrently in Windows 95.

To prepare for this exercise, minimize the Paint window again. Then, click on the Start button to display the Start menu. Move your mouse pointer to the Programs option. After Windows 95 displays the Programs menu, move your mouse pointer to the Accessories option. Windows 95, in turn, will display the Accessories menu (see Figure 1.7). Click your mouse on the Accessories menu WordPad option. In response, Windows 95 will run the WordPad program and display the WordPad window on your Desktop, as shown in Figure 1.12.

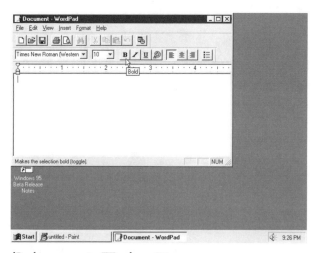

Figure 1.12 Running the WordPad program in Windows 95.

Notice that the Taskbar now has three buttons: the Start button and two program buttons (one for Paint and the other for WordPad). As you have learned, Windows 95 adds a Taskbar button for each program you run. Thus, a glance at the Taskbar tells you which programs are running.

Take a few moments to examine the WordPad program window. As its name suggests, WordPad is a word-processing program. Therefore, you can type text into the WordPad window. The WordPad window has two toolbars along its top edge. The buttons on these toolbars provide quick access to various tasks that the program performs. For example, to open a document in WordPad, click on the toolbar button with the open folder icon (the second toolbar button from the left in Figure 1.12). To print the current document, click on the toolbar button with the printer icon (the fourth toolbar button from the left in Figure 1.12).

If you move the mouse pointer to any of the toolbar buttons and leave it there for a moment, a small text balloon appears on your screen that tells you the button's function. Many Windows 95 programs support this context-sensitive Help feature. You will find this feature handy if you cannot figure out what a button is supposed to do. For example, in Figure 1.12, the mouse pointer is on the button with a capital "B" and the corresponding text balloon says "Bold." When you click this toolbar button, WordPad turns on boldface formatting.

Using Toolbar Buttons

As you have learned, many Windows 95 windows include toolbar buttons you can use to speed up tasks. For example, to preview a WordPad document before you print it, you can move your mouse pointer up to the WordPad window's File menu category, click your mouse, move your mouse pointer down to the File menu Print Preview option, and click your mouse again. Or, you can simply click on the WordPad window Print Preview button (the button with the dog-eared page and magnifying glass).

Before you start to use a Windows 95 program, explore its toolbar. Find out what the program's toolbar buttons can do. Move your mouse pointer on top of each button and read the text balloon that the program displays. Create a document for experimental purposes and try out each toolbar button.

Switching between Programs

When you have two or more programs running at the same time, you can use the Taskbar's buttons to switch from one program to another. For example, click on the Paint program's Taskbar button. Windows 95, in turn, will place the Paint program window above the WordPad window, giving you access to all parts of the Paint window. When the Paint window appears on top, part of the WordPad window is still visible underneath, as shown in Figure 1.13.

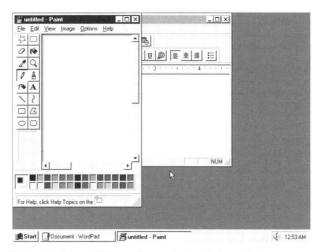

Figure 1.13 Parts of the WordPad window visible underneath the Paint window.

Move your mouse pointer to one of the buttons along the left side of the Paint window. Notice that a small text balloon, similar to those you saw in the WordPad program, pops up and identifies the button's function. Now, click on the WordPad program's Taskbar button. Windows 95, in turn, will move the WordPad window to the top. As you can see, the Taskbar buttons let you switch to a specific program with a single mouse click.

Note: As was the case in Windows 3.1, Windows 95 lets you make a window the active window by simply clicking your mouse on any visible piece of the window.

Moving a Window

Just as you may shuffle papers on the desk at your office, there will be times when you need to move windows around the Desktop. As you have learned, when you run multiple programs at the same time, Windows 95 displays each program's output in its own window. Depending on the number of programs you are running, there will be times when you need to move one program's window out of the way so you can work with another.

So far, you have not moved the Paint and WordPad program windows from where Windows 95 originally placed them on the Desktop. To move the WordPad window, place the mouse pointer in the title bar (where the program's title appears), hold the left-mouse button down, and move your mouse. An outline of the window will move with the mouse pointer. After you move the outline to a suitable position, release the mouse button. Windows 95, in turn, will drop the window into its new location.

Resizing a Window

Earlier in this chapter, you learned to maximize and minimize a program's window. However, there will be times when you need to make the window a specific size. For example, if you work with a spreadsheet in one window and a calculator in another, you might want to multiply some numbers using the calculator, and then use those numbers in the spreadsheet. To view both windows at one time, you would want to make the spreadsheet window large enough for you to do your work, but leave enough room for a calculator window. Fortunately, Windows 95 lets you make windows almost any size you want (there is a limit on how small you can make a window). There are many ways you can resize a window. One of the easiest is to drag the window's lower-right corner—the corner with three diagonal marks.

Place the mouse pointer on the lower-right corner of the WordPad window. In response, Windows 95 will change the shape of the mouse pointer to a diagonal line with arrows at both ends. Now, hold down your left-mouse button and move the mouse around. Windows 95, in turn, will display an outline of the window and resize it as you move the mouse. Release the mouse button when the window reaches the size you desire.

Closing a Window

Each time you run a program, Windows 95 opens a window within which it displays the program's output. When you are done using a program, you simply close that program's window. For example, to close the WordPad window, click on the Close button that appears in the window's title bar. Windows 95, in turn, will close the WordPad program. Next, click on the Close button in the Paint window's title bar. In response, Windows 95 will close the Paint window and leave you with a clean Desktop and nearly bare Taskbar.

Using the Right-Mouse Button

So far, you have used the left-mouse button for various tasks. In Windows 95, you must use the left-mouse button to perform almost all tasks—from selecting menu options to moving and resizing windows. Conversely, you use the right-mouse button for one specific purpose—to display pop-up menus. If you click the right-mouse button on almost anything on the display screen, Windows 95 will display a pop-up menu. Microsoft uses the term *pop-up* to refer to such menus because they appear to pop up at the mouse-pointer location when you click your right-mouse button.

To see how Windows 95 reacts to a right-mouse button click, move your mouse pointer to an empty area of the Desktop and click your right-mouse button. Windows 95, in turn, will display the pop-up menu shown in Figure 1.14.

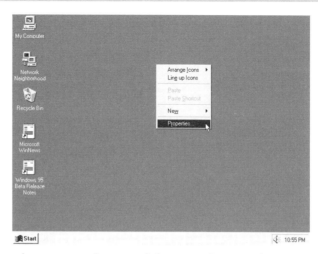

Figure 1.14 *The pop-up menu that appears when you click your right-mouse button on the Windows 95 Desktop.*

In the pop-up menu shown in Figure 1.14, the first two options let you arrange the icons that appear on the Desktop. The last option, Properties, lets you set Desktop characteristics, such as the display screen's background color and pattern, the color scheme of program windows, the fonts Windows 95 uses for window text, and so on. You will explore the Desktop properties in depth in Chapter 5, "Customizing Common Hardware."

Windows 95 displays a different pop-up menu when you click your right-mouse button on different Desktop objects. For example, click on the Taskbar with the right-mouse button. Windows 95, in turn, will display the pop-up menu you see in Figure 1.15.

Notice how the pop-up menu in Figure 1.15 differs from the one in Figure 1.14. As you can see, pop-up menus are context-sensitive—they always include options that apply exclusively to the object on which your mouse pointer rests when you click your right-mouse button.

Note: *Each item on your display screen is an object with a specific set of properties that you can view and set. It is common to use the term **object** to refer to the Taskbar, the Desktop, the icons on the Desktop, and any windows on the Desktop. Because of this object-based view, Microsoft refers to Windows 95 as an **object-oriented** environment.*

Even though pop-up menus are context-sensitive, they share one common feature: every pop-up menu contains a Properties option as its last item.

Figure 1.15 *The pop-up menu that appears when you click your right-mouse button on the Windows 95 Taskbar.*

Later in this book, you will learn how to use the Properties option to set object characteristics. For now, keep in mind that to discover what you can do with an object, all you have to do is click on the object with the right-mouse button. Windows 95 will display the object's pop-up menu. For example, click your right-mouse button on the time object shown at the rightmost edge of the Taskbar. In response, Windows 95 will display the pop-up menu, shown in Figure 1.16.

Figure 1.16 The pop-up menu that appears after you click your right-mouse button on the Taskbar's time object.

RIGHT-CLICKING ON DESKTOP OBJECTS

Whenever you click your right-mouse button on a Desktop object, Windows 95 displays a pop-up menu with options that apply exclusively to that object. For example, when you right-click on the Desktop itself, Windows 95 displays a pop-up menu with options that let you rearrange Desktop icons and set Desktop properties. Likewise, when you right-click on the Taskbar, Windows 95 displays a pop-up menu with options that let you rearrange and minimize program windows and set Taskbar properties.

EXPLORING YOUR COMPUTER

As previously mentioned, although the Windows 95 Desktop looks sparse without the Welcome window, the Taskbar and icons it always contains provide you with enormous functionality. So far, you have examined the Taskbar and learned how the Start menu helps you run programs. Now, you will discover how you can use one of the most important items on the Desktop, the My Computer icon.

Double-click on the My Computer icon. Windows 95, in turn, will open a window, as shown in Figure 1.17. The new window is the My Computer folder. Windows 95 uses *folders* to organize objects. Unlike its paper-based counterpart, a folder on the Windows 95 Desktop can contain a great variety of objects, such as disk drives, printers, calculators, and even other folders. As you can see in Figure 1.17, the My Computer folder contains your computer's hard drives, floppy drives, and CD-ROM drive, as well as two other folders. You can recognize the two folders from their folder-shaped icons. After you open the My Computer folder, a button with the My Computer label appears on the Taskbar. When you open a folder, Windows 95 adds a Taskbar button with the folder's name.

1: WINDOWS 95 IN FIFTEEN MINUTES

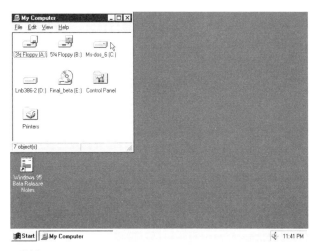

Figure 1.17 The My Computer folder.

EXPLORING YOUR SYSTEM'S HARD DISK

Several of the icons in the My Computer folder represent your system's disk drives. To see the contents of a disk drive, double-click your left-mouse button on the drive's icon. For example, double-click on your hard disk's icon. Windows 95, in turn, will open a new window that displays the contents of the hard disk, as shown in Figure 1.18. In addition, Windows 95 will add a button with the open window's name to the Taskbar .

Figure 1.18 A window showing the contents of the author's hard disk.

In the hard disk window, Windows 95 will display your hard disk's contents as a set of icons—small pictures—with labels. Some of these icons represent folders that contain other items. Other icons represent programs and documents that the programs create.

To open any one of the folders appearing in your hard disk's window, simply double-click on the folder's icon. For example, to open the Windows folder, double-click on it. Windows 95, in turn, will open a new window that displays the contents of the Windows folder, as shown in Figure 1.19.

15

Figure 1.19 *The Windows folder on your hard disk.*

STARTING PROGRAMS FROM FOLDERS

Many of the icons in the Windows folder represent programs. To run one of these programs directly from the Windows folder, double-click on the program's icon. For example, to start the Calc program, double-click your left-mouse button on the Calc icon (the icon looks like a calculator). Windows 95, in turn, will start the Calculator program and display a Calculator window, similar to the one shown in Figure 1.20.

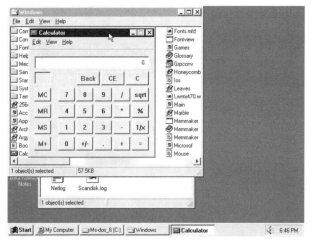

Figure 1.20 *Starting the Calculator program from the Windows folder.*

As you can see from this exercise, you do not always have to use the Start menu to run a program. Instead, you can just double-click on the program's icon in a folder. However, to use this method, you first must locate the folder that contains the program you want to run. As a result, you'll usually find it easier to start a program from the Start menu, because it is easier to move through a sequence of submenus than to open a series of folders.

OPENING A DOCUMENT

Windows 95 emphasizes the notion that you work with documents, not programs. After all, a program is often simply a tool to help you create a document. For example, you use a word-processing program to create a text document; a Paint program to create a drawing; and a spreadsheet program to prepare a spreadsheet. You might say Windows 95 encourages you to work directly with a document. To open any document, all you have to do is double-click on the document's icon. Windows 95, in turn, will start the document's associated program and load the document into the program's window. For example, double-click on the Leaves icon in the Windows folder. (This icon represents a graphics file.) As shown in Figure 1.21, when you double-click on the Leaves icon on your system, Windows 95 starts the Paint program and loads the LEAVES image in that window. After you view the image, use the Close button to close the Paint window.

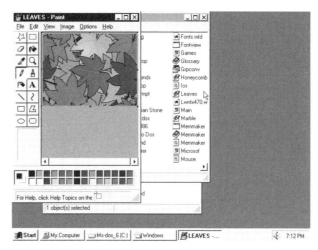

Figure 1.21 The image Windows 95 displays after you double-click on the Leaves icon in the Windows folder.

How to Tell an Icon's Type

As a graphical environment, Windows 95 uses many different icons. Some icons represent documents. Others represent programs. Still others represent objects, such as a printer or a modem. To use Windows 95 completely, you need to recognize these icons. Each icon has a picture to help you identify the object it represents. However, there may be times when you have difficulty associating an icon with a document or a program because the picture on the icon doesn't mean anything to you.

Fortunately, Windows 95 provides you with an easy way to identify the type of object an icon represents. If you are not sure whether a particular icon represents a program or document, place the mouse pointer on the icon and click the right-mouse button. For example, right-click on the Calc icon. Windows 95, in turn, will display a pop-up menu, as shown in Figure 1.22.

Figure 1.22 Right-clicking on the Calc icon in the Windows folder.

> ### RIGHT-CLICKING TO IDENTIFY AN ICON
>
>
> As you have learned, there may be times when you have difficulty associating an icon with an object because you don't recognize the icon's picture. In such situations, right-click on the icon. Windows 95, in turn, will display a pop-up menu. Select the pop-up menu's Properties option. In response, Windows 95 will display a properties sheet that identifies the object's name, type, location, size, and attributes. In addition, the properties sheet tells you when the object was created, last modified, and most recently accessed.

Next, move your mouse pointer to the pop-up menu's last option, Properties, and click your left-mouse button. Windows 95 will display a properties sheet, like the one shown in Figure 1.23.

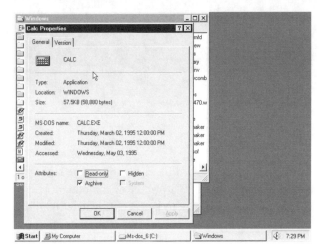

Figure 1.23 *Properties of the Calc icon.*

You will learn more about properties sheets later. For now, simply look at the Type field just below the Calc icon. As you can see, the Calc object is an Application, which is just a fancy way of saying that the Calc icon represents a computer program. To close the Calc Properties sheet, click on the sheet's Cancel button. Try right-clicking on another icon and selecting the Properties option from the pop-up menu that appears. Remember, if you need information about any object in Windows 95, be it a folder, a document, or a program (application), start by right-clicking on its icon.

EASY ACCESS TO A PROGRAM OR A DOCUMENT

You do not have to go through many levels of folders every time you want to run a program. Windows 95 gives you a quicker way—a shortcut. In fact, you should create shortcuts for the programs you run on a regular basis. For example, suppose you want a shortcut to the Calc program. Position the mouse pointer on the Calc icon, hold down your left-mouse button, drag the icon on to an empty spot on the Desktop, and drop the icon (release your mouse button). Figure 1.24 shows the result of this drag-and-drop operation: Windows 95 places a new icon, Shortcut to Calc, on the Desktop. Go ahead and close all open folders. Now, double-click on the Shortcut to Calc icon. Windows 95, in turn, will start the Calc program and display the Calculator window on the Desktop. As you can see, the Shortcut to Calc icon acts the same way as the original Calc icon in the Windows folder. Using the simple shortcut icon on the Desktop, you can start the Calc program with a simple double-click of your mouse. Close the Calculator window and continue with the rest of the session.

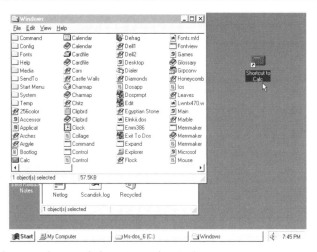

Figure 1.24 The Calc icon after you drag-and-drop it on the Desktop.

> **SHORTCUT ICONS FOR DOCUMENTS**
>
> If you have a particular document that you revise frequently, you may find it a hassle to open a series of folders each time you need to work with it. For example, you may have a spreadsheet to which you add information several times a day. Fortunately, Windows 95 provides you a quick way to open the document and run its corresponding program—you can set up a shortcut icon to the document on your Desktop. To do so, position your mouse pointer on the icon, hold down your left-mouse button, and drag the document's icon to an empty spot on your Desktop. Windows 95, in turn, will place a shortcut icon for the document directly on the Desktop. When you click this icon, Windows 95 will open the document and start the corresponding program.

GETTING HELP

When you started this test drive of Windows 95, the initial Welcome window let you see an example of the online Help available in Windows 95. After you clicked on the Welcome window What's New button, Windows 95 opened a Help window that contained information about the new features in Windows 95. As you will see, there is a lot more online Help information in Windows 95.

You will find online Help useful because it gives you instant access to information. You do not have to rummage through your desk to find the printed manuals. You do not have to strain your eyes on tiny index print or scan hundreds of book pages to find the information you need. All you have to do is start online Help. In addition, nearly all Windows 95 programs provide online Help and use the same format to present such Help information. For example, online Help in WordPad looks and behaves the same as it does in Paint. As such, after you learn how to access the Windows 95 online Help system, you will be able to obtain Help information in every Windows 95 application you use.

The Windows 95 online Help is easy to use. To start online Help, click on the Start button on the Taskbar. In response, Windows 95 will display the Start menu. To display the online Help window, click on the Start menu Help option. Windows 95, in turn, will display the Help Topics sheet Contents page, as shown in Figure 1.25. This page lets you look up general information about Windows 95.

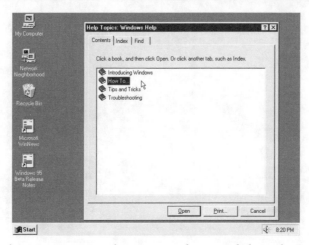

Figure 1.25 The Help Topics sheet Contents page that appears when you click on the Start menu Help option.

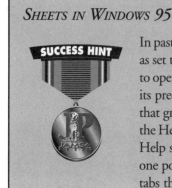

SHEETS IN WINDOWS 95

In past versions of Windows, when users wanted to perform a series of related operations (such as set the properties of dialog boxes), they had to expend lots of time and many mouse clicks to open and close several menus and windows. To make Windows 95 more user-friendly than its predecessors, Microsoft built a substantial number of *sheets*, a specific type of dialog box that groups similar functions together, into the Windows 95 operating system. For example, the Help Topics sheet you just opened gives you easy access to three key portions of the online Help system: the Help Topics Contents, Index, and Find functions. To move quickly from one portion (or *page*) of the Help Topics sheet to another, all you have to do is click on the tabs that appear just beneath the sheet's title bar.

BROWSING THROUGH HELP TOPICS

One way to use the online Help system is to browse through the information it contains, just as you might thumb through the pages of a book. In fact, the Windows 95 online Help system uses a book analogy to display its topics. Notice that each topic in Figure 1.25 has an icon of a closed book next to it. Double-click on the closed book icon next to the "How To..." topic. Help, in turn, will open that topic and display an indented list of subtopics, each with a closed book icon. Double-click on the Run Program topic. In response, Help will open that topic and display the subtopics, as shown in Figure 1.26.

Figure 1.26 Help subtopics in the Run Program topic.

Notice how the icons that accompany the topics have changed from closed books to pages with question marks. To view information on how to start a program in Windows 95, double-click on the "Starting a program" topic. Help, in turn, will display the window you see in Figure 1.27.

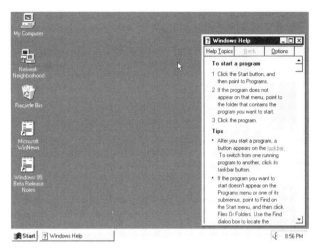

Figure 1.27 Help information on starting a program in Windows 95.

Notice how the Help window in Figure 1.27 provides step-by-step instructions that you can follow to start any program. In some cases, the Help window will also include *jump buttons*. When you click your mouse on a jump button, Windows 95 starts a program you need to perform the Help window's instructions. The Help window in Figure 1.27 also shows a number of tips on starting a program. For most topics, the Help window includes such tips.

To explore another interesting feature of online Help, click on the underlined word, *Taskbar*, in the Help window. Help, in turn, will display a small pop-up window with the definition of the term *Taskbar*. (Click again, and that pop-up window disappears.) Whenever you see an underlined term in a Windows 95 Help window, you can click on the term to learn its definition.

CHECKING OUT THE INDEX

When you need a specific piece of information from a book, you turn to the book's index to find out which pages contain the information you need. The book's index saves you time because you do not have to thumb through every page in the book to find information on a specific topic. Windows 95's online Help system also provides an index. However, the Windows 95 online Help index is easier to use than a conventional book index. To find information on a topic in a conventional index, you must search among a wide range of headings and subheadings. In contrast, the Windows 95 online Help system searches its index for you—all you have to do is enter in the first few letters of the topic about which you want information.

To see the online Help index, first click on the Help window Help Topics button (see Figure 1.27). In response, Windows 95 will open the Help Topics sheet again. Notice that the sheet has divider tabs like the ones you find on file folders in an office. Click on the middle tab—Index. Help, in turn, will open the Help Topics sheet Index page that you see in Figure 1.28.

Using the Help index is straightforward. In the Text field at the top of the Index page, you type in the first few letters of the topic you want Help to find. As you type each letter, Help changes the content of the Index page's list box so that the initial characters of the box's first entry match those you type in the page's text field. When the list box displays the entry you want, you simply click on the entry, and then click the Display button.

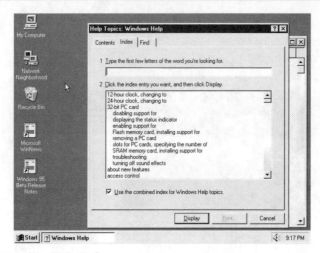

Figure 1.28 The Windows 95 online Help Index.

For example, suppose you want to find information on the Start menu. To do so, enter the words **Start menu** in the Index page's text field. As you enter **s**, the index display in the list box jumps to the first index that starts with the letter *s*. Enter **t**. Help, in turn, moves the index to the first word that starts with *st*. By now, you can see the "Start menu" entry in the index. Click on that entry. Then, click on the Display button. In response, Windows 95 will display a window with a list of all the topics for the "Start menu" index entry. Click on the topic that appeals to you. Now, click on the Display button. Help, in turn, will display a window with the Help information for the topic you selected.

Searching for a Keyword

While the Help index is a handy feature, there will be times when this index doesn't include the text you want to search. Fortunately, using the Help Topics sheet Find page, you can search for any specific word or phrase that appears in a Windows 95 online Help topic—something you cannot easily do in a printed manual.

To search for a specific word or phrase in online Help, click on the Help Topics sheet Find tab. When you click on this tab for the first time, a window opens that tells you Windows 95 must create a list of all the words that appear in the online Help system. (Help will refer to this list of words, called the *search index*, when you ask it to find specific words or phrases in the Help topics.) Figure 1.29 shows this window.

Figure 1.29 Creating a list of Help words.

To build the search index, click on the Next button in the window shown in Figure 1.29. In the next window that Windows 95 displays, click on the Finish button. Windows 95, in turn, will prepare the search index. In addition, the Help Topics sheet Find page will display a list of words that you can search, as shown in Figure 1.30.

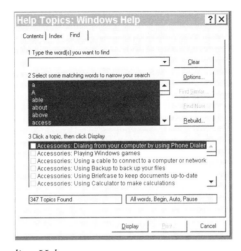

Figure 1.30 *Finding a word in the online Help system.*

To search for a specific word in online Help, begin to enter the word in the text field at the top of the Find page (see Figure 1.30). As you type each letter, Help will display a list of all words that start with the letters you have entered so far. Underneath that list of matching words, Help will display another list with all the Help topics whose text contains the search word. For example, if you are looking for information on the Point to Point Protocol (or PPP, for short), enter **PPP** in the text field. (PPP is a popular protocol that you might use to connect your home computer to the Internet.) Help, in turn, will display all the topics that contain any occurrence of the word PPP, as shown in Figure 1.31.

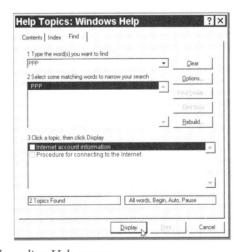

Figure 1.31 *Searching for PPP in the online Help system.*

The Help topics themselves do not have to contain the search word. Windows 95 online Help system will display a topic if the search word appears somewhere in the topic's complete text. As such, although the letters PPP do not appear in the topics that the Index page in Figure 1.31 shows, you will see at least one reference to PPP if you open either topic. To see the text for a Help topic that the Find page displays, click on the topic and then click on the Display button. Help, in turn, will open another window with the online Help information for the topic you selected. As you can see, Windows 95 offers you an extensive online Help system, which you will learn more about in Chapter 4, "Using Online Help."

Ending Your Windows 95 Session

Your 15-minute tour of Windows 95 is almost over. It is now time to end your Windows 95 session. However, before you exit Windows 95, you must initiate the operating system's shutdown procedure. Unlike simple operating systems such as MS-DOS, Windows 95 does not always write everything to disk when you expect it to—instead, Windows 95 stores data in memory as much as possible to avoid accessing the disk too frequently. Windows 95 postpones writing to the disk because the mechanical disk access is much slower than memory access. By reducing the number of times it accesses the disk, Windows 95 makes the system more efficient for you. As such, to ensure that Windows 95 safely stores all work you do, you need to use the operating system's shutdown procedure. To start the shutdown procedure, click on the Start button. In the Start menu, click on the Shut Down option. Windows 95, in turn, will open a window that presents you with four options:

- Shut down the computer?
- Restart the computer?
- Restart the computer in MS-DOS mode?
- Close all programs and log on as a different user?

The first option is the default. Because you want to shut down the system, simply click on the Yes button (or press ENTER). Windows 95, in turn, will shut down your system and display a message that says you can safely turn off your computer.

Note: Never turn off your computer without first shutting down Windows 95. Doing so may damage or destroy the information stored on your disk.

Keys to Success

When you started this chapter, you were like a visitor to a strange and new city (Windows 95). In a whirlwind tour of the new city, this chapter has taught you how to speak the language of the natives—how to use your mouse and the various elements that Windows 95 displays. Likewise, you have discovered how, if you ever get lost and need direction, you can use the Windows 95 online Help system to obtain assistance. In Chapter 2, you will receive further instruction in the language of Windows 95. You will learn how to use and manipulate elements of the Windows 95 display, such as windows, dialog boxes, sheets, and so on. However, before you move on to Chapter 2, make sure you understand the following key concepts:

- ✓ You can use the Start button to start programs in Windows 95.
- ✓ The Taskbar tells you, at a glance, which programs are running. In addition, you use the Taskbar buttons to switch from one program to another.
- ✓ You can use the My Computer icon to explore the documents, programs, and devices on your system.
- ✓ You can use buttons on the title bar to size and close a window.
- ✓ To move a window, drag the window's title bar using your mouse.
- ✓ The online Help system provides you with easy access to information about the Windows 95 operating system.
- ✓ You must use the Start menu Shut Down option to exit Windows 95.
- ✓ Always shut down Windows 95 before you turn off your computer.

Chapter 2
Working with Windows in Windows 95

In Chapter 1, you went on a whirlwind tour of the new city—Windows 95. You saw the major landmarks, learned how to get around, and discovered how to leave the city. However, because Chapter 1 provided so much information, you may not remember all that you saw or learned during your tour. Fortunately, Chapter 1 was only your first fifteen minutes of a much longer Windows 95 tour. In the rest of this book, you will return to the sights and attractions you drove by in Chapter 1. However, during your next visit to these locations, your guide, *Success with Windows 95*, will stop the tour bus and let you explore Windows 95 more thoroughly.

In this chapter, your tour bus will stop at the Windows 95 language academy, where you will learn how to speak conversational Windows 95; in other words, you will learn how to use the windows, menus, and dialog boxes that are at the heart of all you see in Windows 95. A *window* is a rectangular region of the screen with various decorations (for example, the title bar and title-bar buttons) around its border. If you have used earlier versions of Microsoft Windows, you have already seen and used windows. However, Windows 95 changes the appearance of the windows. Because you must use windows to perform most tasks in Windows 95, this chapter teaches you key window operations. By the time you finish this chapter, you will understand the following key concepts:

- Windows 95 runs your programs within a window. Each window has common attributes, such as a menu bar, title bar, and buttons you can click to close or size the window.

- One of the easiest ways to run a program is to choose the program from the Start menu Program option.

- Windows 95 lets you run multiple programs at the same time, each within its own window.

- When you run two or more programs at the same time, Windows 95 lets you exchange information (such as text or pictures) between them.

- To simplify common operations, Windows 95 makes extensive use of menus. The two most common menu types are pull-down and pop-up menus.

- At times, a program cannot continue until it receives information from you, such as the printer you want to use or the file you want to open from your disk. In such cases, the program will display a dialog box that asks you to specify the necessary information.

A Typical Window

In Windows 95, you do most of your work in a window. As such, you need to learn how to use the different parts of a window. To view a typical window, run WordPad, the word-processing program that comes with Windows 95. To start WordPad, perform these steps:

1. Click on the Start button. Windows 95, in turn, will display the Start menu.

2. Move your mouse pointer to the Start menu Programs option. Windows 95 will display the Programs menu.

3. Move your mouse pointer to the Programs menu Accessories option. Windows 95 will display the Accessories menu.

4. Chose the Accessories menu WordPad option. Windows 95 will start the WordPad program.

When WordPad runs, it displays a window within which you can create your document. Additionally, Windows 95 adds a Taskbar button with the label "Document - WordPad." As you learned in Chapter 1, you click on the Taskbar button to activate or select the WordPad program. As shown in Figure 2.1, the WordPad window includes many of the typical window parts that are common to all windows in Windows 95.

Note: *Not every window in Windows 95 displays all the parts shown in Figure 2.1. For example, the Calculator program's window shown in Chapter 1 has no toolbar, status bar, or sizing handle.*

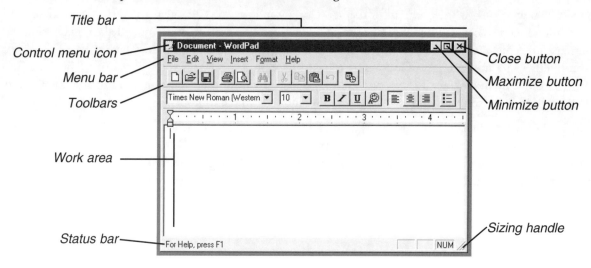

Figure 2.1 Parts of a typical window in Windows 95.

In Chapter 1, you used some of the window parts Figure 2.1 identifies. In the following sections, you will learn more about these parts of a window.

TITLE BAR

Each program you run displays its output within a window. When you run multiple programs at the same time, you need a way to determine which window corresponds to which program. That's where a window's title bar comes in. The *title bar* stretches across the top of the window. The program uses the title bar to display its name (or title). In addition, if you are using a document within the program, the title bar may also display the document name. For example, the WordPad window in Figure 2.1 displays "Document - WordPad" in its title bar, which tells you the WordPad program is currently working with the document named "Document."

MENU BAR

Most Windows-based programs let you perform operations by selecting different menu options. As such, most program windows display a *menu bar* just beneath the title bar. As you can see in the WordPad window, the menu bar lists the names of major menu categories. When you click on a menu category, the program displays a menu. Each menu, in turn, provides a number of options. For example, WordPad's File menu includes options you can select to open, save, or print a document file. Later in this chapter, you will explore menus further.

TOOLBARS

Although you can perform most operations using menus, you may have to make several menu choices. To save you steps (and time), many newer programs display one or more *toolbars* that contain buttons and other items you can use to perform specific tasks quickly. The WordPad program displays two toolbars underneath its menu bar.

Typically, each toolbar button displays an icon that indicates (or at least strongly hints at) what function the button performs. For example, in the WordPad window, you can use the button with the printer icon to print the document that the window currently displays. However, you may not always be able to determine a toolbar button's function just by looking at the icon it displays. Fortunately, most Windows 95 programs have a feature you can use to learn a button's purpose. To see this feature in action, move your mouse pointer to any toolbar button in the WordPad window and let the pointer rest on the button for two to three seconds. The program, in turn, will display a small pop-up window with text that briefly describes the button's function. These pop-up windows are known as *tool tips*.

USING TOOL TIPS

To make common operations quick and easy, many programs use toolbars that contain a number of buttons, each with its own icon. Each toolbar button performs a specific task. By looking at a button's icon, you can usually determine what the button does. However, if an icon's meaning is not clear to you (or you want to make sure you know what the button does), try using the tool tips feature that most Windows 95 programs support. Rest the mouse pointer on a toolbar button for a moment or two. The program, in turn, will display a small pop-up window with text that describes the button's function.

Try the tool tips feature whenever you see a toolbar with buttons.

STATUS BAR

As you use a Windows program to perform different operations, there may be times when the program wants to let you know how it is progressing. In such cases, the program may display status or other informational messages. For example, if you are printing a large document, your word processor may display a status message that tells you what percentage of your document it has printed.

The *status bar*, another optional window element, is the rectangular area that stretches across the bottom edge of a window. The status bar displays helpful hints and other information relevant to the program. For example, in the WordPad window, the status bar tells you to press the **F1** key if you need help. The status bar also indicates when certain keys, such as NUM LOCK and CAPS LOCK, are active. In Figure 2.1, the letters *NUM* appearing in the status bar indicate that the NUM LOCK key is active. As such, keys on your keyboard's numeric keypad will produce numbers, as opposed to directional arrow keys that move the cursor.

WORK AREA

As you use Windows programs to accomplish everyday tasks, the *work area* of a window is where you will spend most of your time. Because WordPad is a word-processing program, you will enter text in the work area. Similarly, in the Paint program, the work area is the canvas on which you will prepare your drawings. Likewise, to perform mathematical operations, you will use the buttons and text field in the Calculator program's work area. In Chapters 12 and 13, you will explore various Windows 95 applications (called accessory programs or accessories), including WordPad, Paint, and Calculator.

CONTROL MENU ICON

In Chapter 1, you learned how to size, move, and close a window. As it turns out, most windows have a special menu, the *Control menu*, that you can use to perform these operations. At the left edge of the title bar, you will find an icon of the program. This icon identifies the program and provides you with a way to display the program's Control menu. As a result, it is called the *Control menu icon*. Click on the Control menu icon in the WordPad window. WordPad, in turn, will display the Control menu, as shown in Figure 2.2.

The Control menu options let you perform basic window operations. The last option, Close, appears in boldface because it is the default option. If you double-click on the Control menu icon, Windows 95 accepts the default option. Thus, if you double-click on the Control menu icon, the window will close and the program will exit. For now, do not close the WordPad window.

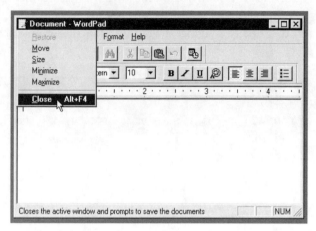

Figure 2.2 The Control menu WordPad displays after you click on the Control menu icon.

BUTTONS ON THE TITLE BAR

Notice the three buttons in the upper-right corner of the window in Figure 2.2. You can use these buttons—the Minimize button, the Maximize button, and the Close button—to perform routine tasks.

MINIMIZE BUTTON

If you run several programs at the same time, the Desktop may become cluttered with program windows. To reduce such clutter and clean up your Desktop, you can use the *Minimize button* (the button with the underscore etched on it) to hide some of the windows. Use the Minimize button when you want to get a window out of the way, but do not want to get rid of it completely (you don't want to close the window).

When you minimize a window, the corresponding program continues to run. As such, you don't need to restart the program or reload document files when you want to use the program again. Instead, you just click on the program's Taskbar button. Windows 95, in turn, redisplays the program window on your Desktop. To see how the Minimize button works, click on the WordPad window's Minimize button. Windows 95, in turn, will hide the WordPad window and show the program's Taskbar button, as shown in Figure 2.3.

Note: *The term* **Taskbar button** *refers to the button that appears on the Taskbar when Windows 95 opens a program window.*

To restore a minimized window to its normal shape and size, click on the window's Taskbar button. For example, click on WordPad's Taskbar button. Windows 95, in turn, will restore the WordPad window to its normal shape and size, making the program's Taskbar button appear "pushed in."

MAXIMIZE BUTTON

Depending on the program with which you are working, there may be times when you want to use your entire screen to display the program's output. For example, if you are using the Paint program to create an illustration, your illustration may be larger than your current window. To expand a program window until it fills your screen, you use the Maximize button.

2: WORKING WITH WINDOWS IN WINDOWS 95

Figure 2.3 *The Desktop after you minimize the WordPad window.*

To see how the Maximize button works, click on the WordPad window's Maximize button. Windows 95, in turn, will expand the WordPad window until it covers your Desktop (except for the Taskbar), as shown in Figure 2.4.

When you maximize a window, Windows 95 changes the Maximize button to a Restore button. As you can see in Figure 2.4, the Restore button has a pair of overlapping rectangles etched on it. To return the maximized window to its normal size and shape, click on the Restore button. For example, in the WordPad window, click on the Restore button. Windows 95, in turn, will return the WordPad window to its previous shape, size, and location.

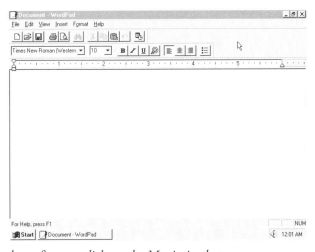

Figure 2.4 *The WordPad window after you click on the Maximize button.*

CLOSE BUTTON

As you learned in Chapter 1, when you finish using a program, you end the program by closing its window. In Windows 95, there are many ways you can close a window. For example, you can double-click on the window's Control menu icon (provided Close is the Control menu's default option) or select the window's File menu Exit option. However, the fastest way you can close a window is to click your mouse on the window's Close button (the button with the "X").

Click on the WordPad window's Close button now to end the program. Windows 95, in turn, will remove both the WordPad window and the WordPad's Taskbar button. Before most Windows programs exit, they typically open a dialog box to give you an opportunity to save any changes you've made to the document or documents with which

29

you have been working. Because you have not done anything with the document in the WordPad window, that program quits immediately.

Running Programs Using the Start Menu

Now that you have examined the parts of a window, you will learn how to use the Taskbar or, more precisely, the Start button to run your programs.

To learn the Start button's purpose, place the mouse pointer on top of the Start button and wait for a moment or two. Windows 95 will display a tool tip that says "Click here to begin." That tip sums up how you use Windows 95; you almost always begin your work at the Start button. When you click on the Start button, Windows 95 displays the Start menu.

Using the Start Menu

In Windows 3.1, the Program Manager was your gateway to the programs on your system. The Program Manager represented your programs as icons and placed these icons into program groups. To start a program, you had to double-click on the program's icon. From extensive testing, Microsoft discovered that new users naturally tried to single-click on such icons. However, to grasp the concept of "double-clicking," most new users needed outside instruction. Additionally, many new users often weren't able to locate specific program groups. To address both of these problems, Microsoft added the Start menu to the Windows 95 user interface. Using the Start menu, you can launch a program with a single mouse click. Furthermore, as you move your mouse pointer on to the submenus that stem from the Start menu, program icons appear in each submenu Windows 95 opens. To see how the Start menu works, click on the Start button. Windows 95, in turn, will display the Start menu, as shown in Figure 2.5.

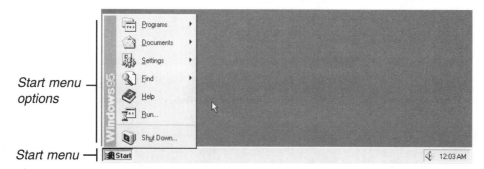

Figure 2.5 The Start menu appears when you click on the Start button.

Note: *As you learned in Chapter 1, the Start menu remains visible even when you move the mouse pointer off the menu. To minimize the number of actions you have to perform to select menu options, Microsoft designed the Start menu, and all other Windows 95 pop-up menus, to remain visible until you click at another location on the Desktop.*

Each Start menu option has an icon and label. You can select one of the last three Start menu options—Help, Run, or Shut Down—by simply clicking on the option. For example, to access the Windows 95 online Help system, you would click on the Start menu Help option.

Each of the first four Start menu options has a triangle that points to the right. When you move your mouse pointer on to a menu option with a right-pointing triangle, Windows 95 opens a submenu immediately adjacent to the menu option. For example, if you place the mouse pointer on the Start menu Programs option, Windows 95 displays another menu—the Programs menu. The Programs menu, in turn, contains other submenus. As you move your mouse pointer from one submenu to another, Windows 95 displays the complete sequence of submenus, as shown in Figure 2.6.

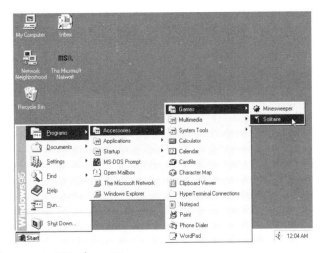

Figure 2.6 A sequence of submenus in Windows 95.

In the sequence of submenus, Windows 95 highlights the menu options you selected with your mouse pointer. For example, in Figure 2.6, Windows 95 highlights the Programs, Accessories, Games, and Solitaire menu options. Thus, you can tell at a glance the path you have taken to reach the Solitaire program. For the menu sequence in Figure 2.6 that selects Solitaire, you may express the path as *Programs> Accessories> Games> Solitaire*.

Pause for a moment and note that you can activate the entire menu sequence of Figure 2.6 with a single mouse click and a few mouse movements. As you have learned, when Microsoft engineers designed Windows 95, they sought to reduce the number of times you'd need to click your mouse to perform most tasks. As a result, you can do practically everything in Windows 95 without any double-clicks.

Use your mouse pointer to duplicate the menu sequence you see in Figure 2.6. After you reach the Games menu, click on the Solitaire option to run the Solitaire card game. As you can see, when you reach the rightmost menu in a menu sequence, all you need to do to select an option is move your mouse pointer on to it and click your left-mouse button. Click on the Solitaire window's Close button to exit the Solitaire game program.

After you know how to navigate through the Start menu and its many submenus, you can start any program easily. If you have your own applications (such as Microsoft Word or Excel) installed on your system, they will appear in the Applications menu, which you access through the Programs menu. Therefore, when you first start using Windows 95, you should go through the various submenus that stem from the Start menu and see what is available on your system.

STARTING PROGRAMS FROM THE START MENU

Using the Windows 95 Start menu, you can run programs with a few mouse movements and a single mouse click. To start a program using the Start menu, perform these steps:

1. Click on the Start button. Windows 95, in turn, will display the Start menu.

2. Move your mouse pointer to the Start menu Programs option. In response, Windows 95 will display the Programs menu.

3. If the program you want to run appears in the Programs menu, move your mouse pointer to the program's option and click your left-mouse button. Windows 95, in turn, will start the program.

If the program you want to run doesn't appear in the Programs menu, move your mouse pointer to one of the Programs menu options with a right-pointing triangle. In response,

> Windows 95 will open another submenu. For example, if you move your mouse pointer to the Programs menu Accessories option, Windows 95 will open the Accessories submenu.
>
> 4. If the program you want to run appears in the new submenu, move your mouse pointer to the program's option and click your left-mouse button. Windows 95, in turn, will start the program.
>
>   If the program you want to run doesn't appear in the new submenu, move your mouse pointer to one of the submenu options with a right-pointing triangle. Windows 95, in turn, will open another submenu.
>
> 5. Repeat step 4 until you find the program you want to run.

RUNNING MULTIPLE PROGRAMS

As you learned in Chapter 1, Windows 95 supports *multitasking*, a feature that lets you run several programs at the same time. For example, suppose you are using WordPad to prepare a newsletter. In addition, imagine that you need an illustration to offset some text on your newsletter's front page. In Windows 95, you can open the Paint program and create that illustration without closing WordPad. Because you don't have to close one application to open another, you can quickly paste the illustration onto the front page of your newsletter to see how it looks, switch to the Paint window to revise the illustration, and then switch back to WordPad to paste the illustration again. You can repeat this process until you find the page's appearance satisfactory.

To start one program while you have another running, just click on the Start button. After Windows 95 displays the Start menu, move your mouse pointer to the appropriate submenu and click your left-mouse button on the program option you desire. Windows 95, in turn, will open a maximized window for the new program. Then, when you want to display the first program's window again without exiting the second program, you click on the first program's Taskbar button.

To get a feel for how Windows 95 multitasking works, start a few of the accessory programs that come with Windows 95. To begin, run the WordPad program. From the Start menu, follow the *Programs> Accessories>* menu sequence and click your mouse on the WordPad option. Windows 95, in turn, will display the WordPad window and place a button on the Taskbar for the WordPad program. Next, run the Paint program. To start Paint, follow the *Programs> Accessories>* menu sequence and click your mouse on the Paint option. Windows 95, in turn, will display the Paint window and place a button on the Taskbar for the Paint program. Notice that your display screen now shows two Taskbar buttons—one for WordPad and one for Paint. Paint's Taskbar button appears depressed, which means that Paint is the active program. In other words, the program with the depressed Taskbar button is the one you are currently using.

Note: *If you have upgraded your system from WIndows 3.1 to Windows 95, you can run older Windows 3.1 accessory programs, such as the Calendar program discussed in the following example. If you bought a new system with Windows 95, your system will not have these older accessory programs.*

Now, start two more accessory programs. To run Calendar and Calculator, perform these steps (if your system does not include the Calendar accessory, simply run WordPad, Paint, and Calculator—three programs instead of four):

1. Click on the Start button. Windows 95 will display the Start menu.
2. Move your mouse pointer to the Start menu Programs option. Windows 95, in turn, will display the Programs menu.

3. Move your mouse pointer to the Programs menu Accessories option. Windows 95 will display the Accessories menu.

4. Position your mouse pointer on the Accessories menu Calendar option and click your left-mouse button. Windows 95 will start the Calendar program.

5. Repeat steps 1 through 3.

6. Position your mouse pointer on the Accessories menu Calculator option and click your left-mouse button. Windows 95, in turn, will start the Calculator program.

Now, you have four programs running: WordPad, Paint, Calendar, and Calculator. As Figure 2.7 shows, a typical display screen looks crowded when you run four programs concurrently.

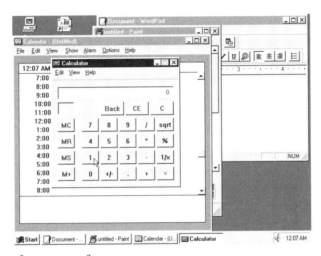

Figure 2.7 *The display screen after you run four programs.*

The Taskbar now has five buttons—the Start button and one button for each program. Notice that the Taskbar button for Calculator—the last program you started—appears depressed. In the next section, you will learn how to manage the windows and switch from one program to another.

Moving Windows

As you work with Windows 95, there will be times when you want to view documents side-by-side so that you can compare their contents. For example, if you are simultaneously preparing a slide show in Microsoft PowerPoint (a presentation program) and supplementary materials for your audience in Microsoft Word, you might want to have the PowerPoint window and the Word window side-by-side so that you can easily transfer information between the two documents. To arrange windows side-by-side, you can move them around.

Note: If your monitor is smaller than 19", you may need to resize one or both windows before they will fit side-by-side on your display screen. Otherwise, one window will always overlap the other. Later in this chapter, you will learn how to resize a window.

To move a window, simply use your mouse to drag the window by its title bar to a new position. To accomplish the drag operation, perform these steps:

1. Place your mouse pointer on some part of the window's title bar, hold down your left-mouse button, and begin moving your mouse. Windows 95, in turn, will display a rectangular outline of the window that moves as you move your mouse.

2. Move your mouse until the window's outline arrives at the location you desire. Then, release the mouse button. Windows 95, in turn, will redisplay the window at the new location.

Try moving some of the windows that you currently see on your Desktop.

> ### PILE OF WINDOWS
>
> When you work with several windows at the same time, Windows 95 arranges the windows in a pile on your display screen—like a pile of papers on an actual desktop. The topmost window has a different colored title bar than the other windows in the pile. When you click on any part of a window, Windows 95 immediately brings that window to the top of the pile.

RESIZING WINDOWS

On occasion, you may need to do more than just rearrange windows to create a well-organized and highly functional Desktop. For example, suppose you want to view the Paint and WordPad windows side-by-side, but your screen display isn't big enough to hold both windows in this manner. On such occasions, you may have to increase or decrease the size of one or more windows on your Desktop. To resize a window, you must use your mouse pointer to drag the window's borders until the window is the size you desire. When you move your mouse pointer on to a window border, the pointer's shape changes to a short line with arrowheads at both ends. The mouse pointer's new shape tells you in which direction the window's size will shrink or grow. To see the different pointer shapes, perform these steps:

1. Move your mouse pointer to the bottom border of any window on the screen. Windows 95, in turn, will change your mouse pointer to an arrow that points up and down.

2. Move your mouse pointer to the left or right edge of a window. Windows 95 will change your mouse pointer to an arrow that points left and right.

3. Move your mouse pointer to the corner of a window. Windows 95, in turn, will change your mouse pointer into a diagonal line with arrows at both ends.

To resize a window, perform these steps:

1. Move your mouse pointer to a side or a corner of the window. Windows 95, in turn, will change the pointer's shape.

2. As soon as the pointer changes, hold down your left-mouse button and begin moving your mouse. In response, Windows 95 will display an outline of the window that changes shape as you move your mouse.

3. Move your mouse until the outline reaches the size you desire for the window. Then, release your left-mouse button. Windows 95, in turn, will redraw the entire window to match the size of the outline.

Note: *Some programs impose a lower limit on the size of the program's window. Don't be surprised if you cannot reduce the size of a window after a certain point.*

2: Working with Windows in Windows 95

Quickly Rearranging the Windows

Although you can move and resize windows to clean up and organize the Desktop exactly the way you want it, you may not always have time to perform such operations. If you need to bring order to your display screen in a hurry, use the Taskbar menu to arrange your windows quickly. For example, to tell Windows 95 to display your windows in a neat pile, perform these steps:

1. Move your mouse pointer to the Taskbar and click your right-mouse button. Windows 95, in turn, will display a pop-up menu (the Taskbar menu), as shown in Figure 2.8.

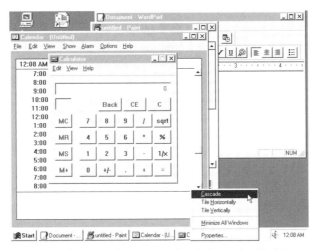

Figure 2.8 The menu that Windows 95 displays when you right-click on the Taskbar.

2. Move your mouse pointer to the Taskbar menu Cascade option and click your left-mouse button. Windows 95, in turn, will arrange (cascade) the windows in a neatly organized, overlapping manner, as shown in Figure 2.9.

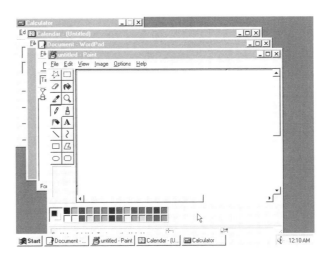

Figure 2.9 A cascaded arrangement of windows on your Desktop.

The other two Taskbar menu arrangement options (see Figure 2.8) are Tile Horizontally and Tile Vertically. When you tell Windows 95 to tile your windows, the operating system places them side-by-side without overlapping, much like tiles on a floor. However, when there are many windows on the Desktop, such tile arrangements are not useful because each window's work area becomes too small for you to use productively.

35

Experiment with the Taskbar menu's Tile Horizontally and Tile Vertically options now. Observe how Windows 95 rearranges the program windows on your Desktop. Figure 2.10 illustrates the Windows tiled horizontally on your screen.

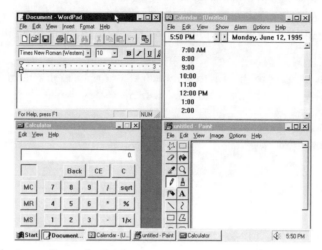

Figure 2.10 Windows tiled horizontally on the Desktop.

Note: *When you select the Tile Horizontally or Tile Vertically option and a window does not resize properly (because the program enforces a minimum size), Windows 95 will attempt to tile the windows. In such cases, the windows on the Desktop will overlap rather than tile properly.*

Minimizing a Window

Another way to reduce the clutter on your display screen is to minimize the windows that you are not using. To minimize a window, click on the Minimize button that appears in that window's title bar. When you want to work with that window again, just click on that program's Taskbar button. Windows 95, in turn, will return the window to its normal size.

Click on the Minimize button in the Paint, Calculator, and Calendar windows.

Note: *If you run several programs at the same time, the Taskbar buttons may not be large enough to show a program's full name. To learn the name of a program that a particular Taskbar button represents, simply place your mouse pointer on the Taskbar button. Windows 95, in turn, will display the program's full name (and the name of any document in the program's window) in a small tool-tip window.*

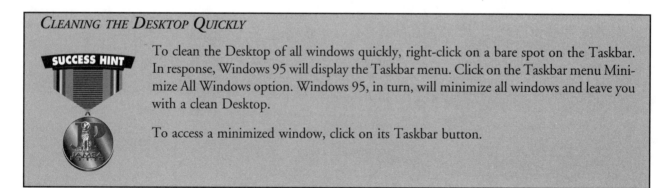

Cleaning the Desktop Quickly

To clean the Desktop of all windows quickly, right-click on a bare spot on the Taskbar. In response, Windows 95 will display the Taskbar menu. Click on the Taskbar menu Minimize All Windows option. Windows 95, in turn, will minimize all windows and leave you with a clean Desktop.

To access a minimized window, click on its Taskbar button.

Maximizing a Window

As you use program windows, there may be times when you need a large work area. For example, suppose you are composing a document in a word-processing program, such as WordPad. If you are like most people, you probably don't just type in all your text, print out your document, and send the hard copy to its destination. More likely, after you finish writing, you revise. Using the window's scroll bars, you make your way through your text, looking for punctuation errors, poor transitions, clarity problems, and so on.

In such document-editing situations, the smaller your program window (and work area), the more you must use the window's scroll bars to view your text. In fact, depending on the exact size and shape of the window, you may not be able to read even a single sentence without clicking your mouse several times on the scroll bar. As such, when you use a word-processing program to write and edit documents, you may want to maximize the program window.

To maximize the WordPad program's window, click on the Maximize button in the window's title bar. WordPad, in turn, will enlarge its window to fill your entire screen. Now the WordPad window will give you as much work area as possible within which you can work.

Switching between Programs

When you have windows scattered on the Desktop, one way to switch to a program is to click on any part of that program's window. However, if another window completely covers the window you want, you must find an alternate window-switching method. Fortunately, Windows 95 provides the Taskbar, which contains a button for each running program. To bring a program's window to the top of all windows, all you have to do is click on that program's Taskbar button.

Switching with the Taskbar

As you have learned, the Taskbar lets you jump to any program with a single click of your mouse. For example, to make the Paint program's window active, locate the Paint program's Taskbar button and click on it. Windows 95, in turn, will bring the Paint window to the top of the window pile and make the Paint program active.

Switching with the Keyboard

So far, you have used your mouse for most Windows 95 tasks. However, you can also use your keyboard to perform many such tasks. For example, Windows 95 offers an interesting keyboard shortcut you can use to switch between programs.

If you have used Windows 3.1, you may be familiar with ALT-TAB program switching. In Windows 3.1, to switch from one program to another, you hold down the ALT key and press TAB. Windows 3.1, in turn, displays a program icon at the center of your display screen. This icon represents the program window that Windows 3.1 will display if you release the ALT key. To change the program icon, you press TAB again.

As you will learn, Windows 95 also lets you use an ALT-TAB keyboard combination to switch between programs. However, unlike Window 3.1, Windows 95's ALT-TAB switching method displays icons for all the open windows on the Desktop. To use the keyboard to switch from one program to another, perform these steps:

1. Press ALT-TAB (hold down the ALT key and then press TAB). Windows 95, in turn, will display a small window with icons that represent the currently running programs, as shown in Figure 2.11. In addition, Windows 95 will place a rectangle around one of the icons. This rectangle indicates the program that will become active when you release the ALT and TAB keys.

Success with Windows 95

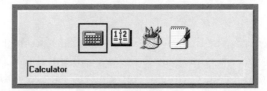

Figure 2.11 *The window that Windows 95 displays when you press* ALT-TAB.

2. As you hold down ALT, press and release TAB. In response, Windows 95 will move the current selection (as indicated by the rectangle) from one icon to the next.

3. When Windows 95 selects the program you want, release the ALT and TAB keys. Windows 95, in turn, will bring that program's window to the top of the window pile.

THREE WAYS TO SWITCH BETWEEN PROGRAMS

As you have learned, Windows 95 lets you run multiple programs at the same time. Furthermore, Windows 95 gives you three easy ways to switch between program windows:

- If the program window you want to activate is visible on the screen, simply click on any portion of the window. Windows 95, in turn, will bring the window to the front of your display screen.

- If the program window you want to activate isn't visible (for example, if the window is completely hidden by a pile of other windows or if it is minimized), click on the window's Taskbar button. Windows 95, in turn, will display the window at the shape and size it was before you minimized it. For example, if the window occupied the entire Desktop before you minimized it, Windows 95 will return the window to a maximized state when you click its Taskbar button.

- If you want to use your keyboard to switch between windows, hold down the ALT key and press TAB. Windows 95, in turn, will display a group of icons that represent the currently running programs. Hold down the ALT key and press and release TAB until Windows 95 places the selection rectangle around the program you want to activate. Then, release the ALT and TAB keys. In response, Windows 95 will bring the program window you selected to the top of the window pile.

WORKING WITH MENUS

As you learned during your quick tour of Windows 95, a menu is simply a list of options. To reach just about anything in Windows 95, you need to access a menu and select one of its options.

TYPES OF MENUS

Windows 95 supports three types of menus:

- Pull-down menu
- Pop-up menu
- Submenu

Pull-down menus appear when you click your left-mouse button on a menu-bar category in any window. *Pop-up menus* appear when you click your right-mouse button on any Desktop object, including the Desktop itself. (Windows 95 also displays a pop-up menu, the Start menu, when you left-click on the Start button.) *Submenus* appear when you move your mouse pointer on to a menu option with a right-pointing triangle.

Pull-down Menu

As you have learned, pull-down menus appear when you click on a menu-bar category. Pull-down menus are a long-time feature of Windows programs and operating systems. As such, if you upgrade to Windows 95 from Windows 3.1, you will have no trouble with the pull-down menus in Windows 95—pull-down menus in both operating systems behave exactly the same. However, if Windows 95 is the first Windows-based system you've used, you may have to practice using pull-down menus before you feel entirely comfortable with them.

To see a typical menu, click on the File category in WordPad's menu bar. (If the WordPad window is not visible, click on WordPad's Taskbar button.) Figure 2.12 shows WordPad's File pull-down menu.

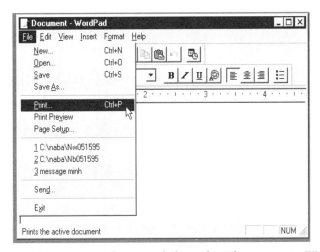

Figure 2.12 The pull-down menu that appears when you click on the File category in WordPad's menu bar.

When you move your mouse pointer on to a menu option, Windows 95 highlights that option. To activate the option, click on it. For example, click on the File menu Exit option; the WordPad program, in turn, will close its window and exit. Almost all Windows 95 programs have the File menu Exit option.

Pop-up Menu

As you have learned, when you click on the Start button, Windows 95 displays a pop-up menu (the Start menu) that lets you access all the programs in your system. Likewise, when you position your mouse pointer on any Desktop object and click your right-mouse button, Windows 95 displays a pop-up menu that you can use to change or manipulate that object's characteristics.

For example, if you right-click on the Taskbar, Windows 95 will display a pop-up menu (the Taskbar menu) with options you can select to change how windows appear on your Desktop. In addition, the Taskbar menu includes an option you can select to change the Taskbar's properties. (For example, using the Taskbar menu Properties option, you can tell Windows 95 to hide the Taskbar when you're not using it.)

Pop-up menus are not new to Microsoft products. For example, many Windows 3.1 programs, such as Word for Windows 6.0, display a pop-up menu when you right-click in the program's work area. However, no prior Microsoft operating system has used pop-up menus as extensively as Windows 95. To see a pop-up menu, click your right-mouse button on the Windows 95 Desktop. As you can see in Figure 2.13, Windows 95 displays a menu at the location where you right-clicked.

Figure 2.13 The pop-up menu that appears when you right-click on the Desktop.

When you right-click on any object on the Desktop, including the Taskbar, Windows 95 displays a pop-up menu. To select an option from a pop-up menu, move your mouse pointer to the option you desire and click your left-mouse button.

SUBMENU

As you have learned, Microsoft engineers included submenus in Windows 95 to reduce the number of steps you need to perform to reach a particular program, device, or operating system function. In past Windows operating systems, you often had to double-click in a series of program windows before you could run a program. In contrast, Windows 95 lets you, with a few movements of your mouse pointer and a single-mouse click, reach all the programs and documents on your system.

To see submenus in action, click on the Start button. Next, move your mouse pointer to one of the options with the right-pointing triangle. For example, move your mouse pointer on to the Start menu Programs option. Windows 95, in turn, will display a submenu (the Programs menu) immediately adjacent to the Programs option.

SOME IMPORTANT MENU FACTS

As you have learned, Windows 95 menus have one thing in common: they all offer you options you can choose to perform tasks and change the way Windows 95 operates. The following list describes some other common menu characteristics and important facts:

- The Control menu appears when you click on the icon at the left edge of a window's title bar.

- The first two items on most menu bars are File and Edit. For example, all the sample programs you have run so far—WordPad, Paint, and Calendar—have File and Edit as the first two items on their menu bars.

- The last option in the File pull-down menu is Exit. To close the window and exit the program, click on the File menu Exit option.

- If you right-click on any Desktop object, Windows 95 will display a pop-up menu. The last option on this menu is always Properties. As you will learn, the Properties option lets you manipulate the object on which you right-clicked. For example, when you click on the Taskbar menu Properties option, Windows 95 displays a sheet you can use to add options to, or remove them from, the Start menu.

- Right-clicking also works in many program windows. For example, right-click on the WordPad window's title bar. WordPad, in turn, will display the Control menu. Right-click on the WordPad window's work area, and WordPad will display a pop-up menu with options that let you change the text style.

- The Taskbar menu, which appears when you right-click on the Taskbar, has options you can select to manage your Desktop's windows. In Chapter 3, "Customizing the Taskbar and Start menu," you will learn how to use the Taskbar menu Properties option to customize the Taskbar.

USING MENUS WITH THE KEYBOARD

Although the mouse is a handy way to interact with menus, there will be times when you'll find it faster and more convenient to use your keyboard. For example, if you're in the middle of entering text into a WordPad window, you may want to use keys to select a menu option because your hands are already on the keyboard.

In Windows 95, you can use your keyboard to access menu bars and pull-down menus. To see how, look at the menu bar of a window, such as the WordPad window. As you can see from Figure 2.14, the first letter of each menu bar category is underlined.

Figure 2.14 *The menu bar of the WordPad window.*

To use your keyboard to display a particular pull-down menu, just press the ALT key and the underlined letter in the corresponding menu bar category. For example, notice that the letter *F* is underlined in the File category in the WordPad window's menu bar. As such, to display WordPad's File pull-down menu, all you need to do is press ALT-F. When you want to remove a pull-down menu from your display screen, press ESC (Escape).

After a program displays a pull-down menu, you can use the UP ARROW and DOWN ARROW keys to select one of the menu's options. To activate the option, press ENTER.

Note: *To open a pull-down menu, you do not have to press* ALT *and the underlined letter simultaneously. Press* ALT *first. Then, to open a menu, press the underlined letter in the corresponding menu bar category.*

There are quite a few other ways to use the keyboard to access menus. Here are a few you can try:

- Press ALT-SPACEBAR. Windows 95, in turn, will display the active window's Control menu.
- Press ALT. Then, press the RIGHT ARROW. The active program, in turn, will highlight a menu bar category. As you press RIGHT ARROW, the program will move the highlight to the next item. To display the pull-down menu for the highlighted item, press ENTER.
- After a menu is open, press the RIGHT ARROW. The active program, in turn, will open the next menu. This is another way you can move from one menu to the next.
- Each option in a pull-down menu has an underlined letter. With the menu open, you can activate an option by pressing ALT and the keyboard key that corresponds to its underlined letter. For example, press ALT-F to see WordPad's File menu. Now press X. WordPad, in turn, will close the window and exit because X is the underlined letter in the File menu Exit option.
- Many menu options display shortcuts (called *hot keys*) you can use to access the options without opening a menu. For example, the characters *CTRL+O* appear next to WordPad's File menu Open option. If you press CTRL-O, WordPad will activate the Open option and display a complicated-looking window (known as the Open dialog box), whether the File menu is open or not. From this new window, you can select a file you want to open.

Working with Dialog Boxes

As you work with a program, there will be times when the program requires you to specify additional information before it can complete an operation. For example, when you print a document, the program may need to know how many copies you want. When a program needs to converse (or carry on a dialogue with you), it displays a dialog box.

Dialog boxes are windows that show you information and request input from you. For example, when you select the File menu Open option in any Windows program, Windows 95 displays the Open dialog box. This dialog box has a text field where you can enter the name of the document you want to open. In addition, the Open dialog box has command buttons, such as Open and Cancel, that you can click on to initiate an action, such as opening a file or closing the window.

To see a common dialog box in action, run the Paint program from the Start menu (remember to follow the *Programs> Accessories> Paint* menu sequence). Then select the File menu Open option. Windows 95, in turn, will display the Open dialog box, as shown in Figure 2.15.

Figure 2.15 *The Open dialog box in Windows 95.*

The Open dialog box lets you specify a document to open. If you want to know how to use the dialog box, click on the title-bar Help button. Windows 95, in turn, will change your mouse pointer to an arrow with a question mark. Now, click on any part of the dialog box. Windows 95, in turn, will display a pop-up window with helpful information about the part of the dialog box on which you clicked. When you want to remove the pop-up Help window, click anywhere else in the dialog box. You can use this Help feature to find out more about the Open dialog box.

As you can see in Figure 2.15, a dialog box contains many varied elements for user input and information display. For example, you use the File name field and Open and Cancel command buttons to input data and send commands to Windows 95. In the work area at the Open dialog box's center, Windows 95 displays the folders in your computer. To close a dialog box, click on the Cancel button or the Close button in the dialog box's title bar.

Properties Sheets in Windows 95

As you have learned, Windows 95 uses a special type of dialog box called a sheet. Each sheet contains one or more pages that you access by clicking tabs that appear near the sheet's title bar. Each page contains a related set of choices.

When you click on the Properties option that appears on most Windows 95 pop-up menus, Windows 95 displays a specific kind of sheet called a *properties sheet*. This sheet lets you view and set the properties of the object on which you originally right-clicked. (As you have learned, to get the pop-up menu in the first place, you must click your right-mouse button on a Desktop object.)

Sheets: A Brief History Lesson

Sheets are a relatively new addition to Windows operating systems. In Windows 3.1, sheets first appeared in programs such as Microsoft Word for Windows. Microsoft engineers began to develop sheets after they realized that the dialog boxes in many Windows applications have far too many controls (command buttons, text fields, list boxes, option buttons, check boxes, and so on), and thus look cluttered and confusing to users. Using sheets, program designers took the controls that used to occupy a single dialog box and spread them out over one or more pages. As a result, you can still access all the same controls in one window (the sheet), but you don't have to look at all of them at the same time.

To see how you can access a properties sheet, assume you want some information about your hard disk. If you don't know where to find the hard disk, double-click on the My Computer icon. In response, Windows 95 will display a window (called a *folder*) that contains icons of all the disks in your system. Locate your hard disk's icon. Next, right-click on the icon and select the Properties option from the pop-up menu. Windows 95, in turn, will display the properties sheet shown in Figure 2.16.

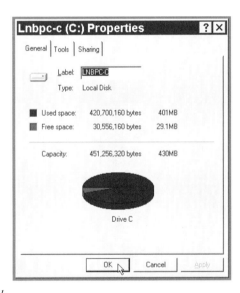

Figure 2.16 Properties of a hard disk.

Pages in Properties Sheets

As you can see from Figure 2.16, a properties sheet contains several *pages*. Each page, in turn, contains a related set of information. For example, in the sheet in Figure 2.16, the General page gives you general information about the disk, such as the disk's name and the amount of free and used space it contains. The Tools page groups together controls you can use to check your disk's error-checking, backup, and defragmentation status. The Sharing page lets you turn on options that allow other users to access your disk. To go to a specific page, simply click on the corresponding tab at the top of the sheet. For example, to display the Tools page, click on the Tools tab.

Some Important Properties Sheets

In Windows 95, you will use properties sheets to perform many important tasks. As such, you should explore various properties sheets. To do so, simply right-click on any object and select the Properties option from the pop-up menu that appears.

> ### Using Sheets
>
>
>
> As you have learned, Microsoft added sheets to Windows 95 so that operating system windows could contain many controls and switches without looking cluttered and confusing to the average user. Just as a book contains chapters that organize and group similar or related pieces of information, a sheet has pages that organize and group similar or related controls and switches. To access a particular page in a sheet, click on the corresponding tab near the sheet's title bar.

Display Properties

One of the important property sheets in Windows 95 is the Display Properties sheet. Using this sheet, you can change your Desktop's background pattern, wallpaper, screen-saver settings, and so on. To explore the Display Properties sheet, right-click on an unoccupied area of the Desktop. Then, select the Properties option from the pop-up menu. Windows 95, in turn, will display the properties sheet shown in Figure 2.17.

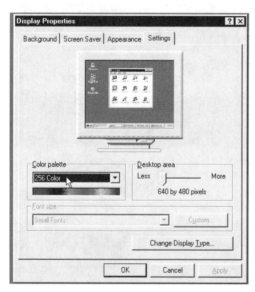

Figure 2.17 The Display Properties sheet in Windows 95.

As you can see from Figure 2.17, the Display Properties sheet groups your display screen's properties into four pages: Background, Screen Saver, Appearance, and Settings. Click on any of the Display Properties sheet's tabs. Windows 95, in turn, will display information for the corresponding page. Figure 2.17 shows the Settings page, which contains information about the colors and the number of pixels on your display screen. You will learn more about the Display properties in Chapter 5, "Customizing Common Hardware."

Taskbar Properties

Another important property sheet is the Taskbar Properties sheet. You can use the Taskbar Properties sheet to customize the Taskbar. For example, this sheet lets you hide the Taskbar when you're not using it, change the size of the icons in the Start menu, and remove the Taskbar clock display. You can open the Taskbar Properties sheet in two ways:

- Right-click on an empty part of the Taskbar and select the Properties option from the resulting pop-up menu.
- Click on the Start button. Then, follow the *Settings> Taskbar* menu sequence to open the Taskbar Properties sheet.

You will explore the Taskbar properties in detail in Chapter 3, where you will learn how to customize the Taskbar and the Start menu.

KEYS TO SUCCESS

In this chapter, you learned how to use the Taskbar, Start menu, and the windows that are the basis of the user interface. In Chapter 3, you will learn how to change the appearance and behavior of the Taskbar and the Start menu. However, before you move on to Chapter 3, make sure that you understand the following key concepts:

- ✓ A window is a framed region of the screen with many components, such as the title bar, the menu bar, the Control menu icon, Minimize and Maximize buttons, and the Close button.
- ✓ The Start menu provides you with a way to start programs in Windows 95.
- ✓ The Taskbar displays buttons for each running program and open folder.
- ✓ Clicking on a window's Taskbar button causes Windows 95 to switch to that window.
- ✓ Right-clicking on any Desktop object displays a pop-up menu whose last option is Properties.
- ✓ Dialog boxes are windows that contain many different components, such as command buttons, fields, and pull-down list buttons.
- ✓ Sheets are a special type of dialog box that Windows 95 uses to display Help information and object properties.

Chapter 3
Customizing the Taskbar and Start Menu

Imagine that you just bought a new car. Picture the shiny chrome bumpers and the immaculate whitewall tires. Smell the leather seats. Feel your right hand on the gear shift with the polished oak knob. Now imagine your disappointment if you discovered, after you just agreed to make car payments that dwarf your rent, that you can't move the leather seats, adjust the rear and side-view mirrors, or tighten the seat-belt straps. Without the ability to customize these basic automobile components, you wouldn't be able to drive the car around. It would just sit in your driveway, perhaps winning you the admiration (or envy) of your neighbors, but not carrying you anywhere.

When Microsoft engineers designed Windows 95, they realized that, like a new car, the operating system would need to have features that users could customize. No matter how sporty the Desktop appeared or how many features the operating system offered, Windows 95 would never become the user-friendly interface Microsoft engineers envisioned unless users could customize some of its basic components. As a result, Microsoft built many programs into Windows 95 that you can follow to make the operating system more effectively meet your needs. In this chapter, you will start to learn some of these procedures. Specifically, you will learn how to customize the Taskbar and the Start menu, two of the most important elements of the Windows 95 user interface.

By the time you finish this chapter, you will understand the following key concepts:

- Using the Taskbar speaker icon, you can control the sound volume used by Windows 95 and your multimedia programs.
- Using the Taskbar clock, you can set your system's date-and-time.
- You will use the Start menu Run option to run most of your programs, using only a few clicks of your mouse.
- Normally, Windows 95 displays the Taskbar at the bottom of your screen. However, you can move the Taskbar to any one of your screen's four edges.
- If you find the Taskbar distracting, Windows 95 lets you hide the Taskbar when you don't need to use it.
- Windows 95 lets you add items to or remove items from the Start menu.

PURPOSE OF THE TASKBAR

If Windows 95 were a car, the Taskbar would be the dashboard and the steering wheel. You essentially "drive" Windows 95 from the Taskbar. Like the fuel gauge on your car's dashboard, the Taskbar shows you the status of the programs you have started. Likewise, you can use the Taskbar to switch from one program to another, just as you turn your car's steering wheel to switch lanes of traffic. Thus, the Taskbar is the focus of your activities when you use Windows 95. In the following section, you will review some of what you've learned about the Taskbar and learn a few new ways to use it.

PARTS OF THE TASKBAR

Before you use the Taskbar again, take a look at the Windows 95 Desktop, as shown in Figure 3.1.

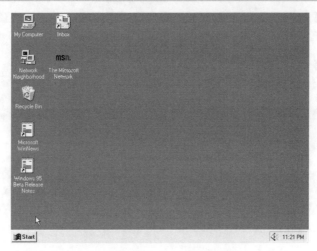

Figure 3.1 The Taskbar in its default location on the Windows 95 Desktop.

In this case, the Taskbar appears at its default location along the Desktop's bottom edge. As you can see in Figure 3.1, the Taskbar initially displays three components:

- The Start button
- The volume control (appears as a speaker icon at the Taskbar's right edge)
- The digital clock next to the speaker icon

As you have learned, you use the Start button to start programs. You use the volume control to adjust the volume at which your computer plays sounds. The clock shows the current time, but you can use it to set your system's date-and-time as well. (Windows 95 maintains a calendar and a clock so that it can timestamp each document you create.) The rest of this section shows you how to use these Taskbar components.

USING THE VOLUME CONTROL

When some important event occurs in your computer system, or when you do something Windows 95 does not like, the operating system makes a sound. (The exact sound Windows 95 makes depends on how you have assigned sounds; you will learn how to assign sounds in Chapter 5, "Customizing Common Hardware.") For example, when Windows 95 first starts, it makes a sound to announce a successful startup. Conversely, when you drag an icon and try to drop it on the Taskbar, Windows 95 makes a sound to let you know you cannot perform that operation.

On occasion, you may find this sound irritating and wish to lower its volume. Other times, especially when your computer has to compete with background noise, you may want to make the sound louder. Fortunately, Windows 95 lets you increase or decrease the volume (loudness) of this sound. To do so, you will use the volume control on the Taskbar. However, before you use the volume control, you need to learn a way to force Windows 95 to make a sound so that you can test various volume settings. As such, you need to perform an operation that Windows 95 dislikes, but also has no negative side effects. To do so, place your mouse pointer on the Recycle Bin icon (see Figure 3.1), hold down your left-mouse button, and move your mouse. Windows 95, in turn, will move the icon in the same direction you move your mouse. Drag the icon over the Taskbar. Windows 95, in turn, will change the icon's shape, as shown in Figure 3.2.

Figure 3.2 The Recycle Bin icon after you drag it on to the Taskbar.

Windows 95 changes the icon's shape to tell you that you cannot drop the Recycle Bin on the Taskbar. Release your mouse button and drop the Recycle Bin anyway. Windows 95, in turn, will make a sound and return the Recycle Bin icon to its original location.

ADJUSTING VOLUME

Now that you know how to force Windows 95 to make a sound, you can try out the volume control. To use the volume control, click your left-mouse button on the Taskbar speaker icon. Windows 95, in turn, will pop up a vertical slider bar, as shown in Figure 3.3.

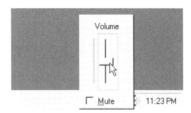

Figure 3.3 *The slider bar for volume control.*

To try out the volume control, move the slider (the rectangular box on the slider bar) all the way to the top. Next, drag the Recycle Bin icon and drop it on the Taskbar. Windows 95, in turn, will make a *loud* sound. Before you continue, set the volume at a comfortable level. Move the slider up to make the sound louder; move it down to make the sound quieter.

MORE VOLUME CONTROLS

As you have learned, you can use the Taskbar speaker icon to adjust the volume of sounds Windows 95 makes. In addition, if your computer has a sound card installed, you can use the speaker icon to control the volume of sound card components.

For example, if your PC has a CD-ROM drive, you can use the speaker icon to set the volume at which Windows 95 plays any sound files your CD-ROMs contain. As such, you may find the speaker icon particularly useful if you play audio CDs in a group setting, such as an office. Depending on the musical preferences of your co-workers, there may be times when you'll want to "crank up" or turn down the volume. On such occasions, you can use the speaker icon to access the Windows 95 extended volume controls, which let you increase or decrease your CD-ROM's audio volume.

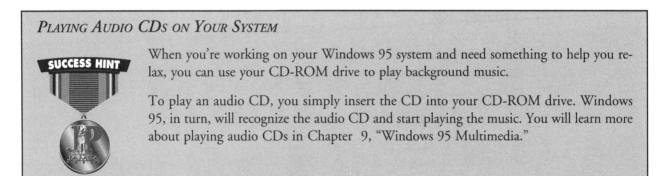

PLAYING AUDIO CDS ON YOUR SYSTEM

When you're working on your Windows 95 system and need something to help you relax, you can use your CD-ROM drive to play background music.

To play an audio CD, you simply insert the CD into your CD-ROM drive. Windows 95, in turn, will recognize the audio CD and start playing the music. You will learn more about playing audio CDs in Chapter 9, "Windows 95 Multimedia."

To see the extended volume controls, double-click your left-mouse button on the speaker icon. Windows 95, in turn, will open a Volume Control dialog box, as shown in Figure 3.4.

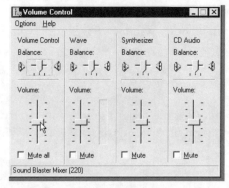

Figure 3.4 *The Volume Control dialog box.*

Notice the rightmost volume control in Figure 3.4. Use that volume control to adjust the volume when you play audio CDs in your CD-ROM drive. To close the Volume Control dialog box, click your mouse on the Close button.

SETTING AUDIO PROPERTIES

As you have learned, the speaker icon lets you set the volume of sounds your computer makes. In addition, the speaker icon lets you access the Audio Properties dialog box, which you can use to adjust the volume at which your sound card records and plays sounds. So far, you have clicked your left-mouse button on the speaker icon to display a vertical-slider bar volume-control, and double-clicked on the icon to open the Volume Control dialog box. Now, to begin your journey to the Audio Properties dialog box, click your right-mouse button on the speaker icon. Windows 95, in turn, will display a pop-up menu, as shown in Figure 3.5.

Figure 3.5 *The pop-up menu Windows 95 displays when you right-click on the speaker icon.*

Now, to view the audio properties, click your left-mouse button on the pop-up menu's Adjust Audio Properties option. (If you click your left-mouse button on the pop-up menu's Volume Controls option, Windows 95 will display the Volume Controls dialog box you saw in Figure 3.4.) Windows 95, in turn, will open the Audio Properties dialog box, as shown in Figure 3.6.

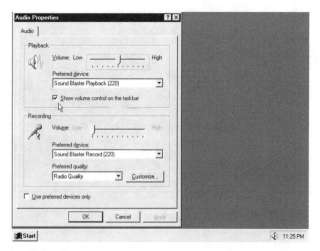

Figure 3.6 *The Audio Properties dialog box.*

3: CUSTOMIZING THE TASKBAR AND START MENU

As previously mentioned, the Audio Properties dialog box lets you adjust the volume at which your sound card records and plays sound. You will learn more about the Audio Properties dialog box in Chapter 9. However, the Audio Properties dialog box does include one feature relevant to this chapter—you can use this dialog box to remove the speaker icon (volume control) from the Taskbar. This feature is especially useful if your system resides in an office, school, or library setting. If you don't want co-workers, students, or library patrons to easily control the volume at which your system plays sounds, just remove the speaker icon. To do so, perform these steps:

1. Click on the check box labeled Show volume control on the taskbar in the dialog box, shown in Figure 3.6. Windows 95 will remove the check mark from that check box.
2. Click on the Apply button. Windows 95 will remove the speaker icon from the Taskbar.

To place the speaker icon back on the Taskbar, perform these steps:

1. Click on the Start button. Windows 95 will display the Start menu.
2. Move your mouse pointer to the Start menu Settings option. Windows 95 will display the Settings menu.
3. Click your mouse on the Settings menu Control Panel option. Windows 95 will display the Control Panel window.
4. Double-click on the Control Panel's Multimedia icon. Windows 95 will display the Multimedia Properties sheet Audio page.
5. Click on the check box labeled "Show volume control on the taskbar." Windows 95 will place a check mark in that check box.
6. Click on the OK button. Windows 95 will close the Multimedia Properties sheet and place the speaker icon back on the Taskbar.

SILENCING YOUR SYSTEM

Imagine that you are married, have two children, and have just purchased a personal computer with Windows 95 preinstalled. You and your spouse use the PC for word processing, personal finance, and an occasional game of Solitaire. Quiet stuff. Your kids, on the other hand, use the PC to play loud video games. During the day, you tolerate the sounds of laser blasts and space-ship crashes. After all, you are a very patient parent. But, come nightfall, you draw the line. You need quiet. You need sleep. Fortunately for you and your kids, you don't have to forbid them to play video games at night so that you can get some rest. Instead, you can use the speaker icon to turn off your system's sound. To turn off your system's sound, perform these steps:

1. Double-click your left-mouse button on the speaker icon. Windows 95 will display the Volume Control dialog box (see Figure 3.4).
2. In the Volume Control dialog box Volume Control section, click on the Mute all check box until a check mark appears.

To make sure your kids can't turn the sound back on, you can remove the speaker icon. Then, after you've had a good night's sleep, you can place the icon back on the Taskbar, return to the Volume Control dialog box, and remove the check mark from the Volume Control section Mute all check box.

ADJUSTING THE DATE-AND-TIME

As you have learned, you can use the Taskbar's volume control to adjust the sounds Windows 95 makes. In the same way, you can use the Taskbar's clock to view and set your system's current date-and-time. By default, your clock displays the current time. However, if you want to see the current date, all you have to do is position your mouse pointer on top of the clock for a moment. Windows 95, in turn, will display a small pop-up window that contains the current day-and-date, as shown in Figure 3.7.

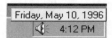

Figure 3.7 Windows 95 displays the current day-and-date after you move your mouse pointer on top of the clock.

Note that if you leave the mouse pointer on top of the clock, Windows 95 removes the day-and-date window after three or four seconds. In addition to viewing the current date-and-time, you can use the clock to set the date-and-time. As with most other settings in Windows 95, you set the date-and-time through a properties page. To view the properties sheet for date-and-time, double-click on the Taskbar's clock. Windows 95, in turn, will open the Date/Time Properties sheet Date & Time page, as shown in Figure 3.8.

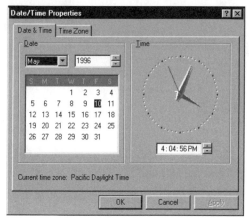

Figure 3.8 The Properties page Windows 95 displays after you double-click on the Taskbar's clock.

From the Date & Time page, you can set the month, day, year, and the current time. You will learn more about this properties page in Chapter 5 when you learn how to set your system's date-and-time.

STARTING PROGRAMS

You have now explored two of the Taskbar's three components—the volume control and the clock. Now, you will examine the Taskbar's final and most crucial component—the Start button. The Start button is the most important Taskbar element, because it lets you run all the programs you need to accomplish tasks on your computer. For example, before you can prepare a text document, you need to run a word-processing program. To read your e-mail, you need to run a Mail program.

In Chapters 1 and 2, you learned how to start programs from the Start menu, which pops up after you click on the Start button. Chapter 2, in particular, provided you with step-by-step instructions for running two or more programs at the same time. In this section, you will review what you've learned about running programs from the Start menu. Note that this section does not describe the programs; you will learn more about them in Chapters 12 and 13. Here, you will only review the mechanics of starting applications in Windows 95.

RUNNING MULTIPLE PROGRAMS

Suppose you want to run concurrently the WordPad word-processing program, the Paint program, and the Calculator program. (Windows 95 includes these accessories, so you should have them in your system.) To run all three programs at the same time, perform these steps:

3: Customizing the Taskbar and Start Menu

1. Click your left-mouse button on the Taskbar's Start button. Windows 95 will display the Start menu.
2. Move the mouse pointer on top of the Start menu Programs option. Windows 95 will display the Programs menu.
3. In the Programs menu, move the mouse pointer to the Accessories option. Windows 95 will display the Accessories menu, as shown in Figure 3.9.
4. Click on the Accessories menu WordPad option. Windows 95 will run the WordPad program.
5. Repeat steps 1 through 3. Then, click on the Accessories menu Paint option. Windows 95 will run the Paint program.
6. Repeat steps 1 through 3. Then, click on the Accessories menu Calculator option. Windows 95 will run the Calculator program.

Figure 3.9 *The Start menu and two (Programs and Accessories) submenus.*

Your system should now be running three programs—WordPad, Paint, and Calculator. In addition, each program should have its own window and Taskbar button. Before you do anything with these program windows, you should learn about another way to run a program from the Start menu.

USING THE START MENU RUN OPTION

As you have learned, you usually can start a program by selecting its name from the Start menu, or more precisely, from the sequence of submenus that stem from the Start menu. However, there will be times when the program you want to run doesn't appear in the Start menu or any of its submenus. For example, when you install a new program, you must first run the Setup program. Because the Setup program will not appear in the Start menu, you need an alternate way to run the program.

If you are a former Windows 3.1 user, you've probably faced this problem before. Undoubtedly, there were times when you wanted to run a program that wasn't in one of the Program Manager's program groups. Fortunately, Windows 3.1 provided you with a solution; it let you use the Program Manager's File menu Run option to start such programs. In a similar way, when you want to run a program that doesn't appear on the Windows 95 Start menu or one of its submenus, you can use the Start menu Run option to initiate the program. For example, suppose you want to install an application from a disk. Furthermore, assume that to install the application, you have to run the SETUP.EXE program the disk contains. In such a situation, you would perform these steps:

1. Place the disk in your floppy disk drive. (Assume that it is the A drive.)
2. Click on the Start button. Windows 95 will display the Start menu, as shown in Figure 3.10.

Figure 3.10 *The Start menu Run option.*

3. Click on the Start menu Run option. Windows 95 will display the Run dialog box, as shown in Figure 3.11.

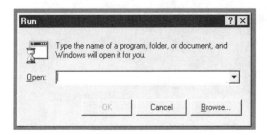

Figure 3.11 *The Run dialog box.*

4. In the Run dialog box Open field, enter **A:\SETUP.EXE**. Then, click OK. Windows 95 will run the SETUP.EXE program from the A: drive.

Switching between Programs

By now, you have seen several ways to start programs in Windows 95. For all the running programs, the Taskbar serves as an information and control center. The Taskbar buttons indicate which program window is active and let you reshuffle the Desktop's window pile with just a click of your mouse. As you learned in Chapter 2, Windows 95 adds to a Taskbar button for each program running on your computer. For example, after you run WordPad, Paint, and Calculator, the Taskbar will include four buttons (the Start button and three Taskbar buttons), as shown in Figure 3.12.

Figure 3.12 *The Taskbar with four buttons.*

When Windows 95 runs several programs simultaneously, the Desktop typically contains a window for each program. Of course, you still use these windows one at a time. At any moment, the window that you use is the *active window*. From the Taskbar buttons, you can tell which window is active. The Taskbar button for the active window appears pushed in. All other Taskbar buttons appear raised. When you want to use another window, click on that program's Taskbar button. Windows 95, in turn, will bring that window to the top of all other windows and make that Taskbar button appear pushed in. You can then use that window's program.

3: Customizing the Taskbar and Start Menu

Changing the Taskbar's Location and Size

In the previous sections of this chapter, you learned how to use the Taskbar and the Start menu. Now, you will learn how to customize the screen's layout. As Microsoft engineers were developing Windows 95, they realized that they could not design a single screen layout that would please every user. As a result, they opted to let you—the user—change many aspects of the Windows 95 user interface. The Taskbar is one of the screen elements you can reposition and alter. (You can also arrange the icons that appear on the Desktop.) As you will learn, Windows 95 lets you move the Taskbar and increase its width.

Moving the Taskbar

The Windows 95 Taskbar is "dockable," which means you can attach the Taskbar to any side of the Desktop, just as you can tie a boat up to any pier in a marina. As such, you can place the Taskbar in one of four possible locations—along the Desktop's top, bottom, left, or right edges. You move the Taskbar with a simple mouse drag-and-drop operation. For example, to move the Taskbar to the left edge of the Desktop, perform these steps:

1. Move your mouse pointer to an empty area (an area without any button or icon) of the Taskbar.
2. Hold down your left-mouse button and move the mouse close to the Desktop's left edge. Windows 95 will display a Taskbar outline along the Desktop's left edge, as shown in Figure 3.13.

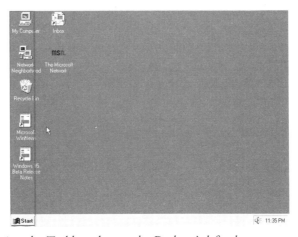

Figure 3.13 The result of dragging the Taskbar close to the Desktop's left edge.

3. Release your left-mouse button to drop the Taskbar in the new location. Windows 95, in turn, will display the Taskbar along the Desktop's left edge, as shown in Figure 3.14.

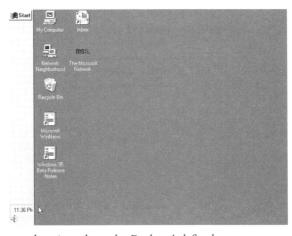

Figure 3.14 The Taskbar in its new location along the Desktop's left edge.

When you move the Taskbar to the Desktop's left edge, the Taskbar does not obscure the icons on the Desktop. Instead, as you can see in Figure 3.14, Windows 95 automatically moves all the icons to the right of the Taskbar. It is really up to you to decide where you want the Taskbar on your Desktop. If you like the Taskbar's default location along the Desktop's bottom edge, you do not have to do anything. However, if you ever want to move the Taskbar to a new location, you know how to do it.

CHANGING THE TASKBAR'S WIDTH

When you move the Taskbar to the Desktop's left or right edge, Windows 95 automatically adjusts the Taskbar's width to provide a reasonable amount of space for the button labels (see Figure 3.14). However, the width may not be adequate for all the labels. For example, in Figure 3.14, the Taskbar is not wide enough for the clock display. If you are willing to give up more of your screen to the Taskbar, you can widen the Taskbar to accommodate the entire clock display. Of course, you can also decrease the width so the Taskbar does not take up quite so much space.

You adjust the Taskbar's width in the same way as you would adjust a window's width. For example, to widen the Taskbar shown in Figure 3.14, perform these steps:

1. Move your mouse pointer on top of the Taskbar's right border. Windows 95 will change the pointer's shape to a horizontal line with arrows at both ends.

2. After Windows 95 changes your mouse pointer's shape, hold down your left-mouse button and move the mouse. Windows 95 will display a rectangular outline that reflects the Taskbar's new width.

3. Release your left-mouse button when the Taskbar's outline reaches the width you desire. Windows 95 will display the Taskbar with the new width, as shown in Figure 3.15.

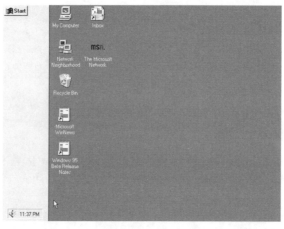

Figure 3.15 *A wider Taskbar along the Desktop's left edge.*

MAKING THE TASKBAR "FIT" YOUR NEEDS

Just as no one shoe fits all people and no one shoe style meets everyone's personal preferences, no one Taskbar width or location can "fit" everyone's computing needs. Fortunately, Windows 95 lets you move the Taskbar and change its width.

To move the Taskbar, position your mouse pointer over an empty area on the Taskbar. Then, hold down your left-mouse button and drag the Taskbar to another edge of the Desktop. Release your left-mouse button to drop the Taskbar into place.

3: CUSTOMIZING THE TASKBAR AND START MENU

> To change the Taskbar's width, position your mouse pointer on top of the Taskbar's inner border (the border facing the Desktop). After Windows 95 changes your mouse pointer to a horizontal line with arrows at both ends, hold down your left-mouse button and pull the border toward the center of the Desktop to widen the Taskbar.
>
> To narrow the Taskbar, pull its border toward the edge of the screen. Windows 95, in turn, will display a rectangle outline that shows the Taskbar's new width. Release your left-mouse button when the Taskbar's outline reaches the width you desire.

When you change the Taskbar's width, the change applies only to the Taskbar's current location. For example, drag the Taskbar to the Desktop's bottom edge. Windows 95, in turn, will display the Taskbar in its horizontal position with the old width. In other words, Windows 95 remembers the width of the Taskbar for each of its four possible locations.

CHANGING THE TASKBAR PROPERTIES

While the Taskbar is functional, it does limit the amount of screen space you have to do your work. As such, an ideal Taskbar would appear only when you need it and stay hidden when you are working in a window. Fortunately, with just a few changes in the Taskbar's properties, you can create an ideal Taskbar. This section shows you how you can customize the Taskbar's behavior.

As previously mentioned, to access an object's properties, all you need to do is move your mouse pointer on to the object and click your right-mouse button. Then, in the pop-up menu Windows 95 displays in response to your right-click, you select the Properties option. To access the Taskbar's properties, you use the exact same method. To work with the Taskbar properties, perform these steps:

1. Move your mouse pointer to an empty area of the Taskbar and click your right-mouse button. Windows 95 will display the Taskbar menu.

2. Click your left-mouse button on the Taskbar menu Properties option. Windows 95, in turn, will open the Taskbar Properties sheet, as shown in Figure 3.16.

Figure 3.16 shows the Taskbar Properties sheet Taskbar Options page. As you can see, this page has a feedback area in which Windows 95 displays a picture of the Taskbar and the Start menu. Four check boxes appear below the feedback area. Windows 95 uses the feedback area to show you how changes you make to the check boxes affect the Taskbar and Start menu.

Figure 3.16 The Taskbar Properties sheet in Windows 95.

As you can see in Figure 3.16, the check boxes labeled "Always on top" and "Show Clock" are selected. In Windows 95, selected check boxes contain check marks.

Before you try to change the check box settings on the Taskbar Options page, read the following descriptions of the check boxes' functions:

- When the Always on top check box is selected, the Taskbar appears on top of all other windows. If you deselect this check box, other windows can obscure the Taskbar.
- If the Auto hide check box is selected, Windows 95 will hide the Taskbar when you aren't using it. To view the Taskbar, bring your mouse pointer close to the Desktop edge where you last saw the Taskbar.
- When the "Show small icons in Start menu" check box is selected, Windows 95 displays small icons in the Start menu. Otherwise, the icons are larger.
- The Show Clock check box controls the Taskbar's clock display. By default, this check box is selected, and the Taskbar includes the clock.

To see how Windows 95 responds when you change the setting of the four check boxes, perform these steps:

1. Click your left-mouse button on the Always on top check box. Windows 95 will remove the check mark. In the feedback area, you will see the Taskbar move behind a window.

2. Click your left-mouse button on the Auto hide check box. Windows 95 will place a check mark in the check box. In the feedback area, the Taskbar will appear as an outline, which indicates that Windows 95 will hide the Taskbar when you don't need it.

3. Click your left-mouse button on the Show small icons in the Start menu check box. Windows 95 will place a check mark in this check box. In the feedback area, Windows 95 will show the Start menu with smaller icons.

4. Click your left-mouse button on the Show Clock check box. Windows 95 will remove the check mark from this check box. If the Taskbar is visible in the feedback area (deselect the Auto hide check box to make the Taskbar visible), Windows 95 will remove the clock from the Taskbar.

Decide which check boxes you want to select. When you have limited screen space, you may want to select the Auto hide check box. Then, after you click on the OK button, Windows 95 will hide the Taskbar and display a thin line in its place. Whenever you want to see the Taskbar, simply move the mouse pointer on to that thin line. Windows 95, in turn, will make the Taskbar visible again.

Finding and Hiding the Taskbar

When some people work on an automobile, they like to spread all their wrenches, sockets, pliers, and other tools neatly on the garage floor before they start to work. They like to have all their tools carefully arranged, much like a physician's instruments on a surgical tray. Other people like to take tools, one at a time, out of their toolboxes and then replace the tools before they reach for more. For such people, tools spread across the garage floor just make it more difficult to locate the exact screwdriver or pair of vice grips they need.

In a similar way, if you share a Windows 95 system with family, friends, or co-workers, you and your system partners may not agree about whether Windows 95 should always display the Taskbar, which contains some of your most important Windows 95 tools. For example, a system partner might decide, because he or she doesn't want Windows 95 to display the Taskbar all the time, to turn on the Taskbar Properties sheet Auto hide check box while you're not around.

3: CUSTOMIZING THE TASKBAR AND START MENU

> If you find yourself in such a situation, look for a thin line along one of the Desktop's edges. Then, move your mouse pointer to that line. Windows 95, in turn, will display the Taskbar.
>
> If you want Windows 95 to display the Taskbar all the time, right-click on the Taskbar and select the Taskbar menu Properties option. Then, in the Taskbar Properties sheet Taskbar Options page, click on the Auto hide check box until the check mark disappears.

CUSTOMIZING THE START MENU

As you already know, the Start menu appears when you click your left-mouse button on the Start button. The Start menu contains options you can select to run programs or open documents. However, there will be times when you'll want to change the options that appear on the Start menu or its submenus. For example, you may use the Paint program often, and grow tired of moving your mouse all the way to the Accessories menu each time you want to run Paint. As a result, you may want to add Paint to an earlier menu, such as Programs, in the Start menu sequence.

Fortunately, in Windows 95, you can easily add programs to the Start menu and all its menus and submenus. Likewise, Windows 95 lets you remove programs from menus. In this section, you'll learn how to customize the Start menu and its submenus to best suit your needs.

Because the Taskbar contains the Start button, you can use the Taskbar Properties sheet to customize the Start menu. To customize the Start menu, first use the steps you learned in the section entitled "Changing the Taskbar Properties" to open the Taskbar Properties sheet. Figure 3.16 shows the Taskbar Properties sheet.

ADDING A PROGRAM TO THE START MENU

To add a program to the Start menu, first click on the Start Menu Programs tab in the Taskbar Properties sheet. Windows 95, in turn, will display the Taskbar Properties sheet Start Menu Programs page, as shown in Figure 3.17.

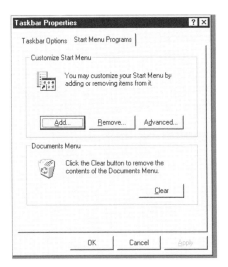

Figure 3.17 The options you can select to customize the Start menu.

For example, suppose you want to add an option for the WordPad program to the Programs menu. To add the option, click on the Add button in the Start Menu Programs page (see Figure 3.17). Windows 95, in turn, will display the Create Shortcut dialog box, as shown in Figure 3.18.

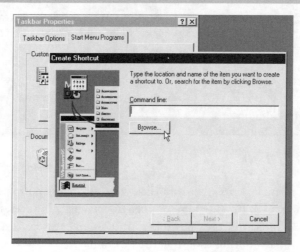

Figure 3.18 Windows 95 prompts for a program name in the Create Shortcut dialog box.

If you do not know the exact location of the program, click on the Browse button. Windows 95, in turn, will display a Browse dialog box. You can use the Browse dialog box to open the appropriate folder on your hard disk and locate the WordPad program. To find WordPad, perform these steps:

1. Double-click on the My Computer icon in the Browse dialog box's work area. Windows 95 will show the disk drives on your system. Double-click on the C: drive's icon. Windows 95 will display the contents of the C: drive.

2. Double-click on the Program Files folder (the icon looks like a folder). Windows 95 will display the contents of the Program Files folder. Double-click on the Accessories folder. Windows 95 will display the programs and folders in the Accessories folder.

3. Click on the WordPad icon. Windows 95 will enter the name in the File Name field.

4. To see the path you have taken to find WordPad, click on the pull-down list in the area underneath the dialog box's title bar. Windows 95 will display a list of icons that indicate the disk and folders you have traversed, as shown in Figure 3.19.

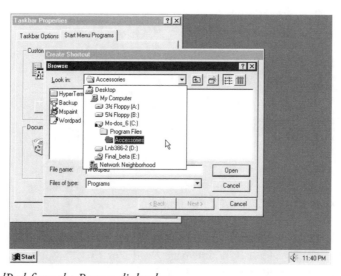

Figure 3.19 Selecting WordPad from the Browse dialog box.

5. Click on the Open button. Windows 95 will remove the Browse dialog box and place the program's name in the Command line field of the Create Shortcut dialog box.

3: CUSTOMIZING THE TASKBAR AND START MENU

After you find the WordPad program, click on the Next button in the Create Shortcut dialog box (see Figure 3.18). Windows 95, in turn, will display the Select Program Folder dialog box, as shown in Figure 3.20.

Each folder in this dialog box represents an item in the Start menu. Because you want to add the WordPad program to the Programs menu, click on the Programs folder. Then, click on the Next button. Windows 95, in turn, will change the Select Program Folder dialog box into Select a Title for the Program dialog box, as shown in Figure 3.21.

Accept the default name of WordPad and click on the Finish button. Windows 95, in turn, will go back to the Taskbar Properties sheet. Click the OK button to exit the sheet.

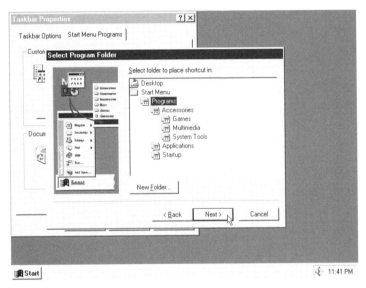

Figure 3.20 The Select Program Folder dialog box.

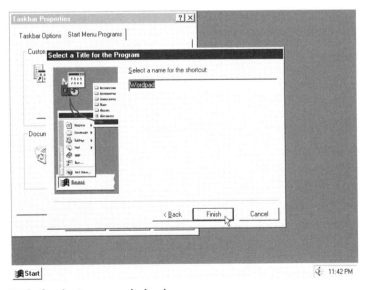

Figure 3.21 The Select a Title for the Program dialog box.

To see the result of this exercise, click on the Start button to display the Start menu. Then, move your mouse pointer into the Programs option to view the Programs menu. As you can see in Figure 3.22, the menu now includes the WordPad option.

SUCCESS WITH WINDOWS 95

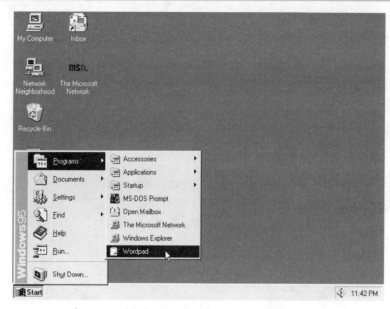

Figure 3.22 The Programs menu after you add the WordPad option.

ADDING A PROGRAM USING DRAG-AND-DROP

In the previous section, you learned how to use the Taskbar Properties sheet to add a program to the Start menu or one of its submenus. However, if you want to add a program or document to the Start menu only (and not to one of its submenus), you don't need to use the Taskbar Properties sheet. Windows 95 offers you an easier way—just drag the program or document's icon and drop it on the Start button. For example, to add the WordPad program in this manner, perform these steps:

1. Double-click on the My Computer icon on the Desktop. Windows 95 will open a new window—My Computer.

2. Double-click on the C: drive's icon. Windows 95 will open a window that shows the contents of the C: drive.

3. Double-click on the Program Files folder. Windows 95 will open a window that shows the contents of the Program Files folder.

4. Double-click on the Accessories folder. Windows 95 will open a window that shows the contents of the Accessories folder.

5. Drag the WordPad icon and drop it on the Taskbar's Start button.

6. Close all the open windows, one by one.

Now, click on the Start button to view the Start menu. As Figure 3.23 shows, the Start menu now includes WordPad as the first entry.

REMOVING A PROGRAM FROM THE START MENU

If you place too many options in the Start menu, the menu may become very long. The longer the Start menu gets, the more difficulty you may have locating and selecting a specific option. As such, if the menu has any options that you do not use regularly, you may want to remove some of them. To remove an option from the Start menu, you have to use the Taskbar Properties sheet Start Menu Programs page (see Figure 3.17).

3: Customizing the Taskbar and Start Menu

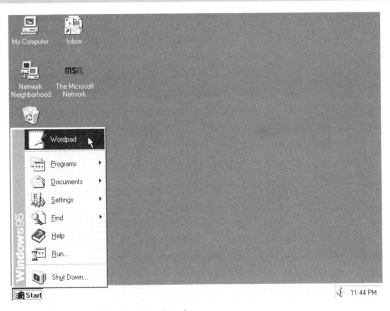

Figure 3.23 *The Start menu after you add the WordPad option.*

To remove an option, click on the Remove button in the Start Menu Programs page. Windows 95, in turn, will display a Remove Shortcuts/Folders dialog box, as shown in Figure 3.24.

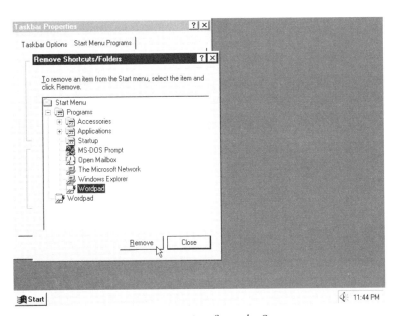

Figure 3.24 *The dialog box you can use to remove an option from the Start menu.*

In Figure 3.24, you can see the two WordPad options that you added through the exercises in earlier sections of this chapter. Click on the WordPad option in the Programs menu (a dotted line connects WordPad to the Programs menu). Then, click the Remove button. Windows 95, in turn, will remove the WordPad option from the Programs menu.

To exit the Remove Shortcuts/Folders dialog box, click the Close button. Windows 95, in turn, will close the dialog box and revert to the Taskbar Properties sheet. Click the OK button to close and exit that properties sheet. You can now verify that the Programs menu no longer contains the WordPad option.

SUCCESS WITH WINDOWS 95

KEYS TO SUCCESS

When you started this chapter, you were somewhat familiar with the Windows 95 Desktop, Taskbar, Start menu, windows, pull-down menus, pop-up menus, and dialog boxes. Just as a tourist in a new city might know his or her way to and from a hotel, a shopping district, or a theme park, you knew enough about these Windows 95 features to make your way through the new operating system. However, before you started to read this chapter, you still only had an outsider's perspective on Windows 95. You had not stopped at the quiet little restaurants and art galleries that the natives of the Windows 95 city love, and visitors seldom notice. You had not experienced the true flavor and power of this city.

When you started this chapter, all that changed. In this chapter, your guide, *Success with Windows 95*, led you off of "Main Street, Windows 95" so that you could explore Windows 95 capabilities that many users (the sightseeing visitors) never discover. Now you know not only how to use Windows features, but also how to customize them to meet your particular needs.

In Chapter 4, you will learn what to do if this book somehow does not have the information you need. As you will see in Chapter 4, you can always turn to Windows 95's online Help system for more information about Windows 95. Before you move on to Chapter 4, make sure that you understand the following key concepts:

- ✓ The Taskbar is where you start your work in Windows 95.
- ✓ You can use the Taskbar's volume-control icon to set the sound volume.
- ✓ You can use the Taskbar's clock to view and set your system's date-and-time.
- ✓ You can drag-and-drop the Taskbar along any one of the Desktop's four edges.
- ✓ You can adjust the Taskbar's width by dragging the Toolbar's outer edge.
- ✓ To customize the Taskbar and the Start menu, right-click on an empty area of the Taskbar, select the Taskbar menu Properties option, and work with the Taskbar Properties sheet.
- ✓ If the Taskbar gets in the way, you can use the Taskbar Properties sheet to hide it.
- ✓ You can add items to or remove them from the Start menu.

Chapter 4
Using Online Help

Even the best tour guide may not have answers to all your questions about a city or a landmark. However, a good tour guide will not leave any of your questions unanswered. Instead, he or she will point you to other resources (such as a book in the library or an information center) you can use to obtain further information. As your Windows 95 tour guide, *Success with Windows 95* will show you most of what you should know. However, there may be times when you have questions that this book does not answer. In this chapter, you will learn how to use the Windows 95 online Help system to find answers to such questions.

By the time you finish this chapter, you will understand the following key concepts:

- Using the Start menu Help option, you can access the Windows 95 online Help system.
- The Windows 95 online Help system provides an index of key terms you can search to locate information on a specific subject.
- Using the Help system's search capabilities, you can find all Help topics that contain a specific word or phrase.
- Most of the dialog boxes Windows 95 displays provide a Help option you can select to answer your questions about dialog-box entries.
- Within the Windows 95 online Help system, you can print Help topics.
- Windows 95 lets you add your own notes to a Help topic.

ABOUT ONLINE HELP

Books, such as *Success with Windows 95*, excel at teaching new concepts to readers. As such, a book can discuss information in a comprehensive, methodical way that helps readers thoroughly grasp a subject. However, due to size limitations, books can contain only a certain volume of information. When authors write books, they must say everything they want to say within a defined number of pages.

Conversely, online Help systems can contain an almost unlimited amount of information. Online information resides on a hard disk, which typically holds about 500 Mb of data (roughly 500 million characters, or the text of 50 average-length novels). In addition, you can always add more hard disk storage space to your computer. As a result, an online Help system can be much more exhaustive than any book.

Even if it were possible to pack all the Windows 95 online Help system's information into one book, you would find it difficult and time-consuming to locate a specific piece of information in such a text. For example, to learn how to change your display screen's wallpaper, you might have to wade through dozens, hundreds, or thousands of pages searching for headings, subheadings, and keywords that will lead you to information you seek (especially if the book doesn't provide a comprehensive index and table of contents). On the other hand, when you need to find a specific piece of information in online Help, Windows 95 can search for you. This feature makes an online Help system particularly attractive as a source of reference information.

Windows 95 comes with an online Help system that includes information about the Windows 95 operating system and its built-in accessory programs. In the following sections, you will learn how to access this online Help system.

> ### ALL WINDOWS 95 HELP SYSTEMS ARE THE SAME
>
>
>
> As you have learned, the Windows 95 operating system and most Windows 95 applications, such as WordPad and Paint, provide extensive online Help. Furthermore, the Help systems in the Windows 95 operating system and in Windows 95 applications share the same structure. All such systems let you access information through the same three pages (Contents, Index, and Find) of the Help Topics sheet. As a result, if you learn how to use the online Help system in Windows 95, you can find Help information in any Windows 95 application. Later in this chapter, you will learn more about using online Help in Windows 95 applications.

HELP AT YOUR FINGERTIPS

The Windows 95 online Help system is literally at your fingertips. As you work in Windows 95, all you have to do to get online Help is press **F1**. To see how the **F1** key works, click your left-mouse button on the Desktop. Then, press **F1**. Windows 95, in turn, will open a Help Topics sheet, as shown in Figure 4.1.

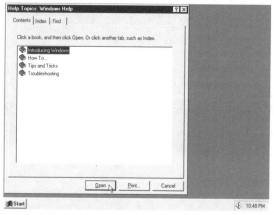

Figure 4.1 The Help Topics sheet Contents page that appears when you press **F1** while using the Desktop.

Soon, you will learn how to navigate the Help Topics sheet. For now, note the contents of the Help Topics sheet. Then, click the Cancel button to close the sheet. Now, use the procedures you learned in Chapter 2 to start WordPad. After Windows 95 opens the WordPad window, press **F1**. WordPad, in turn, will open a Help Topics sheet that displays WordPad-specific Help information, as shown in Figure 4.2.

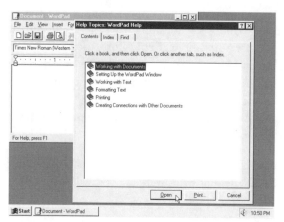

Figure 4.2 The Help Topics sheet that appears when you press **F1** while using WordPad.

4: Using Online Help

Note that the Help Topics sheet now displays Help information on WordPad. Click on the Cancel button to close the Help Topics sheet. From this exercise, you can see that you get Help information on the active program when you press **F1**. After you clicked your left-mouse button on the Desktop, the Windows 95 operating system became the active program. Then, after you pressed **F1**, Windows 95 displayed its Help information in a Help Topics sheet. In the second example, after you ran WordPad and pressed **F1**, WordPad opened a Help Topics sheet that contained WordPad-specific information.

STARTING HELP FROM THE START MENU

As you have learned, to start online Help from your keyboard, all you need to do is press **F1**. However, if you prefer to use your mouse, you can start the Windows 95 online Help system from the Start menu. To use your mouse to start Windows 95 online Help, perform these steps:

1. Click your left-mouse button on the Start button. Windows 95 will display the Start menu.

2. Click your left-mouse button on the Start menu Help option. Windows 95 will open a Help Topics sheet that displays Windows 95 Help information.

The Help Topics sheet on your screen is identical to the one in Figure 4.1. Leave the Help Topics sheet open. You will use the online Help system in the following sections.

STARTING HELP IN A WINDOWS 95 APPLICATION

In most Windows 95 applications, the program window includes a Help category on its menu bar. To access program-specific Help information with your mouse, click your left-mouse button on the Help category. The program, in turn, will display a Help menu from which you can choose one of several Help options. For example, if you click on the Help category in the Paint window's menu bar, Paint will display a Help menu with two options. If you click your mouse on the first option, Help Topics, Help will display a Help Topics sheet with three pages—Contents, Index, and Find—that let you access information about the Paint program. If you click your mouse on the second option, About Paint, Help will display a window that contains information about the Paint program.

HELP ON THE HELP TOPICS SHEET

Imagine that you've just arrived in Paris, France, and need a tour guide to show you around the city. Unfortunately, when you arrive at the Visitor's Bureau, you find there are no guides available who speak your language (and you don't speak French). "You have two options," the Bureau Director says. "You can wait two or three days for a guide who speaks your language, or you can have a French-speaking guide and a translator now. However, the translator will cost you extra."

When you first start to use the online Help system, you may feel like a visitor to Paris with a tour guide who doesn't speak your language. You may not understand how to access the online Help features or use all the controls on the Help Topics sheet well enough to get all the information you need. Fortunately, Help provides you with a "translator" (no extra charge!) that you can access with just a couple of mouse clicks. This "translator" feature lets you obtain information about the various parts of the Help Topics sheet so that you can better understand how online Help presents and organizes information. Before you explore this translator feature, look closely at the Help Topics sheet in Figure 4.1. Notice that the sheet contains three tabs just beneath its title bar. These tabs represent, and let you access, the Help Topics sheet's three pages:

- The Contents page displays a hierarchy of Help topics, much like a book's table of contents lists chapters and sections within each chapter.

- The Index page lets you search for a keyword, much as the index at the back of a book.
- The Find page lets you locate a Help topic that contains a specific word.

Notice the three buttons at the bottom of the Help Topics sheet. Depending on the current page, the first button may have Open, Close, or Display as its label. The next two buttons, Print and Cancel, always appear on the Help Topics sheet. If you click on Cancel, Windows 95 will close the Help Topics sheet. The most interesting part of the Help Topics sheet is the Help button—the title-bar button with a question mark. When you click your left-mouse button on the Help button, Windows 95 activates the previously discussed "translator" feature, which gives you information on the Help system itself. To try Help's "translator" feature, perform these steps:

1. Click on the Help button on the Help Topics sheet's title-bar. Windows 95 will change your mouse pointer's shape to a left-pointing arrow with a question mark (this is the ? pointer).

2. Move your reshaped mouse pointer to an area of the Help Topics sheet and click. Windows 95 will display a pop-up window with Help information on that part of the Help Topics sheet.

Figure 4.3 shows the pop-up window that Windows 95 displays when you click with the ? pointer in the Topics area of the Contents page. You can use the Help button to find out the purpose of each part of the Help Topics sheet. In fact, you will find the Help button in every Windows 95 dialog box. Therefore, you can use the Help button to retrieve context-specific Help information in any Windows 95 dialog box. In short, the Help button lets you ask Help, "What's this?" when you point at an object.

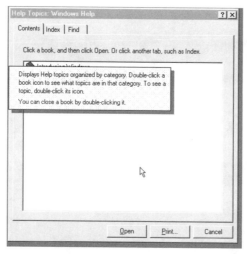

Figure 4.3 The information Windows 95 displays when you click on the Contents page Topics area with the ? pointer.

Using the Help Button

If you've ever purchased a product that required some assembly (such as a bicycle or bookshelf), you know how worrisome it can be when the instructions that accompany the product don't make sense to you. Although Microsoft engineers designed online Help (your Windows 95 instructions) to be extremely user-friendly, they also realized that not all people would at first understand how to use it. As such, Microsoft added the Help button to the Help Topics sheet. Using the Help button, you can get information about the Help Topics sheet itself. When you click your mouse on the Help button and then click on any item in the Help Topics sheet, online Help displays a small pop-up window that describes the item's function. For example, when you click your mouse on the Help button and then on the Help Topics sheet Cancel button, Help displays a pop-up window that says, "Closes this dialog box with-

> out saving any changes you have made." In addition, every Windows 95 dialog box includes a Help button. As such, you can use the Help button to retrieve context-specific Help information in any Windows 95 dialog box.

BROWSING THE CONTENTS

Now that you know how to get information about the Help Topics sheet itself, you can begin to use online Help. The Windows 95 online Help system is almost like a book, only better. Like a book, you can turn from one chapter to another and read the pages that contain the information you need. This section shows you how to browse the Help information like a book. If you look at the Help Topics sheet Contents page in Figure 4.1, you will see a list of topics. This topic list is much like a book's table of contents, except that each Help topic's title appears next to a closed book icon rather than a page number. As such, to access a Help topic, you don't need to find a particular page number. Instead, you just double-click on the topic's title or closed book icon. The online Help system, in turn, will change the book icon from a closed book to an open one and display the topic's contents. To close a topic, double-click on the open book icon. In response, the online Help system will change the icon back into a closed book and hide the topic's contents. As you open a topic, you may see more closed book icons inside it. These closed book icons represent Help subtopics. If you think of a Windows 95 online Help topic as a book, you might think of these subtopics as chapters, sections, and so on. To view Help information, you have to keep opening subtopics (closed book icons) until Windows 95 displays a list of topic pages. (To represent each topic page, Windows 95 uses an icon of a dog-eared page that contains a question mark.) For example, suppose you want to browse the first topic—"Introducing Windows" (see Figure 4.1). To do so, perform these steps:

1. Double-click on the closed book icon for the "Introducing Windows" topic. The online Help system will display two subtopics, "Welcome" and "Using Windows Accessories," each with a closed book icon.

2. Double-click on the closed book icon for the "Welcome" topic. The online Help system will display two topic pages and another topic, "A List of What's New."

3. Double-click on the "A List of What's New" topic. The online Help system will display the topic pages in this topic.

Figure 4.4 shows the Help Topics sheet's contents after you have fully opened the "Welcome" subtopic in the "Introducing Windows" topic.

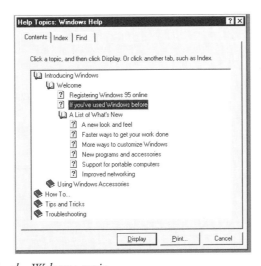

Figure 4.4 The Help topic pages in the Welcome topic.

Whenever a topic page icon (a dog-eared page with a question mark) is visible in the Help Topics sheet, you can open the corresponding topic page and read its contents. To open a topic page, double-click on its icon or on the title next to the icon. (To open a topic page, you can also click once on either the icon or the title and then click on the Display button.) For example, suppose you want to read the "If you've used Windows before" topic. Double-click on that topic page icon. The online Help system, in turn, will hide the Help Topics sheet and open another Help window, as shown in Figure 4.5.

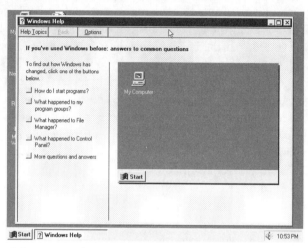

Figure 4.5 *The contents of the "If you've used Windows before" topic.*

Notice the list of questions on the Help window's left side. To get an answer to one of these questions, all you need to do is click on the button that precedes it. For example, click on the button labeled "How do I start programs?" Windows 95, in turn, will display a brief message that explains how you can use the Start menu to run programs. Additionally, Windows 95 will display, directly beneath the message, an illustration of the Start menu. The Help window in Figure 4.5 also includes a toolbar with three buttons—Help Topics, Back, and Options. You will learn more about the Options button later in this chapter. The Back button is useful as you begin reading material in the Help window—as you view multiple topics, you click on the Back button to return to the previous contents of the Help window. Click on the Help Topics button to view the Help Topics sheet from which you opened this topic.

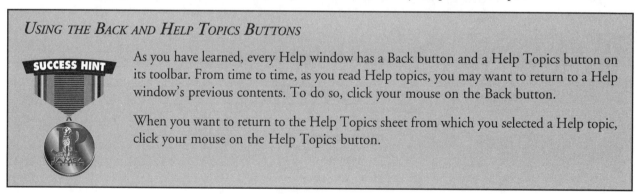

Using the Index

When you want to browse the contents of a book, you simply turn its pages, stopping to read only the material that catches your eye. Similarly, when you want to browse the contents of the Windows 95 online Help system, you click on a series of topics and subtopics until you arrive at a topic page that interests you. However, when you need to find a specific piece of information in either a book or in an online Help system, you might take a different approach. Although browsing is a good strategy when you aren't sure what you're looking for, it's a time-consuming and error-prone way to locate specific references. For example, consider how much time you would have to spend flipping the pages of an American history book to find information about Squanto (a native American who befriended the Pilgrims at Plymouth Rock), especially if you knew nothing about the man except his name. Likewise, imagine how many closed book icons you would have to click your mouse on to find online Help information about the Windows 95 Recycle Bin. Sure, you might get lucky and immediately open a series of topics and subtopics leading straight to the information you need (just as you might, in an American history book, randomly turn to a page that discusses Squanto). But more likely, you'll search for a long time before you get any results. To save you time, most books include an index that you can use to locate the pages that contain the information you want. Likewise, the Windows 95 online Help system provides an index you can use to find specific topics. However, unlike a traditional book index, the Windows 95 online index doesn't give you page numbers that correspond to each index entry. Instead, the online Help index lets you, with just a couple of mouse clicks, advance directly to the information you seek. To view the Windows 95 online Help index, click on the Help Topics sheet Index tab (Figure 4.1). The online Help system, in turn, will display the Help Topics sheet Index page, as shown in Figure 4.6.

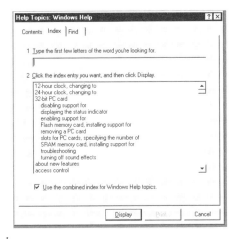

Figure 4.6 The Help Topics sheet Index page.

To search for a specific piece of information in the online Help index, you type a word or words in the text field at the top of the Index page. As you type each letter, Help will display, in the list box directly beneath the text field, the portion of its index that corresponds alphabetically to the sequence of characters in the text field. For example, if you want to look for information on "connecting to the Internet," type in the first few letters in the text field. As you type each letter, the Help system positions the index list on an entry that most closely matches the letters you have entered so far. By the time you enter **conn**, the Help system has already selected the word "connecting" in the index list (see Figure 4.7).

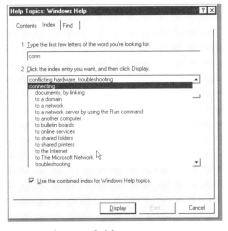

Figure 4.7 The Index after you enter **conn** in the text field.

At this point, you can already see the "to the Internet" entry in the index list. To display the topic that corresponds to this entry, double-click on the entry. The online Help system, in turn, will close the Help Topics sheet and open a new Help window with the topic, as shown in Figure 4.8. In Figure 4.8, Help underlines the text *The Microsoft Network* and *Internet access provider*. If you click on such underlined text, the online Help system displays a pop-up window that contains the definition of the underlined text. Figure 4.9 shows the pop-up window that appears when you click your left-mouse button on the text *Internet access provider*.

Figure 4.8 The Help information on "Connecting to the Internet."

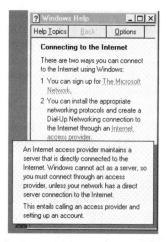

Figure 4.9 The pop-up window with the definition of **Internet access provider**.

From the Help window of Figure 4.9, click on the Help Topics button to go back to the Help Topics sheet (Figure 4.7).

Searching for a Word

When a publishing company needs someone to create an index for a book, they usually hire a professional indexer. The indexer reads the entire text and selects items that he or she feels readers will frequently want to look up. The indexer then places these items in alphabetical order in the index. Microsoft compiled the online index in much the same way—someone read all the Help topics, decided what pieces of information you would find most important, and structured the online Help index accordingly.

Note: Before the online Help system can search for a word, it needs to create an index of all the words it contains. When you click on the Find tab for the first time, the online Help system will display a dialog box and walk you through the process of building this index.

Fortunately, Microsoft also recognized that its online indexing scheme would not always meet your needs. Microsoft realized that Windows 95 users will sometimes seek information that the online Help index just can't direct them toward, no matter how carefully Windows 95 developers structured the online index. As a result, Microsoft added the Find feature, which lets you search the entire online Help system for occurrences of a specific word, even if the search word doesn't appear in the online Help index. To begin your search for a specific word, click on the Help Topics sheet Find tab. The online Help system, in turn, will display the contents of the Help Topics sheet Find page, as shown in Figure 4.10.

Figure 4.10 Finding a word in the online Help for Windows 95.

To find the Help topics that contain a specific word, perform these steps:

1. In the text field at the top of the Find page, type in the word you want to find. The online Help system will display the list of matching words in a list box that appears immediately below the text field.

2. In the list of matching words, click on the word you want. In response, the online Help system will display a list of topics that contain the word you have selected. The list of topics will appear below the list of matching words.

3. In the list of topics, click on the topic you want to display. Help will highlight the topic in reverse video.

4. Click on the Display button. The online Help system will close the Help Topics sheet and open a Help window with the topic you have selected.

For example, suppose you want to look up the Help topics that contain the word *Internet* (because you want to connect your computer to the Internet). Figure 4.11 shows the result of typing **Int** in the text field at the top of the Find page.

Figure 4.11 Finding Help topics with the word **Internet**.

As you can see in Figure 4.11, the online Help system has found quite a few Help topics that contain one or more occurrences of the word *Internet*. Note that the Help topic's title does not necessarily have to include the search word.

Printing a Topic

As you use online Help, there will be times when you will want to print Help's instructions so that you can read the material while you later perform the corresponding action. In such cases, you can print a Help topic easily by using a menu option. To print the current Help topic, click on the Help window Options button. The Help system, in turn, will display a menu, as shown in Figure 4.12.

Note: You can also access the menu shown in Figure 4.12 by right-clicking on the Help topic's text.

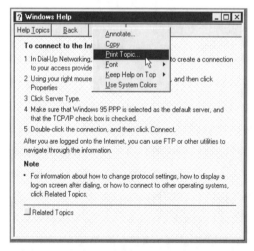

Figure 4.12 The menu that appears when you click on the Help window Options button.

As you can see, the menu in Figure 4.12 includes a Print Topic option. To print the Help topic in the window, click on the Print Topic option. Help, in turn, will display the Print dialog box, as shown in Figure 4.13.

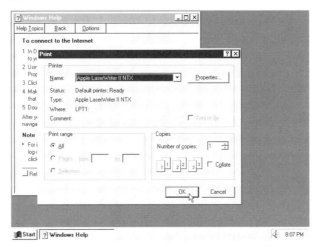

Figure 4.13 *The Print dialog box that appears after you select the Print Topic option.*

Click on the OK button in the Print dialog box. Help, in turn, will print the topic.

COPYING A HELP TOPIC TO THE WINDOWS CLIPBOARD

As you may know, many Windows programs let you cut or copy objects from a document into the Windows Clipboard so you can paste them elsewhere in the same document, in a different document, or even in a different program window. For example, if you want to move an object (such as a block of text in WordPad) to another location, you first use your mouse to select the object. Next, you select the program window's Edit menu Cut option to remove the object from its current location. The program, in turn, stores the object in the *Windows Clipboard*—a memory location that Windows 95 maintains for all programs that let users cut, copy, and paste objects. Then, you click your mouse at the location where you want the object and select the program window's Edit menu Paste option. The program, in turn, removes the object from the Clipboard and pastes the object into your document at the cursor's new location.

When you want to copy (rather than cut) an object and paste the copy at another location, you first use your mouse to select the object. Then, you select the program window's Edit menu Copy option. The program, in turn, sends a copy of the object to the Clipboard without disturbing the original. After you click your mouse at the location where you want the copy, you select the Edit menu Paste option.

Note: *If the new location where you want to paste an object is in another document, you will need to open the document, click your mouse at the new location, and select the Edit menu Paste option in the new document's program window.*

As you use online Help, there may be times when you'll want to copy Help information and paste it into a document or program window. For example, you may want to send to a friend an electronic mail message that contains instructions on setting up a dial-up Internet connection in Windows 95. To save yourself some time, you might want to copy the instructions from the appropriate Help topic and paste that text into the mail message. To copy all the text from a Help topic to the Clipboard, click on the Help window Options button. Help, in turn, will display a menu. Click on the menu's Copy option to copy the entire Help topic. After you copy the topic's text, you can paste that text into almost any open document.

As you paste Help information into your documents, you may not always want to add a Help topic's full text to a document. For example, you may not want your document to include all the steps in a particular Help window. Instead, you may want just one of the tips that appear in the bottom half of the window. On such occasions, you can select a portion of the Help text, copy the selection to the Clipboard, and paste the selection into your document. To do so, perform these steps:

1. Position your mouse pointer at the beginning of the text you want to copy.
2. Hold down your left-mouse button and drag your mouse pointer. Online Help will highlight the text as you move your mouse.
3. Release your left-mouse button when you have selected the text you want.
4. Click on the Option button. Help will display a menu.
5. Click on the menu's Copy option. Help will copy the text you selected to the Clipboard.
6. If you have not done so already, open the document to which you want to add the Help text.
7. In the document, click your mouse at the location where you want the Help text.
8. Select the Edit menu Paste option. The document's program will paste the Help text.

Copying Help Topics

As you have learned, Help lets you copy all or part of a Help topic into a document or program window. To copy all the text from a Help topic, click your mouse on the Help window Options button. Help, in turn, will display a menu. Click on the menu's Copy option to copy the entire Help topic. After you copy the topic's text, you can paste that text into almost any open document or program window.

To copy only a portion of a Help topic, first select the text. To do so, perform these steps:

1. Position your mouse pointer at the beginning of the text you want to copy.
2. Hold down your left-mouse button and drag your mouse pointer. Online Help will highlight the text as you move your mouse.
3. Release your left-mouse button when you have selected the text you want.

Next, you need to copy the text you selected to the Windows Clipboard. To do so, perform these steps:

1. Click on the Option button. Help will display a menu.
2. Click on the menu's Copy option. Help, in turn, will copy the text you selected to the Clipboard.

Finally, you need to select a program window or document and paste the text. To do so, perform these steps:

1. If you have not done so already, open the document to which you want to add the Help text.
2. In the document, click your mouse at the location where you want to insert the Help text.
3. Select the Edit menu Paste option. The document's program, in turn, will paste the Help text.

Adding Your Own Notes to a Topic

One useful aspect of printed manuals is that you can write down, in the margins, personal notes that make sense to you. In these notes, you might correct errors you find in the manual or record simple information, such as your Internet provider's phone number. In a similar way, the online Help system annotation feature lets you add your own notes to a Help topic. Using the annotation feature may not be as easy as scribbling a note in the margins of a book page, but you will find the feature handy.

For example, suppose you want to "jot down" your Internet access provider's phone number in the "Connecting to the Internet" Help topic. To add a note to the Help topic, perform these steps:

1. Click on the Options button. Help will display a menu.

2. Click on the Annotate option in the menu. Help will display the Annotate dialog box, as shown in Figure 4.14.

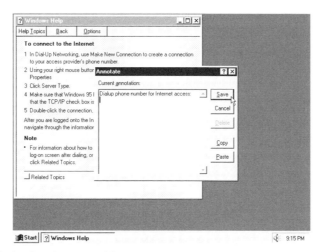

Figure 4.14 *The Annotate dialog box lets you add your own notes.*

3. Enter your note in the Current annotation section of the Annotate dialog box. For this example, enter your Internet dial-up phone number. Then, click on the Save button. Help will close the Annotate dialog box and save the note.

After you add a note to a Help topic, the online Help system displays a paper clip icon next to the title of the Help topic, as shown in Figure 4.15.

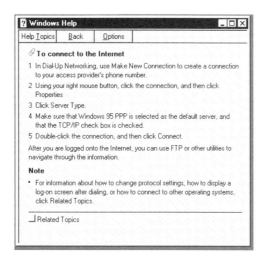

Figure 4.15 *A paper clip icon indicates that you have attached a note to this Help topic.*

To view the note you attached to the Help topic, click on the paper clip icon. The online Help system, in turn, will display the note in the Annotate dialog box. If you want to get rid of the note, click on the Delete button in the Annotate dialog box.

USING ONLINE HELP IN A PROGRAM

Imagine you're visiting a city for the first time. The morning after your arrival, room service delivers a pot of steaming coffee and a newspaper. Due to a late flight, you missed the football game you wanted to watch, so you search the paper for scores and highlights. Using the index on the front page, you quickly locate the Sports section and discover your favorite team, a 21-point underdog going into the game, stomped its opponent.

You know how to find the Sports section because this paper is very similar to the one you subscribe to back home. Although their contents vary, both papers have nearly the same format (a front-page index, Opinion section, Comics section, Sports section, and so on), so you have no more trouble finding information in one than in the other. Similarly, the Windows 95 online Help system and the online Help system in all Windows 95 applications share the same format (again, only the content differs). Just as the Windows 95 online Help system uses a Help Topics sheet with three pages (Contents, Index, and Find), so do the online Help systems in Windows 95 programs. As such, if you know how to use one online Help system to locate information, you know how to use them all.

In a Windows 95 program, you use the program window's Help menu to access the online Help system. Consider, for example, the WordPad program that comes with Windows 95. Run WordPad from the Start menu. In the WordPad window, click on the Help menu Help Topics option. WordPad, in turn, will start the online Help system and display Help information on WordPad, as shown in Figure 4.16.

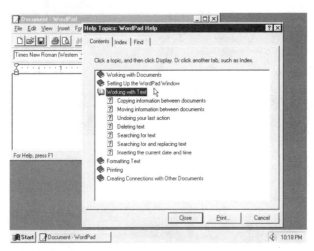

Figure 4.16 *The online Help on WordPad.*

You can see that this is the same dialog box that Windows 95 uses to display the Windows 95 online Help. From the previous sections of this chapter, you should be familiar with this dialog box. You can now use that knowledge to look up Help information in any Windows 95 program.

JUMP BUTTONS IN WINDOWS 95 ONLINE HELP

Imagine that you've just reached your vacation destination only to discover the airline lost your luggage. Until the airline tracks down your suitcases, you'll be without extra clothes, a toothbrush, and so on. In such a situation, you need help. A good tour guide might give you directions to the nearest store. But you need more than just information. You need a personal assistant, someone who'll purchase clothes and supplies for you so you don't have to lose a minute of your vacation time.

In Windows 3.1, online Help was like a good tour guide—in a crunch, it would give you the instructions you needed. In Windows 95, online Help is more like a personal assistant because, in addition to providing you with information, it actually performs tasks for you. To make Windows 95 online Help perform tasks, you click your mouse on *jump buttons,* which appear periodically in the text of Help windows. When you click on a jump button, online Help automatically starts the program or opens the window you need to perform the Help window's instructions, saving you time and effort. To see a jump button in action, select the Start menu Help option. In response, Windows 95 will open the Help Topics sheet. Click on the Help Topics sheet Index tab. Help, in turn, will display the Index page (see Figure 4.6). In the Index page's text field, type **inst**. Help will position the index list at the "installing" entry. Scroll down the list and select the "modems" entry. Help, in turn, will highlight the entry, as shown in Figure 4.17.

Figure 4.17 Windows 95 highlights the "modems" entry in the index list.

Click on the Display button. Help, in turn, will display the online Help information about how to set up a modem, as shown in Figure 4.18.

Figure 4.18 Windows 95 online Help information about how to set up a modem.

The Help window instructs you to click on a small button with a left-pointing arrow. That button is a jump button. Click on the jump button to install a modem. Help, in turn, will open the Modems Properties sheet, similar to the one shown in Figure 4.19.

Figure 4.19 After you click on the jump button, Help opens the Modems Properties sheet.

As you can see, the Modems Properties sheet in Figure 4.19 shows that the system already has a modem installed. If your system does not have a modem, the sheet won't list one. To begin installing a modem, you would click on the Add button. (You will learn how to install a modem in Chapter 5, "Customizing Common Hardware.") The "Setting up a modem" topic page is just one example of how jump buttons make it easier for you to perform online Help instructions. The Windows 95 online Help system includes many such jump buttons throughout its topic pages.

Note: Online Help also uses conversation buttons in Help windows that simply provide information. In such cases, you use the buttons to advance to the next piece of Help information, rather than answer Help system questions.

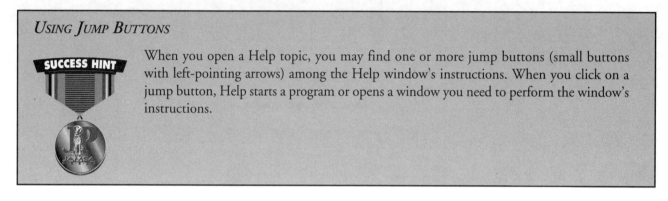

USING JUMP BUTTONS

When you open a Help topic, you may find one or more jump buttons (small buttons with left-pointing arrows) among the Help window's instructions. When you click on a jump button, Help starts a program or opens a window you need to perform the window's instructions.

CONVERSATION BUTTONS

When you're feeling sick and visit your doctor to find out what's wrong, your doctor usually asks you a series of questions—"How have you been sleeping? How have you been eating? Where does it hurt? Can you describe it to me?" Based on your responses (and, often, a few tests), the doctor makes a diagnosis and prescribes a treatment. In a similar way, when you have a problem and seek assistance from one of online Help's troubleshooting topic pages, online Help converses with you, gathering input until it has enough information to make a diagnosis and suggest a solution. To let you answer its questions, online Help provides a special kind of jump button, which this book calls a *conversation button*. A conversation button is a plain, square button with a label that states a possible response to a question Help asks you. For example, suppose you install a new modem and, each time you use your modem, your mouse stops working. Or, when you move your mouse, your modem hangs up. In this case, your modem and mouse have a hardware conflict. To begin troubleshooting this problem, start with the Help Topics sheet Index page. Enter the text **confl** in the text field. Help will select the "conflicting hardware, troubleshooting" index entry. Click on the Display button. Help, in turn, will display the Help information in a window, as shown in Figure 4.20.

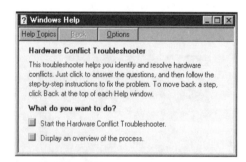

Figure 4.20 Getting help with troubleshooting hardware conflicts.

As you can see, after Help explains what the Hardware Troubleshooter does, the Help window asks you what you want to do. To answer Help's question, you click on one of the two conversation buttons. Click on the conversation button that says "Start the Hardware Conflict Troubleshooter." Help, in turn, will display a new Help topic, "Start Device Manager," as shown in Figure 4.21.

4: Using Online Help

Figure 4.21 *The "Start Device Manager" Help topic.*

In the new Help window, you will see a jump button that lets you view your system's properties. If you click on the jump button, Help will display the System Properties sheet, as shown in Figure 4.22.

After Help displays the System Properties sheet, you can perform the second step in the "Start Device Manager" Help topic (see Figure 4.21).

Figure 4.22 *The System Properties sheet Device Manager page and the Help window side-by-side.*

After you complete that second step, click your mouse on the "Click here to continue" conversation button. The online Help system, in turn, will begin a conversation with you. During this conversation, Help will ask you questions about your system, as shown in Figure 4.23.

Figure 4.23 *Help begins to converse with you.*

To answer Help's questions, refer to the System Properties sheet Help just opened, gather the information Help requests, and click on the appropriate conversation button. Help, in turn, will move on to its next question. This question-and-answer conversation will continue until Help has enough information to diagnose your problem and recommend a solution.

KEYS TO SUCCESS

As your Windows 95 tour guide, this book tells you almost everything you need to know to use Windows 95. However, when you have a question this book doesn't answer, you can always turn to the Windows 95 online Help system. In this chapter, you learned how to access the online Help system and how to use its features to get the information you need.

Chapter 5 will show you how to customize your system's hardware devices, such as your display screen, mouse, and keyboard. However, before you move on to Chapter 5, make sure that you understand the following key concepts:

- ✓ You can access the Windows 95 online Help system from the Start menu Help option.
- ✓ Press **F1** to get online Help information in any program.
- ✓ In any dialog box, click on the Help button, the button with a question mark, to get Help information.
- ✓ You can use the Help index to look up Help information on a specific subject.
- ✓ You can use the Help system Find feature to search for Help topics that contain a specific word.
- ✓ You can add your own personal notes to a Help topic's text.
- ✓ You can copy Help text into your documents.
- ✓ You can print a Help topic.
- ✓ Many Help topic pages include jump buttons you can click on to initiate tasks.
- ✓ When your hardware isn't functioning properly, you can use conversation buttons to describe the problem to online Help. Then, based on the information you provide, Help will diagnose the problem and suggest solutions.

Chapter 5
Customizing Common Hardware

If Windows 95 were a car, Chapters 1 through 4 taught you how to drive it. However, you still have neither looked at many instruments on the dashboard nor seen the engine under the hood. If you are going to operate and maintain your car, you probably need to know a bit more than how to use the steering wheel, accelerator, and brakes. You also need to know how to change the oil, rotate the tires, and set the clock on your dashboard. Likewise, if you plan to use Windows 95 effectively, you will need to learn how to set up your printer and modem, add new fonts, and add new programs. In Windows 95, you use the Control Panel to perform these tasks. Chapters 5 and 6 will teach you how to use the Control Panel to access and modify some of Windows 95's "under the hood" machinery. Chapter 5 focuses on some of the simpler tasks, such as setting your system's date-and-time and working with your printer. In Chapter 6, "Customizing Advanced System Settings," you will learn how to add new hardware and work with some more advanced system settings. By the time you finish this chapter, you will understand the following key concepts:

- To access the Windows 95 Control Panel, you select the Start menu Settings Option and choose Control Panel.

- Using the Control Panel's Date/Time entry, you can set your system's date-and-time.

- The Windows 95 Control Panel lets you customize your screen display, changing its resolution, number of colors displayed, and the colors Windows 95 uses for items such as menus.

- Using the Control Panel Mouse entry, you can speed up or slow down your mouse.

- The Control Panel Modem entry lets you add a modem or change an existing modem's settings.

- Using the Control Panel Printer entry, you can add a new printer or change an existing printer's settings to better suit your needs.

- If your system has a sound card and speakers, you can use the Control Panel Sound entry to make Windows 95 play sounds for specific system events.

Exploring the Control Panel

When you work with a car's engine, you need many different tools. For Windows 95, the Control Panel is your toolbox. In the Control Panel, you will find the tools you need to tinker with and fine tune Windows 95. You can get to the Control Panel in two different ways. First, double-click on the My Computer icon. Windows 95, in turn, will open the My Computer folder, as shown in Figure 5.1.

Figure 5.1 Double-click on the My Computer folder to access the Control Panel.

Note the Control Panel icon in Figure 5.1. To open the Control Panel, double-click on the Control Panel icon. Windows 95, in turn, will open the Control Panel folder (shown in Figure 5.3).

The second way you can access the Control Panel is through the Start menu. Click on the Start button to view the Start menu. Then, move your mouse pointer to the Start menu Settings option. Windows 95, in turn, will display the Settings menu, as shown in Figure 5.2.

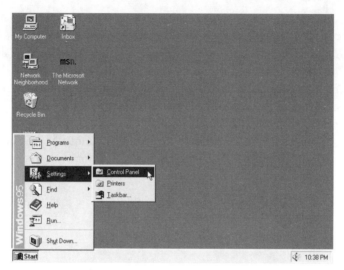

Figure 5.2 *The Settings menu Control Panel option.*

To open the Control Panel, click on the Settings menu Control Panel option. Windows 95, in turn, will open the Control Panel folder. Figure 5.3 shows a typical Control Panel folder.

Figure 5.3 *The Control Panel folder contains the tools you use to customize Windows 95.*

Each icon in the Control Panel folder represents a tool you can use to configure something in Windows 95. Table 5.1 explains the purpose of each tool in a typical Control Panel.

Note: As you read the description of each tool in Table 5.1, don't worry if you don't fully understand what the description means. The rest of this chapter and Chapter 6 will explain and show you how to use most of these tools.

Icon	Purpose
Add New Hardware	Adds new hardware, such as a sound card or a network card, to your system.
Add/Remove Programs	Installs or removes a program, sets up Windows 95 programs (such as Microsoft Network and Microsoft Exchange), and creates a startup disk.
Date/Time	Sets the date, time, and time zone.
Display	Sets the Desktop's colors, display size, and background pattern. It also, turns the screen saver on or off.
Fonts	Displays, adds, or removes fonts from your system.
Joystick	Changes the joystick settings.
Keyboard	Changes the keyboard's key repeat rate, language, and the keyboard type.
Mail and FAX	Sets up Microsoft Exchange (a program to manage your messages and faxes).
Microsoft Mail Postoffice	Manages a Microsoft Mail post office (only if you have Microsoft Mail).
Modems	Adds or removes a modem and sets up an existing modem.
Mouse	Changes mouse settings (such as left-handed or right-handed, and the double-click speed).
Multimedia	Changes audio, video, MIDI, and audio CD playback settings.
Network	Configures network hardware and software.
Passwords	Changes your password.
Printers	Adds, removes, or configures a printer.
Regional Settings	Specifies how all Windows 95 programs display numbers, dates, times, and currencies.
Sounds	Changes the sounds that Windows 95 makes when certain events (such as error or shutdown) occur.
System	Displays system information, as well as manages all system devices (this is an advanced option).
Accessibility Options	Provides additional keyboard, sound display, and mouse support to improve user accessibility.

Table 5.1 *The function of the Control Panel tools.*

Success with Windows 95

Accessing the Control Panel

As you have learned, the Control Panel contains the tools you'll need to customize Windows 95. As such, when you want to change the way Windows 95 functions, you'll usually need to access the Control Panel and click on its icons. Windows 95 gives you two ways to reach the Control Panel:

- Double-click on the My Computer icon. Windows 95, in turn, will open the My Computer folder. Next, double-click on the Control Panel icon.

- Click on the Start button. Then, move your mouse pointer to the Start menu Settings option. Finally, move your mouse pointer to the Setting menu Control Panel option and click your left-mouse button.

Setting the Date-and-Time

From cars to VCRs, almost everything comes with a clock. Your computer is no exception. Your system uses its date-and-time function for many tasks, such as to time-stamp the documents and e-mail messages you create.

For example, if you have a fax/modem, you can send faxes from Windows 95. In the United States, there is a law—The Telephone Consumer Protection Act of 1991—that requires your faxes to include the date-and-time, as well as the name of the fax sender. When you send a fax from your computer, the date-and-time comes from the operating system. If you were not convinced before why you need to set your system's date-and-time, now you have a legal reason to do so—at least if you live in the United States.

To see if your system's date-and-time is accurate, all you have to do is look at the clock on the Taskbar. The Taskbar clock shows the time only. To display the date, momentarily rest your mouse pointer on the clock:

If your system's date-and-time is wrong, you can set it through the Date/Time Properties sheet. To access the Date/Time Properties sheet, double-click on the Control Panel's Date/Time icon. Windows 95, in turn, will open the Date/Time Properties sheet, as shown in Figure 5.4.

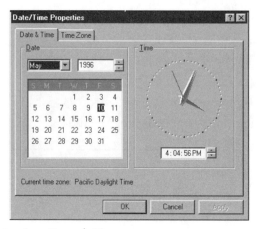

Figure 5.4 *The Date/Time Properties sheet Date & Time page.*

As you can see from Figure 5.4, the Date/Time Properties sheet has two pages:

- The Date & Time page lets you set your system's date-and-time.
- The Time Zone page lets you specify your system's time zone.

SETTING THE DATE

In the Date/Time Properties sheet, the controls you use to set your system's date reside on the Date & Time page's left side. To set the date, perform these steps:

1. To set the month, click on the pull-down list button next to the text field in which the month appears. Windows 95 will display a list of months.
2. In the pull-down list, click on the current month. Windows 95 will place the month's name in the text field next to the pull-down list button. In addition, Windows 95 will also change the monthly calendar to reflect the current month.
3. To set the day of the month, click on the current day from the monthly calendar. Windows 95, in turn, will highlight the selected day.
4. To change the year, click on the spin button next to the text field that shows the year. Windows 95 will adjust (increment or decrement) the year by one as you click on the arrows in the spin button.
5. To set the date, click on the Apply button.

Note: *A spin button is a pair of adjacent buttons with up and down arrows. To increase a value, click on the up-arrow button. To decrease a value, click on the down-arrow button.*

SETTING THE TIME

To set your system's time, you use the controls that appear underneath the clock on the Date & Time page's right side (see Figure 5.4). A simple way to set the time is to enter the current time in the text field beneath the clock. Or, you can use the spin button that appears next to the text field.

To set the time, perform these steps:

1. To set the AM or PM indicator, click on AM or PM in the text field. Windows 95, in turn, will highlight the indicator's letters.
2. Click the spin button's up-arrow or down-arrow. Windows 95, in turn, will change the AM or PM text.
3. To change the hour, click on the hour in the text field (for example, if the time is 6:45:47 PM, click on the "6"). Windows 95, in turn, will display a blinking cursor in the hour field.
4. Click on the spin button's up-arrow or down-arrow. Windows 95 will increment the hour when you click on the up-arrow and decrement it when you click on the down-arrow.
5. To change the minutes, click on the minutes in the text field (for example, if the time is 6:45:47 PM, click on the "45"). Windows 95, in turn, will display a blinking cursor in the minutes field.
6. Click on the spin button's up-arrow or down-arrow. Windows 95 will increment the minutes when you click on the up-arrow and decrement them when you click on the down-arrow.

7. To change the seconds, click on the seconds in the text field (for example, if the time is 6:45:47 PM, click on the "47"). Windows 95, in turn, will display a blinking cursor in the seconds field.

8. Click on the spin button's up-arrow or down-arrow. Windows 95 will increment the seconds when you click on the up-arrow and decrement them when you click on the down-arrow.

9. To set the time, click on the Apply button.

SETTING THE TIME ZONE

The local time is different in different parts of the world. When someone starts work at 8:00 AM in Washington, D.C., it is already 1:00 PM in London, England. As such, when a computer in London, England communicates with one in Washington, D.C., the two computers need a standard reference time.

For example, assume your computer resides in Washington, D.C. and, during the course of one day, you receive two messages—one from London, England (with a 7:00 PM local timestamp) and the other from Madrid, Spain (with a 7:30 PM local timestamp). Furthermore, assume you want your system to sort these messages by the order of their arrival. Without a standard reference time, each of these messages will be stamped only with the sender's local time. As such, your system may list the London message that actually arrived at 2:00 PM your time before a Madrid message that arrived at 1:30 PM.

As you might know, Greenwich Mean Time (or GMT, for short) is the standard reference time that all computers (and most government, business, and military organizations) use. In various circles, GMT is known as Zulu time or Universal Coordinated Time (the acronym is UTC, from the French equivalent of the words *Universal Coordinated Time*). The local time in Greenwich, England is the standard because the zero meridian of longitude passes through Greenwich.

When you specify a time zone, you tell Windows 95 how early or late your local time is relative to GMT. Your computer then uses the time zone information to convert local time to GMT and vice versa. For example, if you reside in Washington D.C., you live in the Eastern time zone, which is five hours earlier than GMT. Thus, when a computer that resides in the Eastern time zone wants to calculate GMT, it adds five hours to its local time.

To set your system's time zone, you use the Date/Time Properties sheet Time Zone page. Click on the Date/Time Properties sheet Time Zone tab (see Figure 5.4). Windows 95, in turn, will display the Time Zone page, as shown in Figure 5.5.

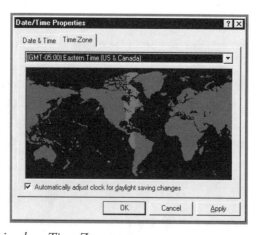

Figure 5.5 The Date/Time Properties sheet Time Zone page.

At the top of the Time Zone page, a text field displays the current time zone's name. Additionally, in the world map that occupies much of the page, Windows 95 highlights the current time zone. To set your system's time zone, just click at your approximate location on the world map. Windows 95, in turn, will highlight your time zone. Furthermore, in the text field at the top of the page, Windows 95 will display your time zone's name and indicate your location. (Sometimes, the text field will contain your country or region's name. Other times, it will list major cities in your region.)

Another way you can set your system's time zone is to click on the pull-down list button in the Time Zone page's top-right corner. Windows 95, in turn, will display a list of time zones, as shown in Figure 5.6.

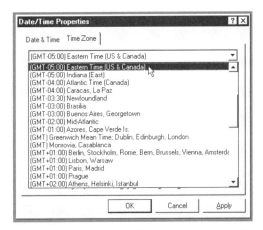

Figure 5.6 *The list of time zones that appears when you click on the pull-down list button.*

To select a time zone from the list, click on the time zone's name. Windows 95, in turn, will display that name in the text field and highlight the new time zone in the world map.

As you may know, in places that use Daylight Savings Time, people reset their clocks twice a year (one hour forward in the spring and one hour back in the fall) to make the most use of the daylight hours. You do not have to explicitly tell Windows 95 if your time zone uses Daylight Savings Time. When you click at your location on the world map (see Figure 5.5) or select your time zone's name from the time zone list (see Figure 5.6), Windows 95 automatically knows if Daylight Savings Time applies to your system.

For example, Washington, D.C.; Toronto, Canada; Richmond, Indiana; Bogota, Colombia; and Lima, Peru are all in the same time zone. However, only Washington, D.C. and Toronto use Daylight Savings Time. As such, for this time zone, the time zone list has three entries: "Eastern Time (US & Canada)," "Indiana (East)," and "Lima, Bogota." When you click on Washington, D.C. or Toronto in the world map, the text box at the top of the Time Zone page shows "Eastern Time (US & Canada)." When you click on eastern Indiana, the text box shows "Indiana (East)." When you click on Colombia or Peru, the text box shows "Lima, Bogota."

If your system resides in an area that uses Daylight Savings Time, Windows 95 will automatically adjust your system's time when Daylight Savings Time is in effect. To switch off this feature, click on the check box at the bottom of the Time Zone page until the check mark disappears.

Customizing the Display

As you probably know, every car has the same basic features. For example, every car has an engine, some doors, a steering wheel, a rear-view mirror, and a brake pedal. However, as soon as you go beyond the basic features, you get into details that differentiate one car from another—the number of doors, the type of body styling, the number of cylinders in the engine, and so on. Car manufacturers offer these variations because customers want cars that fit their lifestyle. Like a car, Windows 95 has some basic features: dialog boxes, command buttons, icons, and so on. However, because computer users, like car buyers, want a product that meets their specific needs, Microsoft engineers built utilities into Windows 95 that you can use to customize the operating system. In this section, you will explore the utilities you can use to change the Windows 95 Desktop. As you will learn, although Windows 95 provides default colors, fonts, and icon sizes, you don't have to stick with them. If, for any reason whatsoever, you are unhappy with your Desktop's default settings, you can quickly change some or all of them. To change your Desktop's appearance, you use the Display Properties sheet. To access the Display Properties sheet, double-click on the Control Panel's Display icon. Windows 95, in turn, will open the Display Properties sheet, as shown in Figure 5.7. As you can see in Figure 5.7, the Display Properties sheet has four pages:

- The Background page lets you select a wallpaper or pattern for the Desktop (instead of a solid color).

- The Screen Saver page lets you select a screen saver for your display screen.

- The Appearance page, as the name indicates, lets you control the appearance of Windows 95, including the Desktop, icons, windows, menus, and message boxes.

- The Settings page lets you specify the maximum number of colors your monitor and video card can support (16 colors to 16 million colors) and the size of your Desktop (how many *pixels* wide by how many pixels tall).

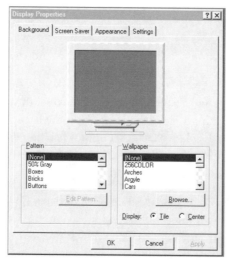

Figure 5.7 The Display Properties sheet.

UNDERSTANDING PIXELS

Monitors display characters and images by illuminating small dots on the screen, called picture elements or pixels. Each pixel, in turn, is made up of a red, green, and blue element. By illuminating the red, green, and blue elements at different intensities, the monitor is able to change the pixel's color. Depending on the size of your monitor, your display screen will have anywhere from 640 to 1280 pixels horizontally and 480 to 1024 pixels vertically. The more pixels your video card and monitor use (in other words, the higher their *resolution*), the sharper your resulting image. Using the Display Properties sheet Settings page, you can adjust your video resolution.

5: Customizing Common Hardware

Selecting a Background Pattern and Wallpaper

In many ways, your Desktop's background is much like the interior walls of a new house. When you first move into a new house, the walls are often blank and unadorned. Some people like their walls that way—a sparse, simple decor. You might be such a person. However, if you're not, you'll likely feel at least some need to decorate your new living environment to make it more eye-pleasing and reflective of your personality. Likewise, the first time you start Windows 95, the Desktop will be plain and solid-colored. If you want your screen to have a simple look, the Desktop's default background may suit you fine. However, you don't have to settle for the plain look. Just as you might swirl plaster on to the walls of your living room to create an eye-catching pattern, you can select a Windows 95 *background pattern* to add some life to your Desktop's background. Each background pattern is an 8x8 (8 pixels wide by 8 pixels tall) pattern of dots that Windows 95 repeats across the Desktop. Or, you may want Windows 95 to place a *wallpaper* at the center of your screen (like hanging a large picture on a bare wall), or tile (repeat) the wallpaper across your Desktop. Each wallpaper is an image, such as a picture of your dog, commonly referred to as a *bitmap*. Windows 95 places wallpaper over any pattern that fills the Desktop.

Whether you choose a pattern or wallpaper to fill your Desktop's background is really a matter of personal preference. However, there are certain advantages to using each. For example, if you opt for a pattern, you can use the Pattern Editor dialog box to change the color (from your Desktop's background color to black, and vice versa) of any of the sixty-four pixels in the pattern's 8x8 block of dots. As such, if you edit the patterns that come with Windows 95, you can create a nearly limitless number of custom Desktop patterns. Wallpaper, on the other hand, normally contains a more sophisticated image. Windows 95 provides several wallpapers you can use. In addition, Windows 95 lets you use any bitmap image as wallpaper. For example, you can use the Windows 95 Paint program to create your own bitmap image and then place that image as wallpaper on your Desktop. If you have a *scanner* (a device that can create a bitmap file from a photograph), you can scan any image you want and use the image as a wallpaper. On the Display Properties sheet Background page (see Figure 5.7), Windows 95 has two groups of controls: one for selecting a background pattern and the other for picking a wallpaper. Initially, Windows 95 highlights the word *(None)* in both the Pattern and Wallpaper list boxes because, by default, Windows 95 uses no pattern or wallpaper. Above the Pattern and Wallpaper list boxes, Windows 95 displays a picture of a monitor, which this book will refer to as the *sample monitor*. When you choose a pattern or a wallpaper, Windows 95 uses the sample monitor to show how your selection will appear on your Desktop.

Trying Out Background Patterns

To see how background patterns change the look of the Desktop, click on a pattern's name in the Background page Pattern list box. Windows 95, in turn, will highlight the pattern's name and use the small monitor to show you the pattern. When you find a pattern you like, click the Apply button. For example, select the Paisley pattern and then click on the Apply button. Windows 95, in turn, will change the Desktop's background to the Paisley pattern, as shown in Figure 5.8.

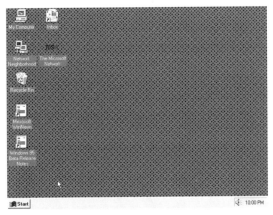

Figure 5.8 The Windows 95 Desktop with the Paisley pattern.

If you do not like any of the patterns in the Pattern list box, you can pick a pattern and edit it. To edit the current pattern, click the Background page Edit Pattern button. Windows 95, in turn, will open a Pattern Editor dialog box, as shown in Figure 5.9.

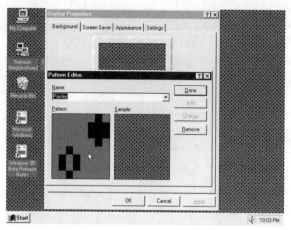

Figure 5.9 *The Pattern Editor dialog box.*

The Pattern Editor dialog box Pattern area contains an 8x8 array of rectangles. Each rectangle represents a dot (or pixel) in the 8x8 pattern of dots. To change the pattern, click on the rectangles to toggle (or switch) their color. If you click on a black rectangle, its color changes to the color of the Desktop. Conversely, if you click on a colored rectangle, it turns black. As you change the pattern, Windows 95 shows you the results in the Pattern Editor dialog box Sample area. Click on the Done button when you are satisfied with the pattern. For more information on editing or creating background patterns, refer to the book *1001 Windows 95 Tips*, Jamsa Press, 1995.

TRYING OUT WALLPAPERS

As you decorate or redecorate your Desktop, there will be times when you'll want more than a simple 8x8 pattern for your Desktop's background. For example, you may want Windows 95 to display a large picture of a peacock at the center of your Desktop. Or, you might want Windows 95 to tile a highly complex, multi-colored image (such as the Tartan wallpaper) across your display screen. To apply a wallpaper, you must select one from the Background page Wallpaper list box (see Figure 5.7). Windows 95 can display a wallpaper in one of two ways:

- Place one copy of the wallpaper bitmap at the center of the Desktop. Click on the Background page Center option button to use wallpaper this way.

- Fill the Desktop with the selected wallpaper as a tile (Windows 95 repeats the same image across the Desktop). Click on the Background page Tile option button to cover the Desktop with a wallpaper.

To see how a wallpaper looks, select the Leaves item from the Background page Wallpaper list box. Next, click on the Tile option button. Finally, click on the Apply button. Windows 95, in turn, will fill the Desktop with the Leaves wallpaper, as shown in Figure 5.10.

In addition to the listed wallpapers, you can use any bitmap image as the Desktop's background. To browse the files on your disk for an image, click on the Browse button (see Figure 5.7). Windows 95, in turn, will display a Browse dialog box from which you can select the bitmap you want as wallpaper.

5: Customizing Common Hardware

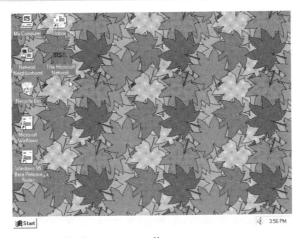

Figure 5.10 The Windows 95 Desktop with the Leaves wallpaper.

Adding Wallpapers to Windows 95

If you don't like any of the wallpapers that Windows 95 provides, you can use the Browse dialog box to add other bitmaps to the Background page Wallpaper list box.

For example, if you are a good artist, you can use the Paint program to prepare a sketch and save it as a bitmap. Or, if you want your Desktop's background to display a picture of your dog, you can run the picture through a *scanner*—a device that can create a bitmap file from a photograph. (When you save the scanned image, make sure you save it as a bitmap file.)

If you have neither artistic talent nor an available scanner, you may want to purchase a commercial clip-art collection. Many of these collections include images in bitmap file format. You can use any of these bitmap images as wallpaper.

Turning on the Screen Saver

In the early days of personal computers, if you left an image on a display screen for too long, the image got "burned in" on the screen. You could see a burned-in image on a screen even after you turned off your display screen. To prevent burn-in damage, everyone used *screen savers*.

A screen saver, which activates only after your computer is idle for a set period of time, fills your screen with some changing pattern. However, as soon as you press a keyboard key or move your mouse, the screen saver restores your screen's previous contents.

Screen savers are still immensely popular because they provide you with a convenient way to prevent others from reading your screen's contents, and they also provide you with password protection. When you want to prevent prying eyes from reading your screen while you're away from your PC, you can password-protect your screen saver to make sure Windows 95 doesn't deactivate your screen saver unless it receives the correct password.

To select a screen saver and turn it on or off, use the Display Properties sheet Screen Saver page. To access the Screen Saver page, click on the Screen Saver tab. Windows 95, in turn, will display the Display Properties sheet Screen Saver page, as shown in Figure 5.11.

Success with Windows 95

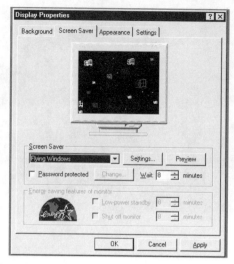

Figure 5.11 The display Properties sheet Screen Saver page.

The Screen Saver page shows a small picture of a display monitor and two groups of controls underneath the monitor's picture:

- The Screen Saver controls let you select a screen saver, change its settings, set password protection, and specify when the screen saver should automatically turn on.

- The "Energy saving features of monitor" controls let you specify when your monitor should switch to low-power mode and when it should turn off automatically. Windows 95 disables these controls if your monitor does not have energy saving features.

Selecting a Screen Saver

Windows 95 comes with several screen savers, each with a unique design. To select a screen saver, perform these steps:

1. Click on the pull-down list button in the Screen Saver controls. Windows 95, in turn, will display a pull-down list of available screen savers.

2. Click on the screen saver you want, or click on "(None)" if you want no screen saver. Windows 95, in turn, will select the screen saver and show you a preview of it in the sample monitor above the controls.

To password protect your screen saver, click on the Password protected check box. Windows 95, in turn, will place a check mark in the check box and enable the Change button. To specify a password, click on the Change button. Windows 95, in turn, will display a dialog box to prompt you for the password.

Password Protection in Windows 95

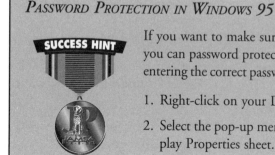

If you want to make sure no one sees what's on your display screen while you're away, you can password protect the screen saver to make sure no one can deactivate it without entering the correct password. To password protect your screen saver, perform these steps:

1. Right-click on your Desktop. Windows 95 will display a pop-up menu.

2. Select the pop-up menu's Properties option. Windows 95 will open the Display Properties sheet.

3. Click your mouse on the Display Properties sheet Screen Saver tab. Windows 95 will open the Display Properties sheet Screen Saver page.

4. Click your mouse on the Settings button. Windows 95 will display a Setup dialog box that contains the name of your current screen saver in its title bar.

5. Click your mouse on the Password protected check box until a check mark appears. Windows 95 will enable the Set Password button.

6. Click your mouse on the Set Password button. Windows 95 will display the Change Password dialog box.

7. In the Old Password field (if present), type your old password.

8. In the New Password field, type your new password.

9. In the Retype New Password field, type your new password again.

10. Click your mouse on the OK buttons in the Change Password dialog box, Setup dialog box, and Display Properties sheet. Windows 95 will password protect your current screen saver.

After you activate the password protection feature, your screen saver will turn on as it always did. However, when someone types on your keyboard or moves your mouse to restore your original screen, Windows 95 will not stop the screen saver. Instead, Windows 95 will display a dialog box that asks for the password.

As you have learned, a screen saver turns on automatically if no one uses the mouse or keyboard within a set period of time. To set the amount of time Windows 95 will wait before it starts the screen saver, use the Wait spin button. Click on the arrows in the Wait spin button to increase or decrease the wait time.

Most of the Windows 95 screen savers have settings that you can change. These settings control some aspects of the screen saver's appearance and behavior. To change the current screen saver's settings, click on the Settings button. Windows 95, in turn, will display a dialog box you can use to specify the screen saver's settings. For example, if you select the Flying Windows screen saver and then click the Settings button, Windows 95 will open a dialog box that lets you set the options for Flying Windows, as shown in Figure 5.12.

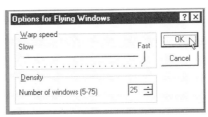

Figure 5.12 The dialog box that lets you set the options for the Flying Windows screen saver.

As you can see in Figure 5.12, you can set the number of flying windows and the speed at which the "windows fly" in the screen saver. After you set these options, click on the OK button to use the settings.

OPTIONS FOR THE ENERGY SAVING FEATURES

Although screen savers are very convenient, they have one major shortcoming. When the screen saver is active, so is your monitor. In an effort to reduce the amount of energy that inactive computer systems consume, hardware and software developers created "energy saver" monitors and printers. When these devices are not in active use, they either shut off or change to a "stand by" mode that consumes less power.

If your monitor has energy saving features, Windows 95 will enable the "Energy saving features of monitor" controls. To turn on Windows 95's energy saving features, you can use the Low-power standby and Shut off monitor check boxes:

- If you select (place a check mark in) the Low-power standby check box, Windows 95 will reduce power to the monitor after a specified amount of time.

- If you select (place a check mark in) the Shut off monitor check box, Windows 95 will turn off power to the monitor after a specified amount of time.

Next to each check box, the Screen Saver page includes a spin button you can use to set the time for the corresponding Windows 95 energy saving feature.

Customizing the Desktop's Appearance

As you have learned, Windows 95 makes it easy for you to change your Desktop's background. However, just as there is more to the appearance of a house than the color of its outside walls, there is more to the appearance of your display screen than the Desktop's background color. When you decorate (or redecorate) the exterior of a house, you must consider the color of door and window trims, shutters, fences, and so on. If you don't, the hot pink you select for your house's exterior walls might clash with your orange shutters. Likewise, when you change the appearance of your Desktop, you must think about the color of the windows, title bars, menu bars, and window work areas that Windows 95 displays. If you don't, the Windows 95 default color for window title bars might clash with the lime green you select for your Desktop's background. Fortunately, the Display Properties sheet Appearance page lets you customize all the Desktop's items to create the total look that is just right for you. To access the Display Properties sheet Appearance page, click on the Display Properties sheet Appearance tab. Windows 95, in turn, will open the Appearance page, as shown in Figure 5.13.

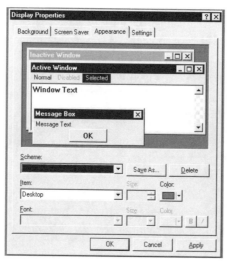

Figure 5.13 The Display Properties sheet Appearance page.

In the upper-half of the Appearance page, Windows 95 displays a sample area that depicts Desktop items (such as active window title bars, inactive window title bars, message box title bars, window text, and so on) with the currently selected colors and fonts. As you change colors and fonts for various Desktop items, Windows 95 uses the sample area to show you how your changes affect the appearance of the items.

Using an Appearance Scheme

As you know, when you paint your house, the job isn't as simple as picking up a few cans of paint, some brushes, and perhaps a roller. You know that, for your house to look great, you need to choose colors carefully. If you pick

5: Customizing Common Hardware

the wrong combination of colors, your door frames, shutters, and roof trim may all clash, making your house an eyesore to all your neighbors. Similarly, your display screen could become an eyesore, one that you'd have to look at as you work with your computer, if you choose the wrong combination of colors for your Desktop. However, you don't need to spend hours experimenting with different color combinations to create an attractive, eye-pleasing Desktop. Instead, you can use one of Window 95's predefined *appearance schemes*.

Like a color scheme, an appearance scheme contains a set of predefined colors that complement one another. However, unlike a color scheme, an appearance scheme also defines the size of fonts that appear in the title bars, menu bars, buttons, and labels that appear on your Desktop. To see a list of appearance schemes available in Windows 95, click on the Appearance page Scheme pull-down list button. Windows 95, in turn, will display a pull-down list of predefined appearance schemes, as shown in Figure 5.14.

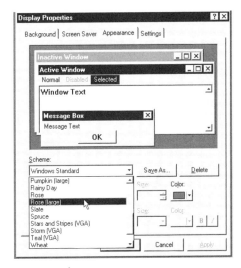

Figure 5.14 The list of predefined appearance schemes.

If you click on one of the schemes, Windows 95 will immediately display the result in the Appearance page sample area. For example, click on the "Rose (large)" appearance scheme. Windows 95, in turn, will use the sample area to show you how the scheme looks (see Figure 5.15). If you look closely at Figure 5.15, you will find that the font size has increased and the color shades are different from those shown in Figure 5.14.

Figure 5.15 The "Rose (large)" appearance scheme in the Appearance page sample area.

As you can see from Figure 5.15, when you select a scheme, Windows 95 selects not only the colors of various items, but also the fonts that appear in title bars, menu bars, and buttons.

When an appearance scheme's name contains the word *(large)*, the scheme will specify large font letters. If you have a large display screen with 800x600 or 1024x768 pixels, you may want to try the schemes with large fonts. On large displays, the letters in small fonts are often too small to read; a large font might help.

ALTERING A SCHEME

One way to get your Desktop's appearance just right is to start with an appearance scheme that closely matches the color and font combinations you desire. Then, you can alter the color or font of specific Desktop items to get a display screen look that you can call your own. To change the appearance of a specific Desktop item, first select the item. Click on the Item pull-down list button. Windows 95 will display a pull-down list of items, as shown in Figure 5.16.

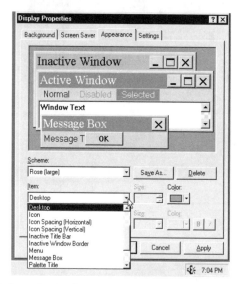

Figure 5.16 The list of Desktop pull-down items that you can customize.

To select the Desktop item you want to change, click your mouse on its name in the Item pull-down list. Windows 95, in turn, will make your selection the current item and place its name in the Item field. You can also select some Desktop items directly from the sample area in the upper-half of the Appearance page. For example, click your mouse on the title bar of the inactive window that Windows 95 displays in the sample area. Windows 95, in turn, will make the inactive title bar the current item and place the words *Inactive Title Bar* in the Item field.

Depending on the item you select, Windows 95 will enable certain Appearance page controls, such as Font, Size, and Color. After Windows enables these controls, you can use them to change the current item's appearance. After you have set the colors and fonts of all the Desktop items to your liking, click on the Apply button to have Windows 95 implement your new settings.

If you develop a group of settings you like, you may want to save them as a new appearance scheme. That way, if you want to use the settings in the future, you don't have to select each item again and reassign colors, font sizes, and so on. To save an appearance scheme, click on the Save As button. Windows 95, in turn, will open a dialog box. In that dialog box, enter the name of the new scheme and click on the OK button. Windows 95, in turn, will add your new scheme to the Scheme pull-down list you saw in Figure 5.14.

5: Customizing Common Hardware

Changing the Display Settings

All computer systems have some fundamental display characteristics (or *display settings*) that limit how much you can alter your Desktop's appearance. For example, if your display hardware (video card) doesn't support more than 16 colors, you simply cannot have more than 16 colors on your Desktop. Likewise, if your display hardware allows no more than 640 pixels horizontally by 480 pixels vertically, you cannot have a Desktop with dimensions larger than 640x480.

During installation, Windows 95 is supposed to automatically recognize your system's display adapter and retrieve your display settings. As such, when installation goes perfectly, you don't need to specify these settings for Windows 95. However, sometimes Windows 95 may not properly identify your system's display adapter. On such occasions, Windows 95 assumes that your adapter is a plain vanilla 16-color VGA (this is an adapter type called Video Graphics Array). As a result, you may have to correct your system's display settings to get all the colors (and resolution) that your display hardware supports.

To change your system's display settings, you use the Display Properties sheet Settings page. Click on the Display Properties sheet Settings tab. Windows 95, in turn, will display the Settings page, as shown in Figure 5.17.

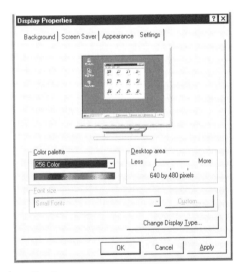

Figure 5.17 The Display Properties sheet Settings page.

Using the Settings page, you can specify the number of colors your monitor displays, as well as your display screen's size (in terms of number of pixels horizontally and vertically). You can also specify your system's display type.

Saving Your Appearance Schemes

If you're happy with the predefined appearance schemes that come with Windows 95, customizing the Desktop is a relatively easy process. Whenever you want to change your Desktop's look, you simply select another appearance scheme from the Appearance page Scheme pull-down list. However, if you prefer a more personal look, you may spend hours (even days) experimenting with item settings until you come up with just the right combination of colors and fonts. On such occasions, don't let your hard work go to waste. Save your new settings as an appearance scheme. Then, when you want to use the settings again, all you need to do is select your appearance scheme from the Scheme pull-down list.

SETTING YOUR SCREEN COLORS AND DEFINING THE DESKTOP AREA

In the Settings page Color palette field, Windows 95 specifies the number of colors your system displays. The number of colors your monitor displays depends on your system's display adapter—the video card. To find out how many colors your system's display adapter supports, consult the literature that came with the adapter (if you installed the display adapter yourself) or with your computer (if the display adapter came preinstalled on your system).

To change the color palette setting, click on the Color palette pull-down list button. Windows 95, in turn, will display a pull-down list from which you can select another color palette. After you select a palette, click on the Apply button. In the Settings page Desktop Area section, Windows 95 displays your Desktop's size in terms of the number of pixels it displays horizontally and vertically. For example, if the Desktop has 640 pixels in the horizontal direction and 480 in the vertical direction, then the Desktop's size (or *Desktop Area*) is "640 by 480 pixels," or 640x480, for short. As you have learned, the higher your monitor's resolution, the sharper your screen image.

To change the Desktop Area resolution, move the slider that appears in the Desktop Area section. For example, to increase your Desktop resolution, drag the Desktop Area slider to the right. Windows 95, in turn, will move the slider to the next mark and specify, just beneath the slider, the new area's measurements (in pixels). Additionally, in the small monitor that appears in the upper-half of the Settings page, Windows 95 will show the effect of changing the Desktop area.

To implement the new Desktop Area, click on the Apply button. Windows 95, in turn, will display a dialog box (see Figure 5.18) that explains the operations Windows 95 or you must perform next. Click on the OK button in the dialog box. Windows 95, in turn, will resize the Desktop and display another dialog box that asks you if you want to use the new settings. If you click the OK button, the changes will take effect. If you click on the Cancel button or do nothing for several seconds, Windows 95 will revert back to the previous Desktop Area.

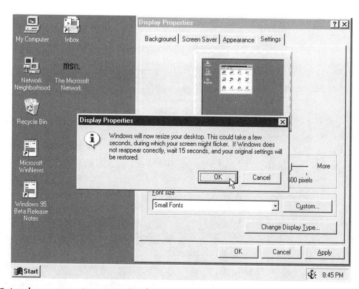

Figure 5.18 Windows 95 is about to resize your Desktop.

SCALING FONTS

If you make your Desktop Area larger, you may find the fonts too small to read. One way to solve the problem is to scale up all fonts (increasing their size). If your hardware supports font scaling, Windows 95 enables the Settings page Custom button. To scale fonts, click on the Custom button. Windows 95, in turn, will display the Custom Font Size dialog box, as shown in Figure 5.19.

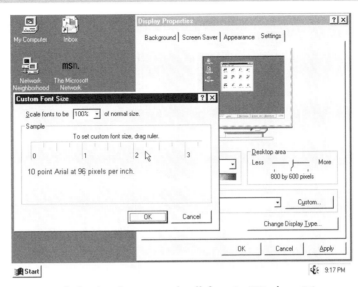

Figure 5.19 The Custom Font Size dialog box lets you scale all fonts in Windows 95.

To scale up all fonts, simply drag the ruler at the center of the Custom Font Size dialog box. As you drag the ruler, Windows 95 changes the font scaling. When the scale factor is what you want, release your mouse button. In response, Windows 95 will show, immediately beneath the ruler, a line of sample text with the new font scaling.

SELECTING A DISPLAY ADAPTER AND MONITOR

If you know that you have a 256-color Super VGA card, and the Settings page shows only 16 colors in the Color palette field, you may need to correct your system's display adapter setting. To check your system's current display adapter and monitor settings, click on the Settings page Change Display Type button. Windows 95, in turn, will open the Change Display Type dialog box, as shown in Figure 5.20.

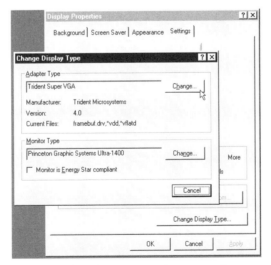

Figure 5.20 The Change Display Type dialog box shows you information about your system's display adapter and monitor.

In the Change Display Type dialog box, you can specify the type of display adapter (video card) and monitor your system uses. If any of the information in this dialog box appears to be wrong, you should correct it.

For example, to change the display adapter setting, click on the Change button next to the Adapter Type field. Windows 95, in turn, will display the Select Device dialog box. In that dialog box, click on the Show all devices option button. Windows 95, in turn, will show the names of all known (known to Windows 95, that is) display adapter manufacturers and models. Figure 5.21 shows a typical list.

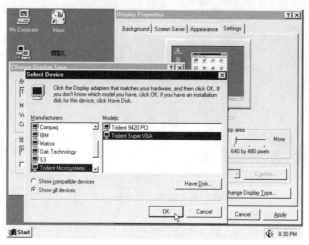

Figure 5.21 *The Select Device dialog box lets you select your system's display adapter.*

To select your display adapter's manufacturer and model number, perform these steps:

1. Look through the Manufacturers list box. Locate and click on the name of your display adapter's manufacturer. Windows 95, in turn, will highlight the manufacturer's name and display a list of models.

2. Click on your display adapter's model.

3. Click on the OK button. Windows 95, in turn, will try to copy certain files from the Windows 95 installation disks. Windows 95 will then prompt you to insert a specific disk from the set of Windows 95 installation disks.

4. Insert the requested disk and click on the OK button. Windows 95, in turn, will copy the necessary files from the disk.

Note: *Before Windows 95 can fully utilize your video card capabilities, you may need to get a Windows 95 device driver (special software that lets Windows 95 use the card) from your video card manufacturer. If your display adapter comes with a Windows 95 driver disk, click on the Have Disk button. Windows 95, in turn, will display a dialog box that prompts you to insert the disk.*

CONTROLLING THE KEYBOARD

For most people, a keyboard works right out of the box and does not need any customizing. However, there are some situations when you may need to change your keyboard's settings. For example, if you use a word-processing program (such as WordPad), there may be times when you'll want to control how fast Windows 95 repeats a character when you hold down a key. For example, if you press the BACKSPACE key and hold it down, the word-processing program will begin deleting the characters one by one as if you pressed the BACKSPACE key repeatedly. However, if the BACKSPACE key repeats too quickly, you may find yourself frequently deleting more characters than you had intended. Also, if you want to work with your computer in a language other than English, you may need to reconfigure your keyboard to that language. When you associate a language with the keyboard, certain key combinations generate foreign characters.

In addition, as you work with Windows 95 applications, you may find that altering the cursor's blink rate makes it easier to locate the cursor on your screen. (The *cursor* is the blinking object that appears at the screen location where Windows 95 will add characters if you type on your keyboard.)

Although Windows 95 is supposed to detect automatically your keyboard's type—whether it is a standard 101-key keyboard or an old 84-key keyboard—during installation, Windows 95 does not always do so correctly. On such occasions, you need to explicitly specify your keyboard's type.

To change all the previously mentioned keyboard settings (key repeat rate, language, cursor blink rate, and keyboard type), you use the Keyboard Properties sheet. To access the Keyboard Properties sheet, double-click on the Control Panel's Keyboard icon. Windows 95, in turn, will open the Keyboard Properties sheet, as shown in Figure 5.22.

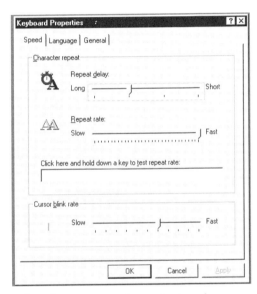

Figure 5.22 *The Keyboard Properties sheet lets you control your keyboard.*

As you can see in Figure 5.22, the Keyboard Properties sheet contains three pages:

- The Speed page, which lets you adjust the rate at which Windows 95 repeats a key when you hold it down. You can also adjust how fast the text-insertion cursor (the cursor that appears when you type text) blinks.
- The Language page, which lets you specify the language of the keyboard and its layout.
- The General page, which lets you set the keyboard type.

As previously mentioned, you won't normally need to change your keyboard's properties. Typically, Windows 95 resolves the important keyboard properties—such as language (English, Swedish, Afrikaans, and so on) and keyboard type (101-key standard keyboard or 84-key PC-AT keyboard)—during installation.

Additionally, for the other keyboard properties (such as key repeat rate and cursor blink rate), Windows 95 provides default values that most people find acceptable. As such, the only keyboard characteristics you might need to adjust are the key repeat-rate and the cursor blink-rate.

The keyboard's key repeat-rate, which you use the Speed page to adjust, has two parameters:

- The *repeat delay*, which specifies how long Windows 95 will wait before it begins to repeat a key.
- The *repeat rate*, which specifies how fast Windows 95 will repeat a key that you hold down.

In the Keyboard Properties sheet Speed page, you can use the Repeat delay and Repeat rate sliders to set the key repeat parameters. To test your new settings, click in the text field immediately below the Repeat delay slider and then hold down a keyboard key. When you are satisfied with your new settings, click your mouse on the Apply button.

If you want to change the cursor blink rate, drag the Speed page Cursor blink rate slider. After you move the slider and release the mouse button, Windows 95 will provide immediate feedback by changing the blink rate of a test cursor that appears to the left of the slider.

> ### Making the Keyboard Match Your Typing Skills
>
>
>
> Before the advent of personal computers and word processors, novice and expert typists alike generally had to work on typewriters with fixed-key repeat-delay parameters. (As you have learned, the repeat-delay parameter specifies how long a typewriter or keyboard will wait before it begins to repeat a key.) As a result, some skilled typists had to work with machines that hindered their performance because the machines' repeat-delay parameter was too slow. Likewise, fast repeat-delay parameters frustrated many novice, "hunt-and-peck," typists because they couldn't lift their fingers off keys quickly enough to type only a single character. (Instead of an "e", the novice typist would sometimes get "eee" when he or she pressed the *e* key.) To make sure your keyboard and your typing skills match, Windows 95 lets you set your keyboard's repeat-delay and repeat-rate (how fast Windows 95 will repeat a key that you hold down) parameters. To change the repeat-delay and repeat-rate parameters, open the Keyboard Properties sheet Speed page. Then, use the Repeat delay and Repeat rate sliders to set the parameters. To test your new settings, click in the text field immediately below the Repeat delay slider and then hold down a keyboard key. When you are satisfied with your new settings, click your mouse on the Apply button.

Customizing the Mouse

Because Windows 95 is a graphical operating system, you use the mouse, rather than the keyboard, to perform most operations. For example, to open many of the Windows 95 properties sheets, you double-click your mouse on icons in the Control Panel. Depending on your reflexes, you may or may not like how fast you have to click to produce a double-click. Fortunately, you can adjust the double-click speed and quite a few other mouse properties from the Mouse Properties sheet. To access the Mouse Properties sheet, double-click on the Control Panel's Mouse icon. Windows 95, in turn, will display the Mouse Properties sheet, as shown in Figure 5.23.

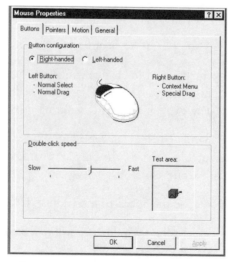

Figure 5.23 The Mouse Properties sheet lets you customize your mouse.

5: Customizing Common Hardware

The Mouse Properties sheet contains four pages:

- The Buttons page lets you configure the mouse buttons and set the double-click speed.
- The Pointers page lets you view and change the pointer shapes.
- The Motion page lets you control the speed of the pointer's movement. You can also enable a feature that causes Windows 95 to show a pointer trail.
- The General page lets you specify the type of mouse. Typically, you do not have to change the mouse type unless you decide to change the mouse.

Managing the Buttons

As you have learned, you use the left-mouse button to perform most mouse actions. However, if you happen to be a left-handed user, you might find it cumbersome to click on the left button. After all, when you hold the mouse in your left hand, your index finger naturally rests on the right-mouse button.

Fortunately, Windows 95 lets you swap the roles of the left-and-right-mouse buttons so that left-handed users can use the mouse easily. The top half of the Mouse Properties sheet Buttons page provides two option buttons—Right-handed and Left-handed. Select the option that suits you.

> ### Creating a Left-Handed Mouse
>
>
>
> If you're left-handed and have ever sat in a classroom that contains desks built for right-handed people, you know how uncomfortable it is to have continually to lift your arm to write notes. Likewise, when you use your system's mouse (which, by default, is set for right-handed users), you know how unnatural the mouse-button positions feel. Fortunately, Windows 95 lets you switch the roles of your mouse buttons. To do so, perform these steps:
>
> 1. Double-click your mouse on the Control Panel's Mouse icon. Windows 95 will open the Mouse Properties sheet.
> 2. Click your mouse on the Mouse Properties sheet Buttons tab. Windows 95 will open the Mouse Properties sheet Buttons page.
> 3. Select the Left-handed option button. Windows 95 will reverse the roles of your mouse buttons.
>
> After you reverse the roles of your mouse buttons, remember to adjust your actions when you read any literature about your system or its programs. For example, when *Success with Windows 95* tells you to double-click your mouse, remember to double-click your right-mouse button. Likewise, when this book tells you to right-click, click your left-mouse button instead.

The Mouse Properties sheet Buttons page lets you control another important setting—the double-click speed. The double-click speed determines how fast you have to click the mouse button twice for Windows 95 to interpret the two successive clicks as a double-click. If your system's double-click speed setting is too fast, you may have trouble clicking quickly enough to make Windows 95 think you have double-clicked. Move the Buttons page Double-click speed slider to adjust your system's double-click speed.

For your convenience, the Buttons page includes a test area with a picture of a jack-in-the-box. Double-click your mouse in the test area. If you click fast enough, Windows 95 will open the jack-in-the-box, as shown in Figure 5.24.

Selecting Pointer Shapes

As you work with Windows 95, you may notice that the mouse pointer changes shape during certain activities. For example, the pointer turns into an hourglass when Windows 95 is busy. Although you may not have a need to change pointer shapes frequently, Windows 95 lets you customize the pointer shape. You can use the Pointers page to assign different pointer shapes to different tasks.

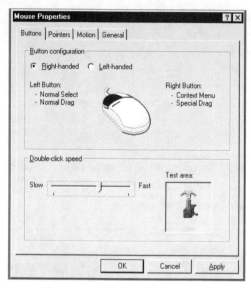

Figure 5.24 *The result of a double-click in the Test Area.*

To view the Pointers page, click on the Mouse Properties sheet Pointers tab. Windows 95, in turn, will display the Pointers page, as shown in Figure 5.25.

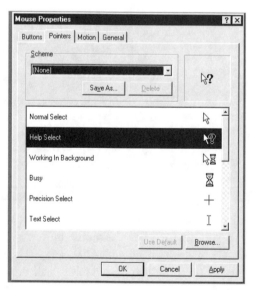

Figure 5.25 *The Mouse Properties sheet Pointers page.*

On the Pointers page, shown in Figure 5.25, Windows 95 displays a Scheme pull-down list button and a list box with fourteen pointer names and shapes. When you first open the Pointers page, the word (None) appears in the Scheme field, and Windows 95 displays its default pointer shapes in the list box.

5: Customizing Common Hardware

To change a pointer shape, perform these steps:

1. Locate the pointer you want to change (scroll down the list, if necessary).

2. Double-click on the pointer's entry in the list. Windows 95, in turn, will show the selected pointer in the upper-right corner of the page. Windows 95 will also display a Browse dialog box with the contents of the Windows folder.

3. Double-click on the System folder. Windows 95, in turn, will show the .CUR or .ANI files and other folders in the System folder.

4. Double-click on an .ANI file (you will see a pointer shape in the Browse dialog box). Windows 95, in turn, will use the selected pointer shape and show it in the Mouse Properties sheet Pointers page.

If you change one or more pointer shapes and like the new combination of pointer shapes that the list box displays, you can save your pointer scheme under a name. To do so, click your mouse on the Save As button and type in your scheme name. Then, the next time you want to use the pointer shapes scheme, just click on the Scheme pull-down list button and select your scheme. After you change a pointer shape from its default, Windows 95 will activate the Use Default button. Any time you want to change a pointer back to its default shape, click on the Use Default button.

Controlling Pointer Motion

As you know, Windows 95 moves the mouse pointer on the screen as you move your mouse (or some other physical pointing device, such as a trackball). In this section, you will learn how to adjust the speed at which the pointer moves on your screen relative to the speed at which you move your mouse. To adjust the pointer speed, you will use the Mouse Properties sheet Motion page. Click on the Mouse Properties sheet Motion tab. Windows 95, in turn, will display the Motion page, as shown in Figure 5.26.

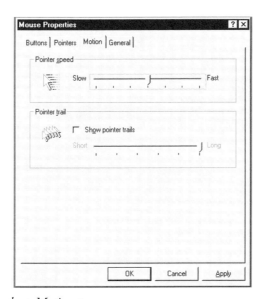

Figure 5.26 The Mouse Properties sheet Motion page.

To increase your system's pointer speed, drag the Pointer speed slider to the right. To decrease the pointer speed, drag the slider to the left. Then, click on the Apply button. You can immediately try out how the new mouse speed feels. In addition to setting your mouse pointer's speed, you can use the Motion page to activate the Windows 95 pointer trail feature. A *pointer trail* consists of additional mouse pointers that appear to chase your primary pointer across the screen as you move your mouse. To turn the pointer trail feature on, click on the Show pointer trails check box. (If the check box and label appear gray, your hardware does not support the pointer trail feature.) Windows 95, in turn, will leave a few old images of the mouse pointer on the screen as you move the mouse. Because the pointer trail makes the mouse pointer easy to locate, the pointer trail feature is especially helpful to laptop users with a passive-matrix LCD display.

Setting up Your Modem

A *modem* is a hardware device that lets two computers communicate over standard phone lines. When you use a modem, one computer calls a second computer, much as you would make a long-distance phone call. Using modems, you can exchange files, chat with other users, send electronic mail, access online services (such as Microsoft Network, CompuServe, and America Online), and connect to the Internet through an Internet access provider.

Note: Windows 95 will configure your modem during installation, regardless of whether or not you used the modem under another operating system (for example, DOS or Windows 3.1). Likewise, Windows 95 doesn't care if you purchased the modem pre-installed or added it later on. To detect and configure your modem, Windows 95 requires only that the modem is physically connected to your system during Windows 95 installation.

Understanding Modem Speeds

As you may know, when computers speak to one another, they do so in terms of 0s and 1s—bits (binary digits). As such, when your system uses a modem to communicate with another system, the modem's transmission speed is measured in bits per second (bps). A 2400 bps modem can send or receive 2400 bits of information per second. Likewise, a 9600 bps modem can send or receive 9600 bits per second. As you can see, the 9600 bps modem is four times faster than its 2400 bps counterpart, which can save you a lot on phone bills. If you plan to connect to online services, such as Microsoft Network or the Internet, you will find a high-speed modem (9,600 bps or greater) essential. Most online information is in graphical form, which is much more voluminous than textual data. For example, 25 lines of text with 80 characters per line can be stored in 16,000 bits. On the other hand, a typical online image, such as a home page, may require anywhere from 240,000 bits to 1,200,000 bits, even when a system stores and transmits such data in a compressed format, known as the Graphics Interchange Format (GIF). As a result, if you want to use online services effectively, you need at least a 9600 bps. (Nowadays, modems can operate at 14400 bps or even 28800 bps.) As such, if your current modem operates at less than 9600 bps, you may want to add a new one soon.

If your system came preinstalled with Windows 95 and a modem, you should not have to do anything to set up the modem. Likewise, if you install a modem and then upgrade to Windows 95, Windows 95 should detect and configure the modem during installation. However, if you neglect to turn the modem's power on (applies only if you have an external modem) when you install Windows 95, or purchase the modem after you install Windows 95, you will need to add the modem to your system and configure it for use. To do so, you have to use the controls in the Modems Properties sheet. To access the Modems Properties sheet, double-click on the Control Panel's Modems icon. Windows 95, in turn, will open the Modems Properties sheet, as shown in Figure 5.27. The first page in the Modems Properties sheet is the General page. The top part of the page lists the modems currently installed on your system. Typically, Windows 95 will list your current modem here. Underneath the list, there are three buttons:

- The Add button lets you add a new modem.
- The Remove button lets you remove the modem currently selected in the list.
- The Properties button lets you view or change the properties of the modem currently selected in the list.

5: CUSTOMIZING COMMON HARDWARE

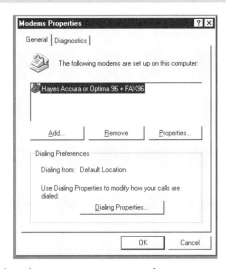

Figure 5.27 *The Modems Properties sheet lets you set up your modem.*

You can use the General page Dialing Properties button to specify how your modem makes a phone call. Specifically, when you click on the Dialing Properties button, Windows 95 displays the Dialing Properties sheet. From this sheet, you can specify how your modem will dial out from your location. For example, if you use your system in an office, your modem may need to specify an access code, such as a 9, to get an outside telephone line. Using the Dialing Properties sheet, you provide Windows 95 with such essential dialing information.

ADDING A NEW MODEM

As you have learned, before you can access online services (such as Microsoft Network, Compuserve, and America Online) or connect to the Internet through an Internet access provider, your system must have a modem. As such, if your Windows 95 system doesn't have a modem, you may want to install one. Or, if your system has a modem, you want to upgrade to a faster model may sometime in the future. Either way, you will need to follow Windows 95's modem installation procedure to add a new modem to your system. Fortunately, Windows 95 makes modem installation relatively painless.

If you plan to install a modem with no outside assistance, you may want to purchase an external, rather than an internal, modem. To install an external modem, you do not have to open up your computer. Also, you can move the external modem to a new computer more easily than you can an internal modem.

Note: *Internal modem installation is beyond the scope of this book. For more information about installing external and internal modems, refer to the book* ***Rescued by Upgrading Your PC, Second Edition****, Jamsa Press, 1996.*

UNDERSTANDING YOUR SYSTEM'S SERIAL AND PARALLEL PORTS

In *Success with Windows 95*, you will encounter many references to your system's serial and parallel ports. To help you understand such references, the following list provides some important facts about serial and parallel ports:

- Serial ports transmit and receive data one bit (binary digit) at a time. Parallel ports transmit and receive data eight bits (binary digits) at a time, over eight wires. As such, devices that are connected to parallel ports transmit data much faster than their serial counterparts.

- Most systems use serial ports to connect to modems and mice. Parallel ports, on the other hand, are usually reserved for printers.

- PCs support up to four serial ports (named COM1, COM2, COM3, and COM4) and three parallel ports (named LPT1, LPT2, and LPT3).
- Serial ports can be either 9- or 25-pin ports. In either case, the serial port uses a male connector. Parallel ports always use a 25-pin female connector.

Normally, to install a new external modem, you simply connect it to a serial port (COM1 or COM2) on your system, connect the modem's power, and turn it on. (Some newer modems let you connect them to either a serial or parallel port.) Then, open the Modems Properties sheet General page (see Figure 5.27), and click on the Add button. Windows 95, in turn, will open the Install New Modem wizard, as shown in Figure 5.28.

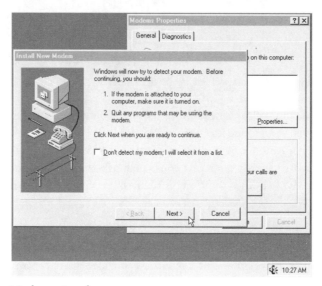

Figure 5.28 *The Install New Modem wizard.*

To make complex operations easy, Windows 95 provides step-by-step dialog boxes, called *wizards*, that walk you through the operation. The Install New Modem wizard walks you through the process of installing the modem.

WIZARDS IN WINDOWS 95

As Microsoft engineers developed Windows 95, one of their goals was to automate as many tasks as possible. They didn't want to force users to follow long lists of steps, search through product manuals for device information, and open and close dozens of windows just to install hardware and software. They wanted to make such installation tasks easy for you, the user. To accomplish their goal, Microsoft engineers built a number of wizards into Windows 95.

A *wizard* is a set of functions within a program or operating system that helps you perform a specific task. After you start a wizard, it gives you step-by-step instructions, requesting all the information the task requires (in the order the task requires), and presenting you with all your options. For example, Windows 95 includes wizards that lead you through hardware and software installations.

To proceed with the modem installation process, click on the Next button. Windows 95 will display a message that tells you it is searching for your modem. When Windows 95 detects a modem, Windows 95 will display the results in the Verify Modem dialog box, as shown in Figure 5.29.

5: Customizing Common Hardware

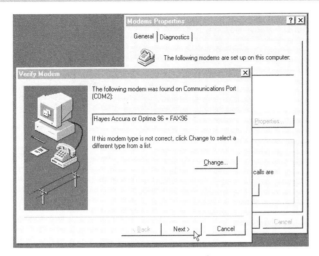

Figure 5.29 A dialog box that shows you the modem Windows 95 detects.

If the modem name in the Verify Modem dialog box is correct, click on the Next button to continue the installation process. Windows 95, in turn, will install the modem and display a message in the Install New Modem dialog box, as shown in Figure 5.30.

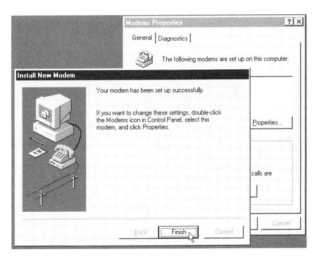

Figure 5.30 The Install New Modem dialog box after Windows 95 successfully installs your modem.

Read the message and click on the Finish button to complete the installation process.

Specifying a Generic Modem

As you have learned, Windows 95 makes modem installation easy. To add a new modem to your system, all you have to do is connect the modem to one of your system's serial ports (COM1 or COM2), connect the modem's power, turn on the modem, and ask Windows 95 to detect it. Most of the time, Windows 95 will detect your new modem and complete the installation without a glitch.

However, in rare cases, Windows 95 may not detect your modem correctly. On such occasions, you can try to select your modem's manufacturer and model from a pair of lists. To access the Manufacturers and Models lists, click on the Add button in the Modem Properties sheet General page (see Figure 5.27). Windows 95, in turn, will display the Install New Modem dialog box (see Figure 5.28). Then, click on the check box, labeled "Don't detect my modem. I will select it from a list" until a check mark appears. Finally, click on the Next button. Windows 95, in response, will display two list boxes: one with modem manufacturers and the other with models for each manufacturer. If the Manufacturers and Models list boxes do not include your modem's manufacturer or model, select "(Standard modem types)" in the Manufacturers list box. Windows 95, in turn, will display modem speeds in the Models list box. Then, pick your modem's speed in the Models list box. For example, if you have a 14.4Kbps modem, choose "14400 bps Modem" as the model.

Note: *If Windows 95 fails to identify your modem, contact your modem manufacturer and ask them if they have software (a device driver) that lets you use their modem with Windows 95.*

INSPECTING PROPERTIES OF A MODEM

As you work with your Windows 95 system, you may encounter modem problems that, with some detailed information, you can easily solve. For example, assume you've just connected a new modem but can't get it to work. If you inspect the modem's properties, you may discover that, although you physically connected the modem to COM1, Windows 95 thinks it's connected to COM2. In such a situation, you may only need to change the modem's serial port setting (from COM2 to COM1) to fix the problem. To inspect and change a modem's properties, select the modem from the list box that appears at the top of the Modems Properties sheet General page (see Figure 5.27). Then, click on the Properties button. Windows 95, in turn, will open a properties sheet with the modem's name in the title bar, as shown in Figure 5.31.

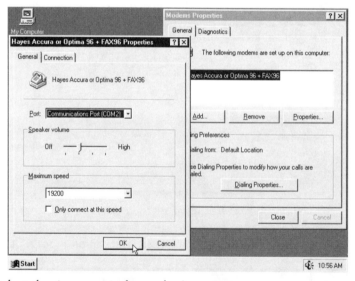

Figure 5.31 A Properties sheet showing a particular modem's properties.

As you can see in Figure 5.31, the new properties sheet (which this book will call the Specific Modem Properties sheet) General page shows the following information:

- The serial port (COM1 or COM2) to which the modem is connected.
- The speaker volume that controls the noises your modem makes when connecting to another computer. If you don't want to hear these noises, simply move the slider to Off.
- The maximum speed at which your modem can communicate.

To see even more modem properties, click on the Specific Modem Properties sheet Connection tab. Windows 95, in turn, will open the Connection page, as shown in Figure 5.32.

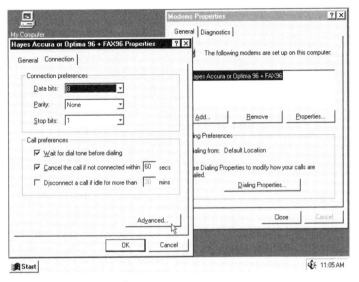

Figure 5.32 The connection properties for a modem.

The Connection page Connection preferences section contains three serial communication settings (Data bits, Parity, and Stop bits) that your modem uses. When two computers communicate, both computers must use the same values for these serial communication settings. Because most systems use 8 data bits, no parity, and one stop bit (8N1), you normally don't have to change these settings. However, if you experience errors when you connect to a remote system, you need to verify your settings match those of the remote computer.

In addition, you may find the three check boxes in the Connection page Call preferences section interesting. For example, notice the "Wait for dial tone before dialing" check box. If your phone has voice mail, for example, the phone line might not have a dial tone when you have messages waiting. If you want your modem to dial out without waiting for a dial tone, turn off the "Wait for dial tone before dialing" check box.

Using the Call preferences section's second check box, you can specify how long the modem will try to call a number. Additionally, you can decide to disconnect a call if the modem is idle (is not sending or receiving any data) for more than a specified number of minutes. You may find this feature especially useful if you connect to online services (such as CompuServe or America Online), pay for your connection by the hour, and want to make sure that you do not inadvertently leave your modem connected overnight.

The Connection page Advanced button gives you access to some modem properties that you really do not have to change. You can look at these properties if you wish, but this book does not cover them in detail. For more information on these advanced modem properties, see Robert L. Hummel's *Data and Fax Communications*, Ziff-Davis Press, 1993.

SETTING THE DIALING PROPERTIES

When a Windows 95 system comes pre-installed with a modem, many of the modem's properties (for example, the modem's manufacturer, model number, and serial port) are preset for you. However, regardless of how you acquired your modem, you must always set your modem's dialing properties, which determine how your modem makes a call. To view or change the dialing properties, click on the Dialing Properties button on the Modems Properties sheet General page (see Figure 5.27). Windows 95, in turn, will open the Dialing Properties sheet, as shown in Figure 5.33.

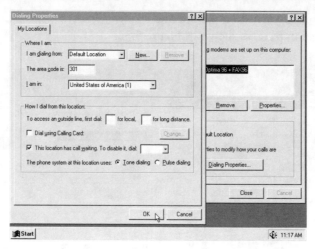

Figure 5.33 Use the Dialing Properties sheet to set up how your modem dials a phone call.

The Dialing Properties sheet has only one page: My Locations. Using the My Locations page, you can specify where you are calling from (such as your home or office), and Windows 95 will automatically adjust settings for you. For example, to place a modem call from your office, you may need your modem to first dial 9 to access an outside line, and 99 to access a long-distance line. If you have a long-distance calling card, you can use the My Locations page to specify your card type and number. When you place modem calls, Windows 95 will dial the appropriate numbers to automatically bill your card.

Note: *For more information about how to use the Dialing Properties sheet, refer to the book* **1001 Windows 95 Tips,** *Jamsa Press, 1995.*

Modem Diagnostics

If your modem isn't working correctly and you need more information to determine the problem, open the Modems Properties sheet Diagnostics page. Click on the Modems Properties sheet Diagnostics tab. Windows 95, in turn, will display the Diagnostics page, as shown in Figure 5.34.

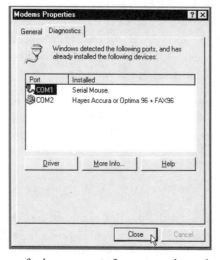

Figure 5.34 The Diagnostics page lets you find out more information about the modem.

At the center of the Diagnostics page, Windows 95 lists your system's communication ports and the devices installed on each port. To obtain information on a particular port, click on the port name and then click on the More Info button. Windows 95, in turn, will display a More Info dialog box with more diagnostic information. Figure 5.35 shows the diagnostic information for a typical 14.4Kbps modem connected to the COM1 port.

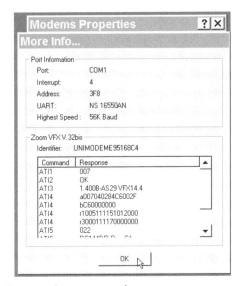

Figure 5.35 Diagnostic information for a modem connected to a port.

Working with Your Printer

Usually, you do not have to do anything special to make your printer work with Windows 95. In particular, if you upgraded from Windows 3.1, all you have to do is provide the printer's make and model and Windows 95 will set up the printer. However, you may run into situations where you have to add and configure a new printer. For example, you may want to replace an old dot-matrix printer with a new laser printer. To add a printer or control a currently installed printer, use the Printers folder. To open the Printers folder, double-click on the Control Panel's Printers icon. Windows 95, in turn, will display the Printers folder, as shown in Figure 5.36.

Figure 5.36 The Printers folder shows currently installed printers and lets you add a new printer.

Note: To access the Printers folder, you can select the Start menu Settings submenu Printers option.

Installing a Printer

Unlike the other icons in the Control Panel, the Printers icon is a folder. Therefore, when you double-click to open it, Windows 95 shows the folder's contents. (Most other Control Panel icons open a properties sheet.) The Printers folder contains icons for each printer currently installed on your system. Additionally, the folder contains an Add Printer icon that you can use to install and set up a new printer.

To install a printer, double-click on the Add Printer icon in the Printers folder. Windows 95, in turn, will open the Add Printer Wizard window, as shown in Figure 5.37.

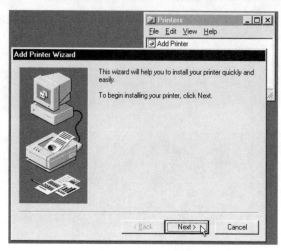

Figure 5.37 The Add Printer wizard guides you through the installation of a printer.

As discussed, Windows 95 provides a number of "wizards" that guide you through the steps for a specific task. The initial Add Printer Wizard window simply informs you that this wizard helps you install your printer. Click on the Next button to proceed. The Add Printer wizard, in turn, will ask you whether the printer is connected to a local parallel port or to another computer on the network. The default selection is the local printer. Assume that you want to set up a local printer and click on the Next button to continue. The Add Printer wizard, in turn, will display a list of known printer manufacturers and printer types, as shown in Figure 5.38.

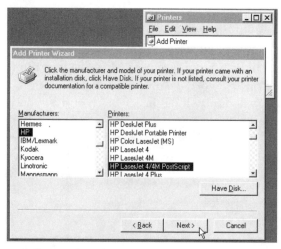

Figure 5.38 The Add Printer wizard shows a list of known printers.

Select your printer's manufacturer and a printer name. Then, click on the Next button to continue the installation. The Add Printer wizard, in turn, will ask you to click on the port to which the printer is connected. Figure 5.39 shows how the wizard prompts you to specify a port. As you can see in Figure 5.39, the Add Printer wizard lets you choose COM ports (serial ports) and LPT ports (parallel ports). In addition, the wizard lets you connect a printer to a file on the disk. When you connect a printer to a file, Windows 95 stores the output that would have gone to the printer in a file. This print-to-file feature is handy if you're working on a system that doesn't have a printer or if you want to create a file you can later print outside an application. For example, if you connect a PostScript printer to a file, you can create a PostScript file, which you can print later by sending it to a PostScript printer. Sometimes this approach is used to send the "ready-to-print" copy of a book or brochure to a printing company. The printing company can simply send the PostScript file to a typesetter and generate the final printed version.

5: CUSTOMIZING COMMON HARDWARE

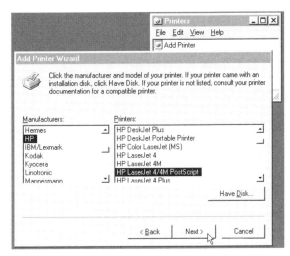

Figure 5.39 The Add Printer wizard prompts you for the port to which the printer is connected.

If your printer is connected to the parallel port, click on the LPT1 port and then click on the Next button. The Add Printer wizard, in turn, will show you the printer's name and let you choose if you want Windows programs to use the printer by default.

Click on the Next button to continue the installation. The Add Printer wizard, in turn, will ask you if you want to print a test page after installation. If you accept the default choice, click Next to proceed. The Add Printer wizard, in turn, will initiate the actual installation process, which requires copying some special files from the Windows 95 installation disk. As such, the Add Printer wizard will use a message box to ask you for the disk, as shown in Figure 5.40.

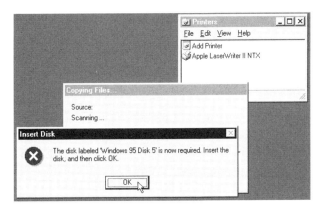

Figure 5.40 The Add Printer wizard prompts you for a Windows 95 installation disk.

Insert the disk and click on the OK button in the message box. If you have the Windows 95 CD instead, insert it into your CD-ROM drive and click on the OK button. The wizard, in turn, will display another dialog box that asks you for the location of the files. In that dialog box, enter the driver letter of your CD-ROM drive. Then, click on the OK button.

The Add Printer wizard, in turn, will copy the necessary files and complete the installation process. After the wizard exits, Windows 95 adds an icon for the newly installed printer in the Printers folder, as shown in Figure 5.41.

117

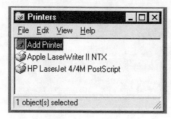

Figure 5.41 *Windows 95 shows an icon for the newly installed printer in the Printers folder.*

Controlling a Printer

Usually, you do not have to do anything special to manage the printer. In most programs, all you do is select the File menu Print option and Windows 95 takes care of the rest. However, sometimes you may want to cancel printing because you inadvertently started printing a lengthy document. Or, you may want to pause the printing so that you can clear a paper jam. For such "printer control" tasks, open the Printers folder and double-click on your current printer's icon. Windows 95, in turn, will display a window with the printer's name in the title bar, as shown in Figure 5.42.

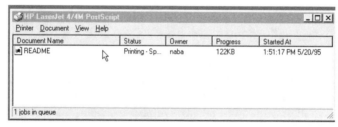

Figure 5.42 *A printer window that shows the status of documents scheduled to print.*

Printer windows, like the one you see in Figure 5.42, show the status of any currently printing document and any documents that are scheduled to print later. In addition, such windows include pull-down menus with options you can select to control printer operations. For example, to pause the printing of a document, click on the Printer menu Pause Printing option. To stop a specific document from printing, select the document in the list that appears in the center of the printer window. Then, select the Document menu Cancel Printing option.

As you print documents in Windows 95, there may be times when you need to stop or pause a printing job quickly. On such occasions, you may not have time to go through the Control Panel and the Printers folder to reach the correct printer window. Fortunately, Windows 95 provides you with a quick way to access the printer window that contains information on the currently printing document. When you print a document, Windows 95 adds a printer icon next to the Taskbar's clock, as shown in Figure 5.43.

Figure 5.43 *The printer icon appears when you print a document.*

If you double-click on the Taskbar's printer icon, Windows 95 will open the printer window (see Figure 5.42). You can then cancel or pause the printing from that information window.

5: Customizing Common Hardware

>
>
> ### Pausing or Stopping a Print Job
>
> As you print documents in Windows 95, there may be times when you'll need a quick way to pause or stop a printing job. For example, you may need to pause a printer operation to clear a paper jam. Or, you may want to stop Windows 95 from printing a lengthy word-processing document after you discover an error that occurs throughout the text. In such situations, you can use the Taskbar's printer icon to pause or cancel a printer operation. To do so, perform these steps:
>
> 1. Double-click on the Taskbar's printer icon. Windows 95 will display the printer window that contains information on the currently printing document.
>
> 2. In the printer window, click your mouse on the document's name.
>
> 3. To pause the printer, select the printer window's Printer menu Pause Printing option. To stop the printing, select the printer window's Document menu Cancel Printing option.

Assigning System Sounds

As you may have observed, Windows 95 makes sounds when certain system events occur. For example, Windows 95 makes a sound when your system starts and a different sound when your system shuts down. If you don't like the default sounds that Windows 95 associates with system events, you can change them. For example, you can have Windows 95 sound trumpets, play the sound of a car engine starting, or even make your computer bark.

To view (and change) how Windows 95 associates sounds to system events, double-click on the Control Panel's Sounds icon. Windows 95, in turn, will open the Sounds Properties sheet, as shown in Figure 5.44.

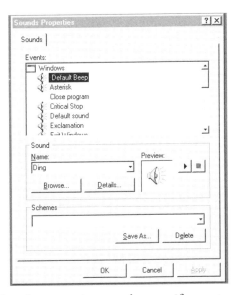

Figure 5.44 The Sounds Properties sheet lets you assign sounds to specific events.

The Sound Properties sheet Events list box shows system events with which Windows 95 associates sounds. Table 5.2 briefly describes eight of these system events.

Event Name	Description
Default Beep	Occurs when Windows 95 would normally sound a beep to get the user's attention.
Asterisk	Occurs when Windows 95 displays an informational dialog box.
Close program	Occurs when you end a program.
Critical Stop	Occurs when Windows 95 displays a dialog box before ending an application due to a critical error.
Default Sound	Plays for events for which you have not specified a sound.
Exclamation	Occurs when Windows 95 displays a dialog box containing a warning message.
Exit Windows	Occurs when you end Windows 95.
Start Windows	Occurs when you start Windows 95.

Table 5.2 Eight system events with which Windows 95 associates sounds.

To see the name of the sound that Windows 95 associates with a particular system event, click on the event in the Events list box. Windows 95, in turn, will display the associated sound's name in the Name field. To hear the sound, click on the button with a right-pointing triangle. Windows 95, in turn, will play the sound.

If you want to associate a different sound with the event you selected, click on the Browse button. Windows 95, in turn, will display a Browse dialog box. To specify a different sound, you have to select a file with the WAV (for sound wave) extension. If you have a sound card and a microphone, you can actually record your own sounds, save them in WAV files, and assign them to various events through the Sounds Properties sheet.

KEYS TO SUCCESS

When you started this chapter, you knew how to drive your shiny new car—Windows 95—but you did not know how to change the oil, rotate the tires, or set the dashboard clock. This chapter has shown you how you can use the tools in the Control Panel to work with the inside machinery of Windows 95—the display, keyboard and mouse, modem, and printer.

In Chapter 6, you will learn how to customize your system in more advanced ways. For example, Chapter 6 will teach you how to add new hardware to your system. However, before you move on to Chapter 6, make sure you understand the following key concepts:

- ✓ The Control Panel contains tools that let you tinker with Windows 95.
- ✓ Many tools in the Control Panel let you access the properties sheets for Windows 95 objects.
- ✓ You can use the Date/Time Properties sheet to set your system's date, time, and time zone.
- ✓ You can use the Display Properties sheet to specify the number of colors your monitor displays and control the Desktop's appearance.
- ✓ You can change how your mouse and keyboard behave.
- ✓ Windows 95 lets you easily add a new printer or modem to your system.
- ✓ You can change the sounds Windows 95 makes when system events occur.

Chapter 6
Customizing Advanced System Settings

Imagine that you're purchasing a new car, but, for one reason or another, you aren't able to get all the extra features (CD player, sunroof, and so on) you desire. Perhaps you don't have enough money. Or, maybe the particular options aren't available for your car model yet. Whatever the reason, you'll have to add those extra features later.

Likewise, when you first start to use Windows 95, your computer may not have all the hardware and software you want or need. Perhaps, when you purchased your system, you didn't have enough money to install a sound card or CD-ROM drive. Or, maybe the software you wanted your computer vendor to pre-install on your system wasn't available yet. (Undoubtedly, the release of Windows 95 will prompt software manufacturers to develop many Windows 95-specific programs that you may want to add to your system.) Regardless of the reason, you'll likely install some new features (sound card, CD-ROM drive, software, and so on) after you purchase your Windows 95 system or upgrade to Windows 95.

In Chapter 5, you learned how to set up common hardware, such as a new printer or a modem. In this chapter, you'll learn how to add other new hardware, as well as new fonts and Windows 95 programs, to your system. Additionally, this chapter will show you how to perform some infrequent but necessary tasks, such as setting up Windows 95 for use in a specific country.

By the time you finish this chapter, you will understand the following key concepts:

- How to add new hardware to your Windows 95 system
- How to add or remove a program
- How to view your system's fonts and add new ones
- How to customize Windows 95's international settings

ADDING NEW HARDWARE

If you bought your computer recently, you probably had the manufacturer configure it with all the popular options—sound card, CD-ROM drive, and a fax/modem. In addition, most new systems include at least 4 Mb (megabytes) of RAM and a large hard disk (from 300 Mb to 1 Gb). You probably chose the sound card and CD-ROM drive so that you can enjoy multimedia programs—applications with many sounds and images. You may have opted for the fax/modem because you want to access online services, such as America Online or CompuServe. You selected the large hard disk and additional RAM because many of the programs you want to run require a lot of memory and disk space. With such a well-equipped system, you may not need to add more hardware in the near future.

However, if you just upgraded to Windows 95, the story may be different, especially if your system is several years old. Typically, older systems have smaller hard disks and less memory than those manufactured today. Furthermore, older systems often lack sound cards and CD-ROM drives. Although many older systems have modems, most of these modems transmit between 2400 to 9600 bps (that's bits per second, a measure of how fast a modem can send or receive data). Today, modems can operate at 14400 bps to 28800 bps or faster. As such, if you have an older system, you will probably need to add some hardware soon.

To install new hardware in your Windows 95 system, you must perform two basic steps:

1. You must follow the hardware manufacturer's instructions and physically install the hardware.
2. You must use the Control Panel to add the new hardware to your Windows 95 system. You must perform this step before you can access and use the new hardware in Windows 95.

This section focuses on the second step—how you add new hardware to Windows 95. (For more information on physically installing hardware, refer to the book *Rescued by Upgrading Your PC, Second Edition*, Jamsa Press, 1996.) When you want to add new hardware to your Windows 95 system, double-click on the Control Panel's Add New Hardware icon. Windows 95, in turn, will run the Add New Hardware wizard, which guides you through the installation steps.

USING THE ADD NEW HARDWARE WIZARD

As you learned in Chapter 5, a wizard is a set of operations within a program or operating system that helps you perform a specific task. For example, after you physically install a new hardware device, the Windows 95 Add New Hardware wizard detects the hardware and guides you through any further installation steps. To see the Add New Hardware wizard in action (you can try the wizard even if you do not have any device to install), double-click on the Control Panel's Add New Hardware icon. Windows 95 will start the Add New Hardware wizard, as shown in Figure 6.1.

Figure 6.1 The Add New Hardware Wizard dialog box that helps you install new hardware.

To begin the installation, click your mouse on the Next button. The Add New Hardware wizard, in turn, will display further options for installing new hardware, as shown in Figure 6.2.

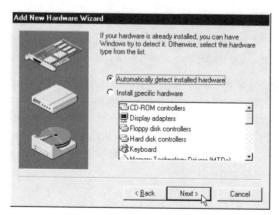

Figure 6.2 The Add New Hardware Wizard dialog box with options for installing new hardware.

Typical Hardware Additions

If you want to enjoy new multimedia software or surf the Internet, you may want to add or upgrade your PC's hardware. Here are some typical hardware additions:

- *Additional memory.* Although Windows 95 will run with as little as 4 Mb of RAM, you will experience significantly improved performance if your system uses 8 Mb or even 16 Mb of RAM. The quickest way to make Windows 95 run faster is to add memory.

- *A second hard-disk drive.* As programs like Windows 95 become larger and more complex, they consume more disk space. Luckily, the prices for hard-disk drives continue to drop. To estimate the size of the disk you need, multiply your current disk space requirements by three.

- *Sound card.* Most newer programs use sounds (voice and music) to improve their user interfaces. To fully use and enjoy such programs, you should install a sound card.

- *CD-ROM drive.* As programs increase in size and complexity, it is common for manufacturers to ship the programs on CD-ROM. In addition, all multimedia programs that use video ship on CD-ROM only. Lastly, using your sound card and CD-ROM drive, you can make your computer play audio CDs.

- *Network adapter.* If you work in an office environment, your PC is likely connected to other PCs in the office. Windows 95 makes network operations very easy. As a result, most small businesses can install and maintain their own local area network.

If you have followed the hardware manufacturer's instructions and physically installed the hardware, you can have Windows 95 try to detect the hardware.

Why Windows 95 Needs to Detect Hardware

All your PC's peripheral devices (hard disk, sound card, CD-ROM drive, modem, printer, keyboard, serial ports, and so on) need to access some system resources. For a device to function properly, Windows 95 must know exactly which system resources the device uses. As such, Windows 95 detects a hardware device to learn three key pieces of system resource information:

- The Interrupt Request (*IRQ*) number the device uses to get the attention of your system's microprocessor (the CPU), which oversees all your PC's operations. Think of the IRQ as the direct line between a device and the microprocessor.

- The Input/Output Port addresses (*I/O addresses*) your system's microprocessor uses to send data to and receive data from the peripheral device. Usually, to work properly, a device needs a whole range of unique I/O addresses, though you only specify the base or starting address.

- The Direct Memory Access (*DMA*) channel the device uses to access your system's memory directly rather than go through the microprocessor.

As you will learn, when Windows 95 fails to detect a device you want to add to your PC, you will need to manually specify this information to Windows 95. To determine your card's settings, you must examine the jumpers and switches that reside on the card itself.

To let Windows 95 detect the hardware, simply click on the Next button to continue the installation. The Add New Hardware wizard, in turn, will display a message informing you that the detection process takes several minutes. Additionally, this message warns you that your system could "lock" during the detection. (When your system locks, you may need to shut down and restart Windows 95 before you can use any programs or perform any system operations.) Don't let this message scare you. Instead, take a moment to close all currently running programs. That way, if your system does lock, you won't lose any work-in-progress.

What to Do When Your System Locks

When you ask Windows 95 to perform certain operations, such as detect a new hardware device on your PC, your system may "lock." When your system locks, it will not respond to any commands you issue, no matter where you move your mouse pointer or click your mouse buttons.

As a result, you cannot use any of your computer's programs or access Windows 95 functions. To unlock your system, press **CTRL-ALT-DEL**. Windows 95, in turn, will display the Close Program window. Then, select one of the following options:

- In the list box at the top of the Close Program window, select the task (program or operating system function) that caused your system to lock. Then, click your mouse on the End Task button.

- Click your mouse on the Shut Down button to exit Windows 95.

- Press **CTRL-ALT-DEL** again to restart your system.

Click the Next button to continue with the hardware installation. The Add New Hardware wizard, in turn, will begin checking all your system's devices and display a progress indicator, as shown in Figure 6.3.

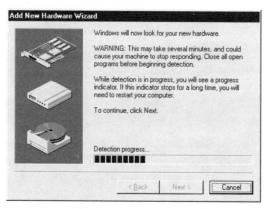

Figure 6.3 The progress indicator in the Add New Hardware Wizard dialog box.

As the Add New Hardware wizard proceeds through the detection process, it gradually fills the progress indicator. When the wizard finishes, it instructs you to click on the Details button to learn more about the devices it detected. Click on the Details button. The wizard, in turn, will display a list of new devices, as shown in Figure 6.4.

In Figure 6.4, the Detected list box shows a new modem. If the Detected list box on your display screen shows your new hardware, select the device from the list box. Then, to install the hardware, click your mouse on the Finish button.

Note: *As the current example will demonstrate, you can use the Add New Hardware wizard for modem installations. However, when you add a new modem to your system, you should use the Install New Modem wizard you learned about in Chapter 5.*

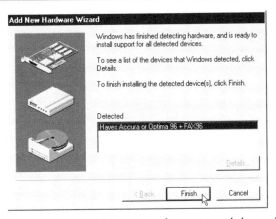

Figure 6.4 *The list of new hardware devices the Add New Hardware wizard detected.*

After you click on the Finish button, the Add New Hardware wizard will display certain device settings and give you an opportunity to confirm or change them. For the modem example, Figure 6.5 shows how the wizard responds when you click on the Finish button.

Note: *If the hardware device you want to install doesn't appear in the Detected list box, click your mouse on the Cancel button. Then, restart the Add New Hardware wizard. Finally, click the Next button and select the Install specific hardware option button. In the next section, you will learn how to use the Install specific hardware option to add devices to your system if the Add New Hardware wizard fails to detect them.*

In Figure 6.5, the Add New Hardware wizard uses the Verify Modem dialog box to show the modem's manufacturer and model name. If the information in the Verify Modem dialog box (the dialog box's full name will vary depending on the type of device you're installing) on your screen is correct, you click on the Next button to confirm the reported settings and continue with the installation. In response, the wizard will, depending on the hardware you are installing, complete the installation or continue with additional installation steps.

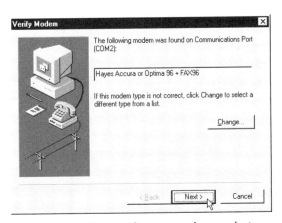

Figure 6.5 *The Add New Hardware wizard verifying information about a device.*

However, if any of the Verify Modem dialog box's information is wrong, click on the Change button. The Add New Hardware wizard, in turn, will display a dialog box you can use to correct the information. For example, assume the modem information in Figure 6.5 is incorrect, and you click on the Change button. The wizard, in turn, will display the Install New Modem dialog box, which contains list boxes from which you can select the modem's correct manufacturer and model (see Figure 6.6).

After you select the device's (in Figure 6.6, the modem's) manufacturer in the Manufacturers list box, the Add New Hardware wizard will highlight the manufacturer's name and show a list of models for that manufacturer in the Models list box. From the Models list box, you pick your device's model.

After you select your device's manufacturer and model, you click on the OK button. The wizard, in turn, will close the dialog box (in the current example, the Install New Modem dialog box in Figure 6.6) and return to the Verify Modem dialog box (see Figure 6.5). When you click on the Next button, the Add New Hardware wizard closes its dialog box and exits.

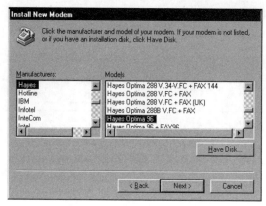

Figure 6.6 *The Install New Modem dialog box.*

For some hardware, such as a printer, Windows 95 needs additional software (known as a printer driver) to control the hardware. The necessary software is normally on the Windows 95 installation disks or the Windows 95 CD. If a hardware device needs additional software, the Add New Hardware wizard will open a dialog box (after you click on the Next button) to request that you provide the Windows 95 installation CD or disk. At this point, the installation steps are the same as those shown in the "Working with Your Printer" section of Chapter 5 (see Figure 5.40).

As you can see, how the Add New Hardware wizard functions depends on the hardware you are installing. For most hardware, the wizard can detect the device and perform installation tasks automatically. For other hardware, the wizard must copy additional software from the Windows 95 installation CD or disks.

INSTALLING HARDWARE WITH A VENDOR-SUPPLIED DISK

As you have learned, there may be times when the Add New Hardware wizard fails to detect the device you want to add to your system. Fortunately, many hardware devices come with a setup disk your system can use to configure the device for use with Windows 95. (Some hardware vendors include several such disks with a device. As such, before you use a setup disk, make sure it contains software specifically for Windows 95.)

To use a setup disk, click on the Add New Hardware Wizard dialog box Install specific hardware option button (see Figure 6.2). Next, scroll to the bottom of the Install specific hardware list box and click your mouse on the "Unknown hardware" item. Finally, click your mouse on the Next button. The wizard, in turn, will display a new dialog box, as shown in Figure 6.7.

Within the new dialog box, the wizard asks you to identify the device's manufacturer and model number. Using this information, Windows 95 will try to determine the device's system resource settings (IRQ number, I/O addresses, and DMA channel) so it can complete the installation.

However, if you have a setup disk from the device's manufacturer, you don't need to select anything from the Manufacturers or Models list boxes. Instead, you can just click your mouse on the Have Disk button. In response, the wizard will ask you to specify the drive where you placed the disk. Indicate the drive and click your mouse on the OK button. The hardware manufacturer's installation software, in turn, should guide you through the installation process.

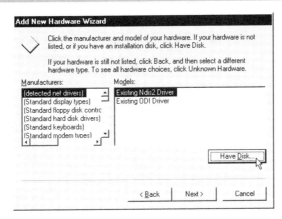

Figure 6.7 Installing unknown hardware.

ADDING AND REMOVING PROGRAMS

Only a few years ago, program installation was a fairly simple process. To install a program, you simply copied a bunch of files into a directory. Likewise, when a program had outlived its usefulness, you could easily remove it from your system by deleting the contents of the program's directory.

However, with the advent of Windows 3.1, program installation and removal became much more complicated. In Windows 3.1, a program's files are not localized in a single directory. Most programs have files in their own directory, as well as in the WINDOWS directory. Furthermore, upon installation, most Windows 3.1 programs added settings to the WIN.INI file. (Windows 3.1 stores the program's font, hardware specifics, and Desktop settings in the WIN.INI file.) As a result, you practically have to be a computer expert, someone who knows exactly which files go where, to remove a program from Windows 3.1. Or, you have to invest in one or more "Windows deinstallation" programs. To help make program installation and removal easier, Windows 95 includes program installation and deinstallation utilities you can access through the Add/Remove Programs Properties sheet.

To access the Add/Remove Programs Properties sheet, double-click on the Control Panel's Add/Remove Programs icon. Windows 95, in turn, will open the Add/Remove Programs Properties sheet, as shown in Figure 6.8.

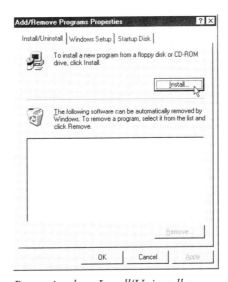

Figure 6.8 The Add/Remove Programs Properties sheet Install/Uninstall page.

As you can see, the top part of the Install/Uninstall page tells you to click on the Install button to add a new program. When you click on the Install button, Windows 95 looks for an installation program on your system's A: drive. If Windows 95 doesn't find anything in the drive, Windows 95 will prompt you for an installation program to run. You can easily start the installation program from the Start menu Run option. The lower part of the Install/Uninstall page lists programs that Windows 95 can automatically remove. To deinstall a program, you select it from the list and click on the Remove button. Unfortunately, the Windows 95 deinstallation utility has two limitations. One, the deinstallation utility can only remove programs you installed using the Install/Uninstall page Install button. Two, the original installation software that came with the program must support the Windows 95 deinstallation utility. As a result, if you just upgraded to Windows 95 from another operating system (such as Windows 3.1), you may not be able to use the deinstallation utility to remove many (or any) of your current programs. However, as software manufacturers design more programs for use with Windows 95, the deinstallation utility will become increasingly useful.

INSTALLING NEW WINDOWS 95 PROGRAMS

As you work with Windows 95, there may be times when you want to add new programs to your system. For example, you may want to install the Windows 95 versions of the popular word processing (Word), slide show presentation (PowerPoint), and spreadsheet (Excel) programs on your PC. To do so, perform these steps:

1. Insert the program's setup disk into your A: drive.

2. Double-click on the Control Panel's Add/Remove Programs icon. Windows 95 will display the Add/Remove Programs Properties sheet Install/Uninstall page.

3. Click on the Install/Uninstall page Install button. Windows 95 will guide you through the program installation.

ADDING WINDOWS 95 COMPONENTS

As you know, an automobile is made up of many component parts. Every automobile has systems for engine cooling, suspension, ignition, braking, passenger safety (seat belts and airbags), passenger comfort (air conditioning), and so on. Although, on the surface, an automobile may look and function like a single machine, it is actually a collection of cooperative, and often interdependent, systems. In a similar way, Windows 95 is not simply one huge program that tells your computer how to operate. Instead, Windows 95 is a collection of many different components—software modules—that provide specific capabilities and often function in concert with one another. Table 6.1 lists the nine components that comprise the Windows 95 operating system.

Component	Description
Accessibility Options	Lets you change keyboard, mouse, and display characteristics to accommodate people with hearing, vision, or movement impairment.
Accessories	Includes Windows 95 accessory programs, such as Calculator, Paint, and WordPad.
Communications	Lets you connect your computer to other systems by modem or by a direct-cable connection.
Disk Tools	Includes the program to backup your system's disk.
Microsoft Exchange	Lets you send and receive electronic mail.

Table 6.1 Windows 95 components. (continued on the next page)

Component	Description
Microsoft Fax	Lets you send and receive faxes.
Multilanguage Support	Lets you write documents in several languages, such as Greek, Polish, Russian, and Slovenian.
Multimedia	Lets you play sound and video clips (provided your system has a sound card and a CD-ROM drive).
Microsoft Network	Lets you use your system's modem to access and use Microsoft's online service.

Table 6.1 Windows 95 components. *(continued from the previous page)*

Each of these Windows 95 components requires some disk space. As such, if you have a limited amount of disk space, you may not want to install all the components. Fortunately, Windows 95 lets you choose only the components you need. For example, if you work only in English, you can safely ignore the Multilanguage Support component. Likewise, if your system has no modem, you don't need to install the Microsoft Fax component.

To give you even greater control over exactly what Windows 95 capabilities you install on your computer, Microsoft divided the operating system's components into subcomponents, which you can install individually. For example, the Communications component contains the following subcomponents:

- The Dial-Up Networking subcomponent, which lets you connect your computer to other computers through a modem.

- The Direct Cable Connection subcomponent, which lets you connect your computer to another computer with a cable between their respective serial or parallel ports.

- The HyperTerminal subcomponent, which lets you connect to other computers and online services (requires a modem).

- The Phone Dialer subcomponent, which lets you tell your computer to dial the phone.

By default, Windows 95 installs only a minimal set of these components. In particular, Windows 95 does not install the Microsoft Network and Microsoft Exchange components. As such, if you want to try the Microsoft Network or send electronic mail, you must install these components yourself. In this section, you will learn how to do so.

To add specific Windows 95 components and subcomponents, you use the Add/Remove Program Properties sheet Windows Setup page. For example, if you install Windows 95 with the default options, your system will not contain several important Windows 95 components, such as Microsoft Network, Microsoft Exchange, and the Briefcase. You would have to use the Windows Setup page to add these components.

Because, in later chapters, *Success with Windows 95* covers Microsoft Network, Microsoft Exchange, and the Briefcase, the following steps show you how to add these components and subcomponents to your system.

First, click on the Add/Remove Programs Properties sheet Windows Setup tab. Windows 95, in turn, will display the Windows Setup page, as shown in Figure 6.9.

The Windows Setup page shows a list of Windows 95 components. Each component in the list has a check box, an icon, and a name. If a check mark appears in a check box, the corresponding component is installed. However, if a marked check box is gray, only parts of the component are installed.

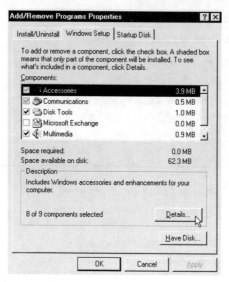

Figure 6.9 The Windows Setup page lets you install Windows 95 components and subcomponents.

In Figure 6.9, the Accessories check box has a check mark. However, the check box is also gray, which means some parts of the Accessories component are not installed. To learn more about which parts of the Accessories components are installed, click on the Details button. Windows 95, in turn, will display the Accessories dialog box, as shown in Figure 6.10.

Note: If you compare the Accessories dialog box (Figure 6.10) with the Add/Remove Programs Properties sheet Windows Setup page (Figure 6.9), you can see that Windows 95 uses the term **component** to refer to both components (such as Accessories) and parts of a component (such as Briefcase, Calculator, and Clipboard Viewer). To minimize confusion, **Success with Windows 95** uses the term **subcomponent** to refer to parts of a component.

Figure 6.10 The Accessories dialog box lists the subcomponents in Accessories.

The Accessories dialog box shows you further details about the Accessories component. Notice that the Briefcase check box is empty. The Briefcase subcomponent lets you synchronize files between two systems, such as a portable computer and a desktop system. Although you won't learn how to use the Briefcase subcomponent until Chapter 11, "Using Windows 95 on Your Portable PC," go ahead and install it now. To install the Briefcase, click your mouse on the Briefcase check box until a check mark appears. Note that the Accessories dialog box also shows the disk space required to install each subcomponent, as well as the total space available on your system's hard disk.

Click on the Accessories dialog box OK button. Windows 95, in turn, will close that dialog box and return you to the Windows Setup page. Notice that the Communications component also appears with a gray check box. To see detailed information about the Communications component, click your mouse on the Communications label and then click the Details button. Windows 95, in turn, will display the Communications dialog box, as shown in Figure 6.11.

The Dial-Up Networking subcomponent includes the software you need to connect to other computers, such as your Internet access provider's computer, using a modem. Since you will use this subcomponent in Chapter 10, "Connecting Windows 95 to the Internet and the World Wide Web," go ahead and install it now. Click your mouse on the Dial-Up Networking check box until a check mark appears. Then, click your mouse on the OK button to close the Communications dialog box and return to the Windows Setup page.

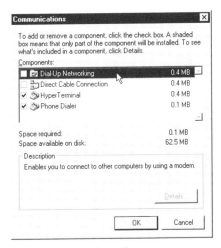

Figure 6.11 The Communications dialog box showing the subcomponents.

In the Windows Setup page Components list box, click on the Microsoft Exchange check box and The Microsoft Network check box (you may need to scroll down the list to see this item). You will use the Microsoft Network component in Chapter 8, "Using Microsoft Networks," and the Microsoft Exchange component in Chapter 17, "Using the Windows 95 Information Center/Microsoft Exchange."

After you have selected all the Windows 95 components you want to add, click on the OK button at the bottom of the Add/Remove Programs Properties sheet. Windows 95, in turn, will try to copy files from an installation disk that it expects to find in your system's A: drive. When it cannot find the disk, Windows 95 displays a message box, as shown in Figure 6.12.

Figure 6.12 Windows 95 asks for a specific installation disk when you add components.

If you installed Windows 95 from floppy disks, insert the disk Windows 95 requests in your system's A: drive and click the message box OK button. If your Windows 95 distribution is on a CD, simply click on the OK button. Windows 95, in turn, will display a dialog box, as shown in Figure 6.13.

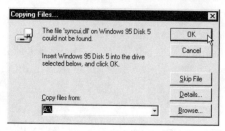

Figure 6.13 *Windows 95 prompts you for the location of installation disk.*

To install the component from a CD, enter your system's CD-ROM drive letter and the name of the directory that contains the installation files. Then, click on the OK button. Windows 95, in turn, will close the dialog box and begin to copy the necessary files. As it copies the files, Windows 95 will display its progress in a dialog box, as shown in Figure 6.14.

Figure 6.14 *Windows 95 shows status of copying files as it adds new components to your system.*

After Windows 95 finishes copying all files, it will display a message box, as shown in Figure 6.15.

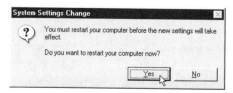

Figure 6.15 *Message box that informs you that you must restart your computer to use the newly added components.*

Click on the Yes button to restart your computer. When the system reboots, Windows 95 will configure the Microsoft Exchange component. (Of the new Windows 95 components you installed, only Microsoft Exchange requires some configuration.) Windows 95 first asks you if you have used Microsoft Exchange before (you can answer either Yes or No). Then, Windows 95 will require you to indicate which information services (such as the Microsoft Network Online Service, Microsoft Mail, Microsoft Fax, CompuServe Mail, and so on) you plan to use. After you specify your information services, Windows 95 will let you select options for each information service. For example, for the Microsoft Network, Windows 95 asks if you want to download mail at startup and use Internet addresses (with embedded @ signs). For Microsoft Fax, Windows 95 asks you to indicate the type of fax/modem your system has. (Windows 95 shows you your system's currently installed modem, which you can simply confirm.) Additionally, Windows 95 asks you to enter your name and phone number (Microsoft Fax uses this information when you send out a fax from your system). After you select options for each information service, Windows 95 will complete the installation and add two new icons (My Briefcase and Inbox) to the Desktop, as shown in Figure 6.16.

Figure 6.16 *Windows 95 adds new icons when you install Microsoft Exchange and Briefcase.*

6: CUSTOMIZING ADVANCED SYSTEM SETTINGS

The Inbox icon lets you access Microsoft Exchange. As you will learn in Chapter 17, you can use this icon to send and receive electronic mail and faxes. The My Briefcase icon lets you synchronize files between two systems, such as a portable computer and a desktop system. Chapter 11 describes how to use the Briefcase. After you install the new components, you will also find a new option, The Microsoft Network, in the Start menu Programs submenu.

REMOVING A WINDOWS 95 COMPONENT

If you never use a particular Windows 95 component (or subcomponent) and want to recover the disk space that it uses, you can use the Add/Remove Program Properties sheet Windows Setup page (see Figure 6.9) to remove the component. In every Windows 95 Components list box, a check mark appears in the check box next to each installed component or subcomponent. To remove an installed component or subcomponent, simply click on its check box. Windows 95, in turn, will remove the check mark. After you select the components and subcomponents you want to remove, click on the OK button at the bottom of the Add/Remove Program Properties sheet. Windows 95, in turn, will remove the components you selected and close the properties sheet.

CHOOSING WINDOWS 95 COMPONENTS EFFECTIVELY

Windows 95 components are to the computer user what a shield and suit of armor are to the medieval knight. Just as a shield and suit of armor can make the knight a more effective combatant, Windows 95 components can make your PC a more effective tool for you to accomplish your objectives. However, in both cases, using such tools has a price. The knight must expend greater energy to move about if he carries a bulky shield and wears a heavy suit of armor. Likewise, the more components you have installed on your system, the more of your PC's memory Windows 95 consumes. As such, when you choose which Windows 95 components and subcomponents to add to or remove from your system, weigh the benefit of using these components against the cost to your system resources.

CREATING A STARTUP DISK

If your Windows 95 system refuses to start, you will need some way to get into the system, locate the problem, and fix it. A Windows 95 startup disk is meant for such emergencies. The startup disk contains the software you need to "boot" or start your PC. In addition, the disk contains several utilities you can use to diagnose and correct problems. To create a startup disk, use the Startup Disk page. To access that page, click on the Add/Remove Program Properties sheet Startup Disk tab. Windows 95, in turn, will display the Startup Disk page, as shown in Figure 6.17.

Figure 6.17 The Startup Disk page lets you create a startup disk.

To create a startup disk, click on the Create Disk button. Windows 95, in turn, will begin to collect the files it needs to create the startup disk. Soon, Windows 95 will display a message box (much like the one shown in Figure 6.12) that asks you to insert Disk 1 of the Windows 95 installation disks. If you installed Windows 95 from floppy disks, insert the disk Windows 95 requests and click on the OK button. Windows 95, in turn, will begin to prepare the files for the startup disk.

If you installed Windows 95 from the CD, insert the Windows 95 installation CD in your CD-ROM drive and click on the OK button. Windows 95, in turn, will display a dialog box, much like the one shown in Figure 6.13. Enter the drive and directory where the installation files are located on the CD. (The drive, of course, is your CD-ROM drive.) Then, click on the OK button. Windows 95, in turn, will close the dialog box and begin to prepare the files for the startup disk. After a few moments, Windows 95 will display a message box, as shown in Figure 6.18, that prompts you to insert a floppy disk into your system's A: drive.

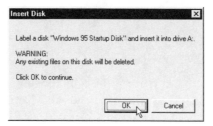

Figure 6.18 Message box that asks you to insert a disk for use as the startup disk.

As the message says, you should provide a disk. (Label the disk to make sure it's easy to locate during an emergency.) Note the message box's warning carefully—Windows 95 will delete all the disk's existing files. As such, make sure the disk you use contains nothing you want to keep. After you insert the disk, click on the OK button. Windows 95, in turn, will close the message box and begin to copy the necessary files onto the startup disk. You should store the startup disk in a safe place. Later on, if you ever need to boot your system with the startup disk, just place the disk in your computer's A: drive and turn on the power. Your system, in turn, should boot from the startup disk and display an A> prompt. When the system boots from the startup disk, you will have to rely on MS-DOS commands to navigate through the system.

Working with Fonts

If you have worked with word-processing programs, you may know that a *font* provides you with a typeface. Windows 95 comes with quite a few fonts. For example, run WordPad and select the Format menu Font option. WordPad, in turn, will display the Font dialog box, as shown in Figure 6.19.

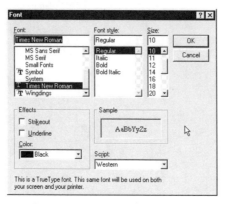

Figure 6.19 Font dialog box that appears when you select WordPad's Format menu Font option.

The Font dialog box Font list box shows the fonts that are currently available in your Windows 95 system. You can scroll through this list to see the font names. Now, suppose you want to use a specific font, such as Adobe Garamond, for the text of a brochure you're preparing. If you don't have the font in your system, you can purchase the font at your local computer store. (Usually, the font will come packaged in a font collection.) However, before you can use the new font in a Windows 95 program (such as WordPad), you have to install the font in your system. The Fonts folder includes the tools you can use to view existing fonts and add new ones. To open the Fonts folder, double-click on the Control Panel's Fonts icon. Windows 95, in turn, will open the Fonts folder, as shown in Figure 6.20.

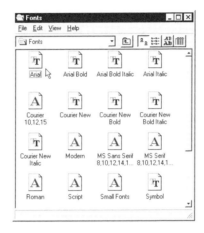

Figure 6.20 The Fonts folder.

The Fonts folder shows an icon for each font in your system. Notice the first row of fonts: Arial, Arial Bold, Arial Bold Italic, and Arial Italic. As you can see, the Fonts folder contains an icon for each style (bold, italic, or regular) of a font such as Arial.

VIEWING A FONT

If you want to view a font in Windows 95, you can run WordPad, select the font, and type some text in the WordPad window. However, this approach may mean a lot of work for you. For example, if you want to see how all letters of the alphabet look in that font, you must type each one of them in the window. Likewise, if you want to see the font at a different point size, you must highlight the work area text, click your mouse on the font size pull-down list button, and select a new size. Fortunately, Windows 95 provides a much simpler way to view a font. If you want to examine a font quickly and easily, double-click on a font's icon. Windows 95, in turn, will open a new window and display the font, as shown in Figure 6.21.

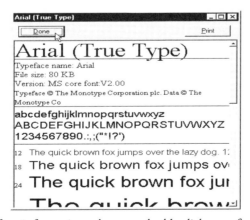

Figure 6.21 Windows 95 displays font information when you double-click on a font's icon in the Fonts folder.

The top part of the font window shows the font's name (Arial), its type (TrueType), the size of the font's file, and the font's copyright information. The rest of the font window shows the font at several point sizes, from 12 points all the way up to 72 points. You must scroll down the window to see the larger point sizes. If you need another user to agree with your font selection, you may want to print the font window's contents. To do so, click on the Print button at the window's upper-right corner. To close the font window and return to the Fonts folder, click on the Done button.

INSTALLING A NEW FONT

To install a font, you must copy the font files to a specific location on your hard disk. While you could probably copy the font files manually, it is much simpler to install the fonts through the Fonts folder. When you use the Fonts folder, Windows 95 copies the font files for you and places them at the correct location in your system.

To install a font, select the File menu Install New Font option. Next, click on the File category in the Fonts window's menu bar. Windows 95, in turn, will display the File menu, as shown in Figure 6.22.

Figure 6.22 *The Fonts folder File menu Install New Font option.*

Click on the File menu Install New Font option. Windows 95, in turn, will display the Add Fonts dialog box, as shown in Figure 6.23.

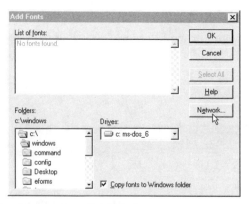

Figure 6.23 *The Add Fonts dialog box lets you install a new font.*

As you can see, the dialog box lets you browse through your system's drives and folders to find the font files. If you have the font on a floppy disk, insert the disk into your system's floppy drive. Then, use the Drives pull-down list button. Windows 95, in turn, will display a pull-down list that contains your system's drives. In the Drives pull-down list, select your floppy drive.

Windows 95, in turn, will list any fonts on the disk. Figure 6.24 shows how the Add Fonts dialog box lists the fonts in a specific folder.

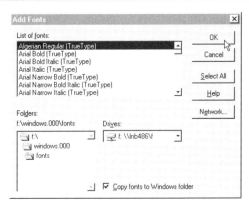

Figure 6.24 Add Fonts dialog box showing the fonts in a specific folder.

To add a specific font to your system, select that font from the list of fonts. Windows 95, in turn, will highlight the selection. Then, click on the OK button in the Add Fonts dialog box. Windows 95, in turn, will copy the necessary font files to the Windows folder. Windows 95 will also add to the Fonts folder an icon that represents the newly added font.

CUSTOMIZING A JOYSTICK

The *joystick* is a hand-held device with several buttons (typically two or more) and an upright, movable stick you can use to interact with certain programs (usually game programs, such as Microsoft Flight Simulator).

Note: *Often, sound cards come with a joystick port. If you have a sound card in your system and you need a joystick for a game, check to see if the sound card already has a joystick port. Under Windows 95, if you calibrate your joystick once, all game programs can use the same calibration. You don't have to recalibrate the joystick for each game program.*

Before you use a joystick, you should calibrate it to tell Windows 95 how far you can move the upright "stick" in any direction. When you calibrate a joystick, game programs you run on your system can properly associate joystick positions with specific values. For example, a game program may want to associate the center joystick position with zero, the far-left joystick position with -10, and the far-right joystick position with 10. The only way a game program can make such associations is if you calibrate your joystick. In Windows 95, you can calibrate a joystick through the Joystick Properties sheet. To access the Joystick Properties sheet, double-click on the Control Panel's Joystick icon. Windows 95, in turn, will open the Joystick Properties sheet, as shown in Figure 6.25.

Figure 6.25 The Joystick Properties sheet lets you calibrate your system's joystick.

The Joystick Properties sheet lets you perform the following tasks:

- Select one of several joysticks (if you happen to have more than one) in your system
- Specify the selected joystick's type (for example, a two-axis, two-button generic joystick or a Gravis Analog joystick)
- Calibrate and test the joystick

To calibrate the joystick (and test it), click on the Calibrate button. Windows 95, in turn, will display a dialog box that guides you through the calibration process. First, the dialog box will ask you to leave your joystick handle alone (in which case, the joystick handle should assume its center position) and click on one of the joystick buttons. Next, the dialog box will ask you to move the joystick in circles several times and then click on one of the joystick buttons again. Finally, the dialog box will again ask you to confirm the joystick's center. To do so, you must leave the joystick handle alone and click one of the joystick buttons. After you complete the dialog box's steps, Windows 95 tells you that you've successfully calibrated your joystick, as shown in Figure 6.26.

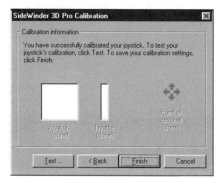

Figure 6.26 Joystick Calibration dialog box that guides you through calibration steps and informs you of success.

To try out the calibration and test the joystick, click on the Test button in the Joystick Calibration dialog box (see Figure 6.26). Windows 95, in turn, will display the Joystick Test dialog box, as shown in Figure 6.27.

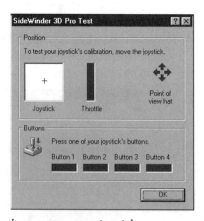

Figure 6.27 The Joystick Test dialog box lets you test your joystick.

Try to move the joystick. As you do so, the small cross-hair cursor should track the joystick's motion. Click on the joystick's buttons. The corresponding button (Button 1 or Button 2) in the Joystick Test dialog box should light up. When you finish testing your joystick, click on the OK button. Windows 95, in turn, will close the Joystick Test dialog box. Click on the Finish button in the Joystick Calibration dialog box. Windows 95, in turn, will save the calibration settings for future use and close the Joystick Calibration dialog box.

Using ODBC (Open Database Connectivity Software)

In a large company, users may store information in many different databases. Often, users will work with a database program with which they are familiar. As a result, the company data may be stored in a file format that is not convenient for your database program. Luckily ODBC can help. Regardless of how the database actually stores the data, ODBC presents a standard table-oriented view of the data. Thus, ODBC makes a database application independent of the specific details of the database. Essentially, ODBC lets the application developer write a database application that can access any database for which an ODBC driver is available. This section briefly describes the ODBC architecture. In addition, this section shows you how to set up the ODBC drivers and data sources so that you can run Windows 95 applications that use ODBC to access databases.

Note: If you do not currently use ODBC, continue your reading at the section entitled "Setting Passwords."

ODBC Overview

Most business applications use databases. Until recently, mainframe computers managed the data centrally. *Terminals*—simple devices with a display screen and a keyboard—let users access the data.

However, the information systems industry is moving to a *client-server architecture*. In such an architecture, a central server-PC manages the data, and users access and manipulate the data using client systems (programs). PCs that run Windows are a popular choice for client systems because they typically include Windows applications that enable users to access data through graphical front-ends.

This is where *Open Database Connectivity* (ODBC) comes into play. ODBC lets such Windows applications use the Structured Query Language (SQL) to access the data many different databases store. ODBC includes several components, one of which is the SQL-based Application Programming Interface (API), that you can use to access and query databases. The ODBC architecture consists of the following major components:

- *ODBC Applications* call the ODBC API functions to store and retrieve data. Usually, applications process and display the data in various formats that make the data more useful to the user.

- The *ODBC API* provides a standard set of functions that applications can call to access data. The access method is similar to the one SQL provides.

- The *ODBC driver manager* loads drivers on behalf of the application.

- *ODBC drivers* are Dynamic Link Libraries (DLL) that process ODBC function calls, send SQL statements to specific databases, and return results to the application. If the Database Management System (DBMS) does not support SQL, the drivers translate SQL statements into requests that conform to the syntax DBMS supports. As a user, you do not have to know how ODBC drivers work, just that you need one for your database.

- *Data sources* represent the files or database tables a driver accesses. A data source can be a Microsoft Access database, an Excel spreadsheet, or even some text files.

A data source is an abstraction of the data that a user wants to access. The amount of work an ODBC driver performs depends on the data source's sophistication. (A sophisticated data source might be a Relational Database Management System (RDBMS) with an SQL front-end.) If a data source is a file, the driver has to act as the DBMS. In contrast, if the data source is a DBMS, the driver merely acts as an agent that transfers SQL requests to the data source.

Setting up ODBC

Before you can use Windows 95 to run a database application that uses ODBC, you must install the ODBC drivers and set up the data sources. Windows 95 does not normally include the ODBC drivers. However, a database program that uses ODBC, such as Microsoft Access, should provide the drivers. Microsoft also provides ODBC drivers for a number of data sources, such as Access and Excel, for a nominal cost.

INSTALLING ODBC DRIVERS

If you have Microsoft's ODBC drivers, the first step is to install them. Insert disk 1 of the ODBC drivers and run the Setup program from the Start menu Run option. The Setup program, in turn, will display its opening screen and ask for confirmation, as shown in Figure 6.29.

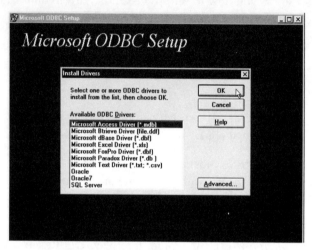

Figure 6.29 *The ODBC Setup program's initial dialog box.*

Click on the Continue button. The ODBC Setup program, in turn, will display a dialog box with a list of available drivers, as shown in Figure 6.30.

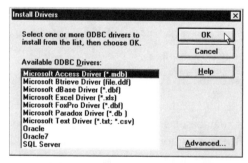

Figure 6.30 *Dialog box that prompts you to select ODBC drivers to install.*

Click on the drivers you want to install. The Setup program, in turn, will highlight the drivers you select. Next, click on the OK button to continue the installation. In response, the Setup program will copy the necessary files onto your system's hard disk. When necessary, the Setup program will prompt you to insert additional disks. After the Setup program copies the files, it will display a message box that announces a successful installation (see Figure 6.31).

6: Customizing Advanced System Settings

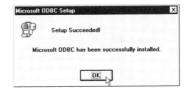

Figure 6.31 Microsoft ODBC setup program announcing success.

After you successfully install the ODBC drivers, Windows 95 will display an ODBC icon in the Control Panel folder, as shown in Figure 6.32.

Figure 6.32 Control Panel folder with the newly-added ODBC icon.

Adding ODBC Data Sources

Before a database application that uses ODBC can access data, you must add data sources. To do so, you must identify an OBDC driver and a database appropriate for that driver. You can perform both tasks through the Control Panel's ODBC icon. To add one or more data sources, double-click on the Control Panel's ODBC icon. Windows 95, in turn, will open a Data Sources dialog box, as shown in Figure 6.33.

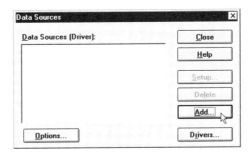

Figure 6.33 The Data Sources dialog lets you add ODBC data sources.

Click on the Add button. Windows 95, in turn, will display a dialog box with a list of installed ODBC drivers, as shown in Figure 6.34.

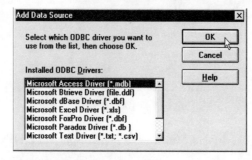

Figure 6.34 Windows 95, showing a list of installed ODBC drivers.

Suppose you want to add a Microsoft Access database as a data source. Click on the Microsoft Access Driver in the Installed ODBC Drivers list box. Windows 95, in turn, will highlight the selected driver's name. Then, click on the OK button. In response, Windows 95 will open the ODBC Microsoft Access Setup dialog box, as shown in Figure 6.35.

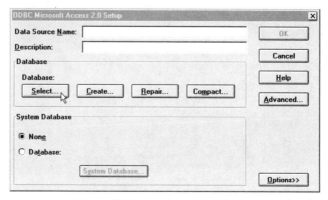

Figure 6.35 The ODBC Microsoft Access Setup dialog box lets you add an Access database as a data source.

In the ODBC Microsoft Access Setup dialog box, click on the Select button. Windows 95, in turn, will display the Select Database dialog box. In the Select Database dialog box, change the drive and select the folder that contains the Microsoft Access database you want to use as a data source. For example, if you were to select the SAMPAPPS folder in the Microsoft Access 2.0 installation directory, you would have the database list shown in Figure 6.36.

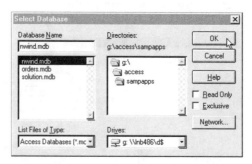

Figure 6.36 The Select Database dialog box lets you pick an Access database.

Click on a database and then click on the OK button. Windows 95, in turn, will close the Select Database dialog box and return you to the ODBC Microsoft Access Setup dialog box (Figure 6.35). In the Data Source Name field, enter a name for the database. Then, if you wish, enter a description of the database in the Description field. Finally, click on the OK button. In response, Windows 95 will close the ODBC Microsoft Access Setup dialog box and return you to the Data Sources dialog box, as shown in Figure 6.37.

6: Customizing Advanced System Settings

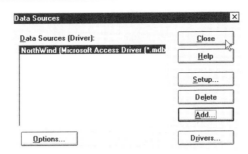

Figure 6.37 The Data Sources dialog box showing a Microsoft Access database as the data source.

Now the Data Sources dialog box displays the name of the Microsoft Access database that you selected as the data source. Click on the Close button to close the Data Sources dialog box and complete the addition of an ODBC data source.

PREPARING YOUR WINDOWS 95 SYSTEM TO USE ODBC APPLICATIONS

Applications that support ODBC let you access, review, and manipulate data contained in a wide variety of databases. However, before your system's applications can use ODBC functions, you must install the ODBC driver manager and ODBC drivers. In addition, you must set up one or more ODBC data sources with the ODBC driver manager.

To install ODBC drivers, perform these steps:

1. Insert disk 1 of the ODBC drivers into your system's floppy disk drive.
2. Select the Start menu Run option and run the Setup program.
3. Follow the Setup program's instructions.

To set up ODBC data sources, perform these steps:

1. Double-click on the Control Panel's ODBC icon. Windows 95 will open the Data Sources dialog box.
2. Click your mouse on the Add button. Windows 95 will display a list of installed ODBC drivers.
3. Select an ODBC driver and click on the OK button. Windows 95 will display a Setup dialog box.
4. Click on the Select button. Windows 95 will display the Select Database dialog box.
5. Select the drive and folder that contain the database you want.
6. Select a database and then click on the OK button. Windows 95 will close the Select Database dialog box and return you to the Setup dialog box.
7. In the Data Source Name field, enter a name for the database and click on the OK button. Windows 95 will close the Setup dialog box and return you to the Data Sources dialog box.
8. Click on the Close button.

SETTING PASSWORDS

If you use an operating system that supports multiple users, such as UNIX, you likely have to "login" each time you want to access the system. When you login, the operating system knows where to place your files (such systems have a separate file storage area for each user) and how to set up the computer for you. (The system stores the background colors, window colors, and so on that each user prefers.)

Although Windows 95 is primarily a single-user system, it does allow multiple users to share the system (one user at a time, however). Like Windows NT and UNIX, Windows 95 requires a user to login. When a user logs in, Windows 95 changes system settings, such as Desktop color, to match the user's preference. Also, Windows 95 can use the password that you provide during login to provide you with access to appropriate network resources, such as printers and disks. For example, your company's network might have a file server that keeps everyone's files so they can be backed up easily from a central location. Or, your company's network might have a few printers that everyone shares. To access and use these network resources, you need a password. If your system is connected to a network, Windows 95 will use your system password to give you access to the network as well.

Note: *Windows 95 does not intend for the password to protect your system from other users. When Windows 95 displays its prompt for a username and password, another user can select the Cancel option and immediately access your system. Windows 95 uses the username and password to control user-profile settings only.*

CHANGING YOUR WINDOWS 95 PASSWORD

You can use the Passwords Properties sheet to change your password and perform a few other system management tasks. To open the Passwords Properties sheet, double-click on the Control Panel's Passwords icon. Windows 95, in turn, will open the Passwords Properties sheet, as shown in Figure 6.38.

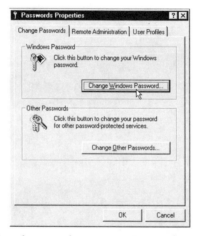

Figure 6.38 *The Passwords Properties sheet lets you change your password.*

The Passwords Properties sheet Change Passwords page has two sections:

- The Windows Password section lets you change your Windows password.
- The Other Passwords section lets you change your password for specific password-protected services, such as Novell Netware servers.

To change your Windows 95 password, click on the Change Windows Password button. Windows 95, in turn, will open the Change Windows Password dialog box, as shown in Figure 6.39.

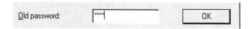

Figure 6.39 *Windows 95 prompting you for a new Windows password.*

In the Change Windows Password dialog box, you must enter your current password, as well as your new one. Furthermore, you also must enter your new password a second time to confirm your change. When you click on the OK button, Windows 95 will change the password.

Specifying a New Password

As you have learned, you can set up Windows 95 as a multiple-user system that requires all users to enter a password before they can use system resources. If you work on a multiple-user Windows 95 system and suspect an unauthorized person has seen your password, you need to change the password immediately. Actually, it's a good standard practice to change your password periodically, even if you don't believe any unauthorized person knows it. Fortunately, you can change your password any time you're logged in to your Windows 95 system. To do so, perform these steps:

1. Double-click on the Control Panel's Passwords icon. Windows 95 will open the Passwords Properties sheet Change Passwords page.
2. Click your mouse on the Change Windows Password button. Windows 95 will open the Change Windows Password dialog box.
3. In the Change Windows Password dialog box, enter your current password and your new password twice.
4. Click your mouse on the Change Windows Password dialog box OK button.
5. Click your mouse on the Passwords Properties sheet Close button.

Setting User Profile Options

As you learned in Chapter 5, Windows 95 lets you customize your system's look and feel. You can choose the colors and fonts your system displays, set the speed at which your mouse pointer moves, and determine how rapidly you have to double-click to initiate a system operation. Using such customization features, you can set up Windows 95 just the way you like it. In addition, if you share your PC with someone else (for example, a roommate, family member, or co-worker) and the other user doesn't like your system settings, you can tell Windows 95 to store system settings on a "per user" basis. As such, each time a user logs in, Windows 95 will change the system settings to match the user's preferences. To set up Windows 95 for "per user" system settings, use the Passwords Properties sheet User Profiles page. To access the User Profiles page, click on the Passwords Properties sheet User Profiles tab. Windows 95, in turn, will display the User Profiles page, as shown in Figure 6.40.

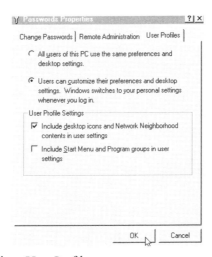

Figure 6.40 The Password Properties sheet User Profiles page.

To make Windows 95 save user settings on a "per user" basis, click on the second option button from the top of the User Profiles page. There are two more check boxes that control the user profile settings. These check boxes determine which items Windows 95 includes in the user settings. For example, if you want each user to have a custom Start menu, click on the last check box to enable it.

Making Windows 95 Please Everyone

If you share Windows 95 with other users, you and your system partners may have different ideas about the correct color for program-window work areas, the right title-bar font size, and a suitable mouse double-click speed. For example, while you may like the Windows 95 defaults, a system partner with poorer eyesight and slower reflexes might desire a larger and brighter work area (so that characters stand out more against the background in word-processing and spreadsheet programs), larger title-bar fonts, and a slower mouse double-click speed. Fortunately, you don't need to argue about the best settings, because Windows 95 lets you set up your system to please everyone. To do so, perform these steps:

1. Double-click on the Control Panel's Passwords icon. Windows 95 will open the Passwords Properties sheet.

2. Click your mouse on the Passwords Properties sheet User Profiles tab. Windows 95 will switch to the Passwords Properties sheet User Profiles page.

3. Select the second option button from the top of the User Profiles page.

4. Click your mouse on the OK button. Windows 95 will close the Passwords Properties sheet. Furthermore, each time a user logs in, Windows 95 will use the system settings the user selected during his or her last session.

Customizing International Settings

Because PC use is now a worldwide phenomenon, software developers can no longer assume that all their customers reside in a single country. As a result, most modern software, including Windows 95, is designed from the ground up for international use. Windows 95 can adjust for the currencies different countries use. Likewise, Windows 95 can accommodate the various ways people around the world write dates and numbers (in some countries, the decimal sign is a comma, not a period, as in the USA). To change these Windows 95 characteristics, you use the Regional Settings Properties sheet. To see how easily you can specify regional settings in Windows 95, double-click on the Control Panel's Regional Settings icon. Windows 95, in turn, will open the Regional Settings Properties sheet, as shown in Figure 6.41. As you can see from Figure 6.41, the Regional Settings Properties sheet has five pages:

- The Regional Settings page lets you select a country or a geographic region that shares common conventions for number, currency, time, and date representation. When you select a region from this page, Windows 95 automatically changes all other settings to reflect the current region. To select a region, click on the world map (see Figure 6.41).

- The Number page shows how positive and negative numbers appear for the currently selected region.

- The Currency page shows the representation of the currency for the currently selected region.

- The Time page shows the representation of time, as well as the AM and PM symbol, for the currently selected region.

- The Date page shows the representation of dates in short (such as 5/25/95) and long (such as Thursday, May 25, 1995) forms for the currently selected region.

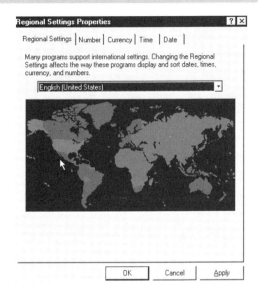

Figure 6.41 The Regional Settings Properties sheet lets you customize Windows 95 for a specific region.

Although you can change settings from individual pages (such as Number, Currency, Time, and Date), the best way to customize Windows 95 for use in a specific region is to simply go to the Regional Settings page and click on your geographic region. Windows 95, in turn, will make that region the current one, provided you have clicked on one of the green areas (those are the only areas for which you can customize Windows 95). Windows 95 displays the currently selected region in light green and shows the name of the region in the text field above the world map.

After you select a region, you can see the current settings from the Number, Currency, Time, and Date pages. If your country or region is not one of the green ones in the map (Figure 6.41), select the country whose settings most closely match your country's conventions. Then, go to each page—Number, Currency, Time, and Date—and change the formats of specific items to come up with the settings that apply to your country.

OTHER CONTROL PANEL ITEMS

In Chapter 5 and the previous sections of this chapter, you have seen how many of the Control Panel icons work. This section gives you a brief description of the Control Panel icons you have yet to explore. You will encounter these Control Panel icons in subsequent chapters of *Success with Windows 95*.

MULTIMEDIA

The Multimedia icon lets you control multimedia devices, such as your system's sound card, video playback, CD Audio playback, and so on. You can also use the Multimedia icon to set up joysticks and MIDI (Musical Instrument Digital Interface) devices and instruments. In Chapter 9, "Windows 95 Multimedia," which covers Windows 95 multimedia in detail, you will learn how to use the Control Panel's Multimedia icon to configure multimedia devices.

NETWORK

Unlike Windows 3.1, Windows 95 has extensive built-in support for a wide variety of networks. You can use the Control Panel's Network icon to configure a wide variety of networks, from Microsoft Networks to TCP/IP over a Dial-Up Network. You will learn the basics of Network configuration in Chapter 10, "Connecting Windows 95 to the Internet and World Wide Web," when the discussions turn to accessing the Internet from within Windows 95.

Mail and Fax

The Control Panel's Mail and Fax icon gives you access to the Microsoft Exchange profiles. Through the Microsoft Exchange profiles, you can set up your personal address book, establish storage areas for all of your messages (electronic mail and fax), and specify your preferences for downloading mail from the Microsoft Network. You will learn more about the Mail Fax icon in Chapter 17, which describes Microsoft Exchange.

Microsoft Mail Post Office

If you have Microsoft Mail, the Mail and Post Office icon lets you access tools you can use to set up and administer a Microsoft Mail Post Office. Like many electronic mail systems, Microsoft Mail uses a central post office—essentially a disk-storage area—to store and forward messages. In Chapter 17, "Using Microsoft Exchange to Send Faxes and E-Mail," you will learn more about electronic post office administration.

System

The Control Panel's System icon lets you see your entire system's settings. When you double-click on the System icon, Windows 95 will open the System Properties sheet. The System Properties sheet General page shows you the version number of your PC's Windows 95 operating system, as well as the computer type and amount of memory. The System Properties sheet Performance page shows the amount of system memory and the percentage of free system resources. The System Properties sheet Device Manager page gives you access to complete details of all devices installed in your system. Chapter 19, "Managing Low-Level Hardware Operations," covers the System settings in detail and shows you how to use the System Properties sheet.

Keys to Success

In the previous chapter, you learned how to customize most of your system's commonly used hardware, such as your system's display screen, keyboard, mouse, modem, and printer. This chapter taught you how to add new hardware (such as a sound card) and how to set up the data source for database access with the Open Data Base Connectivity (ODBC) drivers.

In Chapter 7, you will learn how files and directories organize your system's programs and documents. However, before you move on to Chapter 7, make sure you understand the following key concepts:

- ✓ After you physically install new hardware, such as a network adapter or a sound card, you must setup that hardware in Windows 95.

- ✓ Windows 95 provides a wizard that helps you install new hardware.

- ✓ Some Windows 95 components, such as Microsoft Network and Microsoft Exchange, may not be installed on your system. To add such components, use the Control Panel's Add/Remove Programs icon.

- ✓ If you buy new fonts, you have to use the Control Panel's Fonts folder to install them.

- ✓ Windows 95 lets you easily customize your system for use in a specific geographic region of the world.

- ✓ If you use ODBC for database access, you must use the Control Panel to set up the data sources and drivers.

Chapter 7
Working with Files and Folders

Before the computer age, if you are like most people, you used paper to store information. To save important data, you recorded it on a paper document, placed the document in a folder that contained related information, and then stored the folder in a file cabinet. If you had many folders, you probably used some sort of filing system. For example, you may have labeled each folder's tab and then arranged the folders alphabetically in the file cabinet.

Today, although many companies still use paper for information storage, they typically prefer to keep as much data as possible in electronic files that reside on disk. Electronic files offer users two key benefits over paper documents: electronic files don't consume anywhere near as much physical space as paper documents and electronic files are easier to access than paper documents in file cabinets.

Windows 95 organizes all the information in your computer (programs, documents, and so on) in a manner similar to your paper filing system. Of course, unlike your filing cabinet, the storage medium is not paper. Instead, Windows 95 stores information on devices, such as your system's hard-disk, floppy-disk, and CD-ROM drives.

In this chapter, you will learn your way around the Windows 95 file system. By the time you finish this chapter, you will understand the following key concepts:

- How the Windows 95 file system works
- The relationship between drives, directories, and files
- How MS-DOS users name files
- How to use long filenames
- How to navigate through the Windows 95 file system

UNDERSTANDING THE WINDOWS 95 FILE SYSTEM

No matter which program you use on your Windows 95 system, there will be times when you need to store information in files on your hard disk or on a floppy disk. To help you organize your files, you can create *folders*. Just as you can store related paper documents in a manila folder, you can group similar electronic files together in a Windows 95 folder.

For example, assume you want to place your office, school, and financial records on your hard disk. Furthermore, assume that because you update these records files frequently, you need to store them in a well-structured, easily accessible format. To organize these files, you could create three folders—named Office, School, and Finances—and place each file in the appropriate folder. Windows 95, in turn, would represent each file as an icon in the Office, School, or Finances folder window.

Folders and file icons are visual representations of how you have organized your disk. All operating systems, including Windows 95, come with a behind-the-scenes *file system* that physically stores data (your files) and later presents the information to the user. The Windows 95 file system stores individual files in directories, which it represents as folder icons. A directory (folder), in turn, can contain other directories (folders).

Although Windows 95 lets you work with icons that represent files and directories, you need to understand the file system because it organizes all your documents and programs. If you know how the file system works, you can easily navigate through your system's folders when you want to locate a specific document.

As previously mentioned, the Windows 95 file system is much like a paper-filing system. Your system's devices correspond to file cabinets, your system's directories to file cabinet drawers, subdirectories to manila folders, and electronic files to paper documents. Figure 7.1 illustrates the analogy between a file cabinet and the Windows 95 file system.

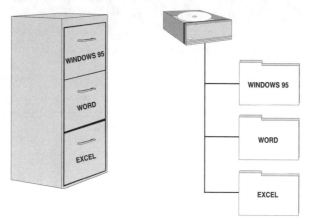

Figure 7.1 The similarities between a file cabinet and Windows 95 file system.

As Figure 7.1 shows, the Windows 95 file system doesn't limit you to four levels, as does a typical file cabinet (cabinet, drawer, folder, paper). While a paper-filing system can contain only one level of drawers and one level of folders, the Windows 95 file system can have many levels of directories. As Figure 7.1 also shows, the Windows 95 file system has the following three key components:

- Drives (hard disk, floppy disk, and CD-ROM), which contain and organize files into directories
- Folders, which contain files and other folders
- Files, which contain the actual information (the data for a program or the program itself)

In the following sections, you will learn how Windows 95 names these components. In addition, you will learn how you can uniquely identify a file by specifying the drive and folders in which the file resides.

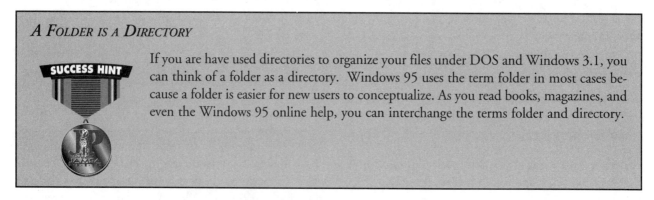

NAMING DRIVES, FOLDERS, AND FILES

If you have used MS-DOS and Microsoft Windows 3.1, you probably know how to refer to your system's drives, folders, and files. If you don't know how to name drives, folders, and files, you'll need to learn because many programs, including Windows 95, expect you to know such details. Although Windows 95 lets you use your mouse to access most of your system's programs and documents, there will be times when you need to understand MS-DOS naming conventions to locate and open a file. For example, when you select the Start menu Run option to run a setup program for new software, you often have to enter a line such as **A:\SETUP** in the Run dialog box's Open field. (The letter *A*, in this case, represents the drive that holds the setup disk. The backslash (\) represents the root directory. SETUP is the name of the installation program.)

DRIVE LETTERS

Windows 95 uses letters to identify your system's storage devices. Typically, a computer has a small number of storage devices, such as one or two floppy drives, a hard-disk drive, and a CD-ROM drive. As a result, Windows 95 identifies each drive by a single letter, such as A, B, C, and so on. In addition, Windows 95 places a colon after the drive letter. Thus, to refer to your system's storage devices, Windows 95 uses names such as *A:* drive, *B:* drive, and *C:* drive.

Like MS-DOS, Windows 95 uses the first few drive letters in a standard way:

- The A: drive is your computer's boot (or startup) floppy drive. If you put a floppy disk in the A: drive and turn on your system's power, your computer will automatically try to start from the floppy disk. (This feature is built into the computer and does not depend on the operating system you installed on your system's hard disk.) On most new systems, the A: drive is a 3.5-inch floppy drive. However, many older systems have a 5.25-inch floppy drive as the A: drive.

- The B: drive is the second floppy-disk drive on a system with two floppy drives.

- The C: drive is your system's first hard-disk drive.

- The D: drive is your system's second hard-disk drive, if you happen to have two hard-disk drives. If your system has only one hard-disk drive and a CD-ROM drive, then the D: drive is the CD-ROM drive.

- Other drive letters represent the CD-ROM drive and any network storage devices (if your system happens to be on a network).

Note: *To organize files better, a user can divide a hard disk into several logical hard-disk drives, each with its own drive letter. For example, a user might divide a 500 Mb hard disk into two logical drives (a 300 Mb C: drive and a 200 Mb D: drive).*

UNDERSTANDING ROOT DIRECTORIES

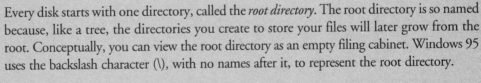

Every disk starts with one directory, called the *root directory*. The root directory is so named because, like a tree, the directories you create to store your files will later grow from the root. Conceptually, you can view the root directory as an empty filing cabinet. Windows 95 uses the backslash character (\), with no names after it, to represent the root directory.

DIRECTORY NAMES AND FILENAMES UNDER MS-DOS

To ensure you can exchange files with other users, Windows 95 continues to support MS-DOS file and directory names. As such, this section explains MS-DOS naming conventions. In MS-DOS, a directory name or filename has three parts:

- A *name* with up to eight characters. The name can use most alphanumeric characters (letters, numbers, and some special symbols such as a hyphen) but no embedded spaces.
- A *dot* (period) that immediately follows the name.
- An *extension* with up to three characters that explains the file's contents (DOC for document, EXE for executable program file, and so on).

Users call this naming scheme "8.3" because it uses an eight-character name, followed by a dot and a three-character extension. Some examples of 8.3 filenames are AUTOEXEC.BAT, CONFIG.SYS, COMMAND.COM, WINWORD.EXE, and WIN.INI. Although directory names can also have extensions, they typically do not. Some examples of directory names are WINDOWS, WINWORD, DOS, and TEMP.

Understanding Extensions

As you have learned, a three-character extension normally appears at the end of every filename. The extension indicates the type of file that the filename represents. For example, the DOC extension in MEMO.DOC tells you that MEMO is a word-processing document. Likewise, the BMP extension in CANVAS.BMP tells you that CANVAS is a graphics bitmap file. Table 7.1 lists and describes commonly used Windows file extensions.

Extension	File Contents
BAT	DOS batch file
BMP	Bitmap graphics image
CAL	Windows calendar file
CRD	Windows card file
DLL	Dynamic link library
DRV	Device driver
EXE	Executable program
FON	Font definition
HLP	Online Help file
INI	Program settings
PIF	Programs Information File for DOS-based programs
REC	Windows macro
RLE	Run-length encoded graphics file
SCR	Screen saver file
TRM	Terminal data communication settings
TTF	TrueType font
TXT	ASCII text file
WAV	Windows sound file
WRI	Write document

Table 7.1 Commonly used Windows file extensions.

PATHNAMES IN MS-DOS

As you know, to locate a document in a file room, you need to know more than just the document's name. You must also know the exact cabinet, drawer, and folder that contains the document. Likewise, to locate an electronic file, you need more than just its filename. You must also know the drive and the directory (which may include subdirectory names). The term *pathname* refers to the complete specification you need to locate a file—the drive letter, directory names, and the filename. To understand pathnames, you must understand the directory structure of the MS-DOS (and Windows 95) file system, as shown in Figure 7.2.

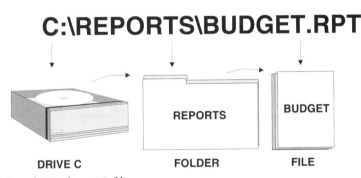

Figure 7.2 The MS-DOS and Windows 95 file system.

As shown in Figure 7.2, the file system has a *root directory* on a specific drive. The root directory contains other directories and files. Each directory, in turn, can have more directories and files under it. You compose a file's pathname by linking the drive letter, directory path, and filename in that order. Figure 7.3 illustrates the pathname components for a Windows 95 (TrueType) font file (ARIAL.TTF).

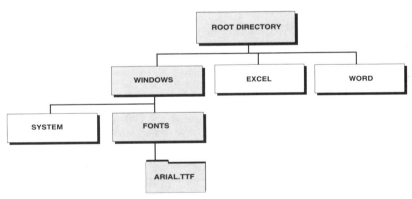

Figure 7.3 The Pathname of a file in MS-DOS and Windows 95.

As you can see from Figure 7.3, the pathname has the following sequence of components:

1. The drive letter, followed by a colon and backslash (\)
2. The directory (WINDOWS), followed by a backslash
3. Additional directories (in this case, just the FONTS directory). In a directory structure, backslashes separate directory names. Additionally, a backslash appears after the last directory name.
4. The filename with a name (up to eight characters) and an extension (up to three characters).

Now, look at Figure 7.2 and compare the pathname C:\WINDOWS\FONTS\ARIAL.TTF with that file's location in the directory structure. As you can see, the pathname contains all the information—drive and directory path—you need to locate the file.

Long Filenames in Windows 95

Imagine that you have a child who's using the Windows 3.1 graphic-drawing (Paint) or word-processing (Write) program for the first time. When the moment comes for your child to save his or her work, you tell your child to select the File menu Save As option. Then, when your system displays the Save As dialog box, your child enters a filename—something like "My report on the rain forest"—and tries to save by clicking the OK button.

In response, the program displays a message: "This is not a valid filename." When your child asks you why, you try to describe the MS-DOS 8.3 naming convention but soon realize you're wasting your breath. It's not easy to explain to the novice user why Windows 3.1 file naming is so inflexible.

While Microsoft engineers were designing the Windows 95 user interface, they conducted extensive usability tests and found that most new users behaved like the previously mentioned child. New users invariably tried to use long descriptive names for their documents, so Microsoft decided to include support for long filenames in Windows 95.

Windows 95 lets you enter file and directory names up to 255 characters long. In addition, you can embed spaces in Windows 95 filenames. However, a long filename cannot contain any of the following eight characters which have special meaning to Windows 95 and MS-DOS:

\ ? : * " < > |

With Windows 95, your child can save a document as "My report on the rain forest" as long as the program he or she is using accepts long filenames. A Windows 3.1 program, when run under Windows 95, will not accept long filenames. In other words, if you use an older program such as the Windows Write word processor, the program itself will not let you use filenames longer than 8.3, even if you are running the program under Windows 95. However, as Windows 95 versions of popular programs appear, you will see more support for long filenames.

Understanding Long Filenames

To name a file, DOS and Windows 3.1 users must abide by certain rules. DOS and Windows 3.1 filenames can have no more than eight characters and include no embedded spaces. As a result, such filenames are often cryptic abbreviations of actual document names. For example, an administrator who is working on a hospital's 1996 budget using Windows 3.1 might give the name HPTBGT96.DOC to the budget document. Now, imagine that administrator is sick one day and you, the administrator's assistant, must find the document without knowing its filename or your supervisor's document naming scheme. Consider how much time you would spend searching through dozens (perhaps hundreds) of documents with such abbreviated filenames.

To help users give their files more descriptive filenames, Microsoft included support for long filenames in Windows 95. In a long filename, you can use embedded spaces and up to 255 characters. As such, you can use the filename HOSPITAL BUDGET FOR 1996.DOC rather than HPTBGT96.DOC.

Note: *If you use older Windows 3.1-based programs, the programs will not let you use the long filenames.*

Using Windows 95 Files in MS-DOS and Windows 3.1

As you begin using Windows 95, some of your friends may continue to use MS-DOS and Windows 3.1—systems that do not support long filenames. Or, you may use Windows 95 at home, but your workplace PCs run Windows 3.1 only. Luckily, because Windows 95 supports the MS-DOS 8.3 naming convention, you can continue to share files between your Windows 95 system and PCs running MS-DOS or Windows 3.1.

In fact, Windows 95 even supports the 8.3 naming convention for files with long filenames. For each file with a long filename, Windows 95 provides an MS-DOS compatible 8.3 name as an alias. For example, for the long filename for the Windows 95 flying windows screen saver "Flying Windows.scr", Windows 95 generates the 8.3 alias "FLYING~1.SCR". Notice that the 8.3 alias uses the long filename's first few letters, converted to uppercase, and adds a tilde character (~) followed by a number. When you copy a Windows 95 file with a long filename on to a disk and read the disk under MS-DOS, you will see the file's 8.3 alias. Although the 8.3 alias may be somewhat cryptic, you can at least use it to share files between Windows 95, Windows 3.1, and MS-DOS.

Understanding the 8.3 Alias

For each long filename on your system, Windows 95 provides an MS-DOS compatible 8.3 alias. As such, to use your Windows 95 files on a DOS or Windows 3.1 system, just load them into the system. DOS or Windows 3.1, in turn, will use the files' 8.3 aliases rather than their long filenames.

Browsing Your System's Drives and Directories

As you may know, to move around directories and access files, MS-DOS users must issue a series of cryptic commands. To make information storage and retrieval tasks easier, Microsoft built the Windows 3.1 File Manager program, which provides users with a graphical view of a disk's contents.

To improve on the File Manager, Windows 95 provides the Explorer program (which you will learn how to use in Chapter 16, "Using the Windows 95 Explorer") and the My Computer icon. This section shows you how to use the My Computer icon to browse and locate files in your system.

Note: After you learn how to browse folders on a drive, you can use that knowledge to find files in the Windows 95 Open dialog box, which Windows 95 applications typically display when you select their File menu Open option.

Looking at the Folders in Your System's Hard Drive

To begin a tour of your system's drives and directories, locate the Desktop's My Computer icon, as shown in Figure 7.4.

Figure 7.4 The My Computer icon on the Windows 95 Desktop.

Double-click on the My Computer icon. Windows 95, in turn, will open the My Computer window, as shown in Figure 7.5.

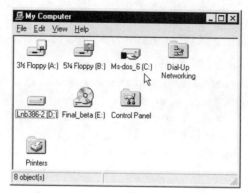

Figure 7.5 *When you double-click on the My Computer icon, Windows 95 opens the My Computer window.*

The appearance of your system's My Computer window will probably be different from the one you see in Figure 7.5. The window will show icons for each of your system's drives, as well as a few special folders, such as Printers and Control Panel. (If you double-click on the Control Panel icon, Windows 95 will open the Control Panel window that Chapters 5 and 6 described.)

To view a specific drive's contents, double-click on that drive's icon. For example, if you want to see what's in your system's C: drive, double-click on the C: drive's icon (the drive with a "C:" in parentheses at the end of its label). Windows 95, in turn, will open a window that displays the C: drive's contents, as shown in Figure 7.6.

Figure 7.6 *When you double-click on the C: drive's icon, Windows 95 displays a window with the C: drive's contents.*

The exact contents of the C: drive's window will depend on your system. However, the window will contain icons that represent the directories and files in your C: drive. Each directory appears as a folder icon. Windows 95 uses the folder icon to represent directories because, like the file cabinet folder that organizes paper documents, a directory organizes files and other directories. To view a directory's contents, double-click on its folder icon.

In addition to the folder icons, the C: drive's window shows icons that represent files in the C: drive's root (main) directory. The icon that Windows 95 selects for a file depends on the file's type, which Windows 95 tries to determine from the file's extension. Table 7.2 shows some of the file icons you may encounter in your system's folders.

7: WORKING WITH FILES AND FOLDERS

Icon	File Extension and Description
	QIC (Microsoft Backup file)
	BAS, FRM (Microsoft Visual Basic files)
	BMP (Bitmap graphics image)
	CDA (Audio CD file)
	INI (Program settings)
	CCH, CDR, SHW (CorelDraw! files)
	SET (Microsoft Backup file sets)
	FON (Font definition)
	HLP (Online Help file)
	HT (HyperTerminal file)
	MSG (Mail message file)
	MMM (Media clip, such as sound and video clips)
	MDA, MDB (Microsoft Access file)
	XLC, XLM, XLS, XLT, XLW (Microsoft Excel files)
	MPP, MPV (Microsoft Project files)
	DOC, DOT, RTF (Microsoft Word files)
	MID, RMI (MIDI files; see Chapter 9 for a description of MIDI)
	PPT (Microsoft PowerPoint file)

Table 7.2 File icons you may encounter in a folder window. (continued on the next page)

Success with Windows 95

Icon	File Extension and Description
	REG (Registration database file)
	TXT (Text file)
	TTF (TrueType Font file)
	AVI (Video file)
	WAV (Windows sound file)
	WRI (Write document)

Table 7.2 File icons you may encounter in a folder window.(continued from the previous page)

Learning More about a File Icon

Success Hint

As you browse your system's drives and directories, there may be times when you'll want to know more about a particular file icon before you decide to double-click on it. To locate such information, perform these steps:

1. Click your right-mouse button on the file icon. Windows 95 will display a pop-up menu.

2. Select the pop-up menu's Properties option. Windows 95 will open a properties sheet that tells you the file's type, location, and size. In addition, the properties sheet will tell you when the file was created, last modified, and last accessed.

Browsing Folders the Smart Way

By default, Windows 95 opens a new window every time you double-click on a folder icon. Each open folder window is a Windows 95 task with its own Taskbar button. (For example, in Figure 7.8, you see Taskbar buttons for the My Computer window and the Windows folder.) As a result, each open folder window consumes system resources, such as memory space. In addition, a large number of open windows can quickly clutter your screen.

To conserve system resources as you browse folders, you can tell Windows 95 to reuse the same window each time you open a folder. Then, each time you double-click on a folder icon, Windows 95 will replace the window's contents with those of the folder you just opened. To enable this feature, select the View menu Options option from the My Computer window. Windows 95, in turn, will open the Options sheet shown in Figure 7.7.

As you can see in Figure 7.7, the Options sheet Folder page contains two option buttons that specify how you want to browse folders. The option button that is currently on—the default one—indicates that you want a separate window for each folder. To browse all folders in a single window, click on the other option button. Windows 95, in turn, will place a black dot inside the option button. To close the Options sheet, click on the OK button.

7: Working with Files and Folders

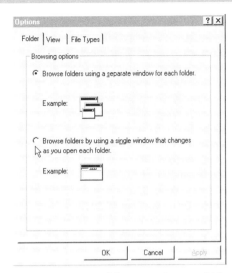

Figure 7.7 The Options sheet Folder page lets you control how you browse folders.

After you set the new browse option, double-click on the Windows folder icon in the C: drive's window (Figure 7.6). Windows 95, in turn, will replace the contents of the C: drive's window with the contents of the Windows folder, as shown in Figure 7.8.

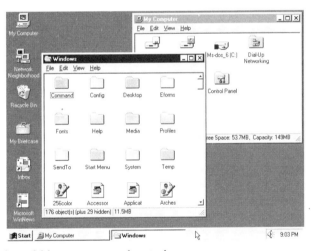

Figure 7.8 Browsing the Windows folder using a single window.

Compare the Taskbar buttons in Figure 7.8 with those in Figure 7.6. Notice that both figures show two Taskbar buttons corresponding to two open windows. As you can see, if you browse folders with a single window, Windows 95 does not create new tasks nor consume additional system resources. In addition, if you use a single window to browse folders, you'll find it easier to keep your Desktop uncluttered.

Note: *If, as a result of your search for a file, you end up with several open folder windows, you can close all the windows in one step by holding down your keyboard SHIFT-key as you close the most recent window.*

Using the Toolbar in a Folder Window

Now that you know how to browse folders with a single window, you still need to know how to perform a crucial step—returning to the parent folder. For example, suppose you open your system's Windows folder and discover other folders, such as Fonts and Cursors. To see your system's fonts, you double-click on the Fonts folder icon. Windows 95, in turn, displays the contents of the Fonts folder in the current window. At this point, if you want to see what the Cursors folder contains, you must return to the Windows folder (the parent folder of Fonts and Cursors) and double-click on the Cursors folder icon.

When you browse folders using a single window, you often must return to a parent folder—the folder from which you opened the current folder. The easiest way to return to the parent folder is to click on the folder window's toolbar Up One Level button. However, before you can do so, you must first turn on the toolbar. To make the toolbar visible, click your left-mouse button on the View category on the folder window's menu bar (see Figure 7.8). Windows 95, in turn, will display the View menu, as shown in Figure 7.9.

Figure 7.9 *When you click on the menu bar's View category, Windows 95 opens the View menu.*

Note the first two options in the View menu: Toolbar and Status Bar. The check mark next to the Status Bar option indicates that the status bar is turned on. In fact, you can see the Help message that Windows 95 displays in the status bar (at the bottom of the folder window).

Click your left-mouse button on the View menu Toolbar option (see Figure 7.9). Windows 95, in turn, will turn on this option and display the toolbar in the folder window. To view the entire toolbar, click on the folder window's Maximize button. Windows 95, in turn, will maximize the window and show you the whole toolbar, as shown in Figure 7.10.

Figure 7.10 *When you click your left-mouse button on the View menu Toolbar option, Windows 95 displays the toolbar.*

Table 7.3 summarizes the purpose of each of the folder window's toolbar buttons.

Button	Purpose
Windows ▼	Takes you to a different folder. Click on the pull-down list button to view other drives and folders in your system.
⬆	Returns you to the parent folder—the folder one level up from the current folder. (This is the Up One Level button.)
	Assigns a drive letter to a network drive.
	Disconnects a network drive.
✂	Cuts items you select from the folder window and pastes them to the Clipboard. (Click on items in the window to select them.)
	Copies items you select to the Clipboard.
	Pastes items from the Clipboard into locations you select in the window.
↶	Undoes the previous file operation.
✕	Deletes items you select from the folder window.
	Displays properties of an item you select.
	Displays items using large icons.
	Displays items using small icons.
	Displays items in a simple list.
	Displays items in a detailed list.

Table 7.3 Purpose of the folder window's Toolbar buttons.

To return to a parent folder, you click on the Up One Level button (the toolbar button that contains a picture of a folder with an arrow).

Note: *The folder window's toolbar is identical to the toolbar that the Windows Explorer uses. You will learn more about the toolbar's buttons in Chapter 16, which covers the Windows Explorer.*

VIEWING THE FULL MS-DOS NAMES

Take another look at Figure 7.10. Notice that the labels beneath the file icons display filenames without extensions. Actually, many of these files use 8.3 names. However, Windows 95, by default, does not show MS-DOS file extensions. If you are familiar with MS-DOS filenames, you may want to view extensions so you can recognize a file. For example, many programs (EXE extension) have associated settings files (INI extension) and Help files (HLP extension) that share the same name but have different extensions. When the extensions are visible, you can easily tell these files apart.

To view full MS-DOS names (including extensions), select the View menu Options option. Windows 95, in turn, will open the Options sheet (see Figure 7.7). Click on the Options sheet View tab. Windows 95, in turn, will display the Options sheet View page, as shown in Figure 7.11.

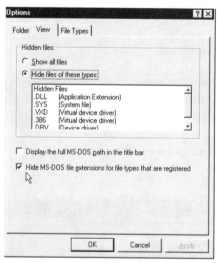

Figure 7.11 The Options sheet View page lets you turn on MS-DOS file extensions.

In Figure 7.11, notice the check box with the "Hide MS-DOS file extensions for file types that are registered" label. To direct Windows 95 to display file extensions underneath the icons, click on the check box to remove the check mark. Then, click on the Options sheet OK button. Windows 95, in turn, will close the Options sheet and update the contents of the folder window, as shown in Figure 7.12.

USING OPEN AND SAVE AS DIALOG BOXES

In previous sections, you learned how Windows 95 structures the files and directories you store on your disk. Additionally, you learned how to use the My Computer icon to browse through your system's folders. In this section, you will see how your newly acquired knowledge about the file system and Windows 95 browsing techniques will serve you each time you try to open or save a document in a Windows 95 application.

This section shows you how to use an Open or Save As dialog box that a typical Windows 95 application displays. (All Windows 95 applications use the same standard Open and Save As dialog boxes.)

7: Working with Files and Folders

Figure 7.12 The Windows folder's contents after you turn on the MS-DOS file extensions.

In Figure 7.12, you can see that full 8.3 format MS-DOS filenames now appear beneath the file icons. For example, the clock icon now has the label "Clock.exe," which is the full name of the file the clock icon represents.

Recognizing Windows 3.1 and Windows 95 Dialog Boxes

If you run a Windows 3.1 application under Windows 95, the dialog boxes you use to open and save files may appear different than the standard Windows 95 Open and Save As dialog boxes. For example, although the Windows 3.1 and Windows 95 Open dialog boxes contain many of the same text fields, these fields reside at different locations within the dialog box. Additionally, whereas Windows 3.1 Open and Save As dialog boxes use list boxes to give users access to disk drives, directories, and files, Windows 95 Open and Save As dialog boxes, by default, fulfill the same purpose by displaying icons in a central work area.

It is important that you distinguish between Windows 3.1 and Windows 95 dialog boxes because Windows 3.1 programs may not let you use long filenames.

To see the Windows 95 Open dialog box in action, start WordPad from the Start menu (follow the path *Programs> Accessories> WordPad*). After the WordPad window appears, select the window's File menu Open option. WordPad, in turn, will display the standard Windows 95 Open dialog box, as shown in Figure 7.13.

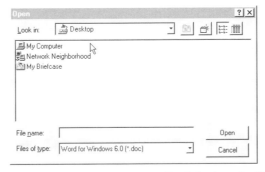

Figure 7.13 After you click on the File menu Open option, WordPad displays the Windows 95 Open dialog box.

163

When you use the Open dialog box, your first step is to find the document (file) you want to open. To do so, you must locate the appropriate drive and then browse the drive's folders. (At this point, you will apply what you learned in previous sections about browsing folders.)

Notice that the large work area that occupies most of the Open dialog box (see Figure 7.13) looks like the Desktop. In the work area, you can see the My Computer icon, as well as two other icons—Network Neighborhood and My Briefcase—that you have not used so far.

To look for a file, double-click on the My Computer icon. Windows 95, in turn, will display My Computer's contents in the Open dialog box's work area, as shown in Figure 7.14.

Compare the drives in Figure 7.14 with those in Figure 7.5. In both figures, you see My Computer's contents.

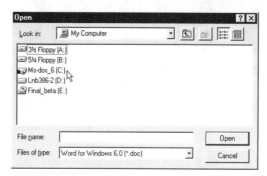

Figure 7.14 When you double-click on the My Computer icon, Windows 95 shows your system's drives.

Now, double-click on the C: drive's icon. Windows 95, in turn, will display the C: drive's contents in the Open dialog box's work area, as shown in Figure 7.15.

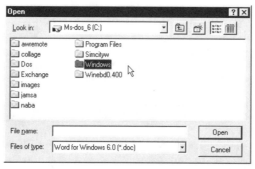

Figure 7.15 When you double-click on the C: drive's icon, Windows 95 shows the C: drive's folders.

Now, compare the Open dialog box's work area in Figure 7.15 with the C: drive's window in Figure 7.6. Notice that, although both figures show the C: drive's contents, the dialog box's work area contains fewer icons than the C: drive's window. The work area has fewer icons because the Open dialog box is set to filter files by extension. In Figure 7.15, the Files of type field at the bottom of the dialog box reads "Word for Windows 6.0 (*.doc)." As a result, the dialog box's work area shows only files with the ".doc" extension. To change the types of files the Open dialog box displays, click your mouse on the Files of type pull-down list button and select a new filter parameter. For example, if you select the All files (*.*) option, the dialog box will display all the files and subfolders the current folder contains.

Next, compare the Open dialog box's toolbar, which appears in the dialog box's upper-right corner, with the folder window's toolbar (see Figure 7.10). As you can see, the dialog box's toolbar and the folder window's toolbar have some of the same buttons. As such, you can navigate through the folders in the Open dialog box the same way you move through folders in the folder window (see Figure 7.10). Using the dialog box's toolbar buttons, you can move up one folder, create a new folder, or connect to a network drive. In addition, you can use the toolbar buttons to control how the Open dialog box displays files and directories (as labeled icons or detailed list items) in the work area.

When you locate the file you want to open, simply click on the file's icon. Windows 95, in turn, will copy that filename into the Open dialog box's File name field. Then, to open the file, click on the OK button.

You use the Save As dialog box much the same way as you use the Open dialog box. (Both dialog boxes share the same basic structure and display the same toolbar buttons.) However, when you use the Save As dialog box, you don't browse your system's folders to locate a file. Rather, you browse to find a folder into which you will place the current document. When you find the folder you want, you double-click on its icon, specify the document's name in the File name field, and click your mouse on the Save button.

To use the Save As dialog box, select the program window's (in this case, WordPad's) File menu Save As option. The program, in turn, will display the Save As dialog box, as shown in Figure 7.16.

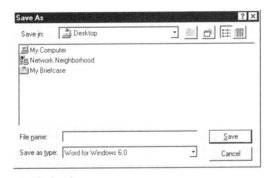

Figure 7.16 The Windows 95 Save As dialog box.

As you can see, the Save As dialog box differs from the Open dialog box (see Figure 7.13) in the following ways:

- The Save As dialog box has a Save button in place of the Open button.
- The Save As dialog box has a Save in field rather than a Look in field. After you find the folder into which you want to save your document, you double-click on the folder's icon. The folder's name then appears in the Save in field.
- The Save As dialog box has a Save as type field instead of a Files of type field.

CREATING A NEW FOLDER FROM THE SAVE AS DIALOG BOX

As you have learned, folders help you organize the files you store on your disk. When you use the Save As dialog box to store a file, there may be times when you want to create a new folder into which you can store the file. On such occasions, click on the Create New Folder button. (The Create New Folder button, which appears on the dialog box's toolbar, contains an icon of a folder with a star at its corner.) Windows 95, in turn, will create a new folder inside the current folder.

Keys to Success

In this chapter, you learned how Windows 95 organizes and represents your system's directories and files. In addition, you discovered several ways you can locate, retrieve, and store files. In Chapter 8, you will switch gears and learn about something new—Microsoft's online service, The Microsoft Network. However, before you move on to Chapter 8, make sure you understand the following key concepts:

- ✓ Windows 95 has a file system with a root directory for each drive. Underneath each root directory, Windows 95 organizes a tree structure of directories and files.

- ✓ A directory can hold other directories or files.

- ✓ Windows 95 stores programs and documents in files.

- ✓ Windows 95 displays directories as folders.

- ✓ MS-DOS uses the "8.3" file-naming convention, which lets MS-DOS users include up to eight characters in a file's name and up to three characters in its extension (for example, AUTOEXEC.BAT).

- ✓ Windows 95 lets you use up to 255 characters and include embedded spaces in a filename (for example, "My trip to the South of France").

- ✓ The Windows 95 file system retains backward compatibility with MS-DOS so that you can use Windows 95 files with long filenames in an MS-DOS or Windows 3.1 system.

- ✓ You can view folders and files through the Desktop's My Computer icon.

- ✓ Most Windows 95 programs use the Open and Save As dialog boxes to let you select a file to open or save.

Chapter 8
Using the Microsoft Network (MSN)

So far, you have learned how to start programs, work with windows and dialog boxes, customize hardware, and browse the folders and files in your Windows 95 system. However, you have not yet learned how to use Windows 95 to take you out on the information highway. If Windows 95 were a car, it is as if you've learned everything about the car—how to drive, how to steer, even how to change the oil—but haven't driven it anywhere yet.

In this chapter, you will learn how to use the Microsoft Network (MSN)—Microsoft's online service, which comes with Windows 95—to "go places." No, MSN can't physically transport you to other cities and countries, but it can help you contact people and access information at locations around the globe. For example, assume you live in Eugene, Oregon and have a child attending college in Cambridge, Massachusetts. When you want to contact your child, you can use MSN to send him or her e-mail messages, which cost less than long-distance phone calls and usually arrive sooner than conventional letters. Or, if you have a child at home that needs help writing a report for school (on rain forests, for example), you can find research material (such as descriptions of tropical plants, pictures of animals, and charts that illustrate the rain forest ecosystem) for him or her in MSN's Education and Reference category.

If you are not at all familiar with online services, do not despair. This chapter will introduce you to MSN and give you step-by-step instructions on how to use it effectively. By the time you finish this chapter, you will understand the following key concepts:

- An online service provides you with worldwide electronic-mail (e-mail) access, the ability to chat with other users, and up-to-date information on domestic and international events, sports, entertainment, and much more.

- The Microsoft Network (MSN) is Microsoft's online network to which you can connect using Windows 95.

- To use the Microsoft Network, you must subscribe. Like all online services, the Microsoft Network charges you a monthly subscription fee.

- Microsoft Network organizes its information using folders that match those you use under Windows 95. To traverse the Microsoft Network, you simply move from one folder to the next.

- Using MSN, you can exchange electronic mail with users worldwide, including users on the Internet.

- MSN provides you with direct access to the such Internet features as newsgroups, mailing lists, and the World Wide Web.

- Using MSN chat groups, you can talk (actually type) online with other users.

MSN—An Online Service

In this section, you will learn the basic concepts behind all online services, including MSN. If you have used other online services (such as CompuServe, America Online, Prodigy, GEnie, MCI Mail, or Delphi), some of the material that follows will not be new to you. However, if you have never used an online service, this section will give you the information you need to start your travels down the information highway.

What Is an Online Service

Think of an online service as a shopping center with a variety of stores, a well-stocked library, a post office, and lots of gathering places. However, you don't have to get in your car to reach an online service, nor do you have to worry about what time it closes. Anytime you want, day or night, you access an online service right from your desk. All you have to do is double-click your mouse on an icon on your computer's screen.

You might wonder about the benefits of the commercial online services. For starters, all online services let you send mail electronically. Electronic mail (or e-mail, for short) is convenient because you can send and read mail anytime, and e-mail usually arrives sooner than letters the Postal Service delivers.

Another benefit of an online service is access to information. If you are a "sports junkie," you can get the latest scores and highlights anytime you want. If you are a salesperson or marketing professional, you can gather demographic information (income levels, educational background, and so on) about a region's population. If you invest in the stock market, you can track your portfolio's value and look for news about companies in which you plan to invest (information that can help you decide when to buy or sell a stock). In short, online services offer you "information at your fingertips."

Online services also let you access the Internet, which links thousands of computer networks around the world in a single, loosely-connected, global information system. Prior to the Internet, each online service was an island unto itself. If you wanted to send e-mail to someone, the other party had to subscribe to the same online service as you did. Now, with the Internet, you can communicate with anyone on any online service (or any other computer on the Internet).

Note: One of the first things to remember about online services is that they will cost you money. Just as you pay for goods and services at the stores in a shopping center, you will have to pay for the privilege of convenient access to information that an online service offers.

Although each online service presents its services to you in a unique manner, they all use a graphical interface. As such, to initiate actions (look for information, send mail, read a bulletin board, and so on) in most online services, you will click your mouse on icons and buttons that appear on your screen. Because the best way to understand an online service is simply to use it, this chapter will take you on a guided tour of MSN, Microsoft's online service.

As you will see in the rest of this chapter, MSN is like other online services. MSN lets you send e-mail, access information, read messages from bulletin boards, and access the Internet. However, if you don't currently subscribe to an online service, MSN does offer you something the other services cannot—an online service you can access using your system's current software. Microsoft built the MSN installation software right into your Windows 95 system. To subscribe to another service, you will need to send away for its installation disk.

Mechanics of Getting Online

Before your MSN tour begins, you might find it helpful to know the typical steps you must perform to get online. That way, you can make sure your computer is ready for MSN, and also learn what you must do to join other online services. At a minimum, you need the following items to access any online service:

- You need a modem and a phone line with which your computer communicates with the online service's computer.

- You need online-service software that runs on your computer. The software differs from one online service to another. As previously discussed, Windows 95 includes MSN's software.

- You will need a credit-card number to pay for the benefits of joining the online service. Usually, you must have a credit card to sign up with an online service.

8: USING THE MICROSOFT NETWORK

MODEMS AND PHONE LINES

To use an online service, your computer must exchange data over telephone lines with the online service's computer. Before you can subscribe to MSN or any other online service, your system must have a modem. When you select a modem (internal or external) for use with online services, you must consider how fast the modem transfers data. Many online services, including MSN, provide information using multimedia (which uses images and sound). As you learned in Chapter 5, such information is much more voluminous than simple text data, and thus takes longer to transmit. As such, you'll want to get the fastest modem you can buy.

Note: *As of this writing, the fastest standard modems are the 28.8Kbps (that means 28,800 bits per second or 28,800 bps) V.34 modems. However, the most popular modems are the V.32bis 14.4Kbps modems. The terms V.34 and V.32bis refer to international standards for modems.*

As you have learned, when two modems communicate, they must operate at the same speed. Thus, if you have a 28,800 bps modem and the online service provider offers only 9600 bps modems, both modems will communicate at 9600 bps. As such, if you plan to purchase a new modem but can't afford the fastest available model, find out your online service's data transmission speed. That way, you can purchase only as much modem speed as you need. However, if money is not an issue, you may want to buy the fastest possible modem anyway. Although many online services support only 14,400 bps modems, it's only a matter of time before 28,800 bps modems become the norm.

As you learned in Chapter 5, Windows 95 makes modem installation easy. To install a modem, all you must do is physically install the device and order Windows 95 to detect it. Windows 95, in turn, automatically detects the modem's manufacturer, model, and essential parameters (speed, parity, number of stop bits, and so on). To connect a phone line to your modem, you simply run a line from the modem to a phone jack. If you get hooked on online services, you may spend much time browsing bulletin boards or downloading files. In that case, if you share a phone line with others and wish to avoid hogging the phone, you may want to install a second line just for your computer to access the online service.

SOFTWARE

As you have learned, to connect to an online service, you need a modem and a phone line. In addition, your system needs software that contains the online service's graphical interface and sends your requests (for example, to read e-mail or download a file) to the online service's computer. Typically, your online service provider (like America Online or CompuServe) sends you a diskette that contains this software. During setup, the software also configures the phone connection by asking you information such as your phone number and modem type. As previously mentioned, Windows 95 already includes all the software you need to connect to MSN. However, the MSN software is not installed by default. You have to install that software before you can use MSN.

Note: *The "Adding Windows 95 Components" section in Chapter 6 describes how to add the MSN software to Windows 95.*

CREDIT CARD

All online services are for-profit businesses that expect you to pay for the use of their services. The first time you connect to an online service, the service's software will ask you for a credit card number. If you do not have a credit card or prefer not to use one, most services offer ways you can sign up and pay with a check. However, if you are in a hurry to join an online service, you will need a credit card number.

SIGNING UP FOR MSN

Now that you know how online services work, you're probably anxious to begin your MSN tour. If you have never used an online service, you might give MSN a try, because your Windows 95 system has everything ready-to-go for MSN. Later on, if you decide not to use MSN, you can always call MSN's customer service and cancel your membership.

Note: *If you currently subscribe to another online service (such as CompuServe or America Online), you can still take this MSN tour.*

Before you can even sign up for MSN, your system must have a modem installed (see Chapter 5 for instructions). Also, make sure that you have installed the MSN software (see Chapter 6 for details). To see if your system has MSN installed, click your mouse on the Start button and move the mouse pointer on to the Programs option. Windows 95, in turn, will display the Programs menu, as shown in Figure 8.1.

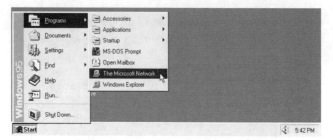

Figure 8.1 *If MSN is installed on your system, the Programs menu has The Microsoft Network option.*

If MSN is installed in your Windows 95 system, the Programs menu will include The Microsoft Network option. To sign up for MSN, click your left-mouse button on the Programs menu The Microsoft Network option. Windows 95, in turn, will start the MSN sign-up process and display the window shown in Figure 8.2.

Figure 8.2 *Initial window for MSN sign-up.*

Click on the OK button. The MSN sign-up program, in turn, will display the dialog box shown in Figure 8.3.

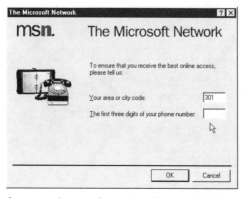

Figure 8.3 *Dialog box that asks you for your phone information during MSN sign-up.*

In the dialog box of Figure 8.3, enter the first three digits of your phone number. (The MSN sign-up program retrieves your area code from the information you provided when you installed your modem.) Then, click on the OK button to continue the sign-up. The MSN sign-up program, in turn, will display some information in the dialog box, as shown in Figure 8.4.

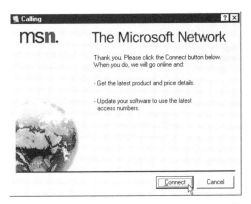

Figure 8.4 Dialog box that asks your permission to connect to MSN and get information needed during sign-up.

The MSN sign-up program now wants to dial up and connect to MSN so it can retrieve a list of access numbers appropriate for your location. An access number is a local telephone number that your system's MSN software dials to connect to the MSN service. Because your access number is normally a local phone call, you will not incur phone charges when you use MSN. Click on the Connect button to proceed. The MSN sign-up software, in turn, will connect to MSN, transfer some information necessary for sign-up, and display the dialog box shown in Figure 8.5

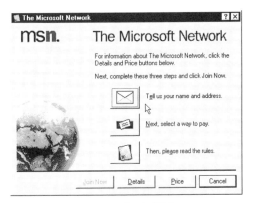

Figure 8.5 Dialog box that requests information necessary for MSN sign-up.

Before you can join MSN, you will have to complete three steps:

1. Provide your name, address, and phone number.
2. Provide a credit card number to pay for your MSN membership.
3. Read and accept the MSN member agreement.

The three buttons in the dialog box of Figure 8.5 let you perform these steps. Notice the grayed-out Join Now button near the dialog box's bottom edge. After you complete the three steps, the Join Now button will become active, and you will be able to join MSN.

Click on the first button labeled, "Tell us your name and address." The MSN sign-up program, in turn, will display a dialog box, as shown in Figure 8.6.

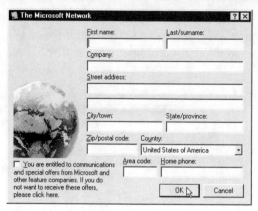

Figure 8.6 Dialog box where you provide your name and address during MSN sign-up.

Enter the requested information and click on the OK button. The MSN sign-up program, in turn, will return you to the dialog box of Figure 8.5. Because you have completed the first step, the sign-up program will place a check mark next to the first button. Next, click on the second button labeled, "Next, select a way to pay" (see Figure 8.5). The MSN sign-up program, in turn, will display a dialog box that shows a list of acceptable credit card names. Click on the credit card you want to use. The MSN sign-up program, in turn, will prompt you for credit card information, as shown in Figure 8.7.

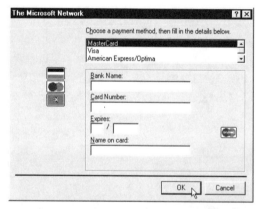

Figure 8.7 Dialog box that prompts you for credit card information during MSN sign-up.

After you fill in the Bank Name, Card Number, Expires, and Name on card fields, click on the OK button. In response, the MSN sign-up program will again display the dialog box of Figure 8.5. Click on the third button labeled, "Then, please read the rules," in the dialog box shown in Figure 8.5. The MSN sign-up program, in turn, will display a dialog box with the MSN membership agreement. To scroll down and read the agreement, use the scroll bar on the right side of the dialog box. If you decide to accept the membership agreement, and you must if you want to use MSN, click on the I Agree button. The MSN sign-up program, in turn, will display a dialog box from which you can join, display additional information about MSN, get MSN pricing, or cancel your signup. At this point, click on the Join Now button and finish your sign-up process.

The MSN sign-up program, in turn, will send your sign-up information to MSN's computer. Additionally, the sign-up program will ask for a member ID (this is the name by which people will know you online) and a password. Pick a meaningful name for your username. If your name, for example, is William Clinton, you might choose the username BClinton. You want to pick a username others can easily remember. Next, choose a password that others won't guess but that you can easily remember. You want to keep your password private because your password prevents others from connecting to MSN as you. If you like canoeing, for example, you might choose the password Whitewater. After you successfully join MSN, Windows 95 will display the Microsoft Network icon on your Desktop, as shown in Figure 8.8.

Figure 8.8 *The Microsoft Network icon appears on the Desktop after you join MSN.*

WHAT DOES MSN COST

The cost of going online varies from one service to another. Of course, with so many online services (such as America Online, CompuServe, and now MSN), there is considerable competition for your business. Most online services offer access for a flat monthly fee (generally around $10-15 per month). However, many services limit the number of hours you can connect to their computer for that flat fee. If you exceed the hour limit, the service will charge you on a per-hour basis. Also, many online companies charge extra fees for additional services, such as news summaries or demographic reports.

A GUIDED TOUR OF MSN

The previous sections showed you how to sign up for MSN and explained what you might expect to pay for MSN. After you join MSN, you can begin your MSN tour at any time. (It will probably take you at least thirty minutes to check out some of MSN's most interesting features.) To start your MSN tour, double-click on the Desktop's The Microsoft Network icon (see Figure 8.8). Windows 95, in turn, will open the MSN Sign In dialog box, as shown in Figure 8.9.

Figure 8.9 *After you double-click on The Microsoft Network icon, Windows 95 displays the MSN Sign In dialog box.*

In the MSN Sign In dialog box, type your member ID and the password. As you type your password, the window will display an asterisk (*) for each character you type. As discussed, you should keep your password private. By displaying an asterisk for each letter of your password, the window prevents another user from reading your password. If you want MSN to remember your password to simplify your future sign-ins, click on the Remember my password check box until a check mark appears. Then, click on the Connect button. The MSN program, in turn, will dial your local access number, which MSN set up when you first signed up for MSN. If the number is busy, the MSN program will dial a second local access number. After the MSN program establishes a connection, MSN will verify your member ID and password. Provided you have typed your username and password correctly, you will be online with MSN.

Starting MSN

The first time you connect to MSN, Microsoft greets you with several welcome messages. Take time to read each message MSN displays on your screen—the messages may contain tips that you can use to better "get around" MSN. Eventually, after you traverse the welcome messages, MSN will display its main window, which MSN refers to as MSN Central, as shown in Figure 8.10.

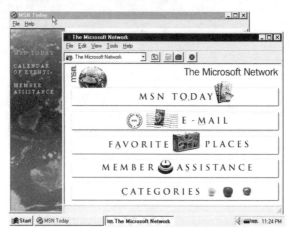

Figure 8.10 *MSN's main window, better known as "MSN Central."*

Browsing MSN is quite similar to browsing the folders on your system's hard-disk drive. In both cases, you double-click on icons to move through folders of information. However, because all your MSN communications must travel over telephone lines, you can't move through MSN as quickly as you can through the folders on your hard disk. A typical MSN connection can transfer data at only 9,600 or 14,400 bits per second (keep in mind that typically eight bits make up a character, so you get somewhat over a thousand characters per second).

The large buttons in Home Base's work area let you access different parts (or *areas*) of MSN. (Microsoft uses the term *area* to encourage us to view MSN as a place that contains many resources you can use, like a shopping mall that has many shops and boutiques you can visit.) Using these buttons, you can perform the following tasks:

- Find out about today's news and upcoming MSN events.
- Send or receive e-mail.
- Get assistance (in case you have problems with MSN).
- Browse the contents of MSN.

In the following sections, you will use the Home Base buttons to visit MSN areas. Note, however, that this tour will focus primarily on teaching you how to navigate through MSN. As such, you will examine only MSN's major features. Later on, you can explore MSN at your leisure and discover all that the online service has to offer.

MSN Today

The first Home Base button is MSN Today. When you click your mouse on the MSN Today button, MSN will display an electronic newspaper that describes today's events, similar to that shown in Figure 8.11.

8: Using the Microsoft Network

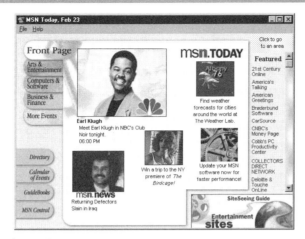

Figure 8.11 The MSN Today electronic newspaper.

Using MSN Today, you can get the latest world and domestic news, information about sports and finance, and much more. To display information on an MSN Today topic, simply click your mouse on the front-page topic. MSN, in turn, will open a window that contains the MSN Today front page, as shown in Figure 8.12.

Figure 8.12 Displaying the MSN Today front page.

Next, click your mouse on the article you desire. MSN, in turn, will display a detailed article within a window. To print the article's contents, click your mouse on the printer icon that appears within the window's toolbar. After you are done reading the article, you can close its window by clicking your mouse on the Close button.

Understanding How MSN Draws Images

When MSN draws an image (such as a picture in the MSN Today window), it doesn't present the entire image at one time. Instead, MSN draws the image in several passes. Initially, MSN draws a fuzzy (low resolution) version of the image. Then, in subsequent passes, MSN gradually fills in the image's details. To you, the whole effect is similar to looking through a camera lens as you bring an image into focus. MSN draws an image in several passes to give the appearance of faster response. If MSN didn't display anything until the image was complete, a long time might pass between when you click the MSN Today button and the moment the image finally appears on your screen.

If you examine the MSN Today window, you will find a Calendar of Events tab. Click your mouse on the tab to learn more about upcoming MSN events. MSN, in turn, will open a window within which it displays its calendar of events as shown in Figure 8.13.

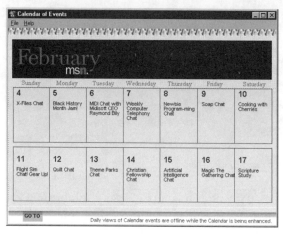

Figure 8.13 The MSN Calendar of events.

After you view the events, click your mouse on the Close button to close the events window. Next, close the MSN Today window to return to MSN Central.

Taking Advantage of Member Assistance

As you travel the Microsoft Network, you will encounter many cool features that you will want to try out. If you have questions regarding a feature, you can normally find an answer within the Member Assistance folder. To view MSN Member Assistance topics, click your mouse on the MSN Central Member Assistance button. MSN, in turn, will display the Member Assistance folder shown in Figure 8.14.

Figure 8.14 The Member Assistance folder.

Within the Member Assistance folder, you can find help on all aspects of MSN. To access specific information on a topic, open the corresponding folder. Within each folder, you will find icons you can click on using your mouse to display help text. As you view the text, you may want to print a copy of the text so that you can refer to it at a later time.

8: Using the Microsoft Network

> **MSN Is Like a Fancy Hotel**
>
>
>
> Microsoft encourages you to think of the MSN online service as a physical place, much like a fancy hotel with its own lobby, help desk, guest lounge, and other amenities. For example, just as many fancy hotels have a help desk where you can obtain the information you need (where to get your clothes dry cleaned, which restaurants to visit and which to avoid, how to get to Bridger Avenue and Main Street, and so on) to make your trip successful and enjoyable, MSN has a Member Assistance area where you can get advice and suggestions that will help you navigate MSN more efficiently and locate the areas you wish to visit more easily. Likewise, just as you can converse with fellow guests in a fancy hotel's guest lounge, you can have online conversations with other MSN members in the MSN Member Lounge. Each of these MSN areas appears in a window with images, texts, and icons that you can click. To move around MSN, use the techniques you learned in Chapter 7 when you browsed through your hard disk's folders.

Online Help in MSN

In addition to the Member Assistance area, MSN provides you with another good source of helpful information—the MSN online Help system. In Chapter 4, "Using Online Help," you learned how to navigate the Windows 95 online Help system. Now you can use that knowledge to get the assistance you need from MSN's online Help.

To access the MSN online Help system, click on the Help menu Help Topics option. MSN, in turn, will open the Help Topics sheet with online Help information for MSN. Use the techniques you learned in Chapter 4 to navigate around MSN's online Help. For example, click on the "Introducing The Microsoft Network" topic to view subtopics and topic pages, as shown in Figure 8.15.

Figure 8.15 *You can access MSN's online Help topic sheet from the MSN window's Help menu.*

To see the "What you can do on MSN" topic page, click on the topic page icon and then click on the Display button. The MSN online Help system, in turn, will open the selected topic page in a window, as shown in Figure 8.16.

Notice the underlined word *services* in Figure 8.16. As discussed in Chapter 4, when you click your left-mouse button on the underlined word, the Help system will display the word's definition in a pop-up window.

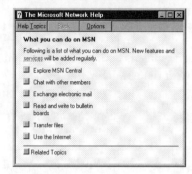

Figure 8.16 MSN's online Help showing "What you can do on MSN."

E-Mail

When they arrive at the office, the first thing many people do (besides turning on their computers) is check electronic mail (e-mail). E-mail messages bring them notes from colleagues, instructions from the boss, the week's calendar for important meetings, an announcement of the upcoming company picnic, and more.

In addition, for many people, much of a day's work activity involves sending and receiving e-mail messages. For example, in the morning, an e-mail message from your boss might instruct you to drop everything and work on that month's progress report. During the day, you might use e-mail to request information from associates across the nation and around the world. Finally, at the end of the day, you might submit the report to your boss as an attachment to an e-mail message.

So many people find e-mail indispensable that it is the staple of all online services. Like all popular online services, MSN lets you send and receive e-mail. MSN uses another Windows 95 component, Microsoft Exchange, to handle e-mail operations. In a nutshell, Microsoft Exchange is a message center where you can read or send messages via e-mail or fax. Although you won't examine Microsoft Exchange in depth until Chapter 17, "Using Explorer for Faxes and E-Mail," you will see some of its features in this section.

To send e-mail from MSN or read e-mail, click on the MSN Central E-Mail button. MSN, in turn, will start Microsoft Exchange, which will open a window, as shown in Figure 8.17. For more instruction on Microsoft Exchange, turn to Chapter 17.

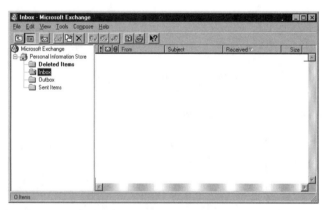

Figure 8.17 When you click on the MSN Central E-Mail button, the Microsoft Exchange window appears.

As you have learned, each time you wish to connect to MSN, you must sign in. Often, after you sign in, you will find new e-mail messages waiting for you. (Even after you first sign in, you might find some welcome messages from the Microsoft Online Staff.) If you happen to have any new e-mail, MSN displays a message box to tell you so. In addition, the message box asks you if you want to open your Inbox, as shown in Figure 8.18.

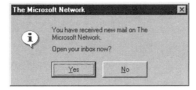

Figure 8.18 If you have new e-mail, MSN informs you with a message when you sign in.

To read your new e-mail messages, click on the Yes button. MSN, in turn, will start Microsoft Exchange, which will open a window and display the Inbox's contents. As Microsoft Exchange starts, it also detects that you have new mail and displays a dialog box, as shown in Figure 8.19.

Figure 8.19 If you have new e-mail, Microsoft Exchange asks you if you want to read it.

To read the new mail, click on the Yes button. Microsoft Exchange, in turn, will open a new window and use it to display one of the new messages, as shown in Figure 8.20.

Figure 8.20 Microsoft Exchange displays a new mail message in a window.

To print your message, select the File menu Print option. After you read a message, click on the Close button. In response, Microsoft Exchange will close the message window and display your Inbox's contents in another window, as shown in Figure 8.21.

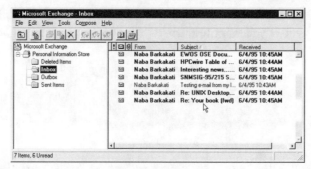

Figure 8.21 Microsoft Exchange displays your Inbox in a window.

Look at the Microsoft Exchange window's left side. Notice how Microsoft Exchange organizes your incoming and outgoing messages in a way similar to how Windows 95 orders files and folders on your system's hard disk. All messages are in the Personal Information Store folder, which contains four separate folders:

- The Deleted Items folder stores messages that you have deleted. (You can set up Microsoft Exchange so that it empties the Deleted Items folder when you exit Exchange. To set this option, select the Tools menu Options option and turn on the appropriate check box in the Deleting Items section.)
- The Inbox folder holds your incoming mail and faxes.
- The Outbox folder holds messages that you have prepared but not sent out yet.
- The Sent Items folder stores messages that you have sent out.

In Figure 8.21, the Inbox folder is open and its contents appear on the Microsoft Exchange window's right side. Your unread messages will appear in boldface. To read a message, simply double-click on its corresponding Inbox list item. Microsoft Exchange, in turn, will open a new window that shows the message's contents.

SENDING AN E-MAIL MESSAGE

To send a message from MSN, click on the MSN Central E-Mail button. MSN, in turn, will start Microsoft Exchange. Then, click on the Compose category in the Microsoft Exchange window's menu bar. Microsoft Exchange, in turn, will display the Compose menu, as shown in Figure 8.22.

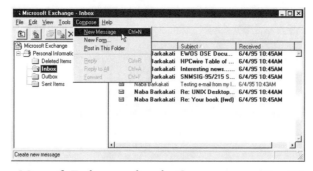

Figure 8.22 To send mail from Microsoft Exchange, select the Compose menu New Message option.

Finally, click your left-mouse button on the Compose menu New Message option. Microsoft Exchange, in turn, will open a message composition window. In the message composition window To field, type the e-mail address of your message's recipient. In the Cc field, enter the addresses of everyone you want to receive a copy of the message. In the Subject field, type a short description of the message's contents. And in the window's work area, you prepare the body of the message.

As an example, I have composed a message to an address at Microsoft that maintains a mailing list of people interested in news about Windows 95. A mailing list is simply a list of e-mail addresses of users who are interested in specific topics. You can add your name to e-mail lists that discuss sports, medicine, Windows 95, and much, much more. Members of a list exchange e-mail messages that discuss the corresponding topic. To subscribe to this WinNews mailing list, all you have to do is send the message shown in Figure 8.23.

Figure 8.23 When you click on the Compose menu New Message option, Microsoft Exchange displays a message composition window.

Note: If you want to send e-mail to a friend at another Internet address, enter the user's Internet address in the message composition window To field. If you want friends on other Internet computers to send you e-mail, tell them to address mail to [your member ID]@msn.com.

To send the message you have just composed, select the message composition window's File menu Send option. After you send a message, Microsoft Exchange will keep a record of your message in your Sent Items folder. Should you ever need to refer back to your message, you can find a copy within the Sent Items folder. To exit Microsoft Exchange, click your mouse the Close button to close the Exchange window.

Browsing MSN Areas the Smart Way

By default, when you go to a new area, MSN opens a new window on your Desktop. As a result, if you browse many areas during an MSN session, your Desktop may become cluttered with windows. Furthermore, each window you open consumes some of your system's memory space and processing power. As a result, the more windows you have open, the slower your system's MSN program will function. To remedy this problem, you can simply tell MSN to replace the contents of the current window (rather than open a new window) each time you visit a new area.

As you learned in the "Browsing Folders the Smart Way" section of Chapter 7, the View menu Options option lets you tell Windows 95 to display all folders in a single window, rather than opening a separate window for each new folder. In a similar way, you can use the View menu Options option to make MSN display all the areas you visit, within a single window. The examples in this chapter use the single window option.

Saving an Area in the Favorite Places

As you move through MSN, there may be times when you'll want to save a specific MSN area so that you can visit that area again without having to look for it. In such cases, you can add the area to your Favorite Places folder. After you do so, you can visit the area by clicking your mouse on the MSN Central Favorite Places button, and then double-clicking the area's icon in the Favorite Places folder.

For example, if you want to visit the Education and Reference category Reference area frequently, you can add the Reference area to your Favorite Places folder by performing these steps:

1. Double-click on the MSN Central Categories button. MSN will open the Categories folder.
2. Double-click on the Education and Reference icon. MSN will open the Education and Reference folder.
3. Double-click on the Reference icon. MSN will open the Reference folder.
4. Click on the Reference folder's File menu Add to Favorite Places option.

VISITING A CHAT AREA

Each of us has a different style when it comes to communicating with others. Some of us like to take everything slow and easy. We write letters to give our communications the personal touch, and then mail them out without much sense of urgency. Others who want a more rapid response send notes through e-mail. Still others, who prefer even more immediate, interactive contact, pick up the telephone. If you are someone who prefers the phone over all other letters and e-mail messages, you will probably enjoy spending time in MSN's chat area. In the chat area, you can have a virtual conversation with other MSN members in real-time. When you "chat" online, you can type in whatever you want to say, and all other parties in the conversation see your words appear on their display screens.

In MSN's chat areas, one or more hosts facilitate the conversation. (Later in this chapter, you will learn how to become a host.) You can either participate or observe. Participants can contribute to the conversation, while observers merely read what others are saying. Some chat areas may control whether you are a participant or an observer. However, most of the time you can choose the role—participant or observer—you want to play.

During your first few online chats, you may find the seemingly random text that scrolls by your system's chat window a bit disconcerting. As such, when you first enter an online conversation, you may want just to observe for a while. Then, if you feel like joining in, you can respond to any questions being posed, or post a comment or question of your own.

UNDERSTANDING THE CONVERSATIONAL DYNAMICS OF AN ONLINE CHAT

Online chats differ from face-to-face conversations in a significant way—in an online chat, you cannot see the people with whom you are "speaking." When you speak with someone face-to-face, you can decide what to say based on the other person's physical reactions (body language and facial expressions) to your previous statements. In addition, face-to-face conversations often have built-in pauses that signal when the next person may speak. Online conversations have no such cues. Everyone "talks" at once. As a result, chats can be very confusing. One way to participate more effectively in a chat is simply to observe for a while and then carefully pick the moments you choose to contribute to the discussion.

As you converse online, keep in mind that anyone can listen in on your conversation. Furthermore, you will not know the exact identities of all the conversation's participants and observers (MSN displays their member IDs, not their full names). As such, you may want to avoid discussing any confidential information in an online chat.

On MSN, you will find numerous chat sessions that continue 24 hours a day. To participate in an online chat, select the MSN Central Categories buttons. MSN, in turn, will display the Categories folder shown in Figure 8.24.

8: Using the Microsoft Network

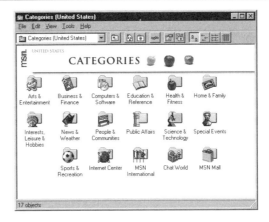

Figure 8.24 The Categories folder.

Within the Categories folder, locate and open the Chat World folder. MSN, in turn, will open the Chat World folder, as shown in Figure 8.25, that contains folders that correspond to various chat sessions you can join.

Figure 8.25 The Chat World folder.

Within the Chat World folder, double-click your mouse on the icon that corresponds to the chat you want to join. Depending on the chat you select, a second folder may appear within which you select a specific chat session. When you select the chat you desire, MSN will display a chat window similar to that shown in Figure 8.26.

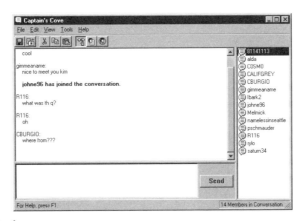

Figure 8.26 An MSN chat window.

As you can see, the top-left portion of a chat window shows what people are saying (actually, typing). The list box on the chat window's right side shows the MSN member IDs of everyone in the chat area. The icon in front of each member ID denotes whether the member is a participant or a host. The gavel (wooden hammer) icon identifies the hosts.

As soon as you join the conversation, the chat window displays a line of text that announces your presence, and the chat area's current host (the Member Lounge chat area has a host) welcomes you. To "talk," you have to first type in your message in the lower-left portion of the chat window, as shown in Figure 8.27.

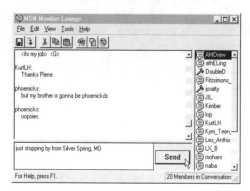

Figure 8.27 To "talk," first prepare the text in the lower-left portion of the chat window.

To send the text, click on the Send button. MSN, in turn, will transmit the text to the MSN computer, and other members will see the message in the upper-left portion of their chat windows. Because you are a participant in the chat, what you "say" also appears in your chat window, as shown in Figure 8.28.

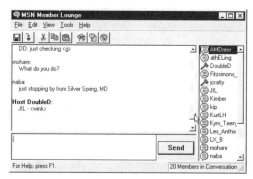

Figure 8.28 When you send your message, all chat participants will see your text in their chat windows.

To exit the chat area, click your mouse on the chat window Close button.

Using a Bulletin Board

Just about everywhere you go, people use bulletin boards to post messages which others will read and respond to. For example, in work situations, employers often post schedules, status reports, and policy changes on bulletin boards, while employees typically tack up solicitations ("Want to adopt three stray aardvarks?") and announcements ("Come One, Come All to J. Alfred Prufrock's retirement party! Please RSVP").

Electronic bulletin boards operate on the same principle as physical bulletin boards. Anyone can post a message on an electronic bulletin board, and MSN members can read and post responses to such messages. Typically, on an electronic bulletin board, members post messages to ask questions, respond to queries, offer opinions, and share files. Although most of MSN's bulletin boards are public, there can be private ones as well. Additionally, some bulletin boards are read-only—you can read, but not post responses to, their messages.

8: Using the Microsoft Network

Electronic bulletin boards differ from e-mail in that anyone can read a bulletin board message that you post. In contrast, your e-mail messages reach only those persons you specifically designate as recipients. Electronic bulletin boards differ from chat areas because bulletin boards are not set up for real-time communication.

Note: Depending on the online service to which you subscribe, electronic bulletin boards may be referred to as message boards, newsgroups, forums, or discussion groups.

The best way to understand MSN bulletin boards is to try one out. In this case, you will use the Members-to-Members bulletin board on which users exchange information about MSN. To display the Members-to-Members bulletin board, perform these steps:

1. Select the MSN Central Member Assistance button. MSN will open the Member Assistance folder.

2. Within the Member Assistance folder, select Member Support. MSN will display the Member Support folder.

3. Within the Member Support folder, click your mouse on the MSN Members-to-Members icon. MSN, in turn, will display the MSN Members-to-Members bulletin board, as shown in Figure 8.29.

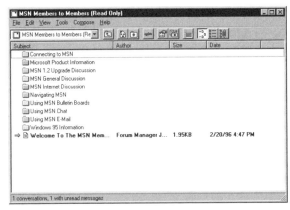

Figure 8.29 The MSN Members-to-Members bulletin board.

4. Click on the folder of the bulletin-board topic that interests you, such as Internet Discussion. MSN, in turn, will display a window of user postings similar to that shown in Figure 8.30.

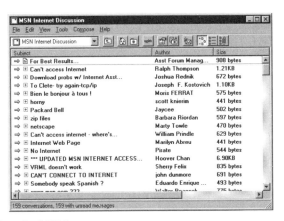

Figure 8.30 Bulletin-board postings in MSN.

To view a user posting, double-click your mouse on the posting's icon. MSN, in turn, will display the posting's text within a window. To post a message to the bulletin-board, select the Compose menu New Message option. MSN, in turn, will open a New Message window. In the New Message window Subject field, enter your message's subject. Then, in the window's work area, type your message's text. After you finish composing the message, select the New Message window's File menu Post Message option to post the message.

FAVORITE PLACES

If you use MSN extensively, you will find some places that you visit regularly. Depending on your interests, these places may be scattered around MSN. As such, you may find it tedious to browse folders each time you want to travel from one favorite place to another. To shorten trips to your favorite MSN areas, you can add shortcut icons to them in MSN's Favorite Places folder. Earlier in this chapter, you learned how to add a location to the Favorite Places list. (Select the area window's File menu Add to Favorite Places option.) When you add a location to the Favorite Places folder, MSN adds a shortcut icon that represents the location to the folder. To visit the location, you simply double-click its shortcut icon. To see the contents of the Favorite Places folder, click on Home Base's Favorite Places button. MSN, in turn, will open the Favorite Places folder, as shown in Figure 8.31.

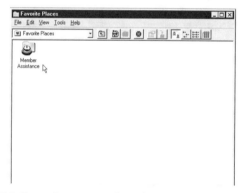

Figure 8.31 When you click the MSN Central Favorite Places button, MSN opens the Favorite Places folder.

CATEGORIES

The biggest attraction of online services is the vast amount of information that they can make available to you. At any time of the day or night, you can connect to an online service and find information about any subject, just as if you had an entire library in your living room. You access MSN's online information through the Categories folder. To open the Categories folder, click on Home Base's Categories button. MSN, in turn, will display the Categories folder, as shown in Figure 8.32.

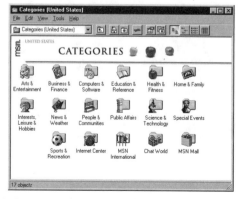

Figure 8.32 When you click on the MSN Central Categories button, MSN opens the Categories folder.

As MSN evolves, Microsoft might regroup the icons in the Categories folder. However, the categories you see in Figure 8.32 are generic enough that most of them should remain in the folder for some time.

Browsing Down a Hierarchy of Folders

In the same way you browse the folders in your system's hard disk, you can browse the categories in MSN's Categories window. To browse a category, double-click on its icon. For example, suppose you want to check out the Computers and Software category (or area) and locate information about Windows 95. Double-click on the Computers and Software icon in the window shown in Figure 8.32. MSN, in turn, will open the Computers and Software folder, as shown in Figure 8.33.

Figure 8.33 Viewing the Computers and Software area in MSN.

To focus on the Software area, double-click on the Software icon. MSN, in turn, will open the Software area, as shown in Figure 8.34.

Figure 8.34 Viewing MSN's Software area.

As you traverse folders, you may encounter files that you can download from MSN to your computer. Before you decide to download a file from this area (or any other MSN area), you may want to find out more about the file. For example, if you have limited space on your system, you may want to know the file's size. Likewise, if you can't afford to tie up your modem phone line for too long, you may want to know how much time the download will require.

As you have learned, to find information on any object in Windows 95, you right-click on the object and then select the Properties option from the object's pop-up menu. If, after viewing the file's properties, you decide you want to download the file, click your mouse on the Properties dialog box Download button.

ACCESS TO INTERNET NEWSGROUPS

Much like MSN bulletin boards, Internet newsgroups let users post information, pose questions, and answer queries. However, unlike the MSN bulletin boards, Internet Newsgroups don't contain the messages and responses of just MSN members. Instead, users from virtually every online service participate in Internet newsgroups. In addition, whereas a conventional electronic bulletin board typically resides at one site, the messages in Usenet Newsgroups are stored and forwarded from one computer to another around the world. As a result, the total Internet newsgroup audience is much larger than that of any individual online service BBS (bulletin board service). Furthermore, due to its immense size, an Internet newsgroup audience is more likely to have experts who can answer just about any question.

In this last part of your MSN tour, you will learn how to access the Internet newsgroups from MSN. To start, access the MSN Central Categories folder. If you are in another folder, click on the toolbar pull-down list button, move your mouse pointer to the pull-down list Categories item, and click on it. MSN, in turn, will take you to the Categories folder. Next, double-click on The Internet Center icon. MSN, in turn, will display The Internet Center's contents, as shown in Figure 8.35.

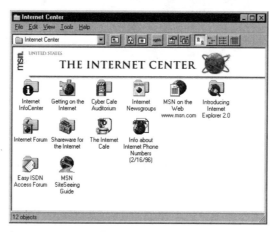

Figure 8.35 The Internet Center gives you access to Internet newsgroups.

Double-click on the Newsgroups icon. MSN, in turn, will display the Newsgroups folder's contents. In the Newsgroups window, double-click on the Usenet Newsgroups icon. (The Internet newsgroups are actually known as Usenet newsgroups; you will learn more about Usenet newsgroups in Chapter 10.) MSN, in turn, will open the Internet Newsgroups folder, as shown in Figure 8.36.

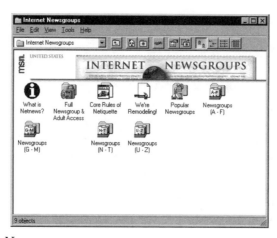

Figure 8.36 Viewing the Usenet Newsgroups.

To help you find the newsgroup that you want quickly, MSN organizes newsgroups alphabetically. For example, if you are looking for a newsgroup that discusses computers, you would first click your mouse on the folders labeled A-F (because computer topics will start with C). MSN, in turn, will display a folder that contains individual folders for each letter. In this case, you would click your mouse on the folder with the letter C. MSN will display the newsgroups that start with the letter C, as shown in Figure 8.37.

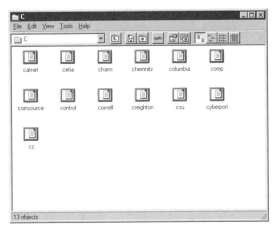

Figure 8.37 Newsgroups that begin with the letter C.

As it turns out, the comp newsgroup corresponds to computers. When you double-click your mouse on the comp folder, MSN will display the folder's topics, as shown in Figure 8.38.

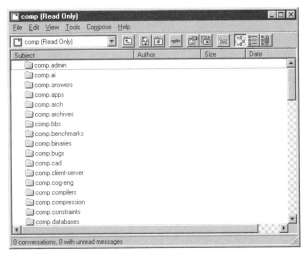

Figure 8.38 The comp folder topics discuss computers.

After you traverse the folders that lead to the topic you desire, you will eventually display newsgroup postings similar to those shown in Figure 8.39. As you can see, a newsgroup displays the subject, author, and date for each of its messages. Of course, when you access this newsgroup, it will contain completely different messages.

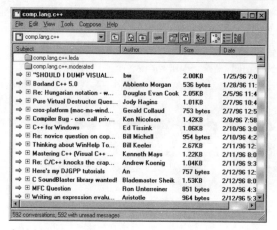

Figure 8.39 *User postings within the computer newsgroup.*

To read a user posting, double-click your mouse on the icon that precedes the posting you desire. To post a message, use the Compose menu New Message option.

KEYS TO SUCCESS

In previous chapters, you learned how to navigate through Windows 95, start programs, work with windows and dialog boxes, and even customize hardware. In this chapter, you begin to learn how to use your Windows 95 system as a productive tool. This chapter taught you how to use The Microsoft Network (MSN)—Microsoft's online service—to contact people and access information at locations around the globe.

In Chapter 9, you will learn how to use Windows 95's multimedia features for both research and instruction. However, before you move on to Chapter 9, make sure you understand the following key concepts:

- ✓ To access an online service, you need a modem connected to a phone line.
- ✓ MSN is one of many online services; other well-known online services include CompuServe, America Online, Prodigy, Delphi, and GEnie.
- ✓ You will have to pay to access and use MSN.
- ✓ MSN is a huge repository of online information.
- ✓ You can use MSN to send and receive electronic mail.
- ✓ You can use MSN to access the Internet.
- ✓ MSN lets you chat with other members online.
- ✓ MSN includes many bulletin boards, including the Internet newsgroups, where you can post messages and read messages others have posted.

Chapter 9
Windows 95 Multimedia

In Chapter 8, you used the Microsoft Network (MSN)—Microsoft's online service—to explore the information highway. As you journeyed through cyberspace, you may have noticed how MSN lays out text and images to enhance each piece of information it presents. The MSN, like most sites across the World Wide Web, makes extensive use of text and images, two key aspects of multimedia. As you might guess, the use of animation, sound, and video—the three other key aspects of multimedia—can make the presentation of information even more interesting. *Multimedia* is the use of text, sound, images (both still and animated), and video to present information.

This chapter examines Windows 95 support for multimedia. You will learn that Windows 95 provides easy installation of multimedia devices such as sound card and CD-ROM drive. (Installation is one of the biggest hurdles a new user faces when adding multimedia capabilities to a PC.) Also, Windows 95 includes built-in multimedia software, such as the Media Player, which lets you play sound or video clips, and the CD Player, which lets you play audio CDs on your PC. This chapter will introduce you to multimedia, the Windows 95 multimedia accessory programs, and ways you can customize your system to improve its multimedia capabilities. By the time you finish this chapter, you will understand the following key concepts:

- Multimedia is the use of text, sound, images, and video to present information.
- Windows 95 provides several new multimedia capabilities and programs.
- Using the Windows 95 Media Player accessory, you can play back audio clips, MIDI music, and even video clips.
- Windows 95 provides you a Volume Control window, within which you can control, individually, the volume for each of your multimedia devices.
- MIDI defines a standard interface for electronic music. Using the Media Player accessory, you can play MIDI music files.
- You use the Media Player to play sound clips and MIDI files.
- Using the Media Player accessory, you can play a video clip within a window on your screen. In fact, Windows 95 provides several sample video clips with which you can experiment.
- If your PC has a CD-ROM drive, Windows 95 provides the CD Player accessory that lets you play an audio CD.
- Using the Sound Recorder accessory, you can record, edit, and mix your own sound files.

WHAT IS MULTIMEDIA?

Taken literally, multimedia is the use of multiple mediums—text, sound, and images—to present information. Of course, multimedia has been around in movies and television for a long time. After all, movies use "moving images" and sound to tell a story. Television brings the images and sound right into your living room. Until a few years ago, personal computers did not really have the computing "horsepower" or the peripheral devices (such as a sound card) to support the kind of multimedia you see in television.

Two components, the sound card and the CD-ROM drive, have contributed most to multimedia's popularity. The CD-ROM provides the storage space for the large number of images and sound files used in a typical multimedia application. The sound card lets the PC generate professional quality sound—a multimedia application's other must-have ingredient.

If your PC does not have a sound card and a CD-ROM drive, you cannot enjoy the multimedia features of Windows 95. One way to jump on the multimedia bandwagon is to buy a multimedia-upgrade kit that typically includes a sound card, two speakers (for stereo sound), a CD-ROM drive, and an installation manual. After you physically install the sound card and CD-ROM drive, use the information in Chapter 6 to set up the sound card and CD-ROM drive under Windows 95. For more information on installing multimedia hardware, turn to the book, *Rescued by Upgrading Your PC, Second Edition*, Jamsa Press, 1996.

Understanding Multimedia

Multimedia is the use of text, sound, and images (both moving video and still pictures) to present information in a meaningful way. Using sound cards that can generate voice, sound, and music, and CD-ROMs that can store over 650Mb of words, pictures, and sounds, the PC has become a very powerful multimedia tool. Over the past year, thousands of multimedia CD-ROMs have entered the software market. With each passing month, the presentation quality and content of new CD-ROM products improve. In the future, almost all PCs sold, both desktop and notebook, will support multimedia.

Taking Windows 95 Multimedia for a Test Drive

If your PC has a sound card and a CD-ROM drive, you may have already experienced multimedia software. However, if you recently purchased your PC (with a sound card and CD-ROM drive) and have not yet tried any multimedia software, Windows 95 includes some sample video clips you should try out. Video clips consist of a sequence of images and sound. In Windows 95, video clips are stored in files with an .AVI extension (AVI stands for Audio-Video Interleaved which is a fancy way of saying the file combines both the video and sound). To play an AVI video file using Windows 95, you use the Media Player Accessory program. For a quick preview of Windows 95's multimedia capabilities, perform these steps:

1. From the Start menu, follow the path *Programs> Accessories> Multimedia> Media Player*. Windows 95 will start the Media Player, as shown in Figure 9.1.

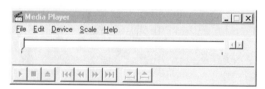

Figure 9.1 *Windows 95 Media Player window.*

2. Select the File menu Open option from the Media Player window. Media Player, in turn, will display the Open dialog box.

3. If you received Windows 95 on a CD-ROM, insert the CD-ROM and open the FUNSTUFF\VIDEOS folder that resides on the CD. Media Player, in turn, will display the contents of the folder in the Open dialog box work area.

4. Double-click your mouse on the GOODTIME.AVI video clip. Media Player, in turn, will display the video clip in a separate window, as shown in Figure 9.2.

9: Windows 95 Multimedia

Figure 9.2 *Playing a video clip within a Media Player window.*

5. To play the video clip, click your mouse on the Play button that appears along the bottom edge of the Media Player window. (Remember, you can rest your mouse pointer on a button to direct Windows 95 display to a pop-up window that tells you the button's purpose.)

Note: *If you did not purchase Windows 95 on a CD-ROM, you may find .AVI video files within the \Windows\Help folder. You will learn more about the Media Player later in this chapter.*

By combining text, sound, images, and video to present information, multimedia captures the attention of its audience. Each day, new multimedia products emerge on the marketplace. You can purchase CD-ROMs that teach you about pets, wines, Vietnam, medicine, and even Windows 95. In the near future, you will find multimedia CD-ROMs for almost any topic.

Windows 95 Provides Several Sample AVI Files

An AVI file combines video and sound to present video information within a window on your screen. Using the Windows 95 Media Player, you can play AVI files provided your PC has a sound card. If you purchased Windows 95 on a CD-ROM, you will find several sample AVI files on the CD. Take time now to play the AVI files using the media player. You will find the videos quite fun. If you installed Windows 95 from a floppy disk, search the Windows\Help folder for several sample AVI files that animate key Windows 95 operations, such as using the Start menu.

Improved Multimedia Support in Windows 95

If you were one of the first users to jump on to the multimedia bandwagon using MS-DOS and Windows 3.1, you probably still vividly recall the difficulties you had getting your sound card and CD-ROM drive to work. To start, you had to install physically a sound card and CD-ROM drive into your PC. Next, you had to configure the devices for use by MS-DOS, which involved adding (often cryptic) lines to the MS-DOS CONFIG.SYS file that told MS-DOS which device drivers to use to access your new devices. Then, you often had to configure the sound card and CD-ROM. Typically, this meant you had to specify detailed information such as the sound card's IRQ and I/O port addresses (see Chapter 6 for a discussion of IRQ and I/O port address). Finally, when you were ready to run the program, you may have found out that your system had too little memory left to run your new programs. I won't go into the details of what you had to do to free up memory, but, as you might guess, running multimedia software under MS-DOS was a lot of work. Worse yet, each time you purchased a DOS-based multimedia program, you had to configure the program to use your system settings.

Luckily, Windows 3.1 changed the situation considerably. Although you still had to install a sound card and CD-ROM drive, you could run most multimedia software without much trouble. This was possible because Windows 3.1 provided a standard way to access multimedia capabilities, such as playing digitized sound or playing a video clip. In other words, Windows-based multimedia software did not have to know details about your sound card and CD-ROM drive to work. Rather, the programs relied on Windows 3.1 to handle most of the details.

In several ways, Windows 95 makes it even easier for you to use multimedia software:

- **Plug-and-Play Support**: The term plug-and-play refers to the idea that you simply plug in new hardware, such as a sound card or CD-ROM, and the device works automatically in Windows 95. In most cases, you can install software support for a new sound card or CD-ROM using the Add Hardware Wizard discussed in Chapter 6.

- **AutoPlay**: This new feature lets you insert a CD in your CD-ROM drive and Windows 95 will load the CD automatically. Of course, only new CD-ROMs that exploit the AutoPlay mechanism will work this way, but you can expect simpler CD-ROM setups in the future. If you insert an audio CD (one that you would normally play using your stereo system), Windows 95 will automatically start playing the CD!

Note: *To implement AutoPlay, Windows 95 automatically spins the CD and looks for a file named AUTORUN.INF. If that file exists, Windows 95 opens it, and follows the instructions in the file. Most Microsoft products, for example, include the AUTORUN.INF file on their CD. When you insert the CD into your drive for the first time, the instructions in the AUTORUN.INF file direct Windows 95 to install the software onto your hard disk. When you insert the CD a second time, the AUTORUN.INF instructions direct Windows 95 to start the program, since they have determined the software is already installed.*

Understanding Plug and Play

In the past, when you installed a new hardware card in your system, you had to configure manually switches and jumpers on the card to set the card's IRQ and I/O port address to a unique value. If two devices used the same settings, the cards would conflict and your system would not work. Plug and play combines hardware and software to simplify installations. To take advantage of plug and play, the card you are installing must use a special chip called the plug-and-play BIOS. When you install the card into your system and power up, the card asks other plug-and-play cards about their settings.

For example, if you install a new sound card, the card's plug-and-play BIOS essentially says, "Hey, is anybody using IRQ 5?" If no other card's plug-and-play BIOS say, "Yeah, I am," the sound card will use IRQ5. Otherwise, the sound card repeats this process until it successfully chooses an unused IRQ and base address.

Because the plug-and-play BIOS does all the work, you no longer have to worry about setting switches and jumpers when you install new hardware cards.

Using the Media Player

While most multimedia programs provide (build in) your ability to play video clips and digitized sound, you can play sound or video without buying any special multimedia software. Windows 95 includes an accessory program—Media Player—that you can use to play various media files. The Media Player can play sound files, video clips, and control the sound volume for various devices.

You can start the Media Player from the Start menu (*Programs> Accessories> Multimedia> Media Player*). When Media Player runs, it displays the main window shown in Figure 9.1. To see the Media Player in action, select the File menu Open option from the Media Player window. Media Player, in turn, will display the Open dialog box. Use the techniques you learned in Chapter 7 to navigate through the folders in your system to the Media folder in your Windows 95 directory. Figure 9.3 shows the typical contents of the Media folder.

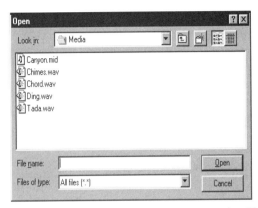

Figure 9.3 *The Media folder in the Windows 95 directory contains some media files.*

Highlight one of the files in the Media folder and click your mouse on the Open button. The Media Player, in turn, will load the file, as shown in Figure 9.4.

Figure 9.4 *The Media Player window after a sound file has been loaded.*

As you can see, the Media Player displays a progress bar that shows you the sound's total duration in seconds. Additionally, Media Player now enables the row of buttons that appear along the bottom edge of its window. Table 9.1 briefly describes the Media Player buttons.

PLAYING SOUND FILES

By default, when you select the Media Player File menu Open option, the Media Player displays the Open dialog box with a listing of all the files in the current folder. At times, you may only be interested in files of a specific type, such as WAV audio files or MIDI music files. In such cases, you can use the Media Player's Device menu to control the list of files the Open dialog box displays. If you open the Device menu in the Media Player, you will see that it can play three types of sounds as well as AVI video:

- **CD Audio** refers to the audio CDs you can buy in music stores.
- **MIDI Sequencer** refers to music files consisting of synthesized musical scores for various instruments.
- **Sound** refers to waveform sound or digitized sound.
- **Video for Windows** refers to AVI video files

These are the common types of sounds used in multimedia applications. It is worth learning about the various types of sound. You may encounter these file types in different multimedia programs or as you journey across the Internet and World Wide Web.

Button	Purpose
▶	Plays the current sound
■	Stops playing the current sound
▲	Ejects a CD-ROM from the drive
◄◄	Moves to the previous CD track or to the start of the current track
◄	Moves to the start of current sound
►►	Moves to the end of the current sound
►►|	Moves to the next CD track
⤓	Marks the start of a sound selection for use in a cut-and-paste operation
⤒	Marks the end of a sound selection for use in a cut-and-paste operation

Table 9.1 *The function of Media Player buttons.*

CD Audio refers to the popular audio compact disc made for your stereo that you can play in your PC's CD-ROM drive. Audio CDs can store high-quality music. Windows 95 includes the CD Player program to play audio CDs. When you insert an audio CD into your drive, Windows 95 recognizes that the CD is an audio CD and automatically starts the CD Player application to play the CD. To disable Windows 95 from automatically playing an audio CD, hold down your keyboard's SHIFT key when you insert the audio CD into your drive.

Digitized sounds can represent any type of sound, no matter how complex. Depending on their quality, however, digitized sound files can consume considerable disk space. For instance, depending on the recording quality, one second of digitized sound can be 8Kb to 172Kb. As such, multimedia applications that make extensive use of digitized sound (WAV files), typically store the files on a CD.

MIDI, which stands for *Musical Instrument Digital Interface*, refers to another type of sound. A MIDI file contains the commands which the sound card's synthesizer (a small chip on the card) uses to imitate musical instruments. Most sound cards support MIDI commands. You cannot use MIDI to record or play back other sounds, such as voices. Because they contain only musical notes and timing information, MIDI files are reasonably small. As such, multimedia programs often use MIDI files to store background music for the programs. However, MIDI is not as flexible as digitized waveform sound because many complex sounds cannot be broken down into simple notes.

MIDI sounds are generally stored in files with a .MID or .RMI file extension. As with .WAV files, to play a MIDI file, simply open the file in Media Player and click your mouse on the Play button. One of the best ways to get a feel for MIDI music is to "test drive" a .MID file. Using the Media Player, open the file CANYON.MID which should reside within the Windows\Media folder. Next, click on the Play button to hear the file's contents.

Video for Windows files are .AVI video files. An .AVI file contains a video sequence stored in *Audio-Video Interleaved* format (.AVI) files. To play video clips under Windows 3.1, you had to purchase, or your programs had to supply, a special program called Video for Windows. Windows 95 includes Microsoft Video for Windows, so you can play video clips with the Media Player.

There are other types of video files in addition to AVI—the most common is QuickTime. Although a QuickTime player does not come with Windows 95, some multimedia programs may install QuickTime for Windows on your system. In most cases, however, when you play video files on your system using the Media Player, the files you play will be AVI. When you select the Media Player's Device menu Video for Windows option, the Media Player will display the names of .AVI files within its file list.

9: Windows 95 Multimedia

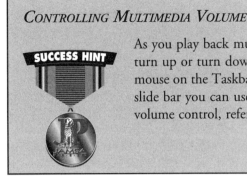

CONTROLLING MULTIMEDIA VOLUME

As you play back multimedia sound, MIDI, CD audio, or video files, you may want to turn up or turn down the volume. To control your system's volume quickly, click your mouse on the Taskbar's speaker icon. Windows 95, in turn, will display a volume control slide bar you can use to adjust the volume. For more information on working with the volume control, refer to Chapter 3, "Customizing the Taskbar and Start Menu."

PLAYING AUDIO CDS

Audio CDs are the popular audio compact discs you normally play in your car or home stereo. If your PC has a sound card and a CD-ROM drive, you can use your PC to play audio CDs. Because people like to play audio CDs in their systems while they work, Windows 95 includes a CD Player program. Although you can play an audio CD from the Media Player, the CD Player is more convenient program to play audio CDs because the controls are more like a regular CD player.

To play an audio CD on your Windows 95 system, place the CD in the CD-ROM drive. Windows 95, in turn, will recognize the audio CD and will start the CD Player program. As you hear the CD's music, you will find that your Taskbar contains a button for the CD Player program:

If you click your mouse on the CD Player button, Windows 95 will display the CD Player window as shown in Figure 9.5.

Figure 9.5 Using the CD Player, you can play audio CDs while you work.

The CD Player's controls are similar to those of a commercial audio CD player (see Table 9.2). To play the CD, click on the large Play button (the one with a right arrow). After the CD begins playing, it will continue to do so even if you close the CD Player window. That is because the CD can play through your sound card without any help from your computer.

Thus, with the CD Player, you can have background music while you work. (Of course, your CD-ROM drive is tied up with the audio CD, so you cannot use any other multimedia CD-ROM while the audio CD plays.) Table 9.2 describes the CD Player buttons.

197

Button	Purpose
▶	Plays the CD
‖	Pauses the CD
■	Stops the CD
■	Starts the current CD track over
◀◀	Skips backward a few seconds
▶▶	Skips forward a few seconds
▶▶|	Starts the next CD track
▲	Ejects the CD from the CD-ROM drive
🗒	Displays the Edit Play List window
🕘	Displays the current track's elapsed playing time
🕘	Displays the current track's remaining playing time
🕘	Displays the disc's remaining playing time
⇄	Plays the CD tracks randomly
↻	Repeats the CD play continuously
≣	Plays only the first few seconds of each track

Table 9.2 *The CD Player buttons.*

If your CD Player window does not contain all the buttons listed in Table 9.2, use the CD Player View menu to enable the toolbar's display.

CUSTOMIZING AN AUDIO CD

Using the CD Player, you can start, stop, or control which CD tracks the CD Plays. In addition, the CD Player lets you customize the current CD by typing in the CD's title, artist, and the name of each song. When you insert the same CD at a later time, the CD Player will remember your entries and will display them automatically. In this way, you can select songs by name as opposed to remembering track numbers.

RECORDING INFORMATION ABOUT AN AUDIO CD

To specify information about an audio CD to CD Player, select the Disc menu Edit Play List option. The CD Player, in turn, will display the Disc Settings dialog box shown in Figure 9.6.

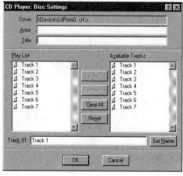

Figure 9.6 The CD Player Disc Settings dialog box.

9: Windows 95 Multimedia

Using the Disc Settings dialog box, you can specify the artist, CD title, and song titles. You can also specify which of the songs (tracks) you want to hear and in what order. To start, click your mouse in the Artist field and type the name of the CD's band or performer. Press the Tab key or click your mouse on the Title field. Type in the CD's title.

The bottom of the Disc Settings dialog box contains two parts. Along the right-hand side of the box, the Available Tracks list tells you all the tracks on the CD. Your Play List, which appears on left-hand side of the box is the list of tracks you want to hear. By customizing the songs in the Play List, you control which tracks the CD Player plays, as well as the order in which the CD Player plays them.

REMOVING ONE OR MORE TRACKS FROM THE PLAY LIST

By default, the CD Player places all of an audio CD's tracks in the Play List. To remove a track from the Play List, click on and highlight the track and then choose the Remove button. If the CD only contains a few songs you want to hear, you can click on the Clear All button and later add back only those songs you desire.

ADDING TRACKS TO PLAY LIST

To add a track to the Play List, click on the track within the Available Tracks list and then click your mouse on the Add button. To add all the tracks to the Play List in one step, click your mouse on the Reset button (which directs the CD Player to restore the Play List to its original contents—all the CD's tracks).

NAMING A CD TRACK

To assign a name to a CD track, click your mouse on and highlight a track within the Available Track list. Next, click your mouse in the Name field that appears at the bottom of the Disc Settings dialog box. Type in the song name that corresponds to the track and click your mouse on the Set Name button.

DEFINING THE TRACK PLAYBACK ORDER

Using the CD Player Play List, you can control the order in which each CD track plays. Also, if you have a favorite song, you can include the song in the Play List two or three times. To move a track up or down in the Play List, click on the track a second time, this time holding down your mouse select button.

The CD Player will display a small arrow to the left of the track. Move your mouse up or down to move the small arrow to the location in the list to which you want to move the song. When you release your mouse select button, the CD Player will move the song to its new location.

TEMPORARILY SUSPENDING AUTOPLAY

As you have learned, to play an audio CD you simply place the CD into your CD-ROM drive. Windows 95, in turn, will recognize the CD is an audio CD and will run the CD Player to play it.

If, for some reason, you don't want Windows 95 to "autoplay" your CD, hold down your keyboard SHIFT key as you insert the CD. When you are later ready to play the CD, you can start the CD Player using the Start menu (*Start> Programs> Accessories> Multimedia> CD Player*).

199

Controlling CD Player Preferences

In addition to customizing the entries for a specific CD, the CD Player lets you specify settings that it uses for all CDs. To begin, select the CD Player Options menu and choose Preferences. The CD Player, in turn, will display the Preferences dialog box as shown in Figure 9.7.

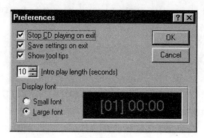

Figure 9.7 The CD Player Preferences dialog box.

The Preferences dialog box Stop CD playing on exit option directs the CD Player to stop playing the CD if you end the CD Player program. If you remove the check mark from this option, an audio CD will continue to play even if you close the CD Player window.

The Save settings on exit option controls whether or not the CD Player saves changes you have made to preferences or display items when you exit the CD Player. If you check this option, the CD Player saves your settings to disk each time you exit the program. If you leave the option unchecked, the CD Player will discard your changes when you close the CD Player window. This option does not correspond to the settings you assign to a specific CD, such as the artist and song names. The CD Player stores that information each time you exit the Disc Settings dialog box.

The Show tool tips option lets you turn on or off the CD Player's display of the small tool tip window that appears when you move your mouse over a CD Player toolbar button:

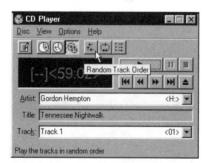

Most users don't use the CD Player buttons on a regular basis, and as such, will normally want the CD Player to display the toolbar tips. If you have not yet named a CD's tracks, you can search for a specific song by directing the CD Player to play the start (introduction) of each track. The Preferences dialog box Intro play length field lets you specify, in seconds, how much of each track the CD Player plays as an introduction. To direct the CD Player to play track introductions only, select the Options menu Intro Play option. The CD Player, in turn, will place a small check mark to the left of the menu option. To turn off the introductory play later, select the menu option a second time, removing the check mark.

Controlling How the CD Player Uses Your Play List

As you have learned, the Play List specifies the list of tracks you want the CD Player to play. Normally, the CD Player plays the tracks in the same order you specify in the Play List. After the CD Player plays the last song in the list, it stops playing the CD. In some cases, you may want the CD Player to continue again at the start of the list. In such cases, select the Options menu Continuous Play option or click your mouse on the Continuous Play button. Likewise, there may be times when you don't care what order the CD Player plays the songs. In such cases, select the Options menu Random Order option or click your mouse on the Random Order option.

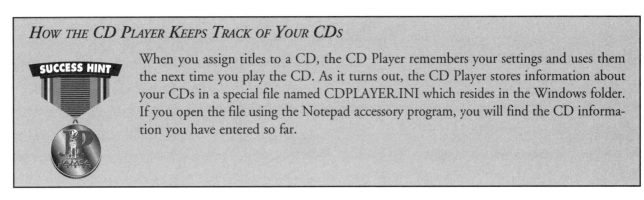

How the CD Player Keeps Track of Your CDs

When you assign titles to a CD, the CD Player remembers your settings and uses them the next time you play the CD. As it turns out, the CD Player stores information about your CDs in a special file named CDPLAYER.INI which resides in the Windows folder. If you open the file using the Notepad accessory program, you will find the CD information you have entered so far.

Using the Sound Recorder

In Chapter 5, "Customizing Common Hardware," you learned that Windows 95 lets you assign sounds to different system events. As you learned, the sounds you assign to events are WAV files that reside on your disk. To help you get started, Windows 95 provides a few sample WAV files. If, however, you have a microphone attached to your sound card, you can use the Windows 95 Sound Recorder program to record your own sounds! To start the Sound Recorder, select the Start menu and select *Start> Programs> Accessories> Multimedia> Sound Recorder*. Windows 95, in turn, will display the Sound Recorder, as shown in Figure 9.8

Figure 9.8 The Windows 95 Sound Recorder.

Think of the Sound Recorder as an electronic tape recorder with buttons that lets you record, play, rewind, fast forward, and stop your recorder. Table 9.3 describes the Sound Recorder buttons.

Button	Function
◄◄	Rewinds your recording
►►	Fast forwards your recording
►	Plays your recording
■	Stops your playback or recording
●	Starts recording

Table 9.3 The function of the Sound Recorder buttons.

Recording a Sound

To record a sound using the Sound Recorder, turn on your microphone. Next, click your mouse on the record button. As you record, the Sound Recorder will display the sound waves that correspond to your recording in its small display window, as shown in Figure 9.9.

Figure 9.9 Displaying recorded sound waves.

To stop recording, click your mouse on the stop button. Next, click your mouse on the rewind button to move to the start of your recording, and then click on the play button to hear the sound.

If you are satisfied with your recording, you can save it to a file on disk. If you are not satisfied, simply record over the recording. To save your recording to a WAV file, perform these steps:

1. Select the File menu Save As option. The Sound Recorder will display the Save As dialog box.
2. Within the Save As dialog box, select the directory within which you want to store the file. Next, type in a filename that describes your recording and that uses the WAV extension.
3. Choose Save.

Recording a New Sound

If you don't like your existing recording and you want to discard it, or if you have saved a successful recording and want to record a new sound, select the File menu New option. If you have recorded or edited sounds and not yet saved your changes to disk, the Sound Recorder will display a dialog box asking you if you want to save or discard the current sound. After you save or discard your changes, you will be ready to record a new sound.

Using the Position Bar

As you record your sound, the Sound Recorder tracks the sound by time, displaying the length of your recording in seconds. In addition, after you stop recording, the Sound Recorder lets you use a scroll bar to select a location within the recording. For example, assume that your recording is 30 seconds in length. Using the position scroll bar, you can select a position that is 10, 15, or even 25 seconds into your recording. Using the position scroll bar in this way, you can play back the last five seconds or record over the last 10 seconds. In short, the position scroll bar is your tool for editing parts of your recording.

Editing Your Sound File

As you record sounds, there may be times when you want to delete part of your recording, increase the volume, combine two or more sound files, or even mix two sound files (possibly mixing a voice sound file over a music background). To perform these editing operations, you will make extensive use of the Sound Recorder's Edit and Effects menus.

Inserting or Appending a Second Sound File

As you edit sound files, it's common to insert or append an existing sound file to your current recording. To insert an existing sound file into your current recording, perform these steps:

1. Use the position scroll bar to select the location in your recording at which you want to place the existing sound.
2. Select the Edit menu Insert File option. The Sound Recorder will display the Insert File dialog box.

9: WINDOWS 95 MULTIMEDIA

3. Within the Insert File dialog box, select the file that contains the sound you want to use.

4. Choose Open.

To append an existing sound to your recording, you simply move the position scroll box to the end of the recording in step 1 and then perform steps 2 through 4.

MIXING AN EXISTING SOUND

When you mix two sounds, you combine the sounds so you hear both sounds at the same time. For example, assume that you have two recordings. The first recording is part of a symphony by Mozart. Your second recording contains a voice description of Mozart's life.

By mixing these two recordings, you can play the symphony as background music for the speaker. To mix an existing sound with your current recording, perform these steps:

1. Use the position scroll bar to select the location within your current document where you want the mix to start.

2. Select the Edit menu Mix with File option. The Sound Recorder will display the Mix With File dialog box.

3. Within the Mix With File dialog box, select the file that contains the sound you want to mix.

4. Choose Open.

DISCARDING YOUR CHANGES

As you edit a recording, there may be times when you will make changes you don't want to keep. In such cases, you can direct the Sound Recorder to revert your recording back to its last saved state—in other words, to the sound you last saved to a file on disk. To revert your sound file to its last saved state, perform these steps:

1. Select the File menu Select Revert option. The Sound Recorder will display a dialog box asking you to verify the reversion.

2. Select Yes.

DELETING PART OF YOUR RECORDING

As you edit, there may be times when you will want to delete sections of your recording. Although the Sound Recorder won't let you delete from the middle, it will let you delete from the beginning and end. To delete from the front or end of your recording, perform these steps:

1. Use the position scroll bar to select the location within your recording before or after which you want to delete sound.

2. Select the Edit menu Delete Before Current Position or Delete After Current Position option. The Sound Recorder will display a dialog box asking you to confirm the deletion.

3. Choose OK.

APPLYING SPECIAL EFFECTS TO YOUR RECORDING

Depending on your recording, there may be times when you will want to change the sound's volume or playback speed. To perform these operations, you use the Effects menu. Table 9.4 briefly describes the Effects menu options.

Option	Function
Increase Volume	Increases your recording's volume by 25%.
Decrease Volume	Decreases your recording's volume by 25%.
Increase Speed	Increases (speeds up) your recording's playback speed by 100%.
Decrease Speed	Decreases (slows down) your recording's speed by 50%.
Add Echo	Adds an echo to your recording.
Reverse	Reverses your recording, so it will play backward.

Table 9.4 The function of Sound Recorder Effects menu options.

CONTROLLING SOUND FILE FORMATS

One of the disadvantages of WAV files is that they can consume considerable space on your disk. For example, if you record one minute of sound at the highest quality (44KHz, 16-bit, stereo), you will consume almost 10Mb of data! To let you choose between sound quality and disk-space consumption, Windows 95 lets you specify the recording quality of your sounds. As you will learn, the lower sound quality you select, the less space your sound files consume.

Changing the Sound Quality

Later in this chapter, you will examine the Control Panel Multimedia dialog box that lets you customize settings for multimedia devices. At that time, you will learn how to set your sound-card's recording and playback formats. When you use these settings to specify your sound-card's playback or recording quality, Windows 95 (and the Sound Recorder) will use these settings as your sound-card's defaults. However, as you will learn next, the Sound Recorder lets you change the quality settings on a file-by-file basis. To change the sound quality for your current recording, select the Sound Recorder File menu Properties option. The Sound Recorder, in turn, will display the Properties for Sound dialog box as shown in Figure 9.10.

Figure 9.10 The Properties for Sound dialog box.

The Properties for Sound dialog box shows you the audio format that the Sound Recorder will use for the current recording. To change the audio format, open the Choose from pull-down list and select All Formats. Next, click your mouse on the Convert Now button. The Sound Recorder, in turn, will display the Sound Selection dialog box as shown in Figure 9.11.

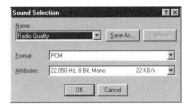

Figure 9.11 *The Sound Selection dialog box.*

The simplest and most common way to select a sound quality is to choose one of Windows 95 predefined settings:

- CD Quality 44KHz, 16-bit, Stereo (172Kb/second)
- Radio Quality 22KHz, 8-bit, Mono (22Kb/second)
- Telephone Quality 11KHz, 8-bit, Mono (11Kb/second)

To choose one of these predefined settings, select the setting from the Name pull-down list. After you select the setting you desire, choose OK to return to the Properties dialog box. Then, choose OK again to return to the Sound Recorder. For more information on defining your own sound quality, turn to the book *1001 Windows 95 Tips*, Jamsa Press, 1995.

MULTIMEDIA CONTROLS

In Chapters 5 and 6, you learned about various tools in the Windows 95 Control Panel. One of the icons in the Control panel, the Multimedia icon, gives you access to various multimedia controls through which you can configure your PC's multimedia devices. This chapter briefly describes these multimedia controls. As you will see, you can typically control the volume of sounds and presentation of video clips with the multimedia controls. To start the multimedia controls, double-click on the Multimedia icon in the Control panel folder (open Control Panel from the Start menu using the path *Settings> Control Panel*). Windows 95, in turn, will open the Multimedia Properties sheet, as shown in Figure 9.12.

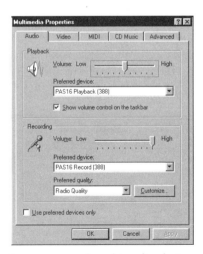

Figure 9.12 *Multimedia Properties sheet lets you control multimedia devices.*

As you can see, the Multimedia Properties sheet consists of five pages:

- **Audio** lets you control the volume and quality of sound recording and sound playback.
- **Video** lets you to set the size of the video playback window.

- **MIDI** provides controls for MIDI instruments.
- **CD Music** lets you set the volume for the audio CD playback through the CD-ROM drive's head phone.
- **Advanced** gives you access to low-level settings for all of the multimedia devices in your system.

CONTROLLING AUDIO DEVICES

The Multimedia Properties dialog box Audio page lets you control the volume and sound quality for WAV files. To adjust the volume control, simply drag the volume slider to the left (to decrease the volume) and right (to increase the volume). This volume control has the same effect as the WAV control you will see later in this chapter when you examine the Volume Control dialog box. This volume control is not the same as the volume control you activate from the Taskbar. The Taskbar volume control sets the volume for all devices, whereas the volume control shown here affects only WAV files. The Audio page lets you control the value for recording and playback. Unless you use a microphone to record your own sounds, you only need to adjust the playback volume. The recording volume lets you control the volume of sounds you record using software such as the Windows 95 Sound Recorder.

As discussed, the higher the quality of your recording, the more disk space your recording will consume. Within the Recording section of the Audio page, you can use the Preferred Quality pull-down list to select the sound quality you want Windows 95 to use as its default. As you learned earlier in this chapter, programs such as the Sound Recorder let you override this default setting. In addition, if one of the predefined settings does not meet your needs, you can create your own setting, specifying the sampling rate, quality (8-bit versus 16-bit), and the number of channels (mono or stereo) that you desire.

CONTROLLING VIDEO PLAYBACK

The Multimedia Properties dialog box Video page lets you control the size at which Windows 95 plays back a video file. In most cases, you will want to select the Original size option that appears within the Window pull-down list. Most programs optimize their video files to play back at a specific size. If you increase the video's size, the video may lose frames and appear choppy. If, however, you have a fast system with a quad-speed (or faster) CD-ROM drive and a video accelerator, you may want to experiment with the video settings until you find a setting that provides you with satisfactory size and speed. To adjust the size of the video playback window, click on the Video tab. Windows 95, in turn, will display the Video page. You can use the option button on the Video page to select whether the video appears in a window or full-screen. If the video is in a window, you can choose the magnification, as shown in Figure 9.13.

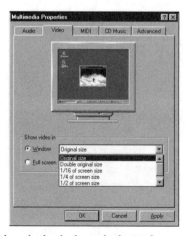

Figure 9.13 *You can adjust the size of video playback through the Video page.*

Controlling Audio CD Playback

The CD Music page provides two simple controls with which you can specify the drive letter that corresponds to your CD-ROM and the sound volume for a headphone that you connect to the CD-ROM drive. To access these CD Music controls, click your mouse on the Multimedia Properties dialog box CD Music tab. Windows 95, in turn, will display the CD Music page, as shown in Figure 9.14.

Figure 9.14 *You can set audio CD properties through the CD Music page.*

As you can see, the headphone volume control is a simple slider. To increase the volume use your mouse to drag the slider to the right. To decrease the volume, drag the slider to the left. Because Windows 95 can normally determine your CD-ROM drive letter, you will normally have no need to use the CD-ROM drive pull-down list.

Controlling MIDI Playback

As you have learned, a MIDI file contains commands that your sound-card's synthesizer uses to imitate different musical instruments. You will normally only need the MIDI page if you are a MIDI enthusiast. However, if you select the Multimedia Properties dialog box, Windows 95 will display the MIDI page as shown in Figure 9.15.

Figure 9.15 *The Multimedia Properties MIDI page.*

The MIDI page refers to your sound-card's synthesizer as an "instrument." Depending on your computer's hardware configuration, there may be times when you have one or more MIDI playback devices (two or more instruments). In such cases, you can use the MIDI page to select the instrument you desire.

Most synthesizers can imitate a variety of instruments. Within a MIDI file, musical commands correspond to specific *channels*, which in turn, correspond to specific instruments. For example, one channel might correspond to a piano while a second channel might correspond to drums. Many sound cards let you customize their playback settings by changing the musical instrument that corresponds to a specific channel. In this way, you can change a song by playing it with instruments the song's composer never imagined—such as Beethoven's Fifth Symphony with drums only. Depending on your sound card type, the steps you must perform to change the channel assignments will differ. Your best source of information is the documentation that accompanied your sound card.

ADVANCED MULTIMEDIA SETTINGS

Depending on the hardware you install in your system, there may be times when a new hardware card conflicts with one of your multimedia devices. You will know when such a conflict occurs because your sound card or CD-ROM will stop working. In such cases, you may need to change the settings for one or more of your multimedia devices. To change such settings, select the Multimedia Properties Advanced tab. Windows 95, in turn, will display the Multimedia devices page as shown in Figure 9.16.

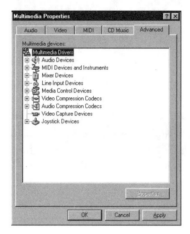

Figure 9.16 The Multimedia devices page.

This page displays your multimedia devices using a tree-like structure similar to that of the Windows 95 Explorer that you will examine in Chapter 14, "Using the Windows 95 Explorer." If you click your mouse on the plus sign (+) that appears in the box that precedes a device name, Windows 95 will expand that branch of the device list to show the next level of detail. For example, if you click your mouse on the plus sign that precedes the Audio Devices entry, Windows 95 will display an entry for your current audio device driver as shown in Figure 9.17.

Figure 9.17 Expanding a branch of the multimedia device tree.

To collapse the branch to its previous level, click your mouse on the minus sign which now appears in the box that precedes the Audio Devices entry. Depending on your hardware and the device driver software you are using, the settings you can view and change for your multimedia devices will differ.

To view or change device settings, highlight the entry you desire within the device list and click your mouse on the Properties button. Windows 95, in turn, will display a Properties dialog box for the device. Depending again on your hardware and software, the Properties dialog box may contain a Settings button you select to view or change various settings. For more information on multimedia device settings, refer to the book *1001 Windows 95 Tips*, Jamsa Press, 1995.

VOLUME CONTROLS

Various multimedia hardware and software, such as a video player, an audio-CD player, and a WAV-file player, all play sound. Each of these devices can have its own volume control that determines the loudness of its sound. Window 95 combines the volume controls for all such multimedia devices into a single dialog box.

You can access the Volume Control dialog box in two ways. One way is to select the Device menu Volume Control option in the Media Player. The second way is to right-click on the Taskbar's loudspeaker icon (next to the clock). Windows 95, in turn, will display a pop-up menu. Select the Volume Control option from the menu. Windows 95 will display the Volume Control dialog box, as shown in Figure 9.18.

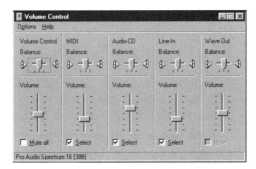

Figure 9.18 *Volume Control dialog box lets you set the volumes for various devices.*

As you can see, there are five volume controls as well as five balance controls (balance refers to the ratio of loudness of the left and right speakers).

You can use each volume control the same way. Drag the Volume slider up to raise the volume and down to lower the volume. To change the balance between the left and right speakers, drag the Balance slider.

The leftmost control, labeled Volume Control, applies to all devices. The other four controls are for specific devices:

- Wave device plays back digitized waveform sound.
- MIDI device plays music in MIDI format.
- CD refers to the audio CD volume.
- Line-In refers to audio signal from an external source (such as a turntable or audio cassette) that you can feed into the sound card.

To turn all sound off, click on the Mute all check box in the leftmost control. When the Mute all check box is enabled, Windows 95 will turn off all sound.

Viewing Information About a Multimedia File

As you encounter WAV, MIDI, and AVI files, there may be times when you are interested in specifics about the file, such as a sound file's quality or an AVI file's frame rate. To display specifics about a multimedia file, right-click your mouse on the file within any Open dialog box. Windows 95, in turn, will display a pop-up menu from which you can select the Properties option. Windows 95 will then display the file's Properties dialog box. For example, using the file WHATSON.AVI which Windows 95 stores in the Windows\Help folder, the Properties dialog box will appear as shown in Figure 9.19.

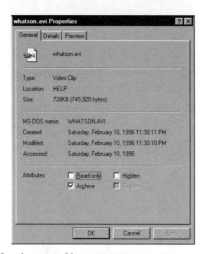

Figure 9.19 The Properties dialog box for the AVI file WHATSON.AVI.

The first page of the Properties dialog box tells you the file contains a video clip. If you select the Details tab, Windows 95 will display specifics about the file, such as its frame rate and video-window size as shown in Figure 9.20.

Figure 9.20 Details about the AVI file WHATSON.AVI.

Finally, using the dialog box Preview page, you can preview the file's contents as shown in Figure 9.21.

9: WINDOWS 95 MULTIMEDIA

Figure 9.21 Previewing an AVI file's contents.

KEYS TO SUCCESS

There is a diversity of Windows multimedia applications that integrate sound, animated graphic images, and video: educational reference material such as dictionaries and encyclopedias on CD-ROM, computer games with animated graphics and digitized sound generated by a sound card (if the system has one), animated product demonstrations, and business presentations.

Windows 95 supports all types of multimedia devices such as sound cards and digital video. Windows 95 also includes accessory programs such as Media Player and CD Player to play digitized sound, video clips, and audio CDs. This chapter showed you how to use Windows 95's multimedia accessories.

In Chapter 10, you will learn about another exciting subject—how to connect to the Internet and "surf the net" with a World Wide Web browser. You will see what it really means to have "information at your fingertips." However, before you move on to Chapter 10, make sure you understand the following key concepts:

- ✓ Multimedia means use of multiple medium—sound, images, and video.
- ✓ Sound card and CD-ROM drive are key the ingredients of a multimedia PC; without a sound card and CD-ROM drive, you cannot fully enjoy multimedia software.
- ✓ Windows 95 provides you a Volume Control window within which you can control, individually, the volume for each of your multimedia devices. In addition, you can use the Taskbar volume button to set the master volume setting.
- ✓ Windows 95 makes it easy to install and use multimedia devices such as sound cards, CD-ROM drives, and video players.
- ✓ You can use Windows 95's Media Player program to play digitized sound and video clips.
- ✓ You can use the CD Player program to play audio CDs on your Windows 95 system.
- ✓ Using the Sound Recorder accessory, you can record, edit, and mix your own sounds.

Chapter 10
Connecting Windows 95 to the Internet and the World Wide Web

In this book's first nine chapters, you have learned a lot about Windows 95—how to navigate its user interface, run programs, set up common hardware, explore its multimedia capabilities, and even how to access the Microsoft Network. In this chapter you will use Windows 95 to access an information source that's much larger than the Microsoft Network—the Internet. As you will learn, Windows 95 makes it easy for you connect to the Internet. In particular, you will learn how to "surf the net" on the World Wide Web (or Web, for short). Using a special program called a Web browser, you will find that the Web brings access to the White House, MTV, ESPN sports, and much more to your PC. Windows 95 provides several software programs you can use to access information across the Internet. This chapter will introduce you to several of the tools. By the time you finish this chapter, you will understand the following key concepts:

- The Internet is a collection of interconnected computer networks that exists across 150 countries.

- Using the Internet, you can exchange electronic mail, share files, or chat with users worldwide.

- The World Wide Web is a collection of related documents you can view by using a special program, called a Web browser.

- Think of the World Wide Web as sitting on top of the Internet. The Internet is made up of computer networks, and the Web consists of the related documents that reside at computers across the Internet.

- To access the Internet from your PC, you need to establish an account with an Internet provider—a company that lets you connect to their computer, using your PC and a modem. The provider's computer is connected to the Internet, which in turn gives your computer Internet access.

- Windows 95 makes it very easy for you to connect your PC to an Internet provider.

- Using the Windows 95 ping program, you can determine if a remote computer is active.

- Using the Windows 95 ftp program, you can download programs and files across the Internet.

- A Web browser is a software program that lets you view documents across the World Wide Web. Microsoft does not include a Web browser in Windows 95. However, in this chapter you will download a browser from across the Internet.

THE INTERNET IS A WORLDWIDE NETWORK OF NETWORKS

If you work in an office, you may already exchange files and electronic mail (e-mail) messages with other users over a local-area network. Networks exist to help users share resources, such as disks, files, and printers. The Internet takes the local-area network's concepts of sharing and magnifies them across the world. Consider, for a moment, how convenient it would be if you could correspond with your customers using the same electronic-mail you use in your office. By sending e-mail messages to your customers, you minimize the effects of "telephone tag," where you miss your customer and leave a message and then they miss you when they call back, so they must leave a message. Instead, by using e-mail, you and your customers can receive mail at just about anytime and anywhere. Next, if you are going to communicate with your customers by e-mail, you may as well do the same with your suppliers.

In the simplest sense, the Internet (or "Net") provides users with a way to interconnect their networks. Today, there are over 30,000 networks connected to the Internet. These networks include businesses, universities, government organizations, research institutions, and much more. In addition to using the Net to send and receive electronic mail, users connect to the Internet to perform a wide variety of activities:

- To research topics that range from agriculture to zoology
- To obtain the latest domestic and international news
- To get sports scores and to order tickets for upcoming events
- To order meals that restaurants deliver to their home or office
- To chat with other users online, either to find answers to questions, or simply to socialize
- To download software programs and games—often for free
- To obtain real-time quotes for their stocks, and even to buy and sell stocks
- To shop for goods and services ranging from airline tickets to a new wardrobe

In short, the Internet has quickly become many different things to many people. The bottom line, however, is that each day, the Internet becomes more a key part of our culture.

The Internet Pays for Itself

The Internet connects computers in over 150 countries worldwide. No one company or individual owns the Internet. Instead, the Internet is somewhat self-sufficient. Assume, for example, that you work for a university that wants to connect its computers to the Internet. To begin, the university must pay the costs to connect their computers physically to the nearest computer that is part of the Internet. This physical connection can be made by cables, phone lines, or even satellites. Each day, millions of users connect their PCs to the Net from their home, from their office, or even from an airplane. Unlike the companies and universities that have expensive (high speed) connections to the Internet, end users connect to the Net by subscribing to a special company, called an Internet provider. In short, an Internet provider is a company that has paid the price to connect its computers to the Net. For a monthly fee, the provider lets you use your PC and modem to connect to their computer, which in turn, gives you access to the Net.

To connect your PC to the Net, your first step is to subscribe to an Internet provider. You will find providers in all major cities. In fact, there are several books that list Internet providers worldwide. The easiest way to find a provider is simply to call a local computer store and ask for a recommendation. Most computer stores should provide you with phone numbers for one or more providers. When you talk to your provider about signing up, let them know that you plan to use Windows 95 and a PPP (point-to-point) protocol. It's not important that you understand what PPP is, but rather, that both you and your provider are using PPP. Recently, the competition among Internet providers has gotten fierce, which has reduced the monthly connection fees. In most cases, your cost-to-connect should be less than $25 a month.

Connecting to the Internet Using an Online Service

If you are a member of an online service such as MSN (see Chapter 8), CompuServe, Prodigy, or AOL, you have access to many Internet features, the most important being e-mail and the World Wide Web. Your advantage in accessing the Net by using an online service is simplicity and cost. Your disadvantage is access speed. Normally, your connection speed through an online service will be half the speed you can get by connecting through an Internet provider. When you "surf" (examine documents across) the World Wide Web, you download many graphics files across the connection to your computer. The slower your connection, the longer your download operations will take, which can become quite frustrating.

YOUR PROVIDER COSTS ARE THE ONLY COSTS YOU WILL PAY

When you search for an Internet provider, find a provider that offers you a local access number—one you can dial without having to place a long-distance phone call. After you connect to the Internet, you can retrieve information from computers around the world for free. For example, if a computer in Japan has a report you desire, you can retrieve the report at no cost. In other words, on the Internet, "long distance" has no meaning. As such, as you send e-mail or chat with other users worldwide, your costs will be no different than if you were to send e-mail or chat with users across town.

In general, the only cost you will incur on the Internet is your monthly provider fee.

WHERE THE WORLD WIDE WEB FITS IN

Across the Internet, there are several million documents whose contents range from medical research papers, to baseball statistics, to the works of Herman Melville (you know, Captain Ahab and Moby Dick). In short, there are documents on the Internet that provide something for everyone. Each day, users, researchers, and companies place over 100,000 new documents on the Net! As a user, your challenge becomes finding the information you need. That's where the World Wide Web fits in.

The World Wide Web goes by several names including WWW, W3, and the Web (which is most common). As you can guess, with millions of documents on computers that reside in over 150 countries, it used to be difficult, at best, to find information on the Net. To help users search for information, programmers created utility programs with names such as Archie, Jughead, Veronica, and gopher. Unfortunately, these programs were too complicated for the masses. Luckily, as a result, programmers developed the World Wide Web.

Using the Web, you view documents graphically within a window. Using a special software program, called a Web browser, users type in the Web address of the document they desire. The browser, in turn, locates and displays the document on the user's screen. For example, Figure 10.1 shows the Web document you will see when you first connect to the Microsoft Web site.

Figure 10.1 Viewing a document at the Microsoft Web site.

Using your Web browser, you can scroll through the document's contents or print a hardcopy to which you can refer at a later time. Across the Web, there are millions of documents you can view which cover a limitless number of topics. Figure 10.2, for example, shows a document at the MTV Web site.

Figure 10.2 Viewing a document at the MTV Web site.

Lastly, Figure 10.3 shows you the opening document at the Jamsa Press Web site.

Figure 10.3 Viewing a document at the Jamsa Press Web site.

To view a site's Web document, you need to know the site's Web address. At first glance, you may find Web addresses a little intimidating. All Web addresses start with the letters http (for hypertext transport protocol), a colon, and two forward slashes (http://). Next, most Web addresses include the letters www (for World Wide Web). For the sites listed in Figures 10.1 through 10.3, the Web addresses are as follows:

    http://www.microsoft.com

    http://www.mtv.com

    http://www.jamsa.com

Note: To obtain Web addresses for thousands of sites which discuss thousands of topics, turn to the books **World Wide Web Directory**, Jamsa Press, 1995 and **1001 Really Cool Web Sites**, Jamsa Press, 1995.

Across the World Wide Web, there are millions of documents, each with its own unique address. Depending on whom you talk to about a Web site, users may say "its **address** is http://www.whitehouse.gov" or "its **URL** is http://www.netscape.com". A URL is a unique resource locator—in short, an address. If you read or hear the term URL, for simplicity, you can replace it with the term address.

10: Connecting Windows 95 to the Internet and World Wide Web

Understanding Homepages

As you surf the Web for information, you will normally start your search at a company's starting page, or *homepage*. From the homepage, you can click on your topics of interest. From the Microsoft homepage, for example, you might click your way to discussions on software, Windows 95, or even employment opportunities. Think of a homepage as a site's main menu, from which you can easily move to other Web documents.

How the Web Simplifies Information Retrieval

The Web makes it easy for you to find information on the Net by linking together related documents. For example, assume that you are interested in reading about Michael Jordan. To start your search, you might try the ESPNet SportsZone (http://espnet.sportszone.com). At ESPNet, you may see highlighted text that discusses basketball. Such highlighted text is a link (the experts call them "hyperlinks"). When you click your mouse on the link, your browser will locate and display the linked document's contents. Within a basketball article, you are bound to find a link that discusses Michael Jordan. What makes the Web so powerful is that the document's links may take you to sites around the world. As you read a document, you don't know (and don't need to know) where the document resides. In the case of the Michael Jordan article, you could find information that resides on a computer in Europe, or even the Far East. By connecting documents that exist around the world, the Web creates a Web of information that spans the globe. As you will find with the Internet, the Web will be much easier for you to understand and appreciate after you have taken it for a test drive. Later in this chapter, you will download a Web browser and do just that.

Important Information You Must Get from Your Internet Provider

As you search for an Internet provider, your monthly connection cost is obviously a consideration. In addition, you want a provider that supports PPP connections. After you sign up with a provider, make sure they tell you the following information:

One or more local phone numbers you can call using your modem to establish your Internet connection

Your username that you must type in each time you connect to the system

Your password that you must type in each time you connect to the system

The Internet address of the site they want you to use for your domain name server. The Internet address which consists of four numbers separated by three periods, such as 123.231.111.3

The hostname of the news server you will use to read newsgroup information

The hostname of the POP3 mail server, your e-mail address, and any username and password information you need to access the e-mail system

---

Understanding Internet Addresses and Hostnames

Across the Internet, every computer that connects must have a unique Internet address (called an IP address, or Internet protocol address). The computer's Internet address is a sequence of four numbers separated by periods. Each number within an IP address must be in the range 0 to 255. For example, the IP address for jamsa.com is 168.158.20.102. In short, the IP address uniquely identifies each computer on the Internet. When you connect to the Internet using your provider, the provider must give you an IP address. Your IP address may change each time you connect. Luckily, the Windows 95 software

217

SUCCESS WITH WINDOWS 95

takes care of getting your IP address for you. All you will need to do is use the Windows 95 dial-up networking software to dial your provider.

As you can imagine, given the millions of users that connect to the Internet each day, and the thousands of businesses and universities that are constantly connected, it would be very confusing if you had to know everyone's Internet address. Luckily, you don't have to. Instead, each site on the Net has a unique domain name, such as ftp.microsoft.com, mtv.com, whitehouse.gov, and jamsa.com. When you run Internet-based programs, you use the site's domain name. Behind the scenes, however, your software uses a special site, called a *domain name server,* to convert the domain name into the numeric Internet address. In short, your software gives the domain name server a name, such as jamsa.com, and the domain name server gives your software back a numeric Internet address.

When you subscribe to an Internet provider, they will tell you the Internet address (the numeric address) of the domain name server they want you to use to connect to the Net.

SETTING UP WINDOWS 95 TO USE DIAL-UP TCP/IP NETWORKING

To access the Internet from within Windows 95, you use a special software that supports a TCP/IP connection. TPC/IP is an acronym for Transport Control Protocol/Internet Protocol. In short, TCP/IP defines the set of rules that software programs follow to communicate over the Internet. Before you can use Windows 95 to connect to your provider, you must prepare Windows 95 to use its built-in TCP/IP support. To setup TCP/IP on your system, perform these steps:

1. Select the Start menu Settings option and choose Control Panel. Windows 95, in turn, will display the Control Panel window.

2. Within the Control Panel window, double-click your mouse on the Network icon. Windows 95, in turn, will display the Network dialog box shown in Figure 10.4.

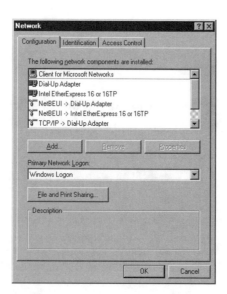

Figure 10.4 The Network dialog box.

Depending on your installation choices and possible changes to your network settings, your system may or may not list the Dial-up Adapter, shown in Figure 10.4. If your system does not list the Dial-Up Adapter, perform these steps:

1. Within the Network dialog box, select the Add button. Windows 95 will display the Select Network Component Type dialog box, as shown in Figure 10.5.

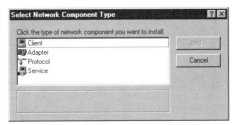

Figure 10.5 The Select Network Component Type dialog box.

2. Click your mouse on the Adapter entry and choose Add. Windows 95 will display the Select Network adapter dialog box, as shown in Figure 10.6.

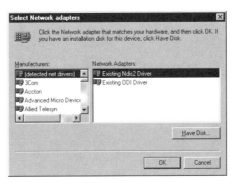

Figure 10.6 The Select Network adapter dialog box.

3. Scroll through the list of manufacturers and select Microsoft.
4. Within the list of Microsoft Network Adapters, highlight Dial-Up Adapter and choose OK.

Next, to add TCP/IP support, perform these steps:

1. Within the Network dialog box Configuration page, highlight Dial-Up adapter and choose Add. Windows 95, in turn, will display the Select Network Component Type dialog box, as previously shown in Figure 10.5.
2. Select the Protocol entry and choose Add. Windows 95 will display the Select Network Protocol dialog box, as shown in Figure 10.7.

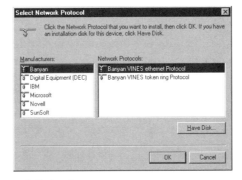

Figure 10.7 The Select Network Protocol dialog box.

3. Scroll through the list of manufacturers and highlight Microsoft. Within the Network Protocols list, highlight TCP/IP and choose OK.

4. Within the Network dialog box, choose OK. Windows 95, in turn, may prompt you to insert one or more of the Windows 95 installation disks. Next, Windows 95 may restart your system to put your network changes into effect.

CONFIGURING YOUR TCP/IP SETTINGS

In most cases, you can use the default TCP/IP settings to connect to your Internet provider. However, should you encounter problems connecting to your provider, you may need to configure your TCP/IP settings. Your provider will give you the settings values you will need to use. Should you need to configure your TCP/IP settings, perform these steps:

1. Within the Network dialog box, select the TCP/IP.

2. Select Properties. Windows 95, in turn, will display the TCP/IP Properties dialog box, as shown in Figure 10.8.

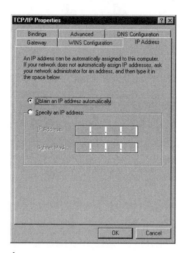

Figure 10.8 The TCP/IP Properties dialog box.

3. Within the dialog box, select the tab that corresponds to the settings your provider wants you to change.

4. Make the changes your provider specifies, and choose OK.

ESTABLISHING A DIAL-UP CONNECTION

After you have obtained your account and account information from your Internet provider, and set up Windows 95 to support TCP/IP networking, you are ready to connect to your provider. Your first step in connecting to your provider is to set up a dial-up connection. To create a dial-up connection for your provider, perform these steps:

1. Select the Start menu Programs option and choose Accessories.

2. Within the Accessories menu, choose Dial-Up Networking. Windows 95, in turn, will display the Dial-Up Networking folder, as shown in Figure 10.9.

10: Connecting Windows 95 to the Internet and World Wide Web

Figure 10.9 The Dial-Up Networking folder.

3. Double-click your mouse on the Make New Connection icon. Windows 95, in turn, will display the Make New Connection Wizard, as shown in Figure 10.10.

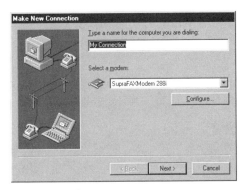

Figure 10.10 The Make New Connection Wizard.

4. Within the Name field, type in a name that corresponds to your Internet provider. Within the Select a modem field, use the pull-down list to select the modem you desire.

5. Click your mouse on the Next button. The Wizard will change its display to prompt you for the phone number you will be dialing, as shown in Figure 10.11.

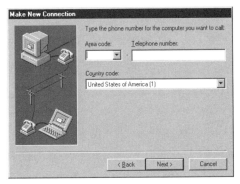

Figure 10.11 The Wizard's prompt for the remote-computer phone number.

6. Within the Area code field, type in the area code for your provider's access number. Within the Telephone field, type in the provider's phone number. Select Next. The Wizard, in turn, will display a dialog box that lets you save your connection information.

7. Choose Finish. The Wizard will add an icon to your Dial-Up Networking folder that corresponds to your provider.

Before you can connect to your Internet provider, you need to configure a few more settings. To complete your provider setup, perform these steps:

1. Within the Dial-Up Networking dialog box, right-click your mouse on the icon that corresponds to your provider connection. Windows 95, in turn, will display a pop-up menu.

2. Choose Properties. Windows 95, in turn, will display a General page similar to that shown in Figure 10.12.

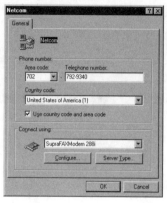

Figure 10.12 The General page for a dial-up connection.

3. Click your mouse on the Server Type button. Windows 95 will display the Server Types dialog box, shown in Figure 10.13.

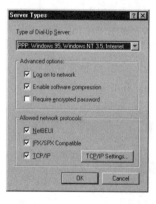

Figure 10.13 The Server Types dialog box.

4. Within the Type of Dial-Up Server pull-down list, select the PPP: Windows 95, Windows NT 3.5, Internet Option.

5. Click your mouse on the TCP/IP Settings buttons. Windows 95, in turn, will display the TCP/IP Settings dialog box, shown in Figure 10.14.

6. Click your mouse on the Specify name server addresses button, and type in the name server addresses given to you by your Internet provider. If your provider did not give you name server addresses, use the following addresses:

```
192.112.36.4        (NS.NIC.DDN.MIL)
128.63.4.82         (AOS.BRL.MIL)
192.36.148.17       (NIC.NORDU.NET)
198.41.0.4          (NS.INTERNIC.NET)
```

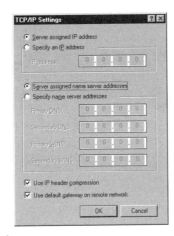

Figure 10.14 *The TCP/IP Settings dialog box.*

7. Choose OK. Within the General page, choose OK.

CONNECTING TO YOUR PROVIDER

After you configure your dial-up connection, you are ready to connect to your Internet provider. To use Windows 95 to connect to your Internet provider, perform these steps:

1. Within the Dial-Up Networking window, double-click your mouse on the icon that corresponds to your provider. Windows 95, in turn, will display the Connect To dialog box shown in Figure 10.15.

Figure 10.15 *The Connect To dialog box.*

2. Within the Username field, type in the username given to you by your provider.
3. Within the Password field, type in the password given to you by your provider.

Note: Should you receive error messages when you try to connect to your provider, which state that your username and password are invalid, contact your provider's technical support and tell them you are trying to connect using Windows 95. In some cases, a provider may tell you to precede your username or password with a special symbol, such as a pound sign (#).

4. Select Connect. Windows 95, in turn, will display a dialog box similar to that shown in Figure 10.16, within which you can monitor your connection.

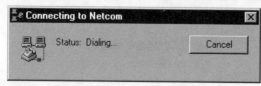

Figure 10.16 *The Connecting dialog box.*

5. When Windows 95 successfully connects you to your provider, Windows 95 will display a Connected dialog box similar to that shown in Figure 10.17.

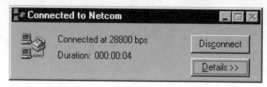

Figure 10.17 *The Connected dialog box.*

The Connected dialog box tells you specifics about your connection, such as your speed and how long you have been connected. Do not close the Connected dialog box until you are ready to end the connection to your provider. However, you can minimize the dialog box to a Taskbar icon to move it out of your way. With your connection in place, you are ready to test drive the Windows 95 Internet software.

WINDOWS 95 INTERNET-BASED SOFTWARE

After you establish your connection to your Internet provider, you can try out several of the Internet-based programs provided with Windows 95. Later, using the Windows 95 ftp program, you will download a Web browser that you can use to traverse the World Wide Web.

TESTING A REMOTE COMPUTER USING PING

When you "surf the net," there will be times when you have trouble connecting to a specific site. In such cases, you can use the ping command to determine whether or not the remote computer is active. To "ping" a site to determine if the site is active, perform these steps:

1. Select the Start menu Run option. Windows 95, in turn, will display the Run dialog box.
2. Within the Open field, type **command**, as shown in Figure 10.18, and press ENTER. Windows 95 will open an MS-DOS window within which you can run the ping command.

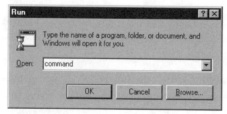

Figure 10.18 *Use **command** to open an MS-DOS window.*

The ping command lets you determine if a remote computer is working. When you issue the ping command, you specify the computer you desire, such as www.microsoft.com. The ping command, in turn, will send a message to the remote computer. If the remote computer is working, it will send ping a response which ping, in turn, will display on your screen. If ping does not receive a response from the remote computer, the remote computer is probably down. Figure 10.19, for example, displays the results of a ping command that tests the state of www.microsoft.com.

Figure 10.19 Using ping to check the state of www.microsoft.com.

In this case, the ping command lets you know that the remote system (in this case, www.microsoft.com) responded. If the remote system is down, ping will either display a message that it did not receive a response, or that your site name is invalid.

Using Telnet to Connect to a Remote Computer

Prior to the World Wide Web, one of the most common ways users surfed the Net was using the telnet command. With telnet, users could connect to a remote computer and run programs. Using telnet, you can connect to several interesting sites. For example, at Colorado University, you can use telnet to list the pro basketball, baseball, and hockey schedules. Likewise, at Columbia University, you can perform law research. In short, when you telnet to a remote computer, it's just as if you are working at that computer. To use telnet to connect to a remote computer under Windows 95, perform these steps:

1. Select the Start menu Run option. Windows 95 will display the Run dialog box.

2. Within the Open field, type Telnet. Windows 95, in turn, will open a telnet window, as shown in Figure 10.20.

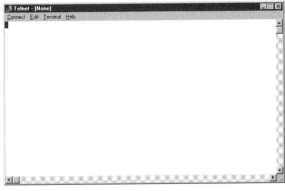

Figure 10.20 Running the telnet command under Windows 95.

3. Within the telnet window, select the Connect menu Remote System option. Windows 95, in turn, will display the Connect dialog box, as shown in Figure 10.21.

Figure 10.21 The Connect dialog box.

4. Within the Host Name field, type in the name of the system to which you want to connect. Table 10.1 lists several interesting telnet sites.

5. Within the Port field, select Telnet, or type in the numeric port number listed in Table 10.1.

6. Choose Connect. The telnet program, in turn, will connect you to the remote computer. Depending on the computer to which you are connecting, you may need to type in a username and password.

Site	Port	Contents	Username
culine.colorado.edu	859	NBA schedules	
culine.colorado.edu	863	NFL schedules	
locis.loc.gov		Library of Congress	
lawnet.law.columbia.edu		Law	lawnet

Table 10.1 Interesting telnet sites.

Figure 10.22, for example, illustrates the NBA schedule you'll find by using telnet to connect to Colorado University.

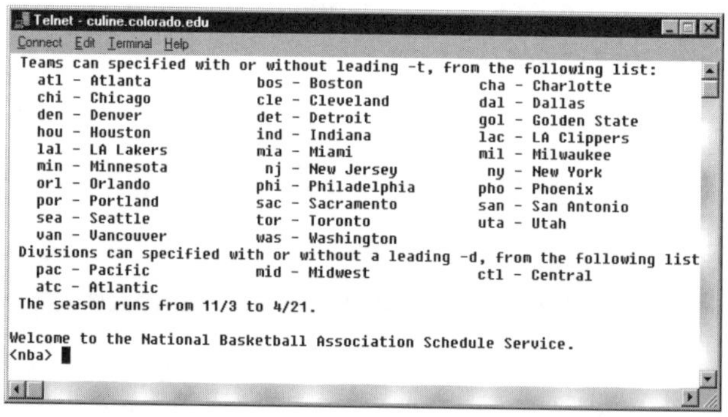

Figure 10.22 Listing NBA team schedules at Colorado University.

TRANSFERRING FILES FROM A REMOTE COMPUTER

Across the Internet, there are hundreds of thousands of files available for you to download to your computer. To download a file across the Internet, you use a special software program called ftp. The letters ftp are an acronym for file transfer protocol—the rules programs follow to exchange files across the Net. To help you get started, Windows 95 provides a simple command-line-based ftp command. To open a DOS window within which you can run the ftp command, perform these steps:

1. Select the Start menu Run option. Windows 95, in turn, will display the Run dialog box.

2. Within the Open field, type **command** and press ENTER.

Table 10.2 lists several interesting sites you may want to visit using ftp to search the Net.

Site	Contents	Directory
ftp.microsoft.com	Software	/pub
ftp.mcom.com	Netscape Web software	/2.0/windows
mthvax.cs.miami.edu	Home brewing	/homebrew
nic.funet.fi	Television	/pub/culture/tv+film

Table 10.2 Interesting ftp sites.

To access an ftp site, type **ftp** followed by the system name at the command prompt. Depending on the site to which you are connecting, you may receive a prompt for a username and password. If you encounter such a prompt, type **anonymous** for the username, and your e-mail address for the password. Most ftp sites provide a directory named /pub within which they will place files that they allow the public to access. In most cases, when you log into an ftp site, the site will start you out in the /pub directory. To list the files within the directory, use the **ls** command. When you locate the file you desire, you can retrieve the file to your computer using the **get** command. For example, Figure 10.23 lists files within the /pub directory at ftp.microsoft.com.

Figure 10.23 Using ls to list files in the /pub directory at ftp.microsoft.com.

USING THE FTP COMMAND TO DOWNLOAD A WEB BROWSER

To access the World Wide Web, you need a special program called a Web browser. Two of the most popular Web browsers are Netscape Navigator and the Microsoft Internet Explorer. Using the ftp command, you can download both of these browsers.

To download the Netscape Navigator browser, perform these steps:

1. Use **ftp** to connect to ftp.mcom.com
2. Use **cd** to select the directory 2.0/windows
3. Use **get** to retrieve the file n32e20.exe
4. Run the n32e20.exe program to extract (decompress) the Netscape-browser setup software

To download the Microsoft Internet Explorer browser, perform these steps:

1. Use ftp to connect to ftp.microsoft.com
2. Use cd to select the directory softlib/mslfiles
3. Use get to retrieve the file msie20.exe
4. Run the msie20.exe program to extract (decompress) the Microsoft-browser setup software

Surfing the World Wide Web

After you install your Web browser, you are ready to surf the World Wide Web. To get started, run your browser program. Next, try out some of the sites listed in Table 10.3. As your browser displays a site, use your scroll bar to view the information the site displays. As you scroll, you will encounter highlighted text and graphics which will link you to other sites. When you click your mouse on a link, your browser will retrieve the linked document. The instant you click on your first link, you are officially surfing the World Wide Web.

Web Address	Contents
http://www.microsoft.com	Information on Microsoft products
http://www.nasa.gov	Information on NASA and the space program
http://www.timeinc.com/si/	Sports Illustrated Online
http://www.shakespeare.com	Many of Shakespeare's works
http://booksonline.com	An online book club
http://virtumall.com/	Online shopping
http://www.realaudio.com	A real audio player
http://www.esrin.esa.it/	European Space Agency
http://www.who.ch/	World Health Organization
http://www.yahoo.com	A search engine for other topics

Table 10.3 Interesting sites on the World Wide Web.

Keys to Success

The Internet and the World Wide Web are becoming two of the most popular pastimes for all types of users. In this chapter you learned that Windows 95 makes it very easy for you to connect to the Internet. In Chapter 11, you will learn how Windows 95 supports notebook PC users. Before you continue with Chapter 11, however, make sure you have learned the following key concepts:

- ✓ The Internet connects networks of computers around the globe.

- ✓ Users connect to the Internet to send and receive electronic mail, share files, or chat with other users.

- ✓ The World Wide Web is a collection of linked documents that make it easier for you to find the information you want across the Internet.

- ✓ To use the World Wide Web, you need a special program called a Web browser.

- ✓ The World Wide Web sits on top of the Internet. In other words, to surf the World Wide Web, you use the cables, computers, and protocols that are the Internet.

- ✓ To access the Internet from your PC, you need to establish an account with an Internet provider.

- ✓ Windows 95 dial-up networking makes it very easy for you to connect your PC to an Internet provider.

- ✓ To help you determine if a remote computer is active, Windows 95 provides the ping command.

- ✓ To let you transfer files to and from remote computers, Windows 95 provides the ftp command.

- ✓ A Web browser is a software program that lets you view documents across the World Wide Web. Although Microsoft does not include a Web browser in Windows 95, you can use the ftp command to download a browser from across the Internet.

Chapter 11
Using Windows 95 on Your Notebook PC

If you make frequent business trips, you probably use (or are thinking about purchasing) a notebook PC. Small and lightweight notebook PCs let you perform—on the road, in the air, at your hotel, and just about anywhere—most of the tasks that your desktop system does. As such, if you have a report due next week and an unexpected business trip comes up, you can save the report on a floppy disk, load the disk into your notebook PC, and work on the report as you travel.

Today, most notebook PCs run Windows 3.1, but Windows 95 includes several features that make it the ideal operating system for your notebook computer. Most notable among Windows 95's notebook-friendly features is the Briefcase, which you can use to synchronize documents between your notebook and desktop computers. In other words, the Windows 95 Briefcase determines whether your notebook or desktop PC contains the latest copy of your document, and automatically updates (synchronizes) the PC with the outdated copy. Before Windows 95, operating systems offered no such synchronization feature. As such, if you had a copy of a file on both your notebook and desktop PC, you were responsible for keeping track of which file was the most recent, and then for selecting the most recent file when it came time to work. As a result, notebook PC users sometimes inadvertently "wiped out" files they'd modified while traveling.

For example, assume a Windows 3.1 user wanted to edit a file on the road. As such, the user copied the file to a floppy disk and used his or her notebook PC to edit the file from the floppy. Then, after the user returned from the trip, he or she copied the latest version of the file to his or her desktop PC. To perform the file copy operation, the user put the disk (with the file) into the desktop PC's floppy drive and started the Windows 3.1 File Manager on the desktop PC. Then, the user opened two windows in File Manager—one with the hard disk's contents and the other with the floppy drive's contents. However, in the final step, the user sometimes made a grievous error. Mentally exhausted from the trip, the user accidentally dragged and dropped the report from the hard disk window to the floppy drive window, instead of the other way around. As a result, the user wiped out all the work he or she put into that report while traveling.

As you will see later in this chapter, with the Windows 95 Briefcase, you no longer have to worry about accidentally overwriting a newer version of a file with an older version. In this chapter, you will learn how to use the Briefcase and other features that make Windows 95 a good choice for your notebook PC.

By the time you finish this chapter, you will understand the following key concepts:

- Windows 95 provides features such as the Briefcase and power management that support notebook PCs.

- Using the Windows 95 Briefcase, you can manage changes to documents you share between your desktop computer and notebook PC.

- If you use a notebook PC, you can connect your notebook to your desktop PC using a network, a direct-cable connection, or Windows 95 dial-up networking.

- To maximize your notebook PC's battery life, Windows 95 provides advanced-power management capabilities.

- To expand your notebook's hardware capabilities, users make extensive use of PCMCIA (or PC card) devices. Windows 95 provides support to help you configure such devices.

Note: *This chapter uses the term* **notebook PC** *as a generic name for any small and lightweight PC that you can easily carry with you. Notebook PCs go by names such as laptops, portables, and even subnotebooks. The term* **PC** *refers to "personal computer."*

NOTEBOOK PCS AND WINDOWS 95

Notebook PCs are convenient because they help you take your work with you when you travel. Likewise, many users take their work with them between their home and office in a notebook PC. However, this convenience comes at a price. To start, the actual cost of a notebook PC typically is higher than its desktop counterpart. Additionally, notebook PCs often use smaller screens, keyboards, and hard disks than desktop PCs. Because notebook PC display screens are flat and small, they use a different technology than desktop PC monitors. As a result, your notebook PC's display may not be as bright and colorful as you like (unless you are willing to pay more money for a notebook PC with an active-matrix display). Furthermore, because many notebook PC screens (especially LCD screens) don't have the contrast of their desktop counterparts, you may find the mouse pointer hard to see on your notebook's monitor. However, using the Control Panel Mouse icon (see Chapter 5), you can enable a Windows 95 feature that leaves a trail as you move the pointer. These mouse trails makes it easy for you to find your mouse pointer if it does not showup clearly on your notebook PC's display screen. Figure 11.1 shows how mouse trails appear on your screen display.

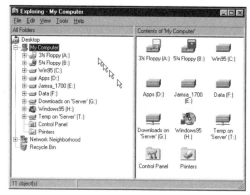

Figure 11.1 Mouse trails help you locate your mouse pointer on the screen.

The notebook PC's small size also limits the physical size of disk drives and other peripherals it can contain. Until recently, most notebook PCs had hard disks with 80 to 120Mb capacity. Because new technology lets notebook PC vendors pack more data into smaller disks, even low-end notebooks now have hard disks with 200 to 300Mb capacity. (Higher-end, and more expensive, notebook PCs can have disk drives with up to 800Mb capacity.) However, many existing notebook computers still have limited disk capacity. As such, an ideal operating system for notebook PCs should use as little disk space as possible. Windows 95 provides a notebook configuration that installs only the files the operating system needs to run on a notebook.

INSTALLING THE WINDOWS 95 PORTABLE PC CONFIGURATION

As you have learned, because notebook computers often have limited disk space, Windows 95 provides a notebook configuration that installs only the files the operating system needs to run on a portable PC. When you install Windows 95, the Setup program displays an option button with the label "Portable." To install the notebook configuration, select the Portable option button. The Windows 95 Setup program, in turn, will copy only those files necessary for a portable (notebook) PC.

To let you connect other peripherals (such as modems, network adapters, and a second hard disk) to your notebook computer, portable PC vendors developed the *Personal Computer Memory Card International Association* (PCMCIA) interface. Windows 95 includes built-in support for PCMCIA.

As you probably know, your notebook PC draws power from a battery. (You can plug your notebook computer into an electrical outlet, but many places you may want to use your notebook computer, such as on an airplane, will not have electrical outlets.) Your notebook PC's battery has a limited amount of electrical power. To help you conserve the power in your Notebook PC's battery, Windows 95 supports Advanced Power Management (APM) Version 1.1, which includes the following features:

- A battery meter shows you the power that remains in your notebook PC's battery.

- The Start menu includes a Suspend option that puts your notebook PC "to sleep." When you select the Suspend option, Windows 95 turns off your notebook PC's disk drives and display screen, but does not completely shut down the notebook system.

- You can shut off your notebook PC's power when you shut down Windows 95 (otherwise, you have to first shut down Windows 95, and then turn off your notebook PC's power switch).

Connecting Your Notebook PC to Your Desktop PC

If you use a notebook PC when you travel, you most likely have a desktop PC at a more permanent location, such as your office or home. When you work on both notebook and desktop systems, you often will need to connect the systems so you can transfer documents between them. Fortunately, Windows 95 offers you several ways to physically connect your notebook and desktop PCs.

Network

If your notebook PC has a network interface (this interface is usually a PCMCIA card) and your office has a *local area network* (LAN), you can use the network to transfer files between your notebook and desktop PCs. The main advantage to using your office's LAN for file transfers is that network connections are high-speed. No other type of connection, including a direct-cable connection between your notebook and desktop PCs, can transfer data as quickly as your office's LAN. Figure 11.2 illustrates a notebook computer connected to a local area network.

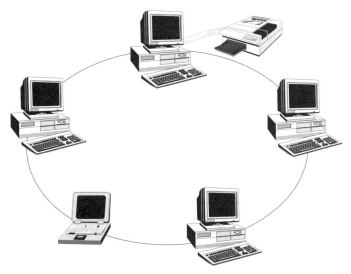

Figure 11.2 *By connecting your notebook computer to a network, you simplify file transfer operations.*

Typically, a LAN has a file-server computer that may store files for all the other computers on the network, including your desktop PC. The *file server* makes it easy for network users to share documents because all files reside at a single location. As such, to use your LAN to transfer files between your notebook and desktop PCs, you might copy documents to and from the file server. Before you leave on a trip, you copy documents from the file server to your notebook PC. Then, after you return from the trip, you copy the documents from your notebook PC back to the file server.

Note: *Depending on your networking expertise, you may transfer files across the network directly between your desktop and notebook PC. To transfer files directly between the two computers, you would map to a drive on the remote (either your desktop or notebook), PC as discussed next.*

To transfer documents between the file server and your notebook PC, you "map a drive letter to the remote network drive." In other words, you map the file server's disk drive to your notebook PC's operating system. After you map a network drive, Windows 95 will view the file server's disk drive as a "new" drive on your notebook (and even assign the file server's disk drive a drive letter). Then, when you copy documents from your "new" hard disk to your notebook PC's floppy-disk drive, Windows 95 will transfer the documents over the network. For example, I have several networked computers; one of them is named LNB486. To access a drive on LNB486 from another computer (such as my notebook PC), I perform these steps:

1. Double-click on the My Computer icon on the notebook PC's Desktop. Windows 95 will open the My Computer folder.

2. Click on the toolbar Map Network Drive button (the third button from the left), as shown by the mouse pointer in Figure 11.3. Windows 95, in turn, will display the Map Network Drive dialog box, as shown in Figure 11.4.

Figure 11.3 The Map Network Drive button.

Figure 11.4 The Map Network Drive dialog box.

3. In the Map Network Drive dialog box Path field, enter the path for the network drive (Windows 95 already fills in the Drive field with the next available drive letter). Drive paths use nearly the same syntax as file pathnames. However, a drive path always begins with the name of the computer (file server) where the network drive resides.

4. Click on the OK button. Windows 95, in turn, will display the network drive's folder, as shown in Figure 11.5.

Figure 11.5 A network drive folder.

In Figure 11.5, note the network drive folder's name: "E$ on 'Lnb486' (F:)." This name means that the notebook PC's drive F is a *shared folder* named E$ in a computer named Lnb486. (You can access a shared folder, which resides on one computer's disk, from any computer on the network.)

> *Learning a Network Computer's Name*
>
>
>
> Before you can connect to a network computer, you need to know the computer's name. To see your own computer's name, double-click on the Control Panel's Network icon. Windows 95, in turn, will open the Network sheet. Click on the Network sheet Identification tab. Windows 95, in turn, will display the Identification page, which contains the computer's name.
>
> To learn the name of a computer that resides on the same network as yours, double-click on the desktop's Network Neighborhood icon. Windows 95, in turn, will open the Network Neighborhood folder. In the Network Neighborhood folder, you will see an icon and a name for each computer connected to the network.

After you map a network drive, you can copy files to or from the network drive, just as if the drive belonged to your local computer. In this case, after you map the file server's drive, you can access the drive using the drive letter *F* on your machine.

> *Understanding Shared Folders*
>
>
>
> Within a local area network, users exchange files by placing the files into shared folders. In short, think of a shared folder as a file cabinet drawer that employees throughout your office can use to store or retrieve files. Just as you can implement controls that limit who can access the file cabinet drawer (for example, you might give five employees keys to the cabinet), Windows 95 lets you control which users can place files into or retrieve files from a shared folder.
>
> To access a shared folder, you map the folder to a drive letter on your PC. After that, you access the files using the mapped drive, just as if the files resided on your own PC.

Docking Bay

Typically, as a notebook PC user, you give up memory space, peripherals, and display screen color and resolution so Wthat you can carry your work with you. To handle tasks your notebook PC can't, you usually need a second system—a desktop system with a high-resolution monitor, lots of memory space, full-size keyboard, network and printer connections, and so on. However, depending on your lottery luck, you may not be able to afford two systems.

A docking bay offers you a way out of this dilemma. Essentially, the docking bay (as the name suggests) is like a desktop PC without the innards you'd normally find in the system's case (the metal box that you call the "PC"). As shown in Figure 11.6, you insert your notebook PC into this bay. Both the metal case and the notebook PC have connectors that hook up when you insert the notebook PC into the docking bay. Then, you operate your notebook PC using the docking bay's larger keyboard, better display screen, serial ports, and parallel ports. Depending on its type, the docking bay may contain a floppy disk, hard disk, and even a CD-ROM drive.

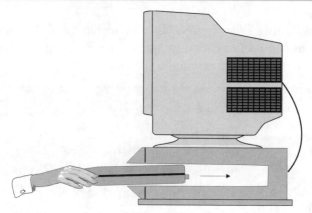

Figure 11.6 Inserting a notebook PC into a docking bay.

When you must travel, you simply remove your notebook PC from the docking bay and go. Because there is only one main disk, you don't need to worry about creating another version of your documents.

DIRECT CABLE CONNECTION

If you do not have a network connection or a docking bay, you can still connect your notebook PC to your desktop PC using a cable between their serial or parallel ports. Figure 11.7 illustrates a notebook and desktop PC connected using a direct cable connection.

Figure 11.7 Connecting a notebook and desktop PC using a direct cable connection.

To begin, you run the Windows 95 Direct Cable Connection wizard on both systems. You access the Direct Cable Connection wizard from the Start menu (*Start> Programs> Accessories> Direct Cable Connection*). To connect two PCs using their serial ports, you must use a special *null modem* cable. To connect the PCs using their parallel ports, you must use a special *bidirectional parallel* cable. You can purchase these cables at most computer stores.

When you use the Direct Cable Connection wizard, you normally designate the desktop PC as the "host" and the notebook PC as the "guest." After the Wizard establishes the connection, you will use the guest system (your notebook PC) to transfer files to or from the host. To establish a direct-cable connection between your notebook and desktop PCs, perform these steps:

1. Connect the two computers using a null-modem or bidirectional-parallel cable. You can either connect the two computers' serial ports or parallel ports.

2. On the notebook PC, start the Direct Cable Connection wizard from the Start menu (*Start> Programs> Accessories> Direct Cable Connection*). Windows 95, in turn, will run the Direct Cable Connection wizard, as shown in Figure 11.8.

11: Using Windows 95 on Your Notebook PC

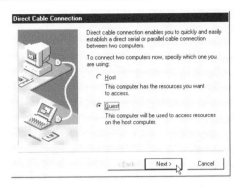

Figure 11.8 The initial dialog box of the Direct Cable Connection wizard.

3. Click on the Guest button and choose Next. The Direct Cable Connection wizard will ask you to specify the port you want to use for the connection.

4. Click on the port you want. The Direct Cable Connection wizard will highlight the port you select, as shown in Figure 11.9.

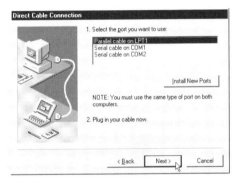

Figure 11.9 The Direct Cable Connection wizard asks you to specify the port you want to use for the direct connection.

5. Click on the Next button. The Direct Cable Connection wizard will inform you that you have successfully set up the guest computer (your notebook PC) and prompt you to set up the host computer (your desktop PC), as shown in Figure 11.10.

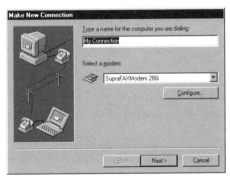

Figure 11.10 The Direct Cable Connection wizard informs you that you have successfully set up the guest computer (on the notebook PC).

6. On the desktop PC, start the Direct Cable Connection wizard and repeat steps 1 through 4, but click on the Host option button in step 3.

7. On the notebook PC, click on the Finish button (see Figure 11.10). The Direct Cable Connection wizard on the notebook PC will establish a connection with its counterpart on the desktop PC.

> ### USING SERIAL AND PARALLEL PORTS IN A DIRECT CABLE CONNECTION
>
>
>
> As you have learned, serial ports transmit and receive data one bit (binary digit) at a time. To connect two PCs using their serial ports, you must use a special null-modem cable. Parallel ports, on the other hand, transmit and receive data eight bits (binary digits) at a time, over eight wires. Therefore, if you want a direct cable connection that carries data at the highest possible speed, connect your notebook and desktop PCs through their parallel ports. To connect the PCs using their parallel ports, you must use a special *bidirectional* parallel cable.

After the connection is set up, you can access your desktop PC's folders from your notebook PC, just as you could with a network connection between the two systems.

THE BRIEFCASE

If you use a notebook PC to work on documents while you travel, you likely have a desktop PC at a more permanent location, such as your home or office. If you're like most people, you store the permanent copies of your documents on your desktop PC. Using your notebook PC, you copy files from your desktop PC and take the files with you as you travel. When you later return to your home or office, you can update both systems with the latest versions of your files. To simplify the process of updating your PCs with the latest versions of each file, Windows 95 provides the Briefcase program.

CREATING A BRIEFCASE

You do not have to do anything to create a Briefcase. The Windows 95 installation program creates a My Briefcase icon on your system's Desktop, as shown in Figure 11.11.

Figure 11.11 The My Briefcase icon on the Desktop.

Note: *If you do not see the My Briefcase icon on your Desktop, the Windows 95 Briefcase component may not be installed on your system. To add the Windows 95 Briefcase component, follow the steps Chapter 6 discusses in the section entitled "Adding Windows 95 Components." You will need the Windows 95 CD or installation disks to add the Briefcase program.*

USING THE BRIEFCASE

Suppose you are taking a trip and want to use your notebook PC to work on a document while you're away from the office. Right now, the document is on your desktop PC. To use the Briefcase, perform these steps:

1. Establish a connection (network or direct cable) between your notebook and desktop PCs.

2. Working at your notebook PC, drag the documents you need from your desktop PC's folder to your notebook PC's My Briefcase icon. For example, in Figure 11.12, the mouse pointer has dragged a document from the network drive's work folder (in this case, the systems are on a network) and is dropping it on the notebook PC's My Briefcase icon.

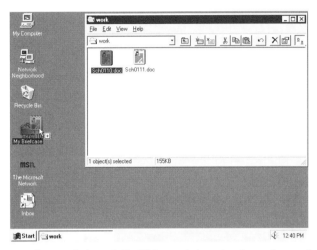

Figure 11.12 Dragging a document from a desktop PC's folder and dropping it on the notebook PC's My Briefcase icon.

3. Disconnect the notebook and desktop PCs. Now you can use your notebook PC to work on the document.

To work on the document on your notebook PC, double-click on the My Briefcase icon. Windows 95, in turn, will open the My Briefcase folder and show its contents. Next, double-click on the document's icon. Windows 95, in turn, will open the document, provided your notebook PC has the program you used to create the document.

UPDATING DOCUMENTS WITH THE BRIEFCASE

When you return from your trip, you use the Briefcase to update, if necessary, the original documents on your desktop PC. To update documents with the Briefcase, perform these steps:

1. Reestablish the connection between your notebook and desktop PCs.

2. On your notebook PC, double-click on the My Briefcase icon. Windows 95 will open the My Briefcase window.

3. Click your mouse on the menu bar's Briefcase category. Windows 95 will display the My Briefcase menu, as shown in Figure 11.13.

Figure 11.13 The My Briefcase window Briefcase menu.

4. Click on the Briefcase menu Update All option. Windows 95 will display the Update My Briefcase dialog box, as shown in Figure 11.14, and recommend an update action.

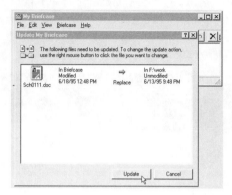

Figure 11.14 *The Update My Briefcase dialog box appears when you select the Briefcase menu Update All option.*

5. If the update action Windows 95 recommends is acceptable, click on the Update button. Windows 95, in turn, will copy the documents in the Update My Briefcase dialog box to update the originals.

If the documents in the Briefcase are identical to the originals (if you did not work on the documents in the Briefcase), Windows 95 will tell you so. On such occasions, Windows 95 will display the dialog box you see in Figure 11.15 when you select the Briefcase menu Update All option.

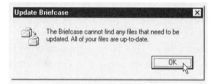

Figure 11.15 *The Update Briefcase dialog box when no files need updating.*

UPDATING A SELECTED FILE

As you work with your notebook PC, there may be times when you'll not want to update all the files that appear in the My Briefcase window. For example, during a business trip, you may not have had time to work on all the files you originally placed in the Briefcase. To update your desktop PC's copy of only one file, click on that file's icon in the My Briefcase folder. Windows 95, in turn, will highlight the file's icon and name. Next, select the Briefcase menu Update Selection option. Windows 95, in turn, will display the Update My Briefcase dialog box and try to update only the selected file.

KEEP YOUR SYSTEM'S DATE-AND-TIME CORRECT

The Windows 95 Briefcase determines which documents to update based on each document's date-and-time stamps. Each time you change and save a document's contents, Windows 95 records the current date-and-time to the file's last modified time stamp. If your desktop or notebook PC is not using the correct date-and-time, its last modified time stamp may be wrong, causing the Briefcase to overwrite the wrong file. To set your system's date-and-time, double-click your mouse on the Taskbar's clock icon and follow the steps discussed in Chapter 5, "Customizing Common Hardware."

11: Using Windows 95 on Your Notebook PC

Overriding the Suggested Update Action

When you select the Briefcase menu Update All option, Briefcase suggests an update action. However, you do not always have to accept the action Windows 95 recommends. For example, assume you have been working with ten documents, but, for some reason, you only want to update the first nine documents on your desktop PC (maybe you've decided to discard your changes to the tenth document). To override the recommended action, perform these steps:

1. Select the Briefcase menu Update All option. Windows 95, in turn, will display the Update My Briefcase dialog box with a recommended action.

2. Right-click your mouse on a document. Windows 95, in turn, will display a pop-up menu, as shown in Figure 11.16.

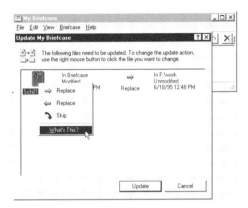

Figure 11.16 When you right-click on a document, Windows 95 displays a pop-up menu.

3. To learn more about the Update My Briefcase dialog box, click on the pop-up menu's What's This? option. Windows 95, in turn, will display a pop-up window with information about the dialog box, as shown in Figure 11.17.

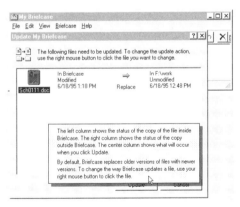

Figure 11.17 When you select the pop-up menu's What's This? option, Windows 95 displays a pop-up window with information about the Update My Briefcase dialog box.

4. Repeat step 2 to display the pop-up menu again. The pop-up menu lets you control how Briefcase updates the file—in other words, you can control which file Briefcase uses for the update, or you can direct Briefcase to skip the update for a specific file.

5. To direct Briefcase to skip a file's update, click your right-mouse button on the file. Within the pop-up menu, choose Skip.

239

6. Note the direction of the update arrows. The arrows tell you which file the Briefcase will use to perform the update. To change the arrow direction (and, hence, which file the Briefcase uses for the update), click your right-mouse button on the file. Within the pop-up menu, choose the arrow direction you desire.

7. To complete your operation, select the Briefcase menu Update All option.

THE BRIEFCASE DOESN'T SUPPORT MULTIPLE UPDATES

The Briefcase program does not perform merge operations. If you have a copy of the same document on two systems and you make changes to both, the Briefcase will not incorporate both sets of changes. Instead, you get one file's changes or the other's. Unless you override the update operation, Briefcase gives you the changes from the file with the most recent time stamp.

SPLITTING A DOCUMENT

Suppose you leave town on business and, while on the road, you work with a document in your Briefcase. In addition, assume that someone edited your original document while you were away from the office. Under such circumstances, you may not want to update either document. Instead, you might simply want to disassociate (or *split*) the document in the Briefcase from the one on your desktop PC. That way, Windows 95 will not even try to update either document. To split a document (in the Briefcase) from its original, perform these steps:

1. Open your notebook PC's My Briefcase folder and click on the document you want to split (from the original). Windows 95 will highlight the document's icon.

2. Click on the menu bar's Briefcase category. Windows 95 will display the Briefcase menu, as shown in Figure 11.18.

Figure 11.18 The My Briefcase folder Briefcase menu.

3. Click your mouse on the Briefcase menu Split From Original option. Windows 95 will display a message box that asks you to confirm that you want to split the document from its original, as shown in Figure 11.19.

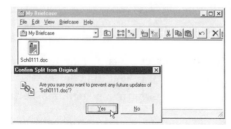

Figure 11.19 Windows 95 displays a message box that asks you to confirm the splitting operation.

4. Click on the Yes button. Windows 95 will split the selected document in the Briefcase from its original.

When you split a document from its original, Windows 95 calls it an *orphan*. When you try to update a Briefcase that contains orphan documents, Windows 95 displays the message box shown in Figure 11.20.

Figure 11.20 *If you try to update a Briefcase with orphan documents, Windows 95 displays this message.*

USING THE BRIEFCASE WITH A FLOPPY DISK

As you use your notebook PC, there may be times when you aren't able (or don't wish) to connect it to your desktop system. For example, the network you normally use to transfer files may be down, and you may not have the right cables for a direct connection. On such occasions, you can still use the Windows 95 Briefcase with a floppy disk. To use a floppy disk for file transfers and keep those files synchronized between your notebook and desktop PCs, perform these steps:

1. On your desktop PC, drag-and-drop the documents (the ones you want to edit on your notebook PC) on the My Briefcase icon.
2. Put a formatted floppy disk into your desktop PC's floppy drive.
3. Double-click the My Computer icon. Windows 95 will open the My Computer folder.
4. Double-click on the floppy drive's icon. Windows 95 will display the contents of the floppy drive.
5. Drag the My Briefcase icon and drop it on the window that displays the floppy drive's contents. Windows 95, in turn, will copy the Briefcase folder's contents on to the floppy disk.
6. Take the floppy to your notebook PC, open the My Briefcase folder, and work with the document directly from the floppy.

If you don't like the speed at which your notebook PC performs when you work with a document directly from the floppy, you can copy the Briefcase from the notebook PC's floppy drive to its hard drive. To do so, perform these steps:

1. Double-click your notebook PC's My Computer icon. Windows 95 will open the My Computer folder.
2. Double-click on the floppy drive's icon. Windows 95 will open a window with the floppy drive's contents.
3. Drag the My Briefcase icon from the floppy drive window and drop the icon at an empty location on the notebook PC's Desktop. Windows 95 will display a message box that asks you if you want to overwrite all files in the notebook PC's Briefcase that have identically named counterparts in the floppy's Briefcase.
4. Click on the Yes button. Windows 95 will copy the contents of the floppy's Briefcase into the notebook PC's Briefcase. In addition, Windows 95 will remove the Briefcase from the floppy.

To transfer the Briefcase back to the notebook PC's floppy drive, drag the My Briefcase icon from the notebook PC's Desktop and drop it on the floppy drive's icon in the My Computer folder. Windows 95, in turn, will copy the Briefcase to the floppy. When you want to update the original documents on your desktop PC, perform these steps:

1. Insert the floppy disk into your desktop PC's floppy drive.
2. Double-click the My Computer icon. Windows 95 will open the My Computer folder.
3. Double-click on the floppy drive's icon. Windows 95 will open a window that displays the floppy drive's contents.
4. Drag the My Briefcase icon from the floppy drive's window and drop it on the Windows 95 Desktop.
5. Double-click on the My Briefcase icon. Windows 95 will open the My Briefcase window.
6. Click on the Briefcase menu Update All option. Windows 95 will display the Update My Briefcase dialog box.
7. Select Update. Windows 95 will copy the documents, as necessary, to update the originals.

After you try the Briefcase, you will find it useful even if you do not have a network or direct-cable connection between your notebook and desktop PCs.

USING WINDOWS 95 POWER MANAGEMENT

To maximize the number of hours you get from your notebook PC's battery, Windows 95 provides power-management support. In short, power management conserves your battery life by turning off your PC's screen or by spinning down your hard disk when they are not in use. Later, when you are ready to use your system, Windows 95 uses its power-management capabilities to power the devices back on. To use Windows 95 power management, open the Control Panel window (*Start> Settings> Control Panel*) and double-click your mouse on the Power icon shown here:

Windows 95, in turn, will display the Power Properties dialog box shown in Figure 11.21.

Figure 11.21 The Power Properties dialog box.

To turn on Windows 95 power management, open the Power Management pull-down list. In most cases, you will want Windows 95 to work aggressively to conserve your battery life. As such, select the Advanced option.

11: Using Windows 95 on Your Notebook PC

Note: *If you later find that one of your devices does not turn back on after Windows 95 turns the device off, the device may not support advanced power management. In such cases, try using the Standard setting to resolve the error.*

As you can see, the Power Properties dialog box provides a Power status bar that indicates your battery's current state. If you battery power your notebook PC on a regular basis, select the Enable battery meter on the taskbar checkbox. Windows 95, in turn, will display a small battery icon on your Taskbar, as shown here:

If you double-click your mouse on the Taskbar Power icon, Windows 95 will display the Battery Meter dialog box shown in Figure 11.22. Using the Battery Meter, you can tell at a glance how much power your battery has left.

Figure 11.22 The Battery Meter dialog box.

Suspending Your Notebook PC

Normally, when you are through using your system, you choose the Start menu Shutdown option to end your session. When you are working with a battery-powered PC, you can direct Windows 95 to suspend (or freeze) your PC when you don't need to use your PC for a while. When you freeze your PC in this way, Windows 95 minimizes your PC's power consumption. Later, when you are ready to use your system, you can resume your work right where you left off. Depending on your system type, the steps you must perform to restart your system may differ. The advantage of suspending your system, over shutting your system down, is that you don't have to end your programs and later restart your system and the programs when you are ready to resume your work which can be a time-consuming task. If suspending your system in this way will be convenient to you, use the Power Properties dialog box to place the Suspend menu option on your Start menu, as shown in Figure 11.23. Using the Power Properties dialog box options, you can direct Windows 95 to display the Suspend option on the Start menu all the time, never, or only when you remove your notebook PC from its docking station.

Figure 11.23 The Suspend option on the Windows 95 Start menu.

Using PCMCIA Cards

Although notebook computers are very convenient for travel, their size limits your ability to add new hardware. When you use a desktop computer, on the other hand, you can open the computer's system unit and install a new modem, sound card, or disk drive. Notebook computers, however, don't offer such expansion slots. As a solution, however, many notebook computers support PCMCIA cards that you insert into a small PCMCIA slot on the side of your computer. You can purchase PCMCIA cards that contain specific hardware. For example, one PCMCIA card might contain a modem, while a second card contains a network interface, and a third SCSI adapter you can use to connect an external CD-ROM or hard drive. Depending on your notebook type, the number and type of PCMCIA cards you can insert into your computer at one time will differ. As such, on an older notebook computer, you might have to remove your PCMCIA modem card before you can insert a PCMCIA network card. To display your current PCMCIA slot use, perform these steps:

1. Select the Start menu Settings option and choose Control Panel. Windows 95, in turn, will open the Control Panel window.

2. Double-click your mouse on the PCMCIA icon. Windows 95 will display the PC Card (PCMCIA) Properties dialog box, as shown in Figure 11.24.

Figure 11.24 The PC Card (PCMCIA) Properties dialog box.

The Properties dialog box tells you which of your PCMCIA slots are in use, and by which cards. If you remove a PCMCIA card and insert another, Windows 95 will immediately update the dialog box to reflect your change. If one of your PCMCIA cards does not appear within the dialog box, you may have not inserted the card properly—remove the PCMCIA card and insert it again. If you use PCMCIA cards on a regular basis, you may want to add a button to you taskbar on which you can double-click your mouse to display the PC Card (PCMCIA) Properties dialog box, as shown here:

To add the PCMCIA button to your Taskbar, select the Show control on taskbar checkbox within the PC Card (PCMCIA) Properties dialog box.

KEYS TO SUCCESS

In this chapter, you learned about the features that make Windows 95 the ideal operating system for notebook computers. Specifically, you learned how to map a network drive, establish direct-cable connections between your notebook and desktop PCs, and use the Windows 95 Briefcase to synchronize documents you transfer between systems. Chapter 12 will discuss the Windows 3.1 accessory programs that are still available under Windows 95. You will learn about programs such as Calculator, Cardfile, and Character Map. However, before you move on to Chapter 12, make sure you understand the following key concepts:

- ✓ Windows 95 has features, such as support for PCMCIA interfaces and APM Version 1.1, that make it a highly effective operating system for notebook computers.
- ✓ You can connect a notebook and desktop PC indirectly with a network, or directly with a cable.
- ✓ If you need the portability of a notebook and the power of a desktop PC, but can't afford two systems, you may want to purchase a docking bay for your notebook PC.
- ✓ You can use the Briefcase to synchronize documents between your notebook and desktop PCs.
- ✓ When you can't connect your notebook and desktop PCs through a network or a cable, you can use the Briefcase with a floppy disk to keep documents synchronized between two systems.

Chapter 12
Using Tried-and-True Windows 3.1 Accessories

As you have learned, Windows 95 refers to the area on your screen where you run your programs as the desktop. Windows 95 uses the desktop analogy to relate your PC operations to tasks you may have performed in the past at a desk in your office. For example, you may have written letters, performed calculations using a calculator, or jotted down notes on a notepad. To improve your PC productivity, Windows 95 provides several accessory programs that let you perform desktop operations using your PC.

Accessory programs are not new to Windows 95. In fact, many of the programs we will discuss in this chapter have existed since the release of Windows 1.0 in 1987! Chapter 13, "Using Windows 95 Accessory Programs," examines accessory programs that are new to Windows 95. Because you can find many books that will discuss these older accessories in detail, this chapter will simply give you enough information to get you started with these accessory programs. If you need the steps to perform a specific operation, you will find that the Windows 95 help system describes these programs in detail. By the time you finish this chapter, you will understand the following key concepts:

- You can perform math operations by using the Calculator accessory program.
- The Character Map accessory makes it easy for you to insert special characters, such as copyright ©, trademark ™, and other symbols into your documents.
- You can track information on electronic 3x5 cards by using the Cardfile accessory.
- The Calendar accessory lets you schedule appointments on a daily or monthly basis.
- Using the Clipboard Viewer, you can view objects that you cut or copy to the clipboard.
- The Notepad accessory lets you create and edit ASCII documents.
  Using the Paint accessory, you can create, edit, and save bitmap graphics images.

Note: *If you upgraded your system from Windows 3.1 to Windows 95, your Accessory folder should contain the programs discussed in this chapter. If, instead, you purchased your system with Windows 95 preinstalled, your system may not have all the accessories this chapter discusses. In that case, continue your reading with Chapter 13, which focuses on the new Windows 95 accessory programs.*

RUNNING AN ACCESSORY PROGRAM

Windows 95 makes it very easy for you to run its accessory programs. To begin, click your mouse on the Start button. Windows 95, in turn, will display the Start menu. Next, select Programs and choose Accessories. Windows 95 will display the Accessories menu, as shown in Figure 12.1.

Figure 12.1 *The Accessories menu options.*

If you find that you use a specific accessory program on a regular basis, create a shortcut for that program on your desktop by performing these steps:

1. Right-click your mouse on an empty spot on your desktop. Windows 95, in turn, will display a pop-up menu.

2. Select New and choose Shortcut. Windows 95, in turn, will display the Create Shortcut dialog box, as shown in Figure 12.2.

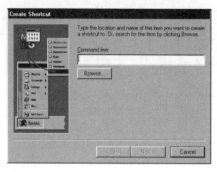

Figure 12.2 *The Create Shortcut dialog box.*

3. Click your mouse on the Browse button. Windows 95 will display the Browse dialog box, shown in Figure 12.3.

Figure 12.3 *The Browse dialog box.*

4. Traverse the folders within the Browse dialog box until you locate the Windows folder.

5. Open the Windows folder and click your mouse on the program file for the accessory program you desire.

6. Choose Open. Windows 95 will display the program's name within the Create Shortcut dialog box.

7. Select Next. Windows 95 will display a dialog box asking you to specify a shortcut name.

8. Type in the name you desire and click Finish. Windows 95 will create the shortcut on your desktop.

USING THE CALCULATOR ACCESSORY

The Calculator accessory lets you perform simple arithmetic, scientific (with support for trigonometric functions, such as sine and cosine), and statistical operations. To start the Calculator, perform these steps:

1. Select the Start menu and choose Programs.

2. Within the Programs menu, select Accessories and choose Calculator. Windows 95, in turn, will open the Calculator window, as shown in Figure 12.4.

12: Using Tried-and-True Windows 3.1 Accessories

Figure 12.4 The standard Calculator.

When you start the Calculator accessory, Windows 95 will normally display the standard calculator, shown in Figure 12.4. However, as you will learn later in this section, Windows 95 also supports a scientific calculator. To enter numbers into the calculator, you can click the corresponding buttons on the Calculator's face or you can type the numbers using your keyboard. To type numbers, you must use the standard numeric keys that appear along the type row of your keyboard, or you can set the NumLock key and enter numbers using your keyboard's numeric keypad.

Performing a Simple Arithmetic Operation

To perform an addition, subtraction, multiplication, or division operation using the Calculator, perform these steps:

1. Enter your first number into the Calculator using your mouse or keyboard.

2. Click your mouse on the symbol that corresponds to the operation you desire, or type the corresponding key (+,-,*,/).

3. Enter your second number into the Calculator using your mouse or keyboard.

4. Click your mouse on the equal-sign button or press your keyboard equal key. The Calculator will display the result of your operation within its numeric window.

Understanding Standard Calculator Buttons

The Standard Calculator lets you perform the same operations as a desktop adding machine or pocket calculator. Table 12.1 describes each of the buttons you will find on the standard calculator, as well as keystrokes you can press to activate the button using your keyboard.

Button	Keyboard	Button Function
C	Esc	Clears the current calculation.
CE	Del	Clears the current value.
Back	Backspace	Clears the current value's rightmost digit.
MC	Ctrl-L	Clears the Calculator's memory.
MR	Ctrl-R	Recalls the Calculator's memory.
M+	Ctrl-P	Adds the current value to the Calculator's memory and stores the result in memory.
MS	Ctrl-M	Stores the current value in the Calculator's memory.
+/-	F9	Changes the current value's sign.
1/x	R	Calculates the current value's reciprocal.
sqrt	@	Calculates the current value's square root.
%	%	Treats the current value as a percentage.

Table 12.1 The standard Calculator buttons and keyboard equivalents.

Using the Scientific Calculator

As briefly discussed, the Calculator accessory provides the standard Calculator you have just seen, as well as a scientific Calculator. The Calculator View menu lets you switch between the two calculator types. When you select the View menu Scientific option, Windows 95 will display the scientific Calculator, shown in Figure 12.5.

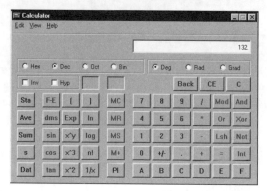

Figure 12.5 The scientific Calculator.

Table 12.2 describes the buttons you will encounter on the scientific Calculator.

Button	Keyboard	Button Function
C	Esc	Clears the current calculation.
CE	Del	Clears the current value.
Back	Backspace	Clears the current value's rightmost digit.
MC	Ctrl-L	Clears the Calculator's memory contents.
MR	Ctrl-R	Recalls the Calculator's memory contents.
M+	Ctrl-P	Adds the current value to the Calculator's memory and stores the result in memory.
MS	Ctrl-M	Stores the current value in the Calculator's memory.
+/-	F9	Changes the current value's sign.
Mod	%	Calculates the remainder from division.
Or	|	Performs a bitwise OR.
Lsh	<	Performs a bitwise shift to the left. Inv+Lsh performs a bitwise shift to the right.
And	&	Performs a bitwise exclusive AND.
Xor	^	Performs a bitwise exclusive OR.
Not	~	Performs a bitwise inverse.
Int	;	Displays the current value's integer portion.
A-F	A-F	Enters a hexadecimal digit.
PI	p	Displays the value of PI. Inv+PI displays 2 times PI.
Sta	Ctrl-S	Activates the Statistics Box.
Ave	Ctrl-A	Displays the average of the Statistics box values.
Sum	Ctrl-T	Displays the sum of the Statistics box values.

Table 12.2 The scientific Calculator buttons and keyboard equivalents. *(continued on the following page)*

Button	Keyboard	Button Function
s	Ctrl-D	Calculates the standard deviation of the Statistics box values.
Dat	Ins	Places the current value into the Statistics box.
F-E	v	Toggles scientific notation on and off.
dms	M	Converts the current value into the degrees-minutes-seconds format. Inv+dms converts the value back.
sin	s	Displays the current value's sine. Inv+sin displays the arc sine.
cos	o	Displays the current value's cosine. Inv+cos displays the arc cosine.
tan	т	Displays the current value's tangent. Inv+tan displays the arc tangent.
( )	( )	Groups expressions.
Exp	x	Enables the entry of exponential numbers.
x^y	y	Displays the value of X raised to the power of Y. Inv+x^y displays the result of X to the Y root.
x^3	#	Displays the value of X cubed. Inv+x^3 displays the cube.
x^2	@	Displays the value of X squared. Inv+x^2 displays the square root of X.
ln	N	Displays the current value's natural logarithm.
log	L	Displays the current value's base 10 log.
n!	!	Calculates the current value's factorial.

Table 12.2 The scientific Calculator buttons and keyboard equivalents. (continued from the previous page)

Performing Statistical Operations

Using the scientific Calculator, you can perform simple statistical operations that use a set of data values. To begin, click your mouse on the Sta (statistics) button. The Calculator, in turn, will display the Statistics Box, shown in Figure 12.6.

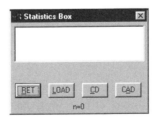

Figure 12.6 The Calculator Statistics Box.

To enter your data values into the Statistics Box, perform these steps:

1. Click your mouse on the Calculator window (not the Statistics Box), or click your mouse on the Statistics Box Ret button to activate the Calculator window.

2. Enter the number you desire.

3. Click your mouse on the Calculator's Dat button or press your keyboard INS key. The Calculator will place the number into the Statistics Box.

4. Repeat steps 2 and 3 to enter your data values.

After you enter the data values you desire into the Statistics Box, you can use the Sum button to add up the numbers within the box, and the Ave button to calculate the average value. Table 12.3 describes the Statistics Box buttons.

Button	Purpose	Keyboard Equivalent
RET	Returns control to the Calculator window	ALT-R
LOAD	Loads the Statistics Box value currently displayed into the Calculator	ALT-L
CD	Deletes the Statistics Box value currently selected from the Statistics Box	ALT-C
CAD	Deletes all values from the Statistics Box	ALT-A

Table 12.3 Statistics Box buttons and their keyboard equivalents.

USING THE CHARACTER MAP ACCESSORY

As you create word processing documents, there may be times when you want to insert unique characters into your document, such as those shown here:

Most newer word processors let you insert such characters within your documents by selecting fonts, such as Symbol, Wingdings, and ZapDingBats. However, if you are using a simplistic word processor, such as the WordPad accessory discussed in Chapter 13, your word processor may not provide you an easy way to insert such characters. In such cases, you can use the Character Map accessory, shown in Figure 12.7.

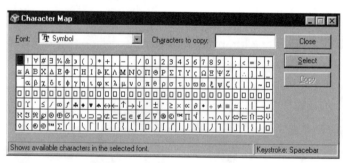

Figure 12.7 The Character Map accessory.

To start the Character Map accessory program, perform these steps:

1. Select the Start menu and choose Programs.

2. Within the Programs menu, select Accessories and choose Character Map.

Using the Character Map, you copy one or more characters to the clipboard. Later, within your word processing program, you paste the characters from the clipboard into your document. To copy one or more characters to the clipboard using the Character Map, perform these steps:

1. Open the Character Map's Font pull-down list and select the font you desire. As you select fonts, the Character Map will display the font's corresponding characters and symbols.

2. To view a specific symbol in detail, hold down your mouse-select button and aim your mouse pointer at the character. The Character Map, in turn, will enlarge the corresponding symbol, as shown in Figure 12.8.

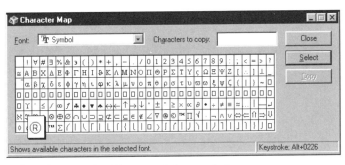

Figure 12.8 Displaying an enlarged view of a Character Map symbol.

3. To select a character that you will later copy to the clipboard, click your mouse on the character and then choose Select. You can use this technique to select as many characters as you desire. As you select characters, the Character Map will display them within the Characters to copy field.

4. After you choose the characters you desire, select Copy. The Character Map, in turn, will copy the characters to the clipboard.

5. Close the Character Map window.

6. Within your word processor, select the Edit menu Paste option to place the characters into your document.

Using the Clipboard Viewer Accessory

As you work with documents, such as a word-processing letter or a spreadsheet, there will be times when you will want to move or copy information from one location within the document to another. To move or copy text in this way, you perform cut-and-paste operations. In general, to perform a cut-and-paste operation, you perform these steps:

1. Within your document, you select the text or object (such as a picture) you want to move or copy.

2. Next, using the Edit menu Cut or Copy options, you move or copy the object to a special storage location, called the clipboard.

3. Use your keyboard arrow keys or mouse to place your cursor at the location within the document at which you want to move or copy the object.

4. Select the Edit menu Paste option to place a copy of the clipboard's contents into your document.

As you cut-and-paste objects to and from the clipboard, there may be times when you want to view or save the clipboard's contents. To do so, you run the Clipboard Viewer accessory, shown in Figure 12.9.

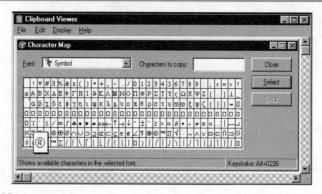

Figure 12.9 The Clipboard Viewer accessory.

Within the Clipboard Viewer, you can display the clipboard's contents, or you can save the contents to a file. In general, you won't use the Clipboard Viewer on a regular basis. However, if you experience problems with your cut-and-paste operations, you may want to open the Clipboard Viewer window during an operation so you can verify that its contents match those you expect.

USING THE NOTEPAD ACCESSORY

If your desk is like mine, you have a notepad readily available where you can jot down today's tasks, or even make notes during a phone call. To help you automate these tasks, you can use the Notepad accessory, shown in Figure 12.10.

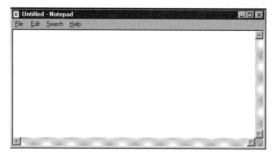

Figure 12.10 The Notepad accessory.

You may be wondering why you would want to automate your note-taking tasks. In short, by moving your notes from paper, which clutters your desk, into one or more files on your computer, you can better organize your tasks. Should you ever need documentation about a specific phone call, you can quickly find and print a copy of your notes.

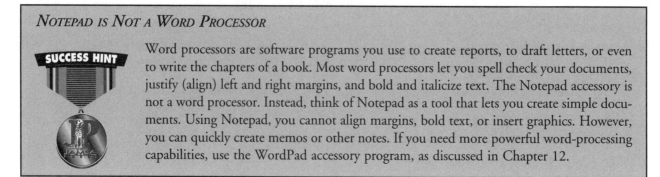

NOTEPAD IS NOT A WORD PROCESSOR

Word processors are software programs you use to create reports, to draft letters, or even to write the chapters of a book. Most word processors let you spell check your documents, justify (align) left and right margins, and bold and italicize text. The Notepad accessory is not a word processor. Instead, think of Notepad as a tool that lets you create simple documents. Using Notepad, you cannot align margins, bold text, or insert graphics. However, you can quickly create memos or other notes. If you need more powerful word-processing capabilities, use the WordPad accessory program, as discussed in Chapter 12.

CREATING A NOTEPAD DOCUMENT

To create a Notepad document, start the Notepad accessory previously shown in Figure 12.10. Next, all you have to do is type. Notepad is not a word processor. As such, Notepad will not automatically wrap your text when you reach the right margin. Instead, you need to press the ENTER key to move text to the start of the next line. After you finish your document, you will want to save the document to a file on disk.

To save your Notepad document to a file on disk, perform these steps:

1. Select the File menu Save As option. Notepad, in turn, will display the Save As dialog box.
2. Within the Save As dialog box, select the folder within which you want to store the document.
3. Within the File name field, type in the filename you desire, and choose Save.

To print your Notepad document, select the File menu Print option. Notepad will immediately print your document to the printer without displaying additional dialog boxes.

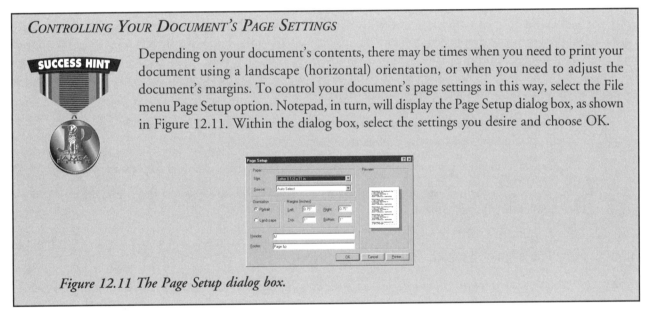

CONTROLLING YOUR DOCUMENT'S PAGE SETTINGS

Depending on your document's contents, there may be times when you need to print your document using a landscape (horizontal) orientation, or when you need to adjust the document's margins. To control your document's page settings in this way, select the File menu Page Setup option. Notepad, in turn, will display the Page Setup dialog box, as shown in Figure 12.11. Within the dialog box, select the settings you desire and choose OK.

Figure 12.11 The Page Setup dialog box.

OPENING AN EXISTING NOTEPAD DOCUMENT

To open a Notepad document that you have previously stored in a file on your disk, perform these steps:

1. Select the File menu Open option. Notepad will display the Open dialog box, as shown in Figure 12.12.

Figure 12.12 The Open dialog box.

2. Within the Open dialog box, select the folder that contains the Notepad document you desire.

3. Within the folder, double-click your mouse on the Notepad document. Notepad, in turn, will open the document file and display the document's contents within its window.

Performing Cut-and-Paste Operations in Notepad

As you edit your Notepad documents, there will be times when you will want to move, delete, or copy text from one location within your document to another. In such cases, you can perform a cut-and-paste operation. Think of a cut-and-paste operation within Notepad as similar to steps you would perform to move text from one page to another using scissors and paste. To start, you select (cut out) the text you want to move, delete, or copy. To select text within Notepad, you can use your mouse or keyboard. To select text using your mouse, click your mouse in front of the first character you want to select. Next, hold down the mouse-select button and move your mouse pointer over the text you desire. As you select text, Notepad will display the text on your screen using reverse video. To select text using your keyboard, use your arrow keys to position the cursor in front of the first character you desire. Next, hold down your keyboard SHIFT key and use your keyboard arrow keys to highlight the text you desire.

After you select your text, you can move or copy the text using a special storage location, called the clipboard. To delete the selected text, you simply press your keyboard DEL key. In general, to move or copy text, you place the text in a temporary storage location called the clipboard. Then, you position your cursor at the location within your document where you want to place the text, and you paste the text from the clipboard to the current location. For example, to move your selected text, perform these steps:

1. Select the Edit menu Cut option. Notepad will remove the selected text from your document, placing the text into the clipboard.

2. Within your document, position the cursor to the location at which you want to place the text.

3. Select the Edit menu Paste option. Notepad, in turn, will place a copy of the clipboard's contents into your document.

The steps to copy text within your document are quite similar, with the exception that in step 1, you select the Edit menu Copy option as opposed to Cut.

Note: *After you place text into the clipboard, you can paste as many copies of the text into your document as you desire.*

Creating a Log File within Notepad

As discussed, Notepad provides you with a convenient way to track phone calls and your daily tasks. If you use Notepad to track such tasks, you can use the Edit menu Time/Date option to insert the current date and time into your document. For example, Figure 12.13 illustrates a Notepad document that contains several phone calls.

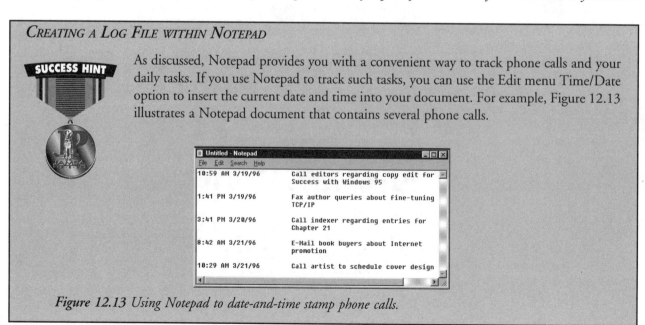

Figure 12.13 Using Notepad to date-and-time stamp phone calls.

Searching Your Notepad Document for Text

As the size of your Notepad documents increases, there may be times when you have trouble locating specific text within your document. In such cases, you can use Notepad's built-in search capabilities. To search for text within your Notepad document, select the Search menu Find option. Notepad, in turn, will display the Find dialog box, as shown in Figure 12.14.

Figure 12.14 *The Find dialog box.*

Within the Find what field, type in the text you desire. Select the direction you want Notepad to search—up toward the start of your document or down toward the end of your document. Click your mouse on the Find Next button. Notepad will search your document for the specified text. If Notepad finds the text, Notepad will highlight the text within your document. If the text Notepad highlights is the occurrence of the text that you desire, select the Cancel button to close the dialog box. Otherwise, click your mouse on the Find Next button, which directs Notepad to search your document for the next occurrence of the text.

Note: *By default, Notepad find operations ignore the case of letters, treating upper and lowercase letters being as the same. If you want Notepad to match letters based on their case, select the Match case checkbox within the Find dialog box.*

Using Notepad to Edit ASCII Files

As you know, word processors let you justify margins, bold and italicize text, change font sizes, and so on. To perform these operations, word processors embed special (hidden) characters within your documents. Although these special characters have meaning to your word processor, your other programs will not understand them. Notepad, on the other hand, is not a word processor. As a result, Notepad does not embed these special characters. As you work with Windows 95, there may be times when a program's instructions ask you to edit an ASCII file, such as AUTOEXEC.BAT or CONFIG.SYS. In general, an ASCII file is a file that contains letters, numbers, and punctuation symbols only—in other words, it contains no special word processing characters. If you edit an ASCII file using your word processor, you may inadvertently introduce hidden characters that corrupt (damage) the file. Your better choice for editing the file is to use Notepad. Because Notepad is not a word processor, Notepad will not embed characters that may damage the file.

Using the Cardfile Accessory

Most desktops have a Rolodex within which you can keep phone numbers and addresses. Unfortunately, few of us travel with our Rolodex. If you use a notebook PC, however, you may find that the Cardfile accessory provides you with a convenient way to track such information. In short, the Cardfile lets you record information on electronic 3x5 index cards.

You organize your index cards by storing related cards within the same file. For example, one file might contain your customer phone numbers and addresses, while a second file tracks employee birthdays. To start the Cardfile accessory, perform these steps:

1. Select the Start menu and choose Programs.
2. Within the Programs menu, select Accessories and choose Cardfile. Windows 95, in turn, will display a blank 3x5 index card, as shown in Figure 12.15.

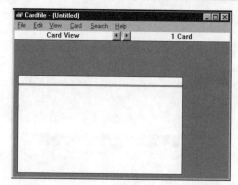

Figure 12.15 A blank index card within the Cardfile accessory.

Within Cardfile, the status line tells you the number of cards your current file contains and how you are displaying those cards (in this case, using card view). Cardfile also provides you with forward and back buttons you can click on with your mouse to cycle through and display the index cards in the current file. Each 3x5 card within Cardfile consists of two parts: an index and an information area. Think of the index as the card's title. The information area is where you store the information you would normally write on a 3x5 card itself. For example, if you are tracking your customer phone numbers and addresses, you might place the customer name within the index area, and the customer's phone number and address within the information area, as shown in Figure 12.16.

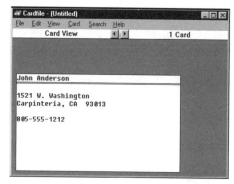

Figure 12.16 Using a Cardfile index card to store customer information.

Adding a Card to Your Deck

To add an index card to the current Cardfile deck, perform these steps:

1. Select the Card menu Add option. Cardfile, in turn, will display the Add dialog box, as shown in Figure 12.17.

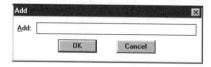

Figure 12.17 The Add dialog box.

2. Within the Add dialog box, type in a meaningful index that describes the contents of your new card. Choose OK. Cardfile will display your new card.

3. Within the information area, type in the text you want the card to store.

Saving Your Card Deck to a File

After you create your card deck, you will want to save the deck's contents to a file on disk. To save your card deck to a file, perform these steps:

1. Select the File menu Save As option. Cardfile, in turn, will display the Save As dialog box.
2. Within the dialog box, select the folder within which you want to store the card-deck file.
3. Within the File name field, type in a meaningful filename that describes the deck's contents.
4. Choose OK.

Opening an Existing Card-Deck File

To access the cards you have previously stored to a file on disk, perform these steps:

1. Select the File menu Open option. Cardfile will display the Open dialog box.
2. Within the Open dialog box, select the folder that contains your card-deck file.
3. Within the folder, click your mouse on the file that contains the card deck you desire, and choose Open.

Moving through Your Card Deck

To move through the cards in your card deck, click your mouse on the forward and back buttons that appear in the Cardfile status bar. In addition, you can use the keystrokes listed in Table 12.4 to move through your card deck.

Keystroke	Operation
PgUp	Moves backward one card.
PgDn	Moves forward one card.
Ctrl+Home	Moves to the first card in the deck.
Ctrl+End	Moves to the last card in the deck.
Ctrl+Letter	Moves to the first card whose index line starts with the letter specified. If two or more lines begin with letter specified, repeat the keyboard combination to move through each of the corresponding cards.

Table 12.4 Keystrokes for moving through a Cardfile card deck.

Deleting a Card from Your Deck

Just as there are times when you will add cards to your card deck, there will also be times when you need to delete a card. For example, if you are tracking customer addresses and your customer goes out of business, you may want to delete the customer's card. To remove a card from your card deck, perform these steps:

1. Display the card you want to delete.
2. Select the Card menu Delete option. Cardfile will display a dialog box asking you to confirm the card's deletion.
3. Select OK.

Changing a Card's Contents

Over time, you may need to make changes to a card's contents. For example, if your card contains a customer's address and phone number, and your customer gets a new fax number and e-mail address, you will want to edit the customer's card. To edit a card within your card deck, perform these steps:

1. Display the card you desire.
2. Click your mouse on the card's information area.
3. Edit the card's contents as you require.

To edit a card's index, perform these steps:

1. Display the card you desire.
2. Double-click your mouse on the card's index area. Cardfile will display the Index dialog box.
3. Within the Index dialog box, edit the index as you desire.
4. Choose OK.

Printing Your Card Deck

Cardfile lets you print the current card or all the cards in your card deck. To print the current card, select the File menu Print option. To print all the cards in your deck, select the File menu Print All option.

Controlling Your Card Deck's Display

As the number of cards in your card deck increases, there may be times when you want Cardfile to display the card indexes only, so that you can quickly locate the card you desire. For example, Figure 12.18 shows only card deck indexes (called a List view).

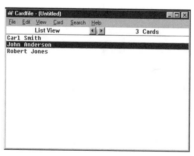

Figure 12.18 Displaying your card deck in List view.

After you click your mouse on the index of the card you desire, you can select Card view to display the card's contents. To switch between Card and List view, use the Cardfile's View menu.

Searching for a Specific Card

As the size of your card deck increases, there may be times when you will have trouble finding a specific card. In such cases, you can take advantage of the Cardfile's search capabilities. Cardfile lets you search card indexes as well as each card's information area. To search card indexes for specific text, perform these steps:

1. Select the Search menu Go To option. Cardfile will display the Go To dialog box.
2. Within the Go To field, type text contained in the index you desire.
3. Choose OK.

To search each card's information area for specific text, perform these steps:

1. Select the Search menu Find option. Cardfile, in turn, will display the Find dialog box.

2. Within the Find What field, type in the text you desire.

3. Select the direction you want Cardfile to search (up toward the start of your document, or down toward the bottom).

4. Choose Find Next. Cardfile will search your document for the specified text. If Cardfile finds the text, Cardfile will highlight the text within your card. If the text Cardfile highlights is the occurrence of the text that you desire, select the Cancel button to close the dialog box. Otherwise, click your mouse on the Find Next button, directing Cardfile to search your document for the next occurrence of the text.

USING CARDFILE TO AUTODIAL

If your PC has a modem to which you have connected your phone, you can use Cardfile to automatically dial the first phone number it encounters on the current card. After Cardfile dials the call and you hear the phone ring, simply pick up your phone receiver. To direct Cardfile to dial the number on the current card, select the Card menu Autodial option.

SETTING UP CARDFILE TO AUTODIAL

Before you can use Cardfile to autodial a phone number that resides on the current card, you need to tell Cardfile about your modem (such as its port, speed, and so on). To setup your modem to support Cardfile's autodial, perform these steps:

1. Select the Card menu Autodial option. Cardfile will display the Autodial dialog box.

2. Within the Autodial dialog box, select Setup. Cardfile will display the Autodial Setup dialog box, shown in Figure 12.19.

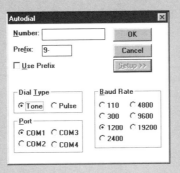

Figure 12.19 The Autodial Setup dialog box.

3. Specify your modem settings and choose OK.

TRACKING YOUR APPOINTMENTS WITH WINDOWS CALENDAR

As you have learned, Windows provides several different accessory programs that provide the same function as items you would normally have on your desktop. To help you manage your appointments, Windows provides the Calendar accessory. To start the Calendar accessory program, perform these steps:

1. Select the Start menu Programs option and choose Accessories.
2. Within the Accessories menu, choose Calendar. Windows 95, in turn, will display the Calendar window, as shown in Figure 12.20.

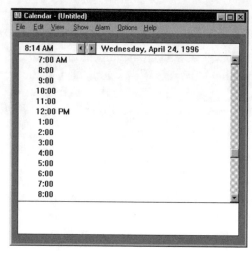

Figure 12.20 *The Calendar accessory's daily appointment.*

Normally, Calendar will display its daily appointment schedule. Use the View menu to toggle between the daily and monthly displays. If you select the View menu's Month option, Calendar will display the monthly calendar, as shown in Figure 12.21.

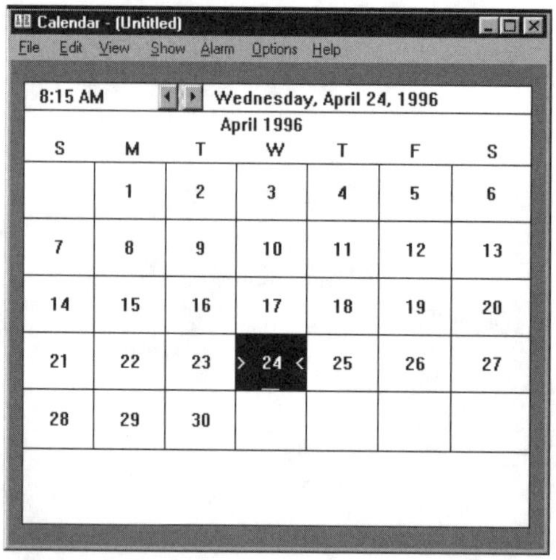

Figure 12.21 *The Calendar accessory's month view.*

For now, use the View menu's Day option to select the daily appointment schedule. To assign an appointment, click your mouse on the desired time and type in a description of the appointment, as shown in Figure 12.22.

If you need to edit an appointment description, click on the description and then change it with your keyboard arrow keys. If you need to delete an appointment, you can click on the appointment with your mouse and then use the DEL or BACKSPACE key to erase the text. If you need to move an appointment, you can perform a cut-and-paste operation, as discussed next.

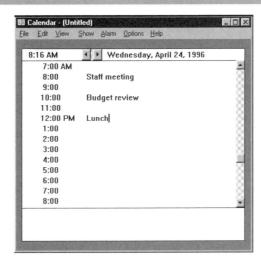

Figure 12.22 *Typing appointments within Calendar.*

CUTTING AND PASTING AN APPOINTMENT

Moving an appointment within Calendar is similar to moving text in the Windows Notepad editor or the Write word processor. To begin, you must select the appointment text you want to move. To do so, click your mouse on the appointment, placing the cursor at the start of the text. Next, hold down a SHIFT key and use the keyboard arrow keys or drag the mouse pointer (move the mouse pointer with mouse-select button held down) across the text you want to select. Calendar will display the selected text in reverse video. Next, select the Edit menu Cut option. Calendar will remove the appointment from your calendar. Next, click your mouse on the desired appointment time. Select the Edit menu's Paste option. Calendar will place the appointment text at the time specified.

SAVING YOUR APPOINTMENTS TO A FILE

When you assign your appointments to a calendar, you must later save the appointments to a file so that Calendar can remember the appointments from one session to another. To save your appointments to a file, perform these steps:

1. Select the File menu's Save As option. Calendar will display the Save As dialog box.

2. Within the Save As dialog box, select the folder within which you want to place your Calendar file. Next, type in a filename that describes your appointments. Calendar appointment files normally use the CAL extension, so you might use a filename such as WORK.CAL or SCHOOL.CAL.

3. Select OK.

PRINTING YOUR APPOINTMENTS

There may be times when you need to print a copy of your appointments. To do so, select the File menu's Print option. Calendar, in turn, will display the Print dialog box, as shown in Figure 12.23, that prompts you for the range of dates for which you want to print your appointments.

SUCCESS WITH WINDOWS 95

Figure 12.23 The Calendar Print dialog box.

Within the *From* field, enter the starting date of the first appointments you desire. In the *To* field, type in the ending date. If you leave the *To* field blank, Calendar will print appointments through the current date.

DISPLAYING THE APPOINTMENTS FOR A SPECIFIC DATE

By default, Calendar displays the appointments for the current day. To display or set appointments for a different date, click your mouse on the right and left arrows that appear in the date bar:

If you are displaying the monthly calendar, you can double-click your mouse on a specific date to display that day's appointments:

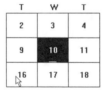

Finally, if you select the Show menu's Date option, Calendar will display a dialog box asking you for the desired date. Type in the date you desire and click on OK. Calendar, in turn, will display the corresponding day's appointments.

SETTING ALARMS WITHIN CALENDAR

When you track your appointments within Calendar, there may be times when you want Calendar to remind you of important appointments. In such cases, Calendar lets you set alarms that notify you before an appointment occurs. To set an alarm for an appointment, click on the appointment within the Calendar. Next, select the Alarm menu and select the Set option. Calendar, in turn, will place a small bell to the left of the appointment to signify that an alarm has been set:

```
     8:00      Staff meeting
     9:00
    10:00      Budget review
    11:00
 ♫  12:00 PM   Lunch
     1:00
```

The Alarm menu's Set option toggles an alarm setting. The first time you select the Set option, Calendar will set an alarm. The second time you select the option, Calendar will clear the alarm. If Calendar is running when the alarm occurs, it will display a dialog box reminding you of the event, as shown in Figure 12.24.

12: Using Tried-and-True Windows 3.1 Accessories

Figure 12.24 *The Calendar accessory's Please remember dialog box.*

If the Calendar program is running, but is not the active window, its menu bar will flash to indicate an alarm has occurred. If Calendar is minimized when an alarm occurs, the Calendar icon will flash. If Calendar is not running, you will not be notified of the alarm. Calendar lets you display the reminder message up to ten minutes before the appointment.

Drawing Simple Illustrations in Windows Paint

As you create documents, there may be times when you need to create simple illustrations or include screen captures (such as a Windows 95 dialog box). To help you create illustrations and work with bitmap images (called BMP files), Windows 95 provides the Paint drawing program. To start the Paint drawing program, perform these steps:

1. Select the Start menu Programs option and choose Accessories.
2. Within the Accessories menu, choose Paint. Windows 95, in turn, will display the Paint window, as shown in Figure 12.25.

Figure 12.25 *The Paint window.*

To simplify your task of drawing images, Paint provides an extensive tool set. Table 12.5 briefly describes each tool in the tool set.

Icon	Tool name	Purpose
	Free-Form Selection	Selects any shape.
	Select	Selects a rectangular shape.
	Eraser	Erases lines and colors.
	Fill with Color	Colors drawn shapes.
	Pick Color	Selects a color from the color palette.
	Magnifier	Magnifies an object's editing area.
	Pencil	Draws free-form.
	Brush	Paints free-form.
	Airbrush	Spray paints color on to the drawing area.
	Text	Inserts text.
	Line	Draws lines.
	Curve	Draws curves.
	Rectangle	Draws rectangles.
	Polygon	Draws polygons (multi-sided closed shapes).
	Ellipse	Draws ellipses.
	Rounded Rectangle	Draws rectangles with rounded corners.

Table 12.5 The Paint tool set.

When you work with Paint, you can rest your mouse on top of a tool, and Paint will display a small tool-tip that tells you the tool's name. To select a Paint tool, aim your mouse at the tool and click:

12: Using Tried-and-True Windows 3.1 Accessories

Likewise, near the bottom of the Paint window, you should find a palette of colors you can use as you draw. To select a foreground color, click your left-mouse button on the color you desire. Likewise, to select a background color, aim your mouse pointer at the color palette and click the right-mouse button:

Note: *For a complete description of the Paint accessory's tools, turn to the book,* **1001 Windows 95 Tips**, *Jamsa Press, 1995.*

Using Paint to Save Screen Captures

When you create documents and presentations, there may be times when you will want to include a screen capture. For example, if you are writing a menu that tells your boss how to turn the display of mouse trails on or off, you might want to include a picture of the Mouse Properties dialog box Motion page, as shown in Figure 12.26.

Figure 12.26 *The Mouse Properties dialog box Motion page.*

To include a screen image within your document, you must first capture the screen image, and then you must save the image to disk. To save the image, you use one of two keyboard combinations: one to copy your current screen contents and a second to copy the active window's contents to the clipboard:

PrintScreen (or PrtSc)   Copies the current screen contents to the clipboard

ALT-PrintScreen (or ALT-PrtSc)   Copies the active window's contents to the clipboard

After you copy the image to the clipboard, you paste the image into Paint, from which you can save the image to a file on disk. For example, to capture and save the Mouse Motion page, you would perform these steps:

1. Within the Control Panel, double-click your mouse on the Mouse icon. Windows 95, in turn, will display the Mouse Properties dialog box.

2. With the Mouse Properties dialog box, select the Motion tab. Windows 95 will display the Mouse Motion page.

3. Hold down your keyboard's ALT key and presss PrintScreen (or PrtSc, depending on your keyboard keys). Windows 95, in turn, will copy the dialog box image to the clipboard.

4. Close the Mouse Properties dialog box.

5. Start the Paint accessory.

6. Within Paint, select the Edit menu Paste option. Paint, in turn, will display the Mouse Properties dialog box image, as shown in Figure 12.27.

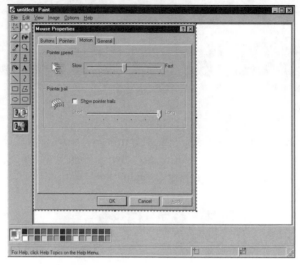

Figure 12.27 A screen capture image within Paint.

7. Select the File menu Save As option to save the image to a file on disk. In this case, you might use the filename MOTION.BMP.

After you save the BMP image to a file, you can insert the image into your documents or presentations. For example, if you are using Microsoft Word or PowerPoint, you can use the Insert menu Picture option to insert the image.

Take Advantage of Clipart and Photo Images

If you are like me, you may have left most of your artistic skills in grade school. If that's your case, you will find that you can improve your illustrations greatly by including clipart images (predrawn images that you buy and use within your documents) and photos. For example, Figure 12.28. contains a small red dog house drawn in Paint.

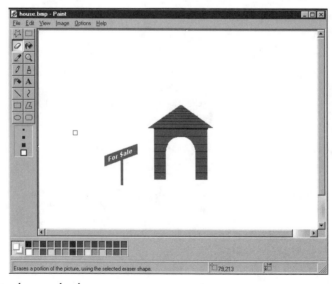

Figure 12.28 Using Paint to draw a dog house.

Note, however, how the image improves when we add a scanned photograph of a dog, as shown in Figure 12.29.

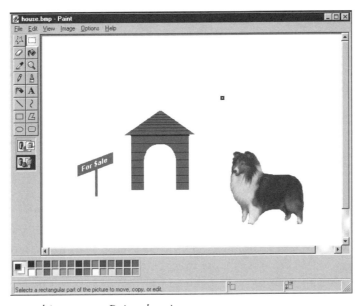

Figuure 12.29 Adding a scanned image to a Paint drawing.

Lastly, note how the image comes together by placing the dog house and the dog into a background image, as shown in Figure 12.30.

Figure 12.30 The final Paint image.

To build a Paint image that uses multiple elements in this way, you first open a file that contains the image you desire and copy the image to the clipboard. Next, you open the Paint drawing you are creating and paste the image from the clipboard into your illustration. By repeatedly cutting and pasting images in this way, you can build a complex illustration in Paint.

Saving Your Paint Image

After you create your image, you must save it to a file. To do so, select the File menu's Save As option. Paint, in turn, will display the Save As dialog box. Within the dialog box, type in a filename that meaningfully describes your picture. Paint image files normally use the BMP extension. For the previous drawing, you might use the filename DOGHOUSE.BMP.

Printing Your Paint Image

To print your image, select the File menu and choose Print. Windows will display the Print dialog box. Select the OK option. If you have a black-and-white printer, Paint will print your colored image using different shades of gray. If you have a color printer, the actual image colors should appear.

Cutting or Copying an Image to the Clipboard

Many users create an illustration within Paint and then cut and paste the image to another document, such as a document produced by Windows Write. To begin, select the Paint Pick tool. Aim your mouse at the upper-left corner of the image you want to copy. Hold down the mouse-select button and move the mouse pointer to the lower-right corner of the image. Next, select the Edit menu and choose Copy. Windows will place a copy of the image on the clipboard. You can now select your Write document, position the cursor within the document, and use Write's Edit menu Paste option to place the image into the document.

Keys to Success

If you upgraded your system from Windows 3.1 to Windows 95, you should find most of the accessory programs discussed in this chapter on your Accessories menu. If, however, your system came with Windows 95 installed, your system may not have several of the programs discussed in this chapter. In Chapter 13, you will examine the accessory programs that Microsoft bundled with Windows 95. Before you continue with Chapter 13, however, make sure you have learned the following key concepts:

- ✓ The Calculator accessory lets you perform math operations, much like a desktop adding machine.
- ✓ Using the Character Map accessory, you can insert special characters and symbols into your documents.
- ✓ The Cardfile accessory lets you track information using electronic 3x5 cards.
- ✓ Using the Calendar accessory, you can schedule appointments on a daily or monthly basis.
- ✓ The Clipboard Viewer lets you view objects you cut or copy to the clipboard.
- ✓ Using the Notepad accessory, you can create and edit ASCII documents.
- ✓ The Paint accessory lets you create, edit, and save bitmap graphics images.

Chapter 13
Using the Windows 95 Accessory Programs

In Chapter 12, "Using Tried and True Windows 3.1 Accessories," you took a quick look at several accessory programs that you may have used under Windows 3.1. If you upgraded your system from Windows 3.1 to Windows 95, the applications discussed in Chapter 12 may appear within the Windows 95 Accessories menu. In this chapter, you will examine several of the accessory programs that are new to Windows 95. By the time you finish this chapter, you will understand the following key concepts:

- Like Windows 3.1, Windows 95 provides a set of accessory programs you can put to immediate use.
- The Backup accessory lets you backup the files on your hard disk to floppy disks or tape.
- To reduce the amount of time your backup operations consume, Backup lets you perform incremental backups that only backup those files you created or changed since the last backup.
- The ScanDisk accessory lets you examine your folders, files, and disk for errors. In most cases, ScanDisk can repair any errors it encounters.
- You should run ScanDisk at least once a week to ensure your disk contains no errors.
- The DriveSpace accessory lets you double a disk's storage capacity by compressing the disk's data. If you are low on disk space, use DriveSpace.
- The Phone Dialer accessory lets you use your modem as a speed dial for the voice calls you place.
- Using the HyperTerminal accessory and your modem, you can connect to remote computers, such as a remote bulletin-board system.
- The WordPad accessory is a simple word processor you can use to create memos and letters.

USING THE WINDOWS 95 SYSTEM TOOLS

To help you maximize your system performance and disk use, and to reduce your chance of lost information due to a disk error, Windows 95 provides several powerful programs it refers to as your System Tools. To display a menu that lists the Windows 95 System Tools, perform these steps:

1. Select the Start menu Programs option.
2. Within the Programs menu, select the Accessories option and choose System Tools. Windows 95, in turn, will display the System Tools submenu, as shown in Figure 13.1.

Figure 13.1 *The Windows 95 System Tools.*

This chapter discusses several, but not all, of the Windows 95 System Tools. Instead, this book presents the remaining System Tools within chapters whose topic better matches each system tool. For example, because the Disk Defragmenter program improves your system performance by repairing fragmented files that reside on your disk, this book presents the Disk Defragmenter in Chapter 21, "Fine-Tuning Windows 95 Performance." Table 13.1 briefly describes the Windows 95 System Tools.

Tool	Purpose	Chapter Discussed
Backup	Backs up files from your hard disk to a tape or floppy.	13
Disk Defragmenter	Improves your system performance by repairing fragmented files.	21
DriveSpace	Increases your disk's storage capacity by compressing data.	13
InBox Repair Tool	Repairs a damaged "in box" that contains Exchange messages.	17
NetWatcher	Monitors your system's use by remote network computers.	18
Resource Meter	Monitors how Windows 95 uses your system resources.	21
ScanDisk	Examines your disks, folders, and files for errors.	13
System Monitor	Monitors Windows 95 behind-the-scenes operations.	21

Table 13.1 Windows 95 System Tools.

BACKING UP YOUR FILES AND FOLDERS

One of the most important, yet most neglected, tasks users must perform is backing up the files on their disk. Although fatal disk errors are less common than they once were, such errors can still occur and result in the loss of all your floppy disks. Also, as you download files you encounter on the Internet and World Wide Web, you increase your risk of downloading a computer virus that destroys your files or damages your disk. In short, your only protection against lost or damaged files is to make backup copies of your files.

Users often use the excuse that "backing up their files simply takes too long." In short, such users are gambling with their files. If the users are wrong and a disk error occurs, they may have to recreate hundreds of files. Depending on their contents, your lost files may mean lost sales, lost productivity, and possibly the loss of your job. It is essential that you backup the files on your disk on a regular basis. Windows 95 provides the Backup accessory program that makes your backup operations easy.

BUY A TAPE DRIVE

One of the easiest ways for you to make backup operations simple and fast is to purchase a tape drive. In the past, hard disks stored much less information than they do today. As such, users could backup the files on their disk using a reasonable number of files. Today, however, most hard disks store several hundred megabytes (Mb), which would require you to use several hundred floppy disks to store your backups.

By using a tape drive, however, you can normally backup your files using one tape, and in only a few minutes each day. Best of all, you can start the backup operation and then let it proceed unattended (since you don't have to swap floppy disks as they fill).

The price of tape drives, like all hardware, has dropped dramatically. You can purchase a tape drive for less than two hundred dollars. The time you save using the tape drive will quickly pay for the drive itself. More importantly, should you ever experience a disk error that destroys you files, your backup tapes may become priceless.

Understanding Backup Operations

When you backup the files on your disk, you have several choices. First, you can perform a full-disk backup operation that makes a copy of every folder and file on your disk. The advantage of performing a full-disk backup operation is that you know you have a copy of every file. The disadvantage of a full-disk backup operation is the amount of time (and floppy disks) the backup consumes. In fact, if you are backing up your files to floppy disks, a full-disk backup operation can easily consume several hours.

Many users, however, will argue that a full-disk backup is unnecessary. Remember, the purpose in backing up your disk is to ensure you have a copy of each file should a disk error occur in the future. As such, when you backup your disk, you don't need to backup program files that you can easily install. For example, if you use Microsoft Word, you will want to backup your document files, but not Word itself. Instead, should a disk error occur in the future, you would simply reinstall Word.

Normally, when you backup the files on your disk, you will only backup specific folders. For example, you would backup word processing documents, spreadsheets, and your database files. Using the Windows 95 Backup program, you can specify which folders and even which files you want to backup. After you select your key folders, you can perform one of two backup operations: a full backup or an incremental backup. When you perform a full-backup, you backup every file the folder contains. The advantage of performing a full backup is that you always have a copy of every file the folder contains in one backup location (such as all the folder's files on one tape). The disadvantage of performing a full backup is the amount of time the backup requires.

As an alternative to the full backup, you can perform an incremental backup operation that backs up only those files you have created or changed since your last backup. If, for example, you perform an incremental backup operation every day, today's backup will complete very quickly, because the only files you need to backup are those you created or changed today. The disadvantage of using an incremental backup operation is that you have to keep track of a set of disks, or possibly a set of tapes, each of which contains the different files you've backed up on a given day.

Most users perform backup operations that combine both incremental and full backups. For example, each Monday, you should perform a full backup of all the files in your key folders. Then, for the rest of the week, you would perform an incremental backup operation at the end of each day. At the end of the week, you would have five days worth of backups. The following Monday, you would repeat this process, again performing a full backup. By combining the full and incremental backups in this way, you reduce the number of files you have to backup each day, and you reduce (to five days worth) the number of backups of which you need to keep track.

Understanding Backup-File Sets

When you use the Backup accessory, you need only to specify the key files and folders you want to backup one time. In general, you tell Backup the list of files and folders you want to backup. You then save your list in a special file, called a *backup-file set*. Later, when you need to backup your files, you open the backup-file set that lists the files and folders you desire. Backup, in turn, will do the rest. Later in this chapter, you will learn how to create your own backup-file sets. For now, however, simply understand that the backup-file set specifies the files and folders you want to backup.

Starting the Backup Accessory

To start the Backup accessory program, perform these steps:

1. Select the Start menu Programs option and choose Accessories.
2. Within the Accessories menu, select System Tools and choose Backup. Windows 95, in turn, may display a Welcome dialog box, similar to that shown in Figure 13.2, that briefly describes the backup process.

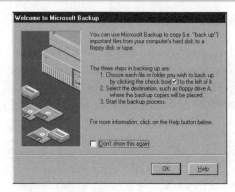

Figure 13.2 *The Welcome to Microsoft Backup dialog box.*

3. If the Welcome dialog box appears, select OK. Windows 95, in turn, will display the Microsoft Backup window, as shown in Figure 13.3.

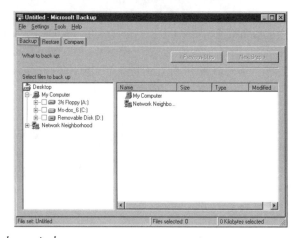

Figure 13.3 *The Microsoft Backup window.*

4. Microsoft Backup may display an additional dialog box that describes a backup-file set named Full System Backup it has created for you. If this dialog box appears, choose OK to remove it.

PERFORMING A FULL-DISK BACKUP OPERATION

As discussed, a full-disk backup operation backs up every file on your disk. You probably only want to perform a full-disk backup operation if you have a tape drive. To make it easy for you to perform a full-disk backup operation, the Backup accessory provides the Full System Backup file set.

To use this backup-file set to backup your entire disk, perform these steps:

1. Select the Backup File menu and choose Open File Set. Backup will display the Open dialog box.

2. Click your mouse on the Full System Backup entry and choose Open. Backup, in turn, will use the Backup File Set entries to select all the files on your disk.

3. Select the Next Step button. Backup, in turn, will change its window contents, letting you select the device to which you want to write your backup, as shown in Figure 13.4.

13: Using the Windows 95 Accessory Programs

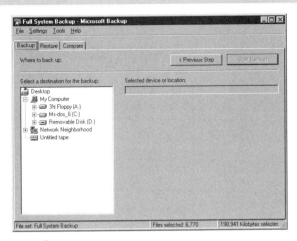

Figure 13.4 Selecting Backup's target device.

4. Within the device list, click your mouse on the tape drive. Select Start Backup. The Backup accessory, in turn, will display the Backup Set Label dialog box, as shown in Figure 13.5, that asks you to specify a name for your backup set.

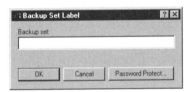

Figure 13.5 The Backup Set Label dialog box.

5. Type in a backup-set name that describes your backup and the date, such as System Disk 3-15-96.

6. Select OK. Backup, in turn, will start the backup operation.

CREATING YOUR OWN BACKUP-FILE SET

As briefly discussed, by creating a backup-file set, you specify the files and folders you want to backup. In addition, you use the backup-file set to specify the type of backup operation you want to perform: incremental or full. To create a backup-file set that specifies the files, folders, and backup type you desire, perform these steps:

1. Within the Backup window, click your mouse on the Backup tab. Backup will display the Backup page.

2. Within the Backup page, click your mouse on the plus sign that precedes the drive that contains the folders you want to backup. Windows 95 will expand the drive to display its top-level folders, as shown in Figure 13.6.

3. To include a folder in your backup-file set, click your mouse within the box that precedes the folder name, placing a check mark in the box. To remove a folder from your backup-file set, click on the folder's box to remove the check mark.

4. Repeat the process selecting folders until you have chosen each of the folders you desire.

5. If you only want to backup specific files within a folder, click on and open the folder to display its file list. Next, click your mouse on the box that precedes the files you desire, placing a check mark within the box.

273

Figure 13.6 Expanding a drive's folder list.

You are now ready to specify the type of backup operation you desire: full or incremental. As briefly discussed, a full-backup operation will backup every file and folder you have selected, every time you perform the backup. An incremental-backup operation, on the other hand, will backup only those selected that you have changed, or new files you have created within a folder, since your last backup operation.

To simplify your backup operations, you probably want to create two backup-file sets: one that performs an incremental backup of your selected files and folders, and a second that performs a full backup of your selected files and folders. To specify your backup type (incremental or full), perform these steps:

1. Select the Settings menu and choose Options. Backup will display the Settings - Options dialog box.
2. Select the Backup tab. Backup, in turn, will display the Backup page, as shown in Figure 13.7.

Figure 13.7 The Settings - Options Backup page.

3. Within the Type of backup field, select a full or incremental backup.
4. Choose OK.

SELECTING YOUR TARGET DEVICE AND SAVING YOUR BACKUP-FILE SET

After you select your files and choose your backup type, you are ready to save your settings to a backup-file set. To save your settings, perform these steps:

1. Select the target device to which you want to write your backup.

13: Using the Windows 95 Accessory Programs

2. Select the File menu Save As option. Backup, in turn, will display the Save As dialog box.

3. Within the File name field, type in a name that describes your backup-file set, such as Work Folders—Incremental Backup.

4. Select Save.

As discussed, you probably want to create two different backup-file sets, one that performs an incremental backup and a second that performs a full backup. If you have just saved your first backup-file set, create your second now, by performing these steps:

1. Select the Settings menu and choose Options. Backup will display the Settings - Options dialog box.

2. Click your mouse on the Backup tab. Backup, in turn, will display the Backup page, previously shown in Figure 13.7.

3. Within the Type of backup field, select the backup type you require.

4. Choose OK.

5. Select the File menu Save As option to save your backup-file set to disk.

USING YOUR BACKUP-FILE SET

The steps you follow to use your backup-file set are very similar to those previously discussed for the full-disk backup operation. To use your backup-file set to back up your previously selected files and folders, perform these steps:

1. Select the Backup File menu and choose Open File Set. Backup will display the Open dialog box.

2. Click your mouse on the entry that corresponds to the backup-file set you desire and choose Open. Backup, in turn, will use the backup-file set settings to identify the folders and files you previously selected.

3. Select the Next Step button. Backup, in turn, will change its window contents, letting you select the device to which you want to write your backup, as previously shown in Figure 13.4.

4. Within the device list, click your mouse on the tape drive. Select Start Backup. The Backup accessory, in turn, will display the Backup Set Label dialog box as previously, shown in Figure 13.5, that asks you to specify a name for your backup set.

5. Type in a backup-set name that describes your backup and the date, such as Work Files—Incremental 3-15-96.

6. Select OK. Backup, in turn, will start the backup operation.

RESTORING YOUR BACKUP FILES

Hopefully, you will never need to restore files from your backups. Think of your backups as an insurance policy. Ideally, you will never need your backups; however, if you do, it's essential that you have them. As you will learn, the Backup accessory makes it very easy for you to restore one or more files. To restore files from a backup set, perform these steps:

1. Within the Backup window, select the Restore tab. Backup, in turn, will change its window to display the list of devices from which you can restore your backup, as shown in Figure 13.8.

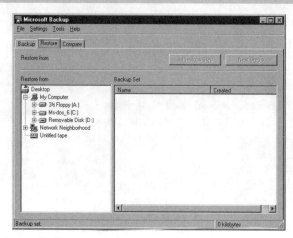

Figure 13.8 Selecting a device from which you can restore backup files.

2. Insert the disk or tape that contains your backup into the corresponding drive.

3. Within the Restore from list, select the device within which you placed your backup-file set, such as your tape drive. Backup, in turn, will display the list of backup-file sets that the device contains. Select the backup-file set you want to restore.

4. Click your mouse on the Next Step button. Backup will display a window similar to that shown in Figure 13.9, from which you can select the folders and files you want to restore.

Figure 13.9 Selecting files and folders to restore from a backup.

5. To select the files and folders you want to restore, click your mouse on the box that precedes the file or folder, placing a check mark in the box.

6. After you select each of the files and folders you want to restore, select the Start Restore button. Backup, in turn, will restore your selected files and folders.

LEARNING MORE ABOUT BACKUP

The Backup accessory provides many advanced settings that you can use to customize your backup operations. This chapter presented the key information you need to backup and restore files and folders using Backup. For more information on how you fine-tune Backup settings, turn to the book *1001 Windows 95 Tips*, Jamsa Press, 1995.

CHECKING YOUR DISKS, FOLDERS, AND FILES FOR ERRORS

Although disk errors occur much less often now than they did a few years ago, your disk can still experience errors which may damage your folders and the files they contain. When such errors occur, you may lose information. Normally, disk errors occur when you turn off your computer without first shutting down Windows 95. In some cases, such as when your office loses power, you can't control when your system shuts down. Unfortunately, when your system loses power in this way, you may very likely encounter disk or file errors. To help you detect and possibly correct disk, folder, and file errors, Windows 95 provides the ScanDisk accessory. To examine your disk using ScanDisk, perform these steps:

1. Select the Start menu Programs option and choose Accessories.

2. Within the Accessories menu, select System Tools and choose ScanDisk. Windows 95, in turn, will display the ScanDisk window, as shown in Figure 13.10.

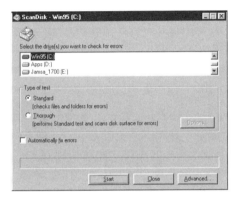

Figure 13.10 *The ScanDisk window.*

Using ScanDisk, you can perform two types of tests. The Standard test, which you will use most often, examines your disk files and folders for errors. The Thorough test, on the other hand, first examines your files and folders and then examines every storage location on your disk. Depending on the size of your disk, ScanDisk's Thorough test can take several hours.

PERFORMING SCANDISK'S STANDARD TEST

ScanDisk's Standard test examines your folders and the files they contain for errors. Such errors normally occur when Windows 95 is about halfway done storing information in a file on disk, and your system loses power. When you perform the Standard test, ScanDisk examines your disk for damaged files and folders. If ScanDisk discovers errors, ScanDisk will display a dialog box that asks you how you want ScanDisk to repair the error. In most cases, you will want ScanDisk simply to delete the damaged file or folder. Then, using your backup files, you can restore the deleted file or folder.

If you are an advanced user, you can direct ScanDisk to salvage as much of the file as it can, storing the recovered file within your disk's root directory, using a name such as FILE0001.CHK, FILE0002.CHK, and so on. Using an editor, such as the Notepad accessory, you may be able to recognize and save part of a damaged file. To run ScanDisk's Standard test, perform these steps:

1. Within the ScanDisk drive list, click your mouse on the disk you want to test.

2. Within the Type of test field, select Standard.

3. Select Start.

ScanDisk, in turn, will examine your disk's folders and files for errors. If ScanDisk encounters an error, ScanDisk will display a dialog box asking how you would like ScanDisk to correct the problem. When ScanDisk completes its test, it will display a Results dialog box, similar to that shown in Figure 13.11.

Figure 13.11 *The ScanDisk Results dialog box.*

As you can see, the ScanDisk Results dialog box tells you your disk's storage capacity, the number of files on your disk and the space they consume, and also your disk's available storage space.

PERFORM SCANDISK'S STANDARD TEST ONCE A WEEK

It is a good habit to run ScanDisk's Standard test once a week to examine your files and folders for errors. If your system has damaged files, you can use ScanDisk to delete the files, which in turn frees up disk space. If you find damaged files on a regular basis, possibly your disk drive may be going bad, or something you are doing (such as turning off your system without shutting down Windows 95) is damaging files. By running ScanDisk's Standard test on a regular basis, you immediately know about such errors.

PERFORMING SCANDISK'S THOROUGH TEST

ScanDisk's Thorough test not only examines each of your disk's files and folders, it also examines every storage location on your disk. To store information, your disk is made up of hundreds (or thousands, depending on your disk size) of circular tracks. Each track, in turn, consists of small storage locations, called *sectors*. A disk sector holds 512 bytes. As such, a large disk may contain over one million sectors!

When you perform ScanDisk's Thorough test, ScanDisk examines every sector on your disk to ensure the sector can store information. Occasionally, due to wear and tear, a sector on your disk may go bad and can no longer store information. If ScanDisk encounters a bad sector, ScanDisk can tell Windows 95 not to use the sector. Because ScanDisk examines each sector on your disk, the Thorough test may be quite time consuming. As such, you may only perform a Thorough test once a month, at most.

To run ScanDisk's Thorough test, perform these steps:

1. Within the ScanDisk drive list, click your mouse on the disk you want to test.
2. Within the Type of test field, select Thorough.
3. Select Start.

ScanDisk, in turn, will first perform a Standard test of your disk's files and folders. Then, ScanDisk will examine the surface of your disk (its sectors). If ScanDisk encounters a damaged location on your disk, ScanDisk will display a dialog box similar to that shown in Figure 13.12.

13: Using the Windows 95 Accessory Programs

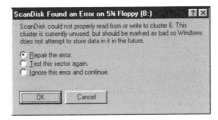

Figure 13.12 A dialog box detailing a disk surface error.

Should ScanDisk encounter a surface error, repeat the test to ensure that the error is valid, and then let ScanDisk correct the error.

Controlling ScanDisk Thorough Test Options

Most users can use ScanDisk's default settings to test their disk. If you are an advanced user, however, you may want to customize how ScanDisk performs its disk-surface examination. To customize one or more Through-test settings, select the Options button. ScanDisk, in turn, will display the Surface Scan Options dialog box as shown in Figure 13.13.

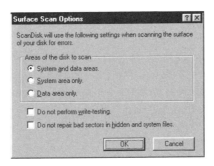

Figure 13.13 ScanDisk's Surface Scan Options dialog box.

For specifics on each option, click your mouse on the help button that contains the question mark, then click your mouse on the option of interest. ScanDisk, in turn, will display a small pop-up window that briefly describes the option. For detailed information on each of the surface scan options, turn to the book *1001 Windows 95 Tips*, Jamsa Press, 1995.

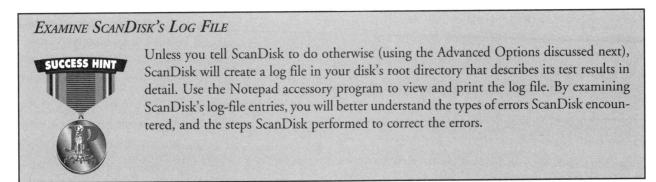

Examine ScanDisk's Log File

Unless you tell ScanDisk to do otherwise (using the Advanced Options discussed next), ScanDisk will create a log file in your disk's root directory that describes its test results in detail. Use the Notepad accessory program to view and print the log file. By examining ScanDisk's log-file entries, you will better understand the types of errors ScanDisk encountered, and the steps ScanDisk performed to correct the errors.

Controlling ScanDisk's Advanced Options

In addition to letting you control its surface scan, ScanDisk also lets you control its display of results, use of a log file, as well as how it handles file errors. To customize the ScanDisk settings, select the Advanced button. ScanDisk, in turn, will display the ScanDisk Advanced Options dialog box, as shown in Figure 13.14.

Figure 13.14 The ScanDisk Advanced Options dialog box.

For specifics on each option, click your mouse on the help button that contains the question mark, then click your mouse on the option of interest. ScanDisk, in turn, will display a small pop-up window that briefly describes the option.

DOUBLING YOUR DISK'S STORAGE CAPACITY

As programs become more powerful and complex, they also increase in size. Likewise, as users become more sophisticated, the files users create also become larger (as users insert charts and other graphics within their documents). As a result, most users never have enough disk space. Using the Windows 95 DriveSpace accessory program, however, you can almost double your disk's storage capacity in minutes. In other words, if you currently have a 200Mb hard drive, by using the DriveSpace program, you can increase your disk's storage capacity to almost 400Mb! The DriveSpace Program increases your disk's storage capacity by compressing the files on your disk. When you compress files in this way, you don't lose any information. Rather, you simply tell Windows 95 to store the files using a technique that consumes less space.

As you may know, your computer works in terms of ones and zeros. When you store information on your disk in a file, your disk drive actually represents the data using ones and zeros only. If you were to look up the ones and zeros that make up your files, you would find that most files contain many groups that are all ones or all zeros. Assume, for example, that your file contained 250 zeros followed by 500 ones. Rather than storing these 250 numbers on your disk, the DriveSpace compression software will place a special code within your file that replaces the string of zeros, and a second code that replaces the string of ones. For example, if you think of the codes as 250(0) followed by 500(1), you can see how these codes can reduce 750 numbers into 12 characters. The DriveSpace software understands these special codes. As a result, when your programs read a file, the DriveSpace software intercepts the codes and converts them back into the correct number of ones or zeros the program expects. In this way, to take advantage of disk compression, you don't do anything any different than you do today. All the compression and decompression takes place behind the scenes. The disadvantage of compressing the files on your disk is that compressing and decompressing does consume processor time. However, if you are low on disk space, you will probably be happy to sacrifice a little speed for twice as much storage capacity.

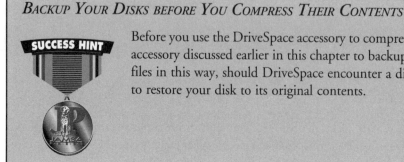

BACKUP YOUR DISKS BEFORE YOU COMPRESS THEIR CONTENTS

Before you use the DriveSpace accessory to compress the files on your disk, use the Backup accessory discussed earlier in this chapter to backup each of your files. By backing up your files in this way, should DriveSpace encounter a disk error, you can use your backup files to restore your disk to its original contents.

COMPRESSING A DISK

To compress a disk using the DriveSpace accessory, perform these steps:

1. Select the Start menu Programs option and choose Accessories.
2. Within the Accessories menu, select the System Tools menu and choose DriveSpace. Windows 95, in turn, will display the DriveSpace window, as shown in Figure 13.15.

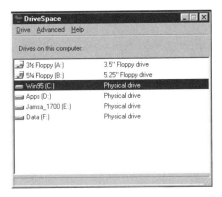

Figure 13.15 *The DriveSpace window.*

3. Within the Drives list, click your mouse on the icon that corresponds to the drive whose contents you want to compress.
4. Select the Drive menu Compress option. DriveSpace, in turn, will display the Compress a Drive dialog box, as shown in Figure 13.16.

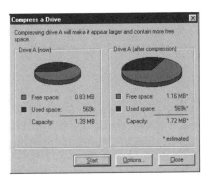

Figure 13.16 *The Compress a Drive dialog box.*

5. Select Start. DriveSpace will display a dialog box telling you it is about to compress the drive.
6. Select Compress Now. DriveSpace will first examine your disk for errors. If errors exist, DriveSpace will display a dialog box that tells you about the error and recommends that you use ScanDisk to correct the error. Depending on the file's contents, you can direct DriveSpace simply to skip this file's compression.
7. After the compression completes, select Close.

UNDERSTANDING HOST AND COMPRESSED DRIVES

When you compress a drive, DriveSpace actually builds one large file within which it places every file it compresses. DriveSpace refers to this file as your compressed drive. As you work, nothing appears to have changed. If, for example, you used DriveSpace to compress drive C, you will still use the drive letter C to access your files and folders. Behind the scenes, however, there's a lot going on. All the files that used to reside on your drive C now reside in the large compressed file. Each time you access a file or folder, the DriveSpace software maps your file reference to compressed data within this one file.

As you examine the disks on your system following a compression operation, you may find a drive with a strange drive letter, such as drive H. DriveSpace refers to this drive as your *host drive*. As you have learned, DriveSpace has compressed all the files on your drive and placed them into the compressed file. However, the compressed file itself needs to reside somewhere. That's where the host drive comes in. Assume that you have compressed drive C's files. The DriveSpace software will compress all the folders and files drive C contains into the large compressed file. DriveSpace will leave, however, part of drive C uncompressed, which becomes the host drive.

If you use the Windows 95 Explorer to examine the hidden files on the host drive, you will find a file named DBLSPACE.000. This file contains your compressed files and folders. Because the DriveSpace software takes care of compressing and decompressing files behind the scenes, you will normally never worry about the host drive. However, because the host drive will appear in every drive list (such as those in an Open or Save As dialog box), it is important that you understand where this new drive came from.

COMPRESSING A FLOPPY DISK IS CONVENIENT

When you exchange files on floppy disks with other users, there may be times when a file is too big to fit on one floppy. In such cases, you can use DriveSpace to compress the floppy. After you double the floppy's storage capacity, you can then copy the large file to the floppy. Then you can hand the floppy off to another Windows 95 user who can simply insert the floppy and use it. If, when the user inserts the floppy, they see the file DBLSPACE.000 as opposed to your large file, have the user select the Advanced menu Mount option to mount the floppy as a compressed drive.

UNCOMPRESSING A DRIVE

Should you decide that your compressed drive consumes too much system performance, you can uncompress the drive. This eliminates the file compression, but also eliminates your extra disk space. To uncompress a drive, perform these steps:

1. Within the DriveSpace drive list, click your mouse on the drive you want to uncompress.
2. Select the Drive menu Uncompress option. DriveSpace, in turn, will display the Uncompress a Drive dialog box, as shown in Figure 13.17.

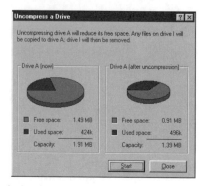

Figure 13.17 The Uncompress a Drive dialog box.

13: Using the Windows 95 Accessory Programs

3. Select Start. DriveSpace will display a dialog box stating that it is about to uncompress your drive.

4. Select Uncompress Now.

Learning More about DriveSpace

Most users who compress their drives simply run the DriveSpace command once and then forget about it. If you are an advanced user, however, you can use DriveSpace settings to control how much of your disk DriveSpace compresses, and how much it leaves uncompressed for the host drive. Likewise, if you have not compressed your hard drive, you can use DriveSpace to mount and unmount compressed floppy drives. In this way, you direct Windows 95 to load and unload the DriveSpace software into and out of memory as you need it. For more information on advanced DriveSpace settings, turn to the book *1001 Windows 95 Tips*, Jamsa Press, 1995.

Speed Dialing Using the Phone Dialer Accessory

If your PC has a modem to which you have connected your phone, you can use the Phone Dialer accessory to speed dial your calls. If you examine your modem, you will find it has plugs for two phone cables. You use the plug labeled Line to connect your modem to the phone outlet on the wall. Next, you use the outlet labeled Phone to connect your telephone to the modem. When you connect your phone to your modem in this way, you can use your phone line for modem connections or for voice phone calls, but not at the same time.

To simplify your voice calls, Windows 95 provides the Phone Dialer accessory. You can use the Phone Dialer to dial your calls. After the Phone Dialer places your call, you simply pick up your phone and talk. To start the Phone Dialer accessory, perform these steps:

1. Select the Start menu Programs option and choose Accessories.

2. Within the Accessories menu, choose Phone Dialer. Windows 95, in turn, will display the Phone Dialer window, as shown in Figure 13.18.

Figure 13.18 The Phone Dialer window.

Using the Phone Dialer to Place a Call

To place a call using the Phone Dialer, simply click your mouse on the numbers you want to dial or use your keyboard to type the phone number. Next, click your mouse on the Dial button. The Phone Dialer, in turn, will dial the number you specify. If your call goes through (the phone you are calling is not busy), Phone Dialer will display a dialog box similar to that shown in Figure 13.19 that tells you to pick up your phone receiver and talk.

Success with Windows 95

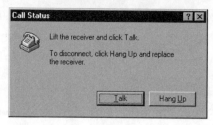

Figure 13.19 *The Phone Dialer Call Status dialog box.*

After you complete your call, simply click your mouse on the Hang Up button and then hang up your phone receiver.

Using Phone Dialer to Speed Dial

The Phone Dialer lets you assign eight phone numbers to its speed-dial buttons. To add a number to the speed dial, click your mouse on the unused button you desire. The Phone Dialer, in turn, will display the Program Speed Dial dialog box, as shown in Figure 13.20.

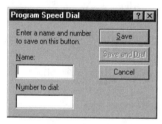

Figure 13.20 *The Program Speed Dial dialog box.*

Within the Name field, type the name you want to appear on the speed-dial button. Within the Number to dial field, type in the corresponding phone number. Choose Save. Later to place a call using your speed-dial entry, simply click your mouse on the speed-dial button.

Changing a Speed Dial Entry

Over time, you may need to change the phone number for one of your speed-dial entries, or you may want to replace an entry with someone else. To change a speed-dial entry, perform these steps:

1. Select the Phone Dialer Edit menu and choose Speed Dial. The Phone Dialer, in turn, will display the Edit Speed Dial dialog box as shown in Figure 13.21.

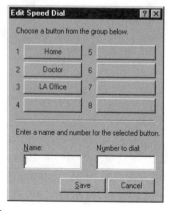

Figure 13.21 *The Edit Speed Dial dialog box.*

2. Click your mouse on the button whose contents you want to edit.

3. Within the Name field, type in the name you want to appear on the speed-dial button.

4. Within the Number to dial field, type in the corresponding phone number.

5. Choose Save.

UNDERSTANDING PHONE DIALER PROPERTIES

The Phone Dialer uses your current modem settings to place phone calls. As you learned in Chapter 5, "Customizing Common Hardware," you can use the Windows 95 Control Panel to specify your modem settings (such as whether you need to dial 9 to reach an outside line, and so on). To access your modem settings from within Phone Dialer, select the Tools menu Dialing Properties option. The Phone Dialer, in turn, will display the Dialing Properties dialog box within which you can select your dialing profile and customize other phone settings.

CONNECTING TO A REMOTE COMPUTER USING HYPERTERMINAL

In Chapter 18, "Windows 95 Networking Operations," you will learn how to use Windows 95 dial-up networking to use your modem to connect to a network server (such as a Windows NT, Novell server, and even Windows 95). If the computer to which you want to connect supports dial-up networking, use the steps Chapter 18 presents to connect to the server. Using Windows 95 dial-up networking, you can access remote disks and printers as if you were part of the local area network. If, however, the computer at your office or school does not support dial-up networking, you can instead use the HyperTerminal accessory. Using HyperTerminal, you connect to the remote computer as if you were using a terminal (monitor and keyboard only). In this way, the programs you run and files you create reside on the remote computer.

You will normally use HyperTerminal to connect to a school computer or to a local bulletin-board system (BBS). With the tremendous growth and popularity of the Internet and World Wide Web, few users require the HyperTerminal accessory. Instead, users who want to connect to a remote computer will use TCP/IP Internet software and a Web browser, as discussed in Chapter 10 "Connecting Windows 95 to the Internet and World Wide Web" or they will connect to an on-line service such as Microsoft Network, as discussed in Chapter 8 "Using the Microsoft Network." However, should you need to connect to a computer that does not support a SLIP or PPP connection (see Chapter 10), or if you want to connect to a bulletin-board system, you can use the HyperTerminal accessory. To start HyperTerminal, perform these steps:

1. Select the Start menu Programs option and choose Accessories.

2. Within the Accessories menu, select HyperTerminal. Windows 95, in turn, will display the HyperTerminal folder, as shown in Figure 13.22.

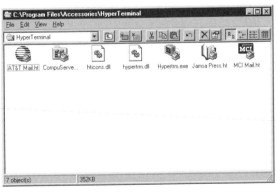

Figure 13.22 *The HyperTerminal folder.*

When you use HyperTerminal, you can store the settings you use to connect to a specific computer within a file. For example, you might store the settings you use to connect your office computer in the file OFFICE.HT (HT is an abbreviation for HyperTerminal), and the settings you use to connect to your school computer in the file SCHOOL.HT. Within the HyperTerminal folder, you can start HyperTerminal with the settings you desire by double- clicking your mouse on the corresponding icon.

For now, however, to create a new connection, double-click your mouse on the icon for Hypertrm.exe. Windows 95, in turn, will display the HyperTerminal window, as shown in Figure 13.23.

Figure 13.23 *The HyperTerminal window.*

As you can see, HyperTerminal displays the Connection Description dialog box within which you can type a name for your connection and choose an icon. For this example, type Microsoft Download Service, choose an icon, and select OK. HyperTerminal, in turn, will display the Phone Number dialog box, as shown in Figure 13.24.

Figure 13.24 *The Phone Number dialog box.*

The Microsoft Download Service is a computer to which you can connect and download sample programs. Normally, most of the programs are examples that show programmers how to use different features of Microsoft programming languages, such as Visual Basic or Visual C++.

In this example, use the phone number 206-936-6735 (be aware, however, that Microsoft may change this number over time). To enter the number, type 206 within the Area code field and 936-6735 within the Phone Number field. Select OK. HyperTerminal will display the Connect dialog box, as shown in Figure 13.25.

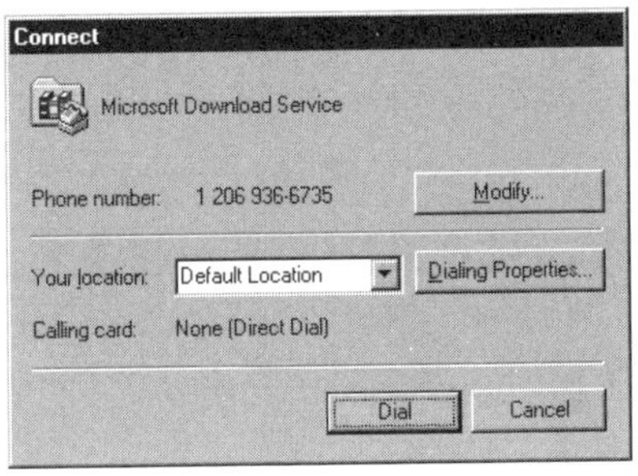

13: Using the Windows 95 Accessory Programs

Figure 13.25 The Connect dialog box.

Note: *Because the Microsoft Download Service resides on a computer at Microsoft in Redmond, Washington, you will need to place a long-distance phone call to connect to the computer. When you use HyperTerminal to place a long-distance phone call, the phone company will bill you for your modem call just as if you had made a voice call.*

Using the Connect dialog box, you can change the location from which you are dialing, and you can change dialing properties (such as whether or not you need to dial a 9 to access an outside line). If your settings are correct, select Dial. HyperTerminal, in this case, will connect you to the Microsoft Download Service. After you connect to the service, you may need to type information, such as your name and the city from which you are calling. Eventually, the Download Service will display its main menu, as shown in Figure 13.26.

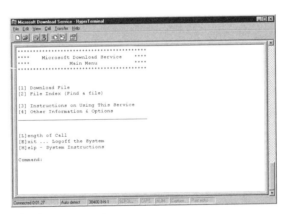

Figure 13.26 The Microsoft Download Service main menu.

From the main menu, you can select options to display lists of files you can download to your computer. For example, if you select the Visual Basic option, the Download Service will display a list of Visual Basic program files you can download, similar to those shown in Figure 13.27.

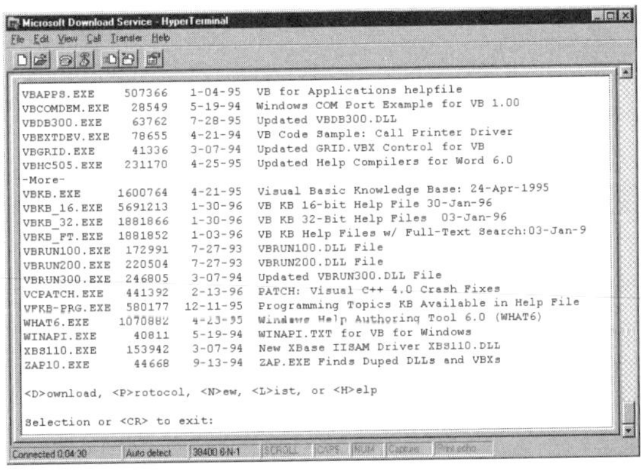

Figure 13.27 Visual Basic files you can download from the Microsoft Download Service.

Using the menu options that appear near the bottom of your screen, you can select and download a file, as discussed next.

DOWNLOADING A FILE

When you download a file from a remote computer, you must tell the remote computer how you want to receive the file and which file you want. To tell the computer how you want to receive the file, you specify a file protocol. In short, a protocol defines a set of rules that your computer and the remote computer follow to exchange the file. The protocol rules, for example, tell how fast the remote computer can send pieces of the file and how big those pieces will be. It's not really important that you understand the specifics of each protocol, but rather, that you use the same protocol on your computer that you select for the remote computer. In other words, if you tell the remote computer to send the file using the Zmodem protocol, you need to receive the file on your computer using Zmodem. Normally, the remote computer will display a menu of options from which you can select the protocol you desire.

Likewise, the remote computer will provide a menu option that lets you start a file download operation. In most cases, when you select the download option, the remote computer will ask you to type the name of the file you desire. After you type in the filename and press Enter, the remote computer is ready to download the file. In other words, it is now waiting for your computer to say "go."

Next, you must tell HyperTerminal to receive the file by selecting the Transfer menu Receive File option. HypterTerminal, in turn, will display the Receive File dialog box, as shown in Figure 13.28.

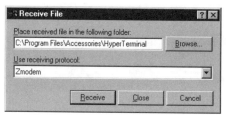

Figure 13.28 *The Receive File dialog box.*

Using the Receive File dialog box, you can tell HyperTerminal the folder within which you want to place the file, as well as the protocol to use for the download. To select the protocol, click your mouse on the pull-down Protocol list and select the protocol that matches the one you selected for the remote computer.

ENDING YOUR HYPERTERMINAL SESSION

To end your session with a remote computer, select HyperTerminal's Call menu Disconnect option. In short, HyperTerminal will end the connection by hanging up your phone line.

LEARNING MORE ABOUT HYPERTERMINAL

As briefly discussed, most users will not use HyperTerminal. Rather, most users will use an online service such as Microsoft Network or a TCP/IP-based Internet connection. The goal of presenting HyperTerminal to you in this chapter was not to explore all of HyperTerminal's capabilities, but rather, to get you connected to a remote computer and to perform a download operation. If you need specifics on other HyperTerminal features, turn to the book *1001 Windows 95 Tips*, Jamsa Press, 1995.

13: Using the Windows 95 Accessory Programs

Using the WordPad Word Processor

A word processor is a program with which you can create letters, memos, reports, and much more. If you have just bought your computer and you have not yet purchased a word processor, such as Microsoft Word, you can use the Windows 95 WordPad accessory program. Take note that although you can use WordPad to perform simple word processing, WordPad lacks key features such as a spell checker, a thesaurus, a grammar checker, and even an ability to fully justify paragraph text. If you plan to use a word processor on a regular basis, put down this book now, run to the store, and buy a professional-quality word processor.

If you only need to create a short letter or memo, you can use WordPad. To start the WordPad accessory, perform these steps:

1. Select the Start menu Programs option and choose Accessories.
2. Within the Accessories menu, choose WordPad. Windows 95, in turn, will open the WordPad window, as shown in Figure 13.29.

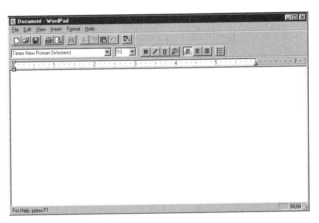

Figure 13.29 The WordPad window.

To get started with WordPad, type the following text:

"I have no particular talent. I am merely inquisitive." Albert Einstein

Should you make a mistake as you type, you can use the BACKSPACE key to erase letters. If you omit a word or letter, use your keyboard arrow keys to move the cursor to the correct location, and then type the missing text. If WordPad does not insert the text you type, but rather, overwrites text, press your keyboard's INS (Insert) key. The INS key works as a toggle. The first time you press the key, WordPad will insert the characters that you type. The second time you press the INS key, WordPad will overwrite existing characters with the new characters you type. Eventually, your WordPad window will appear similar to that shown in Figure 13.30.

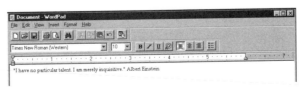

Figure 13.30 Text within a WordPad window.

289

PRINTING YOUR WORDPAD DOCUMENT

To print your WordPad document, select the File menu Print option. WordPad, in turn, will display the Print dialog box. Select OK. Also, you can print your document by clicking your mouse on the Printer icon, which appears on the WordPad toolbar.

SAVING YOUR WORDPAD DOCUMENT

To save your WordPad document to a file on disk, select the File menu Save As option. WordPad, in turn, will display the Save As dialog box, as shown in Figure 13.31.

Figure 13.31 *The Save As dialog box.*

Select the folder within which you want to save your document. Next, within the File name field, type your document's name. In this case, type the filename EINSTEIN.DOC and click your mouse on Save. WordPad, in turn, will create the file on disk, saving your document's contents to the file.

Later, as you make changes to your document, you will need to save your changes to the file on disk. To save your changes, select the File menu Save option. Because you have already specified a filename for your document, WordPad will not ask you for one when you select Save. In short, you use the Save As option when you want to assign a filename to your document, and you use the Save option when you want to store changes to your document to its file on disk.

TYPING WITHIN WORDPAD

When you type using WordPad, you will normally not press the ENTER key when the cursor reaches the right margin. Instead, WordPad will automatically wrap your text to the start of the next line for you. In fact, the only time you press the ENTER key is at the end of a paragraph, or when you want to force WordPad to wrap your line, such as when you type an address. If, when you type, you find that WordPad does not wrap text for you automatically, you can change WordPad's text-wrapping option, as discussed later in this chapter.

ENDING YOUR WORDPAD SESSION

When you are done editing a document and you have saved your changes to a file on your disk, you can end your WordPad session by selecting the File menu Exit option. If, for some reason, you have changes to your document that you have not yet saved to disk, WordPad will display a dialog box asking you if you want to save your changes. If you select Yes, WordPad will save the document's changes to its file on disk, or if you have yet to specify a document file, WordPad will display the Save As dialog box. If you select No, WordPad will discard your changes.

OPENING A WORDPAD DOCUMENT FROM A FILE ON DISK

To work with a document that you have saved to a file on disk, you simply need to open the corresponding document file. To open a document file within WordPad, perform these steps:

1. Select the File menu Open option. WordPad will display the Open dialog box.
2. Within the Open dialog box, select the folder that contains the document file you want.
3. Within the folder, click your mouse on the file that contains the document you want.
4. Select Open.

Note: *To make it easy for you to open the documents with which you have been recently working, WordPad lists your recently used files on the File menu. To open a recently used document, simply select the corresponding file from your file menu.*

CONTROLLING YOUR PARAGRAPH ALIGNMENT

Depending on the type of document you are creating, you may want WordPad to align your text to the right or left margin or to center your text. Unlike other word processors, WordPad will not full-justify your text (so that the margin text is flush on the right and left, as are the paragraphs of this book). To align paragraph text, place your cursor within the paragraph and select the Format menu Paragraph option. WordPad, in turn, will display the Paragraph dialog box, as shown in Figure 13.32.

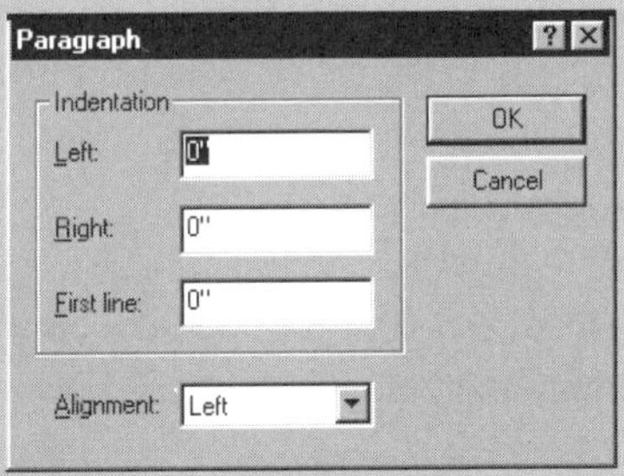

Figure 13.32 The Paragraph dialog box.

Click your mouse on the Alignment pull-down box and choose the paragraph alignment you desire.

CONTROLLING FONTS WITHIN WORDPAD

Using fonts (such as Times, Helvetica, and many others), you control how characters appear within your document. In addition, using font styles, such as italics, bold, and underlining, you can make specific characters stand out from others on your page. As you will learn, WordPad makes it easy for you to change fonts, font styles, and even the colors you assign to text.

To select a font, font size, font style, or even the color you want to use for text, you have two choices. You can either make your font selection and then type your text using that selection, or you can type your text and later apply the font or styles you want to the existing text. To select a font or font style before you type, use the toolbar buttons to select the font, size, style, or color you like. Then, type your text. For example, to type underlined text, you would click your mouse on the underline button, type your text, and then click your mouse on the underline button a second time to turn off underlining. Likewise, to use a 14-point font for the text you will type next, you would use the toolbar to select a 14-point font, type your text, and then use the toolbar to restore the font size to its previous setting.

In most cases, however, you will want to change the appearance of text that already resides within your document. To start, you need to select the text whose appearance you want to change. To select text using your keyboard, use the arrow keys to place the cursor in front of the first character in the text you want. Next, hold down a Shift key and press the arrow keys to select the text you desire. To select text using your mouse, click your mouse in front of the first character in the text you desire. Next, hold down your mouse select button and move your mouse pointer over the characters you want. As you select text, WordPad will display the text in reverse video. For example, if you select the characters in the previous Einstein quote, your WordPad window will appear similar to that shown in Figure 13.33.

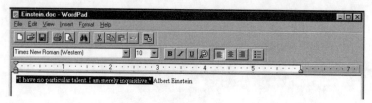

Figure 13.33 Selecting text within a WordPad window.

After you select the text you desire, use the toolbar to choose the font, font size, font style, or color you desire. Then, click your mouse anywhere within your document to turn off your selection. For example, if you assign italics to your Einstein quote, your text will appear as shown in Figure 13.34.

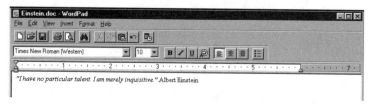

Figure 13.34 The Einstein quotes in italics.

To assign a color other than black to your text, select the text you want, and then click your mouse on the toolbar Color button. WordPad, in turn, will display the color palette, as shown in Figure 13.35.

Figure 13.35 The WordPad Color palette.

Click your mouse on the color you desire.

Searching Your WordPad Document for Specific Text

As the size of your WordPad documents increase, there may be times when you have trouble finding specific text. In such cases, you can direct WordPad to search your document for the text you want. To search your document for a specific word or phrase, perform these steps:

13: Using the Windows 95 Accessory Programs

1. Select the Edit menu Find option. WordPad, in turn, will display the Find dialog box, as shown in Figure 13.36.

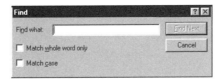

Figure 13.36 *The Find dialog box.*

2. Within the Find what field, type in the text you desire.
3. Choose Find Next.

WordPad will highlight the next occurrence of the text within your document. If WordPad has located the text you desire, select the Cancel option to close the dialog box. Otherwise, click your mouse on the Find Next button until WordPad either locates the text you want, or displays a dialog box that tells you it has reached the end of your document.

Customizing Your Page Settings

SUCCESS HINT Depending on your document, you may want to change your margins or your page orientation (portrait or landscape). To change a document's page settings, select the File menu Page Setup option. WordPad, in turn, will display the Page Setup dialog box as shown in Figure 13.37. Within the Page Setup dialog box, select the settings you desire and choose OK.

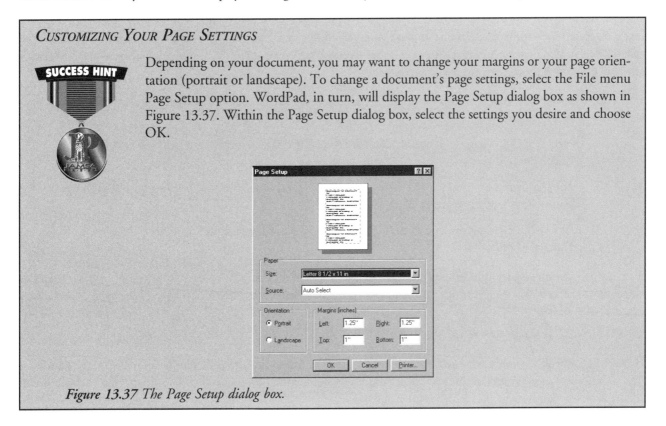

Figure 13.37 *The Page Setup dialog box.*

Replacing Text within Your Document

Just as you can use WordPad to search your document for text, you can also direct WordPad to replace each occurrence of one word or phrase with another. To replace text within your WordPad document, perform these steps:

1. Select the Edit menu Replace option. WordPad will display the Replace dialog box, as shown in Figure 13.38.

293

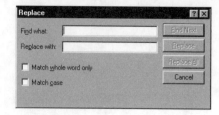

Figure 13.38 The Replace dialog box.

2. Within the Find what field, type in the text you want WordPad to replace.

3. Within the Replace with field, type in your replacement text.

4. If you want WordPad to replace every occurrence of the word or phrase throughout your document, choose the Replace All button. If you want to replace a specific occurrence of the text, select the Find Next button until WordPad highlights the occurrence of the text you desire. When WordPad highlights the text you desire, select Replace.

Moving Text Using a Cut-and-Paste Operation

One of your biggest advantages in using a word processor is the ease with which you can move or copy text. To move or copy text within WordPad, you perform a cut-and-paste operation—so named because it mimics the operation you might perform using scissors and paste to move text on paper. To move text within WordPad using a cut-and-paste operation, perform these steps:

1. Using your mouse or keyboard, select the text you want to move (by displaying the text in reverse video).

2. Select the Edit menu Cut option. WordPad, in turn, will remove your selected text from your document.

3. Using your mouse or keyboard arrow keys, move your cursor to the location within your document where you want to place the text.

4. Choose the Edit menu Paste option. WordPad will place the text back into your document at the cursor location.

To copy text throughout your document, change step 2 to use the Edit menu Copy option instead of Cut. WordPad, in turn, will make a copy of your text that you can place throughout your document by using the Edit menu Paste option.

Customizing WordPad Options

By default, WordPad should wrap text to the start of the next line each time your text reaches your right margin. If WordPad does not wrap text in this way, select the View menu and choose Options. WordPad, in turn, will display the Options dialog box, as shown in Figure 13.39.

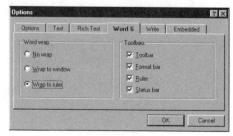

Figure 13.39 The Options dialog box.

13: Using the Windows 95 Accessory Programs

Using the Options dialog box, you can control how WordPad wraps text. Using the tabs that appear at the top of the dialog box, select the format with which you plan to save your document, such as Word 6. Next, choose the text-wrapping technique you desire. In other words, you may want WordPad automatically to wrap the documents you save in Word 6 files, but you may not want WordPad automatically to wrap text that you save as text files.

Keys to Success

Windows 95 provides several very powerful accessory programs you can put to instant use. In fact, most users should use the Backup and ScanDisk accessory programs on a regular basis. In Chapter 14, you will use the Windows Explorer to traverse and manage the folders on your disk. Before you continue with Chapter 14, however, make sure you have learned the following key concepts:

- ✓ Using Backup, you can backup the files on your hard disk to floppy disks or tape.
- ✓ Use ScanDisk at least once a week to examine your folders, files, and disks for errors.
- ✓ If you are low on disk space, you can use the DriveSpace accessory to double your disk's capacity.
- ✓ If you connect your phone to your modem, you can use the Phone Dialer accessory to speed dial the voice calls you place.
- ✓ The HyperTerminal accessory lets you connect your PC to remote computers, such as bulletin-board systems.
- ✓ WordPad provides basic word-processing capabilities you can use to create memos and short letters.

Chapter 14
Using the Windows 95 Explorer

As you know, the programs you run and the documents you create reside on your computer's hard disk. To help you organize the information you store on your disk, Windows 95 lets you place your programs and documents into folders. To help you manage the folders you create, Windows 95 provides a special program called the Explorer. Using the Explorer, you can open folders and display their contents within a window, you can copy, move, and delete files, and you can associate documents of a particular type (such as documents with the DOC extension) to a specific program (such as your word processor). By associating a document type to a program in this way, you instruct Windows 95 to run the program automatically, and to load the document for use, whenever you double-click your mouse on a document of that type.

It is important that you get comfortable with the Windows 95 Explorer. As you will learn, many Windows 95 programs display windows and dialog boxes that offer capabilities similar to those you'll find within the Explorer. By understanding the Explorer, you can maximize your efficiency within other programs. This chapter examines the Explorer in detail. By the time you finish this chapter, you will understand the following key concepts:

- You use the Explorer to open, close, and traverse file folders.
- Using the Explorer, you can copy, move, delete, and rename files and folders.
- You can use the Explorer to view a file's contents or specifics about the file, such as its size and the date and time you created or last used the file.
- The Explorer lets you associate a document type with a specific program. To determine a document's type, look at the document's filename extension. For example, word processing documents use the DOC extension, Excel spreadsheets use XLS, and so on.
- After you associate a document type with a program, you can later double-click your mouse on a document of that type and Windows 95 will automatically run the associated program, loading the document for your use.
- The Explorer provides toolbar buttons that let you quickly move up one folder, create a new folder, delete files, and so on.
- Many Windows 95 programs also provide toolbars that are similar to the Explorer's. By understanding the Explorer toolbar buttons, you can better use other programs that feature similar tools.

STARTING THE WINDOWS 95 EXPLORER

To start the Windows 95 Explorer, select the Start menu Programs option and choose Windows Explorer. Windows 95, in turn, will display the Explorer window as shown in Figure 14.1.

Figure 14.1 The Windows 95 Explorer.

The Explorer window consists of two primary parts. On the left side of the window, Explorer displays a list of disk drives and folders. On the right side of the window, Explorer displays the files and folders that reside within the current disk or folder. You can determine the current disk or folder by examining the name that appears in the bar above the files and folders as shown in Figure 14.2.

Figure 14.2 The Explorer displays the current disk and folder name.

Use the vertical scroll bar that appears next to the list of drives and folders to view the folder names. If you scroll the to the top of the list, you will see icons for the Desktop, My Computer, and your disk drives. Next, scroll through the list until the Explorer displays the Windows folder. Click your mouse on the Windows folder. The Explorer, in turn, will display the files and folders that reside within the Windows folder as shown in Figure 14.3.

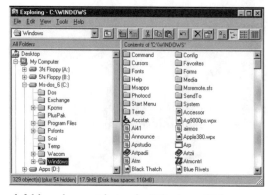

Figure 14.3 Displaying the files and folders that reside in the Windows folder.

Take time now to click your mouse on one or more folders that appear within the Explorer's disk and folders list. Each time you click your mouse on a folder, the Explorer will display that folder's contents within the right-hand side of its window.

> *Explorer Displays Your Disk's Directory Structure*
>
>
>
> In Chapter 7, "Working with Files and Folders," you learned how to use directories (Windows 95 calls them folders) to organize your disk. As you learned, you should think of your disk as a filing cabinet. The first set of directories you create correspond to the cabinet's drawers. Unlike a four-drawer filing cabinet, however, Windows 95 does not restrict the number of directories you can create.
>
> Just as you may further organize the information you place into each drawer using additional files and folders, Windows 95 lets you create additional subdirectories within a directory. When you use the Windows 95 Explorer, you display the files and folders that reside on your disk. Just as you might open the drawer of a filing cabinet and find numerous files, you may click on a folder on your disk to find other folders.
>
> Most books and magazines refer to the process of moving through the folders on your disk as traversing directories. You might, for example, move down into a subdirectory (subfolder) to look for a file. From there you can move down another level (if folders exist within this folder) or you can move back up one level (to the subfolder's parent folder). Also, you can move to an unrelated folder. The Windows 95 Explorer provides you with a vehicle for traversing your disk.

Changing the Explorer's Display

As you view folders using the Explorer, there may be times when you will want to display more information about the files in a folder's list than just the file names. In such cases, you can use the Explorer's View menu to select the display you desire.

If, for example, you have trouble reading the file names, select the View menu Large Icons option. The Explorer, in turn, will increase each file's icon size as shown in Figure 14.4.

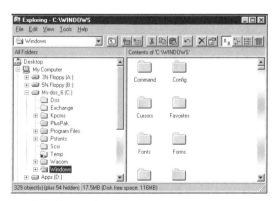

Figure 14.4 Displaying large icons within the Explorer.

In some cases, you may want to know specifics about each file, such as its size, type (such as a spreadsheet or word-processing document), as well as the date and time the file was created or last changed (the file's date and time stamp). To display such file specifics, select the View menu Details option. The Explorer, in turn, will change its file and folder list to include details about each item as shown in Figure 14.5.

Figure 14.5 Displaying file details within the Explorer.

Take time now to experiment with the Explorer's View menu's Large Icons, Small Icons, List, and Details display options.

Controlling the Order in Which Documents Appear Within the Files and Folders List

As you use the Explorer to search for files on your disk, there may be times when you'll want the Explorer to display a folder's contents sorted by name, size, date, or type (based on the file's extension). To control the order in which the Explorer lists files and folders, select the View menu Arrange Icons option. The Explorer, in turn, will cascade a menu of options that let you control the sort order as shown in Figure 14.6.

Figure 14.6 The Explorer's menu of sort options.

Using these sort options, you can arrange files and folders within the list by size, age, name, and type. Take time now to experiment with these sort options. As you will find, within the files and folders list, Explorer always displays your folders before your files.

Expanding and Collapsing Explorer Folders

As you know, folders exist to help you organize the files on your disk. In short, you should group related documents within the same folder, much as you would organize paper documents within the same file folder. When the number of files in a folder becomes too large for you to manage, you can divide the folder into additional subfolders. For example, within the folder that contains your word processing documents, you might create one subfolder to hold your memos, another for documents, and a third to hold your reports.

As you examine the list of folders that appear on the left-hand side of the Explorer window, you will find small boxes to the left of most folders that contain a plus (+) or minus (-) sign. By clicking your mouse on a box that contains a plus sign, you direct the Explorer to *expand* the folder to display its next level of subfolders. For example, Figure

14.7 illustrates a directory folder named School in its *collapsed* form (with a plus sign in the box) and next to it is the same folder in its *expanded* form (with a minus sign in the box). As you can see, when you expand the folder's contents, the Explorer displays the subfolders Math, Spanish, and Science as shown in Figure 14.7a.

Figure 14.7 The Explorer's collapsed and expanded views of the School folder.

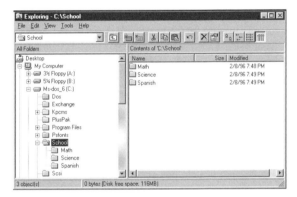

Figure 14.7a Expanding the School folder to display subfolders.

When you click your mouse on a box that contains a plus sign to expand a folder, the Explorer displays the folder's next level of subfolders. In addition, the Explorer changes the plus sign that previously appeared in the box into a minus sign. If you click your mouse on the minus sign, the Explorer will collapse the folder, hiding the subfolders.

As you expand one folder, you may find that the subfolders, too, have boxes preceding their names which contain a plus sign. You can click on the plus sign to expand that folder's view to display its subfolders. If the Explorer does not precede a subfolder with a box and plus sign, the folder does not contain any subfolders.

CREATING YOUR OWN FOLDERS

As you organize the files on your disk, you will eventually need to create additional folders. To use the Explorer to create a folder, perform these steps:

1. Within the Explorer's list of drives and folders, click your mouse on the drive or folder within which you want to create your folder.

2. Select the Explorer File menu and choose New. The Explorer will cascade a menu of options.

3. Choose the Folder option. The Explorer, in turn, will create a new folder within the files and folders list on the right-hand side of the Window.

4. Type in the folder name you desire and press ENTER.

Renaming Files and Folders

Over time, you may find that a folder or file name no longer accurately describes the folder or file's contents. In such cases, the Explorer makes it easy for you to rename folders and files. To rename a folder, for example, perform these steps:

1. Within the Explorer's drives and folders list, single-click your mouse on the folder you want to rename.
2. Select the Explorer File menu Rename option. The Explorer, in turn, will highlight the folder name.
3. Type in the name you desire and press ENTER.

The Explorer also makes its easy for you to rename a file that resides within a folder. To rename a file using the Explorer, perform these steps:

1. Within the Explorer's drives and folders list, select the folder that contains the file you want to rename.
2. Within the files and folders list that appears on the right-hand side of the window, single-click your mouse on the file you want to rename. You may need to scroll through the files and folders list to locate the file.
3. Select the File menu Rename option. The Explorer, in turn, will highlight the file's name.
4. Type in the filename you desire and press ENTER.

Note: In the previous examples, after you selected the file or folder you want to rename, you then selected the File menu Rename option. As it turns out, the Explorer defines the F2 function key as a hot key that corresponds to the Rename option. As such, to rename a file or folder, click on the file or folder, press the F2 function key, and then type the name you desire.

Understanding Explorer Undo Operations

If, while you are using the Explorer, you perform an errant operation, such as moving or deleting the wrong folder, you may be able to "undo" your operation by selecting the Explorer Edit menu Undo option. To successfully undo an operation in this way, you must select the Undo option before you use the Explorer to perform any other operations.

Deleting a File or Folder

Over time, you may no longer need one or more files or folders that reside on your disk. In such cases, you can quickly delete a file or folder using the Explorer. To delete a file from your disk, for example, perform these steps:

1. Within the Explorer's drives and folders list, select the folder that contains the file you want to delete.
2. Within the files and folders list that appears on the right-hand side of the window, single-click your mouse on the file you want to delete. You may need to scroll through the files and folders list to locate the file.
3. Select the File menu Delete option (or press your DEL key). The Explorer, in turn, will delete the file from your disk and will remove the file's name from the files and folders list.

Note: If you inadvertently delete one or more files or folders whose contents you need, you can undelete the files using the Windows 95 Recycle Bin discussed in detail in Chapter15, "Revisiting My Computer and the Recycle Bin."

When you delete a folder from your disk, you delete all the files and subfolders the folder contains. Therefore, you need to be very careful when you delete a folder. Unlike a file delete operation that deletes only one item from your disk, when you delete a folder, you can delete hundreds of files and folders in one step. Before you delete a folder, stop and make sure you no longer need the folder or any of the files the folders may contain. To delete a folder using the Explorer, perform these steps:

1. Within the Explorer's drives and folders list, select the folder whose contents you want to delete.

2. Select the Explorer's File menu and choose Delete. The Explorer, in turn, will display the Confirm Folder Delete dialog box as shown in Figure 14.8 asking you to confirm that you really want to delete the folder.

Figure 14.8 *The Confirm Folder Delete dialog box.*

3. Select Yes to delete the folder. Depending on the folder's contents, the Explorer may display additional dialog boxes asking you to confirm your file deletions. Select Yes or No for each as you desire.

UNDERSTANDING THE RECYCLE BIN

When you delete a file or folder, Windows 95 does not immediately remove the item from your disk. Instead, Windows 95 moves the item into a special storage container called the Recycle Bin. Think of the Recycle Bin as the trash can that sits next to your desk. As you organize your desk, you may throw items away into the trash can. Later, you may realize that you need the item. If someone has not yet emptied your trash can, you can remove the item and place it back on your desk. In a similar way, if Windows 95 has not yet emptied the Recycle Bin, you can pull out files or folders you realize you still need. Chapter 15, "Revisiting My Computer and the Recycle Bin" discusses the Windows 95 Recycle Bin in detail.

VIEWING YOUR DOCUMENT TYPES

As you work, you will create many types of documents ranging from word processing documents, to spreadsheets, to databases. To help you organize your documents, you should use file extensions that describe the document's contents. As you have learned, the file extension follows the period in a filename. For example, you might use the DOC extension for word processing documents (such as CHAPTER14.DOC, INDEX.DOC, and so on). Likewise, you might use the XLS extension for Excel spreadsheets (BUDGET97.XLS).

If you used Windows 3.1 in the past, you may be used to using three character extensions. Under Windows 95, however, your extensions can exceed three characters. You could, for example, use the following filename extensions:

    CHAPTER14.WORD DOCUMENT
    BUDGET97.EXCEL SPREADSHEET
    REPORT.FIRST DRAFT

In this case, the file extensions not only exceeded 3 characters, they included spaces! Although at first glance, these longer file extensions may look appealing, they may actually introduce problems. To begin, you probably already have many word processing documents on your disk that use the DOC extension. As a rule, you should pick one file extension for each document type and stick with that extension. Second, as your document extensions become longer, your chance of misspelling or abbreviating the extension increases if you are in a hurry. Third, if you work in an office, you probably want to use the same file extensions as your coworkers to simplify your exchange of documents. As such, you may want to stick with the three-letter file extensions you used in Windows 3.1. By using a longer filename you can still create a meaningful name that describes the file's contents.

To display file extensions within the Explorer, perform these steps:

1. Select the Explorer View menu and choose Options. The Explorer will display the Options dialog box as shown in Figure 14.9.

Figure 14.9 *The Explorer Options dialog box.*

2. Remove the check mark from the Hide MS-DOS file extensions for file types that are registered checkbox.

3. Choose OK. The Explorer will display the file extensions as shown in Figure 14.10.

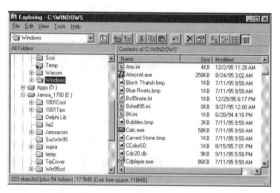

Figure 14.10 *Displaying file extensions within the Explorer.*

REGISTERING (ASSOCIATING) A FILE TYPE WITH A PROGRAM

Microsoft designed Windows 95 with the goal that you quit focusing on the programs you use to create various documents and start thinking more about the documents themselves. As a result, the Windows 95 developers prefer that you not have to run a program and then open a document, but rather, that you simply double-click your mouse on a document so that the program that created the document automatically runs. Before Windows 95 can know

14: Using the Windows 95 Explorer

which program it should run when you double-click your mouse on a specific document type, someone (either the program's software installation or you) must register the file type and program with Windows 95. In other words, you must tell Windows 95, for example, that when you double-click your mouse on a file with the DOC extension, you want Windows 95 to run Microsoft Word. To tell Windows 95 which program to run for a specific document type, you must register the document type with Windows 95 using the Explorer. To register a document type with Windows 95, perform these steps:

1. Select the Explorer View menu and choose Options. Windows 95 will display the Options dialog box previously shown in Figure 14.9.

2. Click your mouse on the File Types tab. The Explorer will display the File Types page as shown in Figure 14.11.

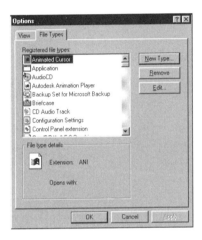

Figure 14.11 The File Types page.

3. Click your mouse on the New Type button. The Explorer, in turn, will display the Add New File Type dialog box as shown in Figure 14.12.

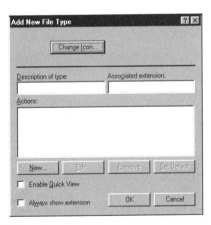

Figure 14.12 The Add New File Type dialog box.

4. Within the Description of type field, type in two or three words that describe the type's typical contents, such as "Report for work."

5. Within the Associated extension field, type in the extension that corresponds to the file type you are registering. Do not precede the extension with a period. For example, to register your work reports, you might use the RPT extension.

305

6. Click your mouse in the Actions box and then click on the New button. The Explorer, in turn, will display the New Actions dialog box as shown in Figure 14.13.

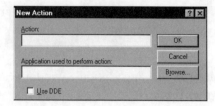

Figure 14.13 *The New Actions dialog box.*

7. Within the Action field, type Open and press the TAB key.

8. Within the Application used to perform action field, type the complete path name to the executable file that corresponds to the program you are registering (such as the pathname C:\WINDOWS\NOTEPAD.EXE).

9. Choose OK. The Explorer will redisplay the Add New File Type page previously shown in Figure 14.12.

10. Choose Close. The Explorer will redisplay the File Types page previously shown in Figure 14.11. Within the list of file types, you will find your new registration.

11. Choose Close.

After you register your file type in this way, you can double-click your mouse on files of that type within the Explorer. Windows 95, in turn, will run the corresponding program, loading your document for your use.

COPYING A FILE OR FOLDER

As you work, there will be times when you will need to copy a file or folder to a new location. You might, for example, copy a file from one folder on your disk to another. Likewise, you might copy a file or folder from your disk to a network disk (Chapter 18, "Windows 95 Networking Operations" discusses Windows 95 network operations). As you will learn, the Explorer gives you two ways to copy files and folders: using cut-and-paste operations discussed here or using drag-and-drop operations discussed later in this Chapter. As you will learn, the steps you perform to copy a file or a folder are the same. However, when you copy a folder's contents, you copy all the files and subfolders the folder contains. As such, by copying a single folder, you may actually copy hundreds of files.

COPYING A FILE OR FOLDER USING CUT-AND-PASTE OPERATIONS

When you use a word processor to move or copy text, you often use cut-and-paste operations. To perform a cut-and-paste operation within your word processor, you first select the text you want to move or copy. Next, you select the Edit menu Cut or Copy option depending on whether you are moving or copying the text. Then, you position your cursor within your document to the location at which you want the text, and you use the Edit menu Paste option to place a copy of the text at that location.

As it turns out, the Windows 95 Explorer lets you move and copy files using cut-and-paste operations. In short, you first select the file or folder you desire and use the Edit menu Cut or Copy option. Next, you select the folder into which you want to move or copy the file or folder and you select the Edit menu Paste option. To copy a file or folder using cut-and-paste operations, perform these steps:

1. Within the Explorer's drives and folders list, select the folder that contains the file or folder you want to copy.

14: Using the Windows 95 Explorer

2. Within the files and folders list that appears on the right-hand side of the window, single-click your mouse on the file or folder you want to copy. You may need to scroll through the files and folders list to locate the item.

3. Select the Edit menu Copy option. The Explorer, behind the scenes, will get information about the file or folder that it needs to perform the copy operation.

4. Within the Explorer's drives and folders list, select the folder or disk to which you want to copy the item.

5. Select the Edit menu Paste option. The Explorer will place a copy of the file or folder into the folder.

UNDERSTANDING PASTE AND PASTE SHORTCUT

When you copy a file or folder using a cut-and-paste operation, you will normally use the Edit menu Paste operation to complete your copy operation. If you examine the Edit menu, however, you will find that it contains a Paste Shortcut option. If you select the Paste Shortcut option during a copy operation, the Explorer won't physically copy your file or folder. Instead, the Explorer will place a shortcut icon in the files and folders list that you can use to access the original file or folder quickly. In this way, you can get to the same information from two places (from its original folder and from the shortcut), but the file or folder actually resides in one location on your disk.

COPYING FILES AND FOLDERS USING DRAG-AND-DROP OPERATIONS

To copy a file or folder using a drag-and-drop operation, you open the folder that contains the file or folder you want to copy. Next, within the files and folders list, you click your mouse on the file or folder and drag the item into a window that corresponds to the folder into which you want to copy the item. When you release your mouse select button, you drop the file copy into the new folder. If the target folder appears in the drives and folders list, you can drag-and-drop the file or folder onto the target folder.

To use a drag-and-drop operation to copy a file or folder, perform these steps:

1. Within the Explorer's drives and folders list, select the folder that contains the file or folder you want to copy.

2. Within the files and folders list that appears on the right-hand side of the window, single-click your mouse on the file or folder you want to copy. You may need to scroll through the files and folders list to locate the item.

3. Within the drives and folders list, locate the drive or folder into which you want to copy the item. You may need to scroll through the list of folders or expand one or two folders to locate the folder you desire.

4. Hold down the mouse select button, press your keyboard CTRL key and drag the item into the drives and folders list, placing the item on top of the target folder you desire.

5. Release your mouse select button and drop the copy of the item into the folder.

Note: *To perform a drag-and-drop file operation, you must hold down your keyboard's CTRL key as you drag the item. Otherwise, the Explorer will perform a move operation.*

307

Moving a File or Folder

As you work, there will be times when you need to move a file from one folder to another. The Explorer lets you move a file or folder using both cut-and-paste and drag-and-drop operations. As you will find, moving a file using the Explorer is very similar to performing a file copy operation. To move a file or folder using a cut-and-paste operation, perform these steps:

1. Within the Explorer's drives and folders list, select the folder that contains the file or folder you want to move.
2. Within the files and folders list that appears on the right-hand side of the window, single-click your mouse on the file or folder you want to move. You may need to scroll through the files and folders list to locate the item.
3. Select the Edit menu Cut option. The Explorer, behind the scenes, will get information about the file or folder that it needs to perform the move operation.
4. Within the Explorer's drives and folders list, select the folder or disk to which you want to move the item.
5. Select the Edit menu Paste option. The Explorer will place the file or folder into the selected folder.

To move a file using drag-and-drop operations, perform these steps:

1. Within the Explorer's drives and folders list, select the folder that contains the file or folder you want to move.
2. Within the files and folders list that appears on the right-hand side of the window, single-click your mouse on the file or folder you want to move. You may need to scroll through the files and folders list to locate the item.
3. Within the drives and folders list, locate the drive or folder into which you want to move the item. You may need to scroll through the list of folders or expand one or two folders to locate the folder you desire.
4. Hold down the mouse select button and drag the item into the drives and folders list, placing the item on top of the target folder you desire.
5. Release your mouse select button and drop the item into the folder.

Running Programs Within the Explorer

In addition to running programs from the Start menu, Windows 95 gives you two ways to run programs from within the Explorer. First, if you locate a program file within the files and folders list, you can simply double-click your mouse on the file's icon. Windows 95, in turn, will open a window within which it displays the program. Second, if you highlight the executable program file within the files and folders list, you can use the File menu Open option to run the program.

Working with Multiple Files

As you work with files, there will be times when you will want to copy, move, or delete two or more files within the same operation. In such cases, the Explorer lets you select multiple files and folders with which you perform an operation. Depending on whether you are selecting files that appear successively within the files and folders list or dispersed throughout the list, the steps you will perform will differ slightly. For example, Figure 14.14 shows a group of selected files that reside in consecutive locations in the file list.

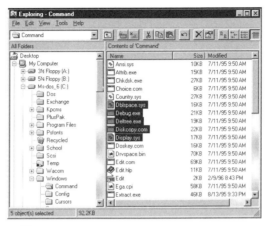

Figure 14.14 A group of consecutive files.

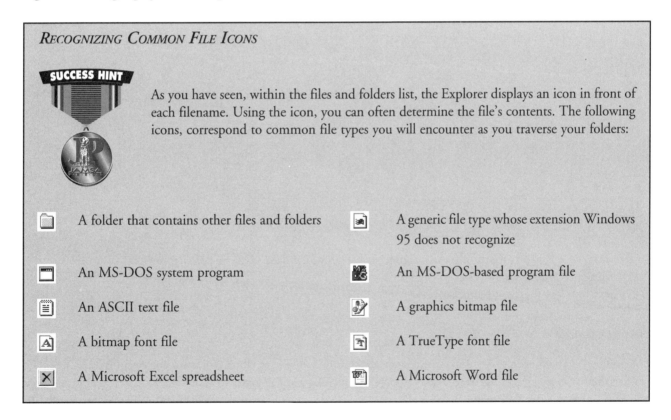

To select a group of consecutive files such as those shown in Figure14.14, click your mouse on the first file in the list. Next, hold down your keyboard SHIFT key and click your mouse on the last file in the list. The Explorer, in turn, will highlight all of the files that appear in between the first and last files. Figure 14.15 on the other hand, shows a group of selected files that reside throughout the file list.

To select a group of files that are dispersed throughout the directory list, simply hold down your keyboard's CTRL key as you click your mouse on each file.

Figure 14.15 A group of dispersed files.

There may be times when you want to select groups of files that reside dispersed throughout the file list, such as those shown in Figure 14.16.

Figure 14.16 Groups of consecutive files dispersed throughout the file list.

In this case, to select the groups of files, you hold down your keyboard CTRL key each time you click on a new file. Next, with the CTRL key depressed, you click on the first file in a list. Then, you hold down both the CTRL and SHIFT keys to select the last file in the list.

INVERTING A FILE SELECTION

Depending on the files in your files and folders list, there may be times when you want to select all but a few files. Rather than selecting files in groups as just discussed, you may find it easier to select the files that you don't want and then to choose the Edit menu Invert Selection option. Also, you may find it convenient to first select all the files in the list, and then to eliminate those files you don't want by holding down your keyboard CTRL key and clicking on the file. To select all the files and folders within a list, choose the Edit menu Select All option.

WORKING WITH TWO EXPLORER WINDOWS

As you have learned, when you click on a folder icon within the Explorer window, the Explorer displays the folder's contents within the current window. There may be times, however, when it is more convenient for you to work with two windows. To open a new Explorer window for a folder, perform these steps:

1. Within the Explorer's drives and folders list, select the folder that contains the folder you want to view.

2. Within the files and folders list that appears on the right-hand side of the window, single-click your mouse on the folder you want to view. You may need to scroll through the files and folders list to locate the folder.

3. Select the File menu Open window. The Explorer, in turn, will open a second window within which it displays the folder's contents as shown in Figure 14.17.

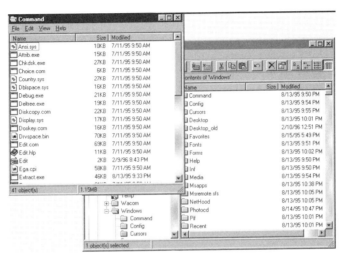

Figure 14.17 To display multiple Explorer windows, use the File menu Open option.

DISPLAYING ALL THE FILES IN A FOLDER

Normally, when you traverse folders, you are looking for a specific document or program file. To reduce the number of files through which you must search, the Explorer suppresses the display of specific file types. As such, the files the Explorer displays for a folder may not be all the files the folder actually contains. Normally, the Explorer hides Windows system files, device drivers, dynamic link library (DLL) files and so on. To direct the Explorer to list all the files a folder contains, perform these steps:

1. Select the Explorer View menu and choose Options. The Explorer will display the Options dialog box as shown in Figure 14.18.

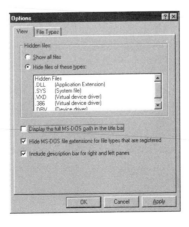

Figure 14.18 The Options dialog box.

2. Within the Hidden Files field, select the Show all files option.

3. Choose OK.

Using the Status Bar

If you examine the bottom of the Explorer window, you will find a small status bar:

If your Explorer window does not contain the status bar, select the View menu Status Bar option, placing a check mark in front of the option. As you perform different operations, the Explorer will display information within this status bar. For example, when you first select a folder, the status bar will display the number of objects in the folder, the amount of disk space the objects consume, and the amount of free space on your disk:

When you later click your mouse on a file or folder, the status bar will tell you the number of objects you have selected and the disk space the objects consume:

Viewing a File's Contents Using Quick View

As you traverse folders on your disk, there may be times when you want to view a file's contents. If you have registered a file's type for use with a specific program, you can double-click on the file and open the corresponding document within the program. However, to open a file in this way, you first have to start the registered program, which can be a time consuming task. As an alternative, the Explorer supports a Quick View capability with which you can view many different file types. If the Explorer's Quick View supports file types you use on a regular basis, you will find using Quick View is much faster than viewing a document by starting the corresponding program. To view a document's contents using Quick View, perform these steps:

1. Within the Explorer's drives and folders list, select the folder that contains the file whose contents you want to view.

2. Within the files and folders list that appears on the right-hand side of the window, single-click your mouse on the file you want to view. You may need to scroll through the files and folders list to locate the folder.

3. Select the File menu Quick View option. The Explorer, in turn, will open a Quick View window within which it displays the document's contents as shown in Figure 14.19.

The Explorer's Quick View capability exists to let you view a document's contents. If you want to edit the document's contents, you must use the program with which you created the document. However, Quick View makes it easy for you to start that program. To start the registered program from within the Quick View window, select the Open File for Editing option. To close the Quick View window, simply click your mouse on the window's Close button.

14: USING THE WINDOWS 95 EXPLORER

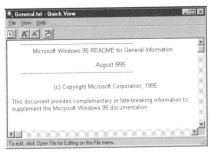

Figure 14.19 *Viewing a document's contents using Quick View.*

UNDERSTANDING THE EXPLORER'S SEND TO OPTION

If you examine the Explorer's File menu, you will find a Send To option that cascades to display several additional options as shown in Figure 14.20.

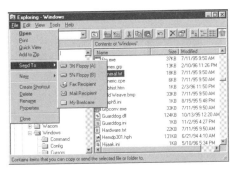

Figure 14.20 *Cascading the Explorer's Send To menu option.*

Using the Send To option, you can send selected files to a floppy disk (a simple file copy operation), to a fax machine or electronic mail recipient via the Windows 95 Exchange (discussed in Chapter 17, "Using Exchange for Faxes and E-Mail") or to Briefcase, previously discussed in Chapter 11. In short, the Explorer's Send To option gives you a convenient way to perform operations from within the Explorer that normally require other programs.

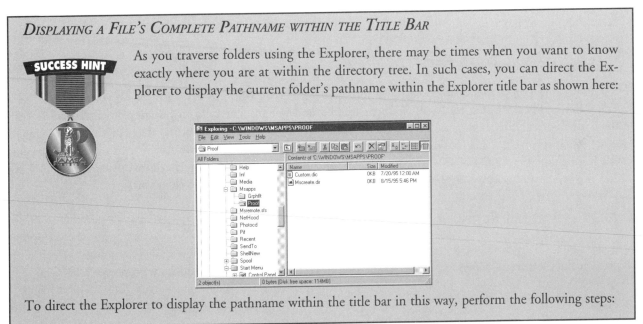

SUCCESS WITH WINDOWS 95

> 1. Select the View menu and choose Options. The Explorer will display the Options dialog box.
> 2. Select the Display the full MS-DOS pathname in the title bar option.
> 3. Choose OK.

DISPLAYING AND CHANGING FILE PROPERTIES WITHIN THE EXPLORER

Every file on your disk has properties such as the file's name, size, type, the date you created and last used the file, and so on. To display a file's properties using the Explorer, perform these steps:

1. Within the Explorer's drives and folders list, select the folder that contains the file whose contents you want to view.

2. Within the files and folders list that appears on the right-hand side of the window, right click your mouse on the file whose properties you want to view and select the pop-up menu Properties option. The Explorer, in turn, will display the Properties dialog box as shown in Figure 14.21.

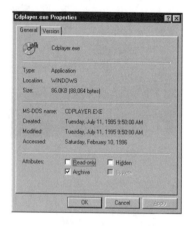

Figure 14.21 The Properties dialog box.

As you can see, the Properties dialog box displays the file's name, size, date and time stamps, and file attributes, which are discussed next.

UNDERSTANDING AND USING FILE ATTRIBUTES

If you examine the Properties dialog box shown in Figure 14.21, you will find that each file on your disk may have several different file attributes: read-only, hidden, archive, and system. The following section briefly describes each of these attributes and when you would use them. For now, however, understand that you can view and change a file's attributes using the Properties dialog box. For example, to assign the read-only attribute to a file (that prevents a user from changing the file's contents), you click your mouse on the read-only checkbox, placing a check mark within the box. To remove an attribute, you click on the checkbox to remove the check mark.

UNDERSTANDING THE READ-ONLY PROPERTY

Depending on a file's contents, there may be times when you want to let users view a file's contents, but you want to prevent the users from changing the file. In such cases, you can use the file's read-only property. When you set a file's read-only property, you cannot delete the file, change the file's contents, or overwrite the file using a file-copy operation. In short, using the read-only attribute is a good way to protect a file. Should you need to change the file's contents in the future, you can clear the read-only attribute, edit the file as you require, and then set the read-only property again.

UNDERSTANDING THE ARCHIVE PROPERTY

When you backup the files on your disk (disk backups are called archives), most software programs let you backup all the files on your disk or only those files that have changed since your last backup operation. To determine which files to backup, the backup software relies on the file's archive property. As it turns out, each time you create or change a file, Windows 95 sets the file's archive property. When you later backup your system, the back-up software clears the archive property. By examining the file's property attribute, you can determine whether or not the file has been backed up or needs backing up. Likewise, by setting a file's archive property, you can force your back-up software to backup the file during your next disk back-up operation.

UNDERSTANDING THE HIDDEN PROPERTY

Depending on a file's contents, there may be times when you don't want the file to appear within a folder's list of files. For example, if you are working on a proposal you don't want other users to see, you can use the file's hidden property to hide the file. A hidden file is simply a file that exists on your disk but normally does not appear within a directory listing. To prevent users from deleting key files, many software programs will hide one or more files.

UNDERSTANDING THE SYSTEM PROPERTY

To prevent users from inadvertently deleting key files, Windows and DOS mark certain files as system files. Like hidden files, system files do not appear within a folder's file list. Likewise, you cannot delete or overwrite a system file. As a rule, you should not clear or set the system property. Instead, reserve the system property's use for Windows 95 or DOS. If you don't want a file to appear within a directory list, use the hidden property. Likewise, if you don't want users to delete a file easily, use the read-only attribute. Then, you don't need to use the system attribute.

SETTING OR CLEARING PROPERTIES FOR MULTIPLE FILES IN ONE OPERATION

As you work with files, there may be times when you want to set or clear similar properties for two or more files. In such cases, select (highlight) each of the files using the techniques previously discussed in this chapter. Next, right click your mouse on one of the selected files and choose the pop-up menu Properties option. The Explorer, in turn, will display the Properties dialog box. Select the properties you desire and choose OK.

UNDERSTANDING THE EXPLORER TOOLBAR

To simplify common operations, the Explorer provides a toolbar whose buttons appear near the top of the window. If your Explorer window does not contain the toolbar, select the View menu Toolbar option. Using the toolbar buttons, you can simplify many of the operations this chapter discusses. Table 14.1 lists the functions of the Explorer toolbar buttons.

Button	Purpose
842460102 (C:)	Lets you access a different folder or drive
	Moves you up one level in the directory tree to the current folder's parent
	Disconnects a network drive
	Cuts selected items to the clipboard
	Copies selected items to the clipboard
	Pastes items from the clipboard
	Undoes the previous operation
	Deletes selected items, placing them into the Recycle Bin
	Displays the Properties dialog box for selected items
	Displays large icons within the Explorer window
	Displays small icons within the Explorer window
	Displays files and folders in list form
	Displays files and folders in detail form

Table 14.1 *The purpose of the Explorer toolbar buttons.*

FINDING A FILE ON YOUR DISK

As you work, there may be times when you misplace one or more files on your disk. Normally, although you can't locate the files, you probably remember either the file name, the date you created the file, or text that appears within the document. In such cases, you can use Windows 95 Find capabilities to locate the file.

FINDING A FILE OR FOLDER BY NAME

If you know the name of the file or folder for which you are searching, you can use Windows 95 to search your disk (or all your disks) for the file by performing these steps:

1. Select the Start menu Find option and choose Files or Folders. Windows 95, in turn, will display the Find: All Files window as shown in Figure 14.22.

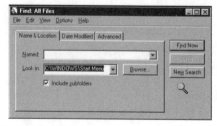

Figure 14.22 *The Find: All Files window.*

2. Within the Named field, type in the name of the file or folder for which you are searching. If you only know part of the filename, you can use the DOS wildcard characters.

3. Within the Look in pull-down list, select the disk you want Windows 95 to search for your files. If you want to search all the disks in your system, select the My Computer option.

4. Select the Find Now option to start your search. If Windows 95 locates a matching file, it will display a dialog box that contains the filename as shown in Figure 14.23.

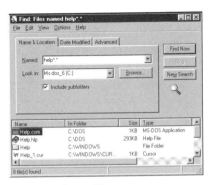

Figure 14.23 *Windows displays a window of matching filenames.*

5. If you have registered the file, you can double-click your mouse on the file to start the corresponding program.

FINDING A FILE OR FOLDER BY DATE

If you know when, or about when, you created a file, you can direct Windows 95 to search for the file by date. For example, if you know the exact date you created the file, you can tell Windows 95 to display all the files created or changed on that day. If you know you created the file within the last month, you can tell Windows 95 to list all the files on your disk that were created within the last month. To search your disk for a file by date, perform these steps:

1. Select the Start menu Find option and choose Files or Folders. Windows 95, in turn, will display the Find: All Files window previously shown in Figure 14.22.

2. Select the Date Modified tab. Windows 95, in turn, will display the Date Modified page as shown in Figure 14.24.

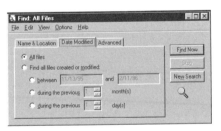

Figure 14.24 *The Date Modified page.*

3. Within the Date Modified page, select the date, range of days, or months for which you want Windows 95 to list files.

4. Select Find Now.

USING ADVANCED FILE SEARCH OPTIONS

There may be times when you can't remember when you created a file or its name, but you can recall one or more words or phrases that appear within the document. For example, you might only recall that you wrote a document to a specific company, such as Jamsa Press, but you can't remember when or what you called the document. In such cases, you can direct Windows 95 to search your disk for files that contain the text Jamsa Press. To perform an advanced search operation, perform these steps:

1. Select the Start menu Find option and choose Files or Folders. Windows 95, in turn, will display the Find: All Files window previously shown in Figure 14.22.

2. Select the Advanced tab. Windows 95, in turn, will display the Advanced page as shown in Figure 14.25.

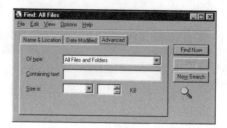

Figure 14.25 *The Advanced page.*

3. Within the Containing text field, type in the text for which you want Windows 95 to search.

4. Select Find Now.

As you can see, using the Advanced page, you can search for files that are bigger or smaller than a specific size. If, for example, you are wondering where all the free space on your disk disappeared to, you can use the Advanced page to search for files that are 1,024Kb (1Mb) or larger. Windows 95, in turn, will display a list of large files that may be consuming much of your free space.

Keys to Success

Using the Windows 95 Explorer, you can create and manage folders on your disk. As you will learn, many Windows 95-based programs provide capabilities similar to those of the Explorer. For example, within the Save As and Open dialog boxes, most programs will let you traverse folders to locate the file you desire or to select the folder within which you want to store a document. In Chapter 15, you will examine the My Computer and Network Neighborhood windows. Before you continue with Chapter 15, however, make sure you understand the following key concepts:

- ✓ The Windows 95 Explorer lets you open, close, and traverse file folders.
- ✓ Using the Explorer, you can copy, move, delete, and rename files and folders.
- ✓ You can use the Explorer's Quick View capability to quickly view a file's contents.
- ✓ By right-clicking your mouse on a file within the Explorer, you can view specifics about the file, such as its size and the date and time you created or last used the file.
- ✓ After you register a document type with a program, you can later double-click your mouse on a document of that type to run the corresponding program.
- ✓ The Explorer provides toolbar buttons that let you quickly move up one folder, create a new folder, delete files, and so on.
- ✓ Many Windows 95 programs also provide toolbars that are similar to the Explorer's. By understanding the Explorer toolbar buttons, you can better use other programs that feature similar tools.
- ✓ To locate a file or folder that resides on your disk, use the Start menu Find option.
- ✓ Using Windows 95 file-search capabilities, you can search for a file by name, by size, or based on the date you created or last changed the file.

Chapter 15
Revisiting My Computer and the Recycle Bin

In Chapter 14, "Using the Windows 95 Explorer," you learned how to traverse the folders on your disk using the Windows 95 Explorer. In addition, you learned how to use the Start menu Find option to locate files and folders on your disk. In this chapter, you will revisit two Desktop items so you can apply your Explorer knowledge: My Computer and the Recycle Bin. As you will learn, the My Computer and Recycle Bin windows are very similar to the Explorer windows you traversed in Chapter 14. By the time you finish this chapter, you will understand the following key concepts:

- Windows 95 uses Explorer-like windows for My Computer, Network Neighborhood, and the Recycle Bin.

- Using the View menu options, you can control how Windows 95 displays files with all Windows 95 folders.

- By double-clicking your mouse on a program-file icon within a folder, you direct Windows 95 to run the corresponding program.

- When you delete a file or folder, Windows 95 moves the file or folder into a temporary folder called the Recycle Bin. In this way, Windows 95 gives you an opportunity to undelete the item.

- The Recycle Bin displays your deleted files and folders using an Explorer-like folder. As such, you can use cut-and-paste or drag-and-drop file-move operations to undelete files from the Recycle Bin.

REVISITING MY COMPUTER

As you have learned, when you double-click your mouse on the My Computer icon, Windows 95 will open a window that contains icons for each of your disk drives as well as folders for your system printers and fonts. Figure 15.1 illustrates a typical My Computer window.

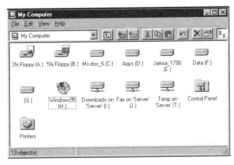

Figure 15.1 The contents of a typical My Computer window.

Examine the menu bar that appears at the top of the My Computer window. The menu bar contains the same options you used in Chapter 14 to traverse Explorer folders. If you click your mouse on the menus, you will find that the menu options match those of the Explorer. As such, starting in the My Computer folder, you can traverse the folders on your disk and perform file copy, move, delete, and rename options.

CONTROLLING MY COMPUTER WINDOWS

When you click your mouse on a folder within the Explorer, Windows 95 normally replaces the current window's contents with that of the new folder. When you double-click your mouse on a folder within My Computer, on the other hand, Windows 95 opens a second window within which it displays the folder's contents as shown in Figure 15.2.

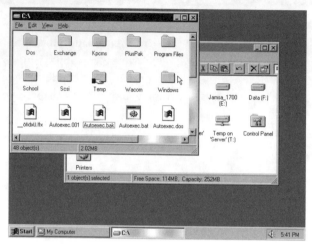

Figure 15.2 By default, Windows 95 opens a window to display each folder you open.

If you traverse through several folders looking for a document, you may end up with several open windows that you must later close as shown in Figure 15.3.

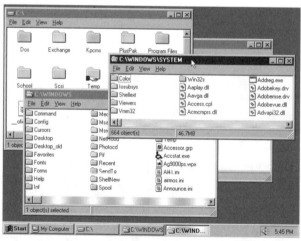

Figure 15.3 A search operation may result in multiple open windows.

Luckily, Windows 95 gives you several ways to manage open folder windows as you will learn next.

First, if your search for a file has opened several windows, such as those shown in Figure 15.3, you can close all the windows in one step by holding down your keyboard SHIFT key as you close the most recent window. Second, if you need to work with two or more folders at the same time, hold down your keyboard's CTRL key and click your mouse on each folder you desire. Next, select the File menu Open option. Windows 95, in turn, will open a window for each folder.

Third, if you don't want Windows 95 to open a new window for each folder, but rather, you want Windows 95 to replace the current window's contents with those of the new folder, hold down your keyboard's CTRL key when you double-click your mouse on the folder. Should you later decide that you want Windows 95 always to replace the current window's contents when you open a new folder, as opposed to opening a new window, perform these steps:

1. Select the View menu and choose Options. Windows 95, in turn, will display the Options dialog box as shown in Figure 15.4.

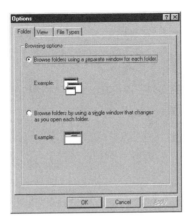

Figure 15.4 *The Options dialog box.*

2. Select the Browse folders using a single window that changes as you open each folder option.

3. Choose OK.

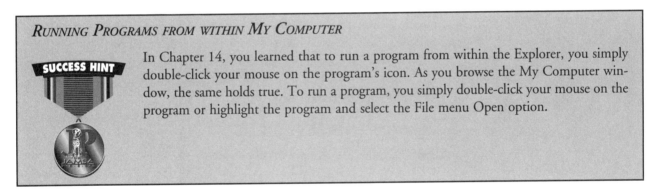

RUNNING PROGRAMS FROM WITHIN MY COMPUTER

In Chapter 14, you learned that to run a program from within the Explorer, you simply double-click your mouse on the program's icon. As you browse the My Computer window, the same holds true. To run a program, you simply double-click your mouse on the program or highlight the program and select the File menu Open option.

ARRANGING ICONS WITHIN THE MY COMPUTER WINDOW

In Chapter 14, you learned that the Explorer lets you display files within a window sorted by size, type, name, or date. Because the My Computer folder includes disk drives, you can arrange the icons using another option: available disk space. When you arrange disk icons by their available disk space, Windows 95 will arrange the disks from least to most available storage space. To arrange your disk icons by their available space, select the View menu Arrange Icons and choose by Free Space.

PERFORMING FILE MOVE AND COPY OPERATIONS

As you traverse My Computer folders, you can perform file move and copy operations using cut-and-paste and drag-and-drop operations. To move or copy a file using a cut-and-paste operation, perform these steps:

1. Open the folder that contains the file you want to move or copy.

2. Click your mouse on the file you want to move or copy.

3. Select the Edit menu and choose Cut if you are moving the file, or Copy if you are copying the file.

4. Open the folder into which you want to move or copy the file.

5. Select the Edit menu Paste option.

As was the case with the Explorer, if you move or copy a folder, Windows 95 moves or copies all the files and subfolders the folder contains. To move or copy a file using a drag-and-drop operation, perform these steps:

1. Open the folder that contains the file you want to move or copy.

2. Open the folder into which you want to move or copy the file.

3. Move the two folder's windows side-by-side.

4. To move the file into a new folder, aim your mouse pointer at the file, hold down your mouse-select button and drag the file into the new folder. When you release the mouse-select button, Windows 95 will drop the file into the folder.

5. To copy the file into the folder, hold down your keyboard CTRL key as you drag the file. Windows 95, in turn, will display a small plus sign next to the file icon as you drag it to indicate a copy operation.

CHANGING MY COMPUTER'S APPEARANCE

Most users have gotten used to seeing large icons within the My Computer window, as previously shown in Figure 15.1. However, because My Computer supports Explorer options, you can change your view of items in the My Computer window. For example, Figure 15.5 illustrates the My Computer window using the Details view.

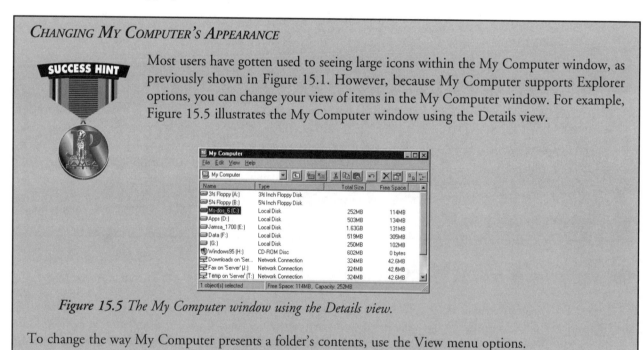

Figure 15.5 The My Computer window using the Details view.

To change the way My Computer presents a folder's contents, use the View menu options.

USING THE RECYCLE BIN

When you delete a file using Windows 95, the file no longer appears within its folder, but is not quite gone from your disk. Instead, when you delete a file, Windows 95 moves the file to a special folder called the Recycle Bin. Think of the Recycle Bin as similar to the trash can beside your desk. When you throw something into your trash can, you can later take it back out provided someone has not emptied your trash. The same is true for the Windows 95 Recycle Bin. When you delete one or more files, you may be able to retrieve the files out of the Recycle Bin provided you or Windows 95 has not tossed out the Recycle Bin's contents. To free up disk space, you can empty the Recycle Bin by selecting the File menu Empty Recycle Bin option. When the Recycle Bin's contents get too full, Windows 95 will toss old files out of the Bin to make room for your recently deleted files.

15: Revisiting My Computer and the Recycle Bin

By examining the Recycle Bin icon that appears on your Desktop, you can determine if your Recycle Bin is empty or if it contains deleted files as shown here:

When you double-click your mouse on the Recycle Bin icon, Windows 95 will display the Recycle Bin window as shown in Figure 15.6.

Figure 15.6 The Recycle Bin window.

The Recycle Bin lists each of your recently deleted files whose contents you can still retrieve. To undelete (retrieve) a file from the Recycle Bin, click your mouse on the file and select the File menu Restore option. Windows 95, in turn, will place the file back into its previous folder and will remove the file from the Recycle Bin list. If you want to restore multiple files in one step, use your keyboard's CTRL and SHIFT keys to select the files you desire and then choose the File menu Restore option.

If you examine the Recycle Bin window, it should look familiar. Because the Recycle Bin uses an Explorer-like window, you can take advantage of features you already know. For example, there may be times when, rather than restoring a file to its original folder, you want to put the file somewhere else. Using Explorer-like cut-and-paste and drag-and-drop operations, you can put the file into any folder you desire. To put a file in a folder other than its original one, use the Explorer or My Computer to open the folder into which you want to place the file. You can then drag-and-drop the file into the new folder, or use the Edit menu Cut and Paste options. There may be times when you want more information about a Recycle Bin file, such as the date you deleted the file or the file size. In such cases, select the file and choose the File menu Properties option. Windows 95, in turn, will display the file's Properties dialog box, as shown in Figure 15.7.

Figure 15.7 The Properties dialog box within the Recycle Bin.

Success with Windows 95

CHANGING THE RECYCLE BIN'S APPEARANCE

By default, the Recycle Bin displays files using the Detail list view, as previously shown in Figure 15.6. Because the Recycle Bin uses an Explorer window, you can change the Recycle Bin's view. For example, Figure 15.8 shows the Recycle Bin's contents using large icons.

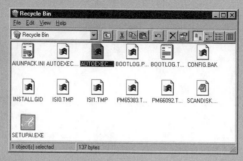

Figure 15.8 Changing the Recycle Bin's view.

In most cases, however, you will find the Details view gives you the most meaningful information about files you might want to retrieve from the Recycle Bin. However, if you want to change the Recycle Bin's appearance, use the View menu options.

Keys to Success

As you learned in Chapter 14, the Explorer lets you traverse the folders on your disk. Many Windows 95 programs use features similar to those of the Explorer. In this chapter, for example, you learned My Computer and Recycle Bin windows support many Explorer-like features. In Chapter 16, you will learn how to customize your system using the Windows 95 Registry. Before you continue with Chapter 16, however, make sure you have learned the following key concepts:

- ✓ Because Windows 95 uses Explorer-like windows for the folders it displays, you can control how Windows 95 displays files with all Windows 95 folders.

- ✓ If you double-click your mouse on a program-file icon within a folder, Windows 95 will run the corresponding program.

- ✓ When you delete a file or folder, Windows 95 moves the file or folder into a temporary folder called the Recycle Bin. In this way, Windows 95 gives you an opportunity to undelete the item.

- ✓ The Recycle Bin displays its contents within an Explorer-like folder. To undelete a file or folder, you can use cut-and-paste or drag-and-drop file-move operations.

Chapter 16
Using the Windows 95 Registry

As you have learned, Windows 95 lets you customize such features as the desktop colors, the Taskbar size and location, as well as the sounds Windows 95 plays when specific system events occur. When you customize your system in this way, Windows 95 uses a special database called the Registry to store your settings. If you have used Windows 3.1 in the past, you may have encountered one or more initialization files that used the INI file extension, such as WIN.INI or SYSTEM.INI. The Windows 95 Registry database replaces INI files. In this chapter you will learn how to use a program called the Registry Editor to view and customize your Registry settings. By the time you finish this chapter, you will understand the following key concepts:

- When you change system settings, such as your desktop colors, Windows 95 stores your settings in a special database called the Registry.

- The Windows 95 Registry database (or Registry for short) contains single-line entries that correspond to these system settings.

- To view or modify Registry entries, you run REGEDIT, the Registry Editor.

- The Windows 95 Registry replaces the INI initialization files used by Windows 3.1.

- To maintain compatibility with Windows 3.1, however, Windows 95 still supports the INI files. However, Windows 95 itself, stores its settings within the Registry.

- You should never change a Registry database entry unless you fully understand the entry's use.

UNDERSTANDING THE WINDOWS 95 REGISTRY

Unlike Windows 3.1 INI files, you cannot edit or view the Registry contents using an ASCII editor such as Notepad. (Later in this chapter you will learn how to export and later import ASCII files that contain Registry settings.) Instead, to edit or view the Registry's contents, you use REGEDIT, the Registry Editor. To run REGEDIT, perform these steps:

1. Select the Start menu Run option. Windows 95, in turn, will display the Run dialog box.

2. Within the Run dialog box, type REGEDIT and press ENTER. Windows 95, in turn, will display the Registry Editor as shown in Figure 16.1.

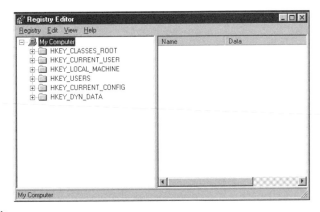

Figure 16.1 *The Registry Editor.*

The Windows 95 Registry organizes your system settings much like a directory tree. In other words, the different Registry branches correspond to related settings. The Registry organizes settings into six branches. Table 16.1 briefly describes the type of entries each Registry branch contains.

Branch	Type of Entry
HKEY_CLASSES_ROOT	Points to the Registry's HKEY_LOCAL_MACHINE branch that describes the software settings for OLE mappings, shortcuts, and user interface settings.
HKEY_CURRENT_USER	Points to the branch that describes the current user's setting preferences in a system shared by two or more users.
HKEY_LOCAL_MACHINE	Points to the branch that describes the computer's current hardware and software configuration in a system that uses two or more hardware profiles.
HKEY_USERS	Points to the branch that describes all users who can log into this computer and their corresponding profiles.
HKEY_CURRENT_CONFIG	Points to the branch that contains information about hardware currently connected to the system.
HKEY_DYN_DATA	Points to the branch plug-and-play (dynamic) information that may change throughout your user session.

Table 16.1 Registry branch entry types.

To view Registry entries, you expand and collapse Registry branches much like you expand and collapse folders within the Windows 95 Explorer. To display (expand) a Registry branch, click your mouse on the plus sign that precedes the branch folder. For example, expand the HKEY_CURRENT_CONFIG branch. The Registry Editor, in turn, will display additional branch folders as shown in Figure 16.2.

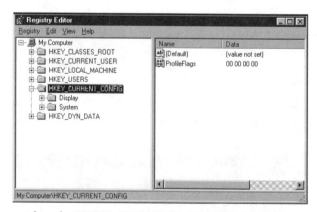

Figure 16.2 Displaying folders within the HKEY_CURRENT_CONFIG branch.

As discussed in Table 16.1, the HKEY_CURRENT_CONFIG branch contains information about the system's current hardware. Click on the plus sign that precedes the Display folder and use a similar technique to open the Settings folder. The Registry Editor, in turn, will display entries that define your current video settings as shown in Figure 16.3.

16: Using the Windows 95 Registry

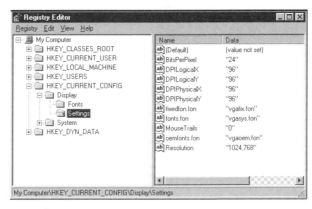

Figure 16.3 Displaying Registry Display settings.

In this case, the Registry Display settings defines the number of bits per pixel Windows 95 uses to represent each pixel's color, the number of screen pixels per vertical and horizontal inch, as well as the screen display font files.

> **OPENING AND CLOSING REGISTRY BRANCHES**
>
>
>
> The Registry database organizes your system settings using a directory-like tree structure. To expand a Registry branch, click your mouse on the plus sign that precedes the branch folder. Later, to close a branch, click your mouse on the minus sign that precedes the branch folder.
>
> Users refer to Registry entries by using a path of branches you must follow to locate the entry. For example, in Figure 16.3, you will find an entry named MouseTrails. When users refer to this entry, they will use a format very similar to a DOS path name. In this case, the entry's name becomes:
>
> \HKEY_CURRENT_CONFIG\Display\Settings\MouseTrails
>
> The entry's name uses a backslash character to distinguish between Registry branches. In this case, to find the MouseTrails entry, you would start with the HKEY_CURRENT_CONFIG branch, select the Display branch, and then select the Settings branch.

The Registry database uses single-line entries to store system settings. Registry entries store their values using one of three formats. Table 16.2 briefly describes the Registry-entry value types.

Value Type	Meaning
String	A value contained within double quotes, such as "Windows 95"
Binary	A value consisting of one or more ones and zeros
DWORD	A 32-bit value that corresponds to an object's address in memory

Table 16.2 Registry-entry value types.

CHANGING A REGISTRY ENTRY

To change a Registry entry, click your mouse on the entry to highlight it. Next, select the Registry Editor's Edit menu and choose Modify. The Registry Editor, in turn, will display a dialog box within which you can type the entry's new value. For example, within the \HKEY_CURRENT_CONFIG\Display\Settings branch, highlight the

MouseTrails entry and choose the Edit menu Modify option (or right click your mouse on the entry and choose Modify from the pop-up menu). The Registry Editor, in turn, will display an Edit String dialog box, as shown in Figure 16.4, within which you can change the entry's value.

Figure 16.4 The Edit String dialog box.

DO NOT CHANGE A REGISTRY ENTRY'S VALUE FOR AN ENTRY YOU DON'T UNDERSTAND

Windows 95 uses Registry entries to store key system and hardware settings. Never change the value of a Registry entry whose purpose you don't fully understand. Should you assign an errant value to a key Registry entry, Windows 95 may not start!

Later in this chapter, you will learn how to backup your Registry entries. Never make changes to the Registry without first backing up its contents.

As you learned in Chapter 5, mouse trails are extra mouse cursors that chase your mouse pointer across the screen as you move your mouse. By enabling mouse trails on a notebook PC, you may make your mouse pointer easier to see. Within the Value data field, type in the value 7 to enable mouse trails. (You can later turn off the mouse trails by assigning the value 0 to the entry's data field or by using the Control Panel Mouse dialog box discussed in Chapter 5). Select the OK button to close the dialog box.

Each time your system starts, Windows 95 examines the Registry's contents. When you use the Registry Editor to change a system setting, you must normally restart your system for your change to take effect.

CREATE A REGISTRY EDITOR SHORTCUT

If you use the Registry Editor on a regular basis, create a desktop shortcut for Registry Editor. In this way, you can run the Registry Editor with a double click of your mouse. To create a Registry Editor shortcut, perform these steps:

1. Open the My Computer folder.
2. Double click your mouse on the drive that contains your Windows folder.
3. Within the Windows folder, locate the program file REGEDIT.EXE.
4. Using your mouse, drag the icon that corresponds to REGEDIT.EXE onto your desktop.
5. Close the folders you opened to locate the REGEDIT.EXE program file.

PRINTING YOUR REGISTRY DATABASE

One of the best ways for you to understand the Windows 95 Registry is to print and examine the Registry's contents. To print your Registry's contents, perform these steps:

1. Select the Registry Editor Registry menu and choose Print. The Registry Editor, in turn, will display the Print dialog box shown in Figure 16.5.

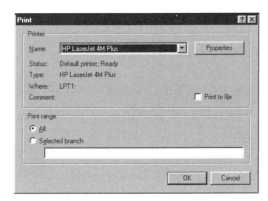

Figure 16.5 *The Registry Editor Print dialog box.*

2. Within the Print Range field, select All.
3. Choose OK. The Registry Editor will print your Registry's contents in a directory-tree-like format.

Keep your Registry printout in a safe place. If, in the future, you make an errant change to one or more Registry entries, you can use the value contained on your printout to restore the Registry's contents.

Before you change a Registry entry's value, you should print a copy of the entry's value. Rather than printing the entire Registry as just discussed, the Registry Editor lets you print only the selected branch. To print a Registry branch, perform these steps:

1. Within the Registry Editor, select the branch that contains the entry whose value you want to change.
2. Select the Registry File menu and choose Print. The Registry Editor will display the Print dialog box as previously shown in Figure 16.5.
3. Within the Print Range field, choose the Selected branch option.
4. Choose OK.

WHERE WINDOWS 95 STORES THE REGISTRY DATA

Although you cannot edit their contents, it is important that you understand that Windows 95 stores the Registry entries within two files that reside within the Windows folder: SYSTEM.DAT and USER.DAT. The file SYSTEM.DAT contains the Registry's system settings. The file USER.DAT contains the setting preferences for each user who can access the system. Windows 95 sets each file's *system* attribute which prevents the file's display within a normal directory listing (use DIR /A:S) or within an Explorer file list (unless you direct Explorer to display all files).

Each time your system starts successfully, Windows 95 copies the contents of SYSTEM.DAT and USER.DAT to backup files in the Windows folder named SYSTEM.DA0 and USER.DA0. Should you ever make a change to your Registry that prevents Windows 95 from starting, you can delete SYSTEM.DAT and USER.DAT and rename the SYSTEM.DA0 and USER.DA0 to files with the DAT extension. Because the DA0 files contain the settings from your last successful start up, you can use their contents to start Windows 95 successfully.

Windows 95 Still Supports Windows 3.1 INI Files

Newer programs designed specifically for Windows 95, such as Microsoft Office 95, will use the Registry to store settings. Older programs, however, that were written for Windows 3.1, don't know about the Registry. Instead, these older programs store their settings in INI (initialization) files that reside within the Windows folder. If you use the Windows 95 Explorer to list files in the Windows folder, you will encounter files such as WIN.INI and SYSTEM.INI.

Although Windows 95 support for INI files lets you run older programs, there may be times when an INI file entry conflicts with a Registry entry. If, for example, you make a change to a Registry entry and your system appears not to have put your change into effect, examine the INI files that reside in your Windows folders and look for a conflicting entry.

Use SYSEDIT to Edit Your INI Files

If you need to edit one or more INI files, use the SYSEDIT program. To run SYSEDIT, perform these steps:

1. Select the Start menu Run option. Windows 95 will display the Run dialog box.

2. Within the Open field, type in the command SYSEDIT and press ENTER. Windows 95 will display the SYSEDIT window as shown in Figure 16.6.

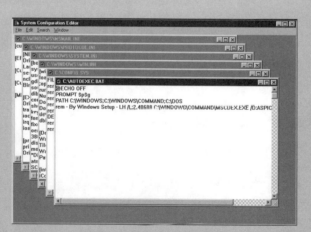

Figure 16.6 The SYSEDIT window.

The SYSEDIT program opens a window for key INI file it locates in the Windows folder, as well as windows for the CONFIG.SYS and AUTOEXEC.BAT files. Within each window, look for an entry that might conflict with your Registry entry. If no entries in a window conflict, simply close the window and continue your search. If you locate the conflicting entry, print a copy of the file's contents (using the SYSEDIT File menu Print option). Next, remove the entry from the file, close and save the file. Then, exit the SYSEDIT program and restart Windows 95.

Finding a Registry Entry

As the number of Windows 95-based programs you install increases, so too will the number of entries in your Registry. Unfortunately, as the number of Registry entries increases, you may find it more difficult to locate a specific entry. Luckily, the Windows 95 Registry Editor lets you search for Registry entries using their name or value. To search the Registry for a specific entry, perform these steps:

1. Select the Edit menu Find option. The Registry Editor, in turn, will display the Find dialog box as shown in Figure 16.7.

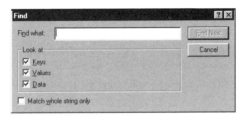

Figure 16.7 *The Registry Editor Find dialog box.*

2. Within the Find what field, type in the name or value for which you are searching. Using the dialog box checkboxes, you can direct the Registry Editor to search only keys (the entry names), values, or data.

3. Select Find Next. The Registry Editor will search your database for the entry you specify, highlighting the first match it encounters. If the Registry Editor has found the entry you desire, you can edit the entry as you need. If the Registry Editor did not find the entry you want, select the Edit menu Find option again. When the Find dialog box appears, select Find Next.

Renaming or Deleting a Registry Entry

As you troubleshoot system errors or conflicts with a company's technical support specialist, you may be told to rename or to delete a Registry entry. Never rename or delete a Registry entry without first backing up your Registry contents or printing a copy of the entry's value.

To rename a Registry entry, perform these steps:

1. Select the Registry entry you want to rename.

2. Select the Edit menu and choose Rename. The Registry Editor will highlight the entry's name in reverse video.

3. Type in the new name you desire and press ENTER.

To delete a Registry entry, perform these steps:

1. Select the Registry entry you want to delete.

2. Select the Edit menu and choose Delete. The Registry Editor will display a dialog box asking you to confirm that you want to delete the entry.

3. Select Yes.

Rename an Entry Before You Delete It

Although you can restore an entry's value using your backup copy of the Registry or your hardcopy printout, you may find it more convenient to rename entries before you delete them. For example, rather than deleting an entry, first rename the entry to a unique name, by preceding the entry's current name with your initials. For example, I would rename the MouseTrails entry as KAJ_MouseTrails. Later, after I restart my system and I am comfortable that it is working properly, I delete the entry I previously renamed. By preceding the entry with my initials, I can quickly locate the entry using a Find operation.

Using an Export Operation to Backup Your Registry Entries

As briefly discussed, Windows 95 stores the Registry entries in two files, SYSTEM.DAT and USER.DAT, which reside in the Windows folder. Each time you successfully start your system, Windows 95 backs up these file's contents to files named SYSTEM.DA0 and USER.DA0. In this way, should you make an errant change to a Registry entry that prevents your system from starting, you can use the Startup disk that you created in Chapter 6 to boot Windows 95. Then, you can delete the files SYSTEM.DAT and USER.DAT which contain the errant entry. Next, you can rename the files SYSTEM.DA0 and USER.DA0 to files with the DAT extension. These two files contain the entries with which your system last started successfully. Using these entries you can get Windows 95 back up and running.

Before you make changes to a Registry entry, you should make your own backup copy of your Registry's contents. An easy way to create a backup of your Registry is to export the Registry's current contents to another file on your disk. To export the Registry's contents to a file, perform these steps:

1. Select the Registry File menu and choose Export Registry File. The Registry Editor, in turn, will display the Export Registry File dialog box as shown in Figure 16.8.

Figure 16.8 The Export Registry File dialog box.

2. Within the dialog box, select the folder within which you want to store your exported Registry file. You may want to create a special folder named Registry. (To create a folder, click your mouse on the toolbar Create new folder button.)

3. Within the File name field, type in the filename you desire. If you export Registry settings on a regular basis, include the date within your filename, such as Registry Contents 7-4-96.

4. Select Save.

As you have learned, Windows 95 stores the Registry's contents in a format only the Registry Editor understands. As a result, you can't edit the Registry database using an editor such as the Notepad accessory program. However, when you export the Registry's contents to a file, the Registry editor creates an ASCII file whose contents you can use Notepad to edit. If you make changes to the exported file using Notepad, you can later import those changes back into the Registry using the Registry Editor.

EXPORTING A REGISTRY BRANCH

If you are only changing one or two Registry entries, you can save disk space by exporting only the corresponding Registry branch to a file on your disk. To export only the branch that contains the entry you are going to change or delete, perform these steps:

1. Select the Registry Branch you want to export.
2. Select the File menu Export Registry File option. The Registry Editor, in turn, will display the Export Registry File dialog box previously shown in Figure 16.8.
3. Within the Export Range field, choose Selected branch.
4. Within the File name field, type in the filename you want to change or delete.
5. Choose OK.

> **EXPORT A BACKUP COPY OF THE REGISTRY DATABASE**
>
> Before you change or delete a Registry entry, make a backup copy of the Registry contents by exporting the Registry entries to a file on disk. Should you later need to restore the Registry settings, you can import the file's contents using the Registry Editor.

IMPORTING A REGISTRY FILE

By exporting the Registry contents to a file as just discussed, you can create an ASCII file you can use as a Registry backup or that you can edit using the Notepad editor. Should you later need to use the contents of your exported file, the Registry Editor lets you import the file's contents back into the Registry database.

When you import a file into the Registry this way, the Registry Editor uses the imported file's contents to replace the current Registry settings. To import a file's contents into the Registry, perform these steps:

1. Select the Registry Editor File menu and choose Import Registry File. The Registry Editor will display the Import Registry File dialog box as shown in Figure 16.9.
2. Within the dialog box, select the folder that contains the file you want to import.
3. Select the file you want to import.
4. Choose OK.

Figure 16.9 The Import Registry File dialog box.

As you have learned, there may be times when you will only export a branch of the Registry. Should you later need to use the branch's contents, you can import the branch from its file using the steps just discussed. The Registry Editor, in turn, will only update that branch of the Registry.

Remember, when you use Control Panel programs to change settings, Windows 95 stores your setting changes within the Registry. Likewise, when you install new software, the installation program may add Registry settings. Just because you haven't used the Registry Editor to change the Registry's contents doesn't mean your Registry contents have not changed. In fact, you might get in the habit of periodically exporting a copy of your Registry contents to a file on your disk.

ADDING A REGISTRY ENTRY

Just as there may be times when you need to delete or rename a Registry entry, there may also be times when you need to add an entry. To create a Registry entry, perform these steps:

1. Within the Registry Editor, select the branch within which you want to create the entry.
2. Select the Edit menu New option. The Registry Editor will cascade the New menu as shown in Figure 16.10.

Figure 16.10 Cascading the New menu.

3. Using the New menu, select the type of entry you want to add. The Registry Editor will display the new Entry.
4. Use the steps previously discussed in this chapter to rename the new entry as you require.
5. Use the steps previously discussed in this chapter to assign the entry's value.

Exploiting the Windows 95 Registry

To understand the true power of the Windows 95 Registry, you need to experiment with a real-world example. As you know, to access the Control Panel programs, you must first select the Start menu Settings option and choose Control Panel. Windows 95, in turn, will display the Control Panel icons. A more convenient way to access the Control Panel programs, however, is to place the programs in the Start menu as shown in Figure 16.11.

Figure 16.11 *Placing Control Panel programs on the Start menu.*

To place the Control Panel entries on the Start menu, you perform steps which ultimately create an entry within the Registry:

1. Right-click your mouse on the Start button.
2. Click your mouse on the Explorer option.
3. Click your mouse on the File menu New Folder option.
4. Type the following long folder name (be very careful to type the name exactly as it appears):

   Control Panel.{21EC2020-3AEA-1069-A2DD-08002B30309D}

5. Press Enter.
6. Close Explorer and display your Start menu. You will find the Control Panel entries at the top of your menu.

As it turns out, the six steps you just performed create an entry in the Registry that corresponds to your new menu option. To locate the entry within the Registry, use a Find operation to search for the numbers 21EC2020. Depending on your Registry contents, you may have to search through a few entries until you find the one whose numbers match exactly the numbers you typed for the folder name.

Accessing Another User's Registry Database

If you responsible for maintaining computers for a number of users within a network, you will be happy to learn that the Registry Editor lets you edit another user's Registry across the Network. To select a remote user's Registry, perform these steps:

1. Select the Registry Editor File menu Connect Network Registry option. The Registry Editor, in turn, will display the Connect Network Registry dialog box as shown in Figure 16.12.
2. Type in the name of the computer whose Registry you want to edit.
3. Select OK.

Figure 16.12 *The Connect Network Registry dialog box.*

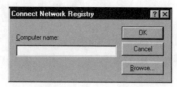

After you make your changes to the Registry, select the File menu Disconnect Network Registry option to end your remote edit session.

KEYS TO SUCCESS

Throughout this book you have learned ways to customize Windows 95. When you change various system settings, Windows 95 stores your changes in a special database file called the Registry. In this chapter you learned how to edit and view Registry entries using the Registry Editor. In Chapter 17 you will learn how to send and receive faxes within Windows 95. Before you continue with Chapter 17, however, make sure you have learned the following key concepts:

- ✓ Windows 95 stores your system settings, such as your desktop colors, display resolution, and mouse attributes in a special database called the Registry.

- ✓ Windows 95 stores settings within the Registry as single-line entries.

- ✓ Although Windows 95 still supports the INI files used in Windows 3.1, Windows 95 stores its own settings within the Registry.

- ✓ To view or modify Registry entries, you run REGEDIT, the Registry Editor.

- ✓ Never change, delete, or rename a Registry entry unless you fully understand the entry's use.

- ✓ Before you change, rename, or delete a Registry entry, you should make a backup copy of your Registry's contents.

- ✓ One way to backup your Registry contents is to export the Registry contents to a file on your disk.

- ✓ Windows 95 stores the Registry entries in two files, SYSTEM.DAT and USER.DAT, that reside in the Windows folder.

- ✓ Each time your system starts successfully, Windows 95 copies the files SYSTEM.DAT and USER.DAT to backup files named SYSTEM.DA0 and USER.DA0.

- ✓ Should you ever make an errant change to your Registry that prevents Windows 95 from starting, you can delete the files SYSTEM.DAT and USER.DAT and rename the files SYSTEM.DA0 and USER.DA0 to files with the DAT extension.

Chapter 17
Using Exchange for Faxes and E-Mail

To be a participant in the information age, you used to need a beeper and a cellular phone. Today, however, you need to have electronic-mail and fax capabilities. In Chapter 8, "Using the Microsoft Network," you learned that by subscribing to MSN, you can exchange e-mail messages with users worldwide. Then, in Chapter 10, "Connecting Windows 95 to the Internet and World Wide Web," you learned that by subscribing to an Internet provider, you can also send and receive e-mail. As you become a true "net surfer," you are likely to have e-mail addresses at several sources. For example, your PC at work my be connected to an Internet provider, while your PC at home may use the Microsoft Network.

To simplify your receipt of e-mail messages, Windows 95 provides the Exchange program. Think of Exchange as a universal inbox for your e-mail and faxes. That's right, by using Exchange, you can receive faxes, using your fax modem, whose contents you can display on your screen or print if your needs require. This chapter examines Exchange, your message manager for the information age. By the time you finish this chapter, you will understand the following key concepts:

- Windows 95 provides a Wizard that will help you setup Exchange.

- Using Exchange, you can send and receive faxes using a fax modem.

- If you use Microsoft Mail within a local area network, you can use Exchange to send and receive your e-mail messages.

- If you use the Microsoft Network, you will send and receive your e-mail messages using Exchange.

- Depending on your Internet provider's software, you may be able to setup Exchange to receive your Internet mail.

- Using Windows 95, you can send a fax by either using Exchange, the Fax accessory, or by printing from within an application to Microsoft Fax, as opposed to a printer.

- To help you create your own custom fax-cover page, Windows 95 provides the Fax Cover Page Editor.

- To help you track the people to whom you fax or e-mail on a regular basis, Windows 95 provides a personal address book.

SENDING AND RECEIVING FAXES

As briefly discussed, Exchange provides a universal inbox for your faxes and e-mail messages. However, if you don't fax or e-mail messages on a regular basis, you may not want to setup and use Exchange. Instead, you can send and request faxes using the Windows 95 Fax accessories. As you will find, Windows 95 provides two Wizards that simplify your process of sending and requesting faxes.

Note: Requesting a fax is different than receiving a fax. When you request a fax, you connect to a fax machine that supports fax-on-demand messages. For example, a company may let you request faxes that describe specific products. Such fax requests are often called "fax backs." To receive an unrequested fax from another user, on the other hand, you need to use Microsoft Exchange.

Sending a Fax

To send a fax using the Windows 95 Fax accessory, perform these steps:

1. Select the Start menu Programs option and choose Accessories.

2. Select the Accessories menu Fax option and choose Compose New Fax. Windows 95, in turn, will display the Compose New Fax Wizard, as shown in Figure 17.1.

Figure 17.1 *The Compose New Fax Wizard.*

The Compose New Fax Wizard's first dialog box lets you specify information about where you are dialing from. If you are composing your first fax, select the Dialing Properties dialog box and make sure your current settings (phone number and dialing instructions) are correct. If you have defined one dialing profile for calling from home, and a second profile for dialing from the office, select the correct profile and choose Next. The Compose New Fax Wizard, in turn, will display a dialog box, as shown in Figure 17.2, that prompts you to specify your fax recipient.

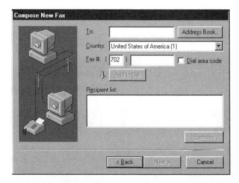

Figure 17.2 *The Compose New Fax Wizard's prompt for your fax recipient.*

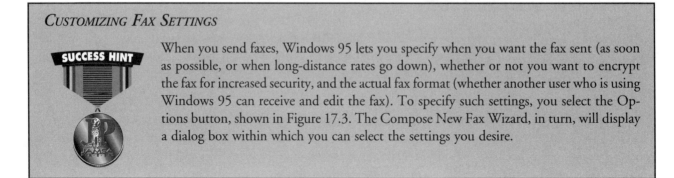

Within the To field, specify the name of the person to whom you are sending your fax. Next, specify the individual's fax number. When you click your mouse on the Add to List button, the Wizard will place the individual within your list of recipients. The Fax Wizard lets you send your fax to more than one recipient. To send a fax to two or more individuals, type in each person's name and fax number, and use the Add to List button to place the individual within your recipient list. To continue, click your mouse on the Next button. The Compose New Fax Wizard will display the dialog box, shown in Figure 17.3, that asks you to select the cover sheet you desire.

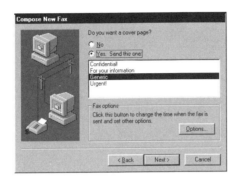

Figure 17.3 *The Compose New Fax Wizard's prompt for a cover sheet.*

Click your mouse on the cover sheet you desire and choose Next. The Compose New Fax Wizard displays the dialog box, shown in Figure 17.4, that lets you specify a subject and note.

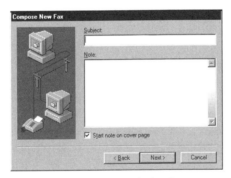

Figure 17.4 *The Compose New Fax Wizard subject and note dialog box.*

If you want to send only a short fax, you can type in your fax using this subject and note dialog box. By default, the text you type will appear on the fax cover sheet. If you want to send a longer document, such as a word processing memo, you leave the subject and note fields blank (by simply tabbing through the fields). After you type in your subject and note, select Next. The Compose New Fax Wizard will display the dialog box, shown in Figure 17.5, that lets you attach a file to your fax.

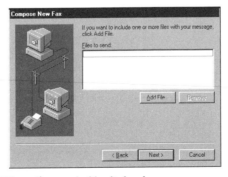

Figure 17.5 *The Compose New Fax Wizard's attach file dialog box.*

Success with Windows 95

If you have a word processing or spreadsheet document that you want to send to your recipient, you can attach that document to your fax. If your fax recipient is using Exchange to receive faxes, they will actually get a copy of the document's file, which they can edit. If, however, the recipient is using a standard fax machine, they will receive a printed copy of the text. To attach a file to a fax, you must use a document that Windows 95 recognizes, such as a Word document or an Excel spreadsheet. For Windows 95 to recognize the document, you must register the document's type with Windows. Chapter 14, "Using the Windows 95 Explorer," tells you how to register a document type. The reason Windows 95 must recognize the document is that Windows 95 will actually use the document's corresponding program to send the document to its fax software. In this way, the program that created the document is responsible for handling formatting, fonts, graphics, and so on.

Click your mouse on the Next button. The Compose New Fax Wizard will display a dialog box telling you that your fax is ready to send. Select Finish. If you instructed the Wizard to send the fax as soon as possible, the Wizard will open a window, similar to that shown in Figure 17.6, within which you can watch the status of your fax transmission.

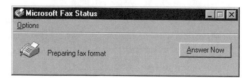

Figure 17.6 *Monitoring the status of your fax transmission.*

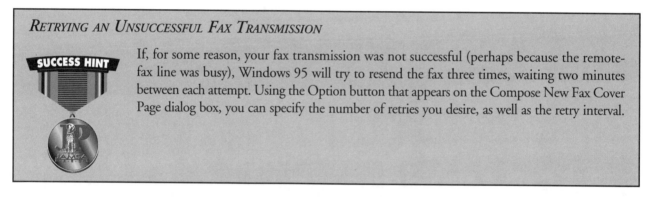

Retrying an Unsuccessful Fax Transmission

If, for some reason, your fax transmission was not successful (perhaps because the remote-fax line was busy), Windows 95 will try to resend the fax three times, waiting two minutes between each attempt. Using the Option button that appears on the Compose New Fax Cover Page dialog box, you can specify the number of retries you desire, as well as the retry interval.

Sending a Fax from within a Program

Using Windows 95's fax support, you can send a fax from any program that lets you select a printer. For example, to fax the contents of a WordPad document, you would perform these steps:

1. Within WordPad, select the File menu Print option. Windows 95, in turn, will display the Print dialog box, as shown in Figure 17.7.

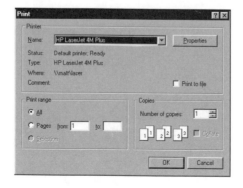

Figure 17.7 *The Print dialog box.*

2. Open the pull-down Printer list and choose Microsoft Fax.

3. Select OK. Windows 95, in turn, will start the Compose New Fax Wizard, as just discussed, to send your fax.

DRAG-AND-DROP FAXING

If you send faxes on a regular basis, you may want to create a shortcut for the Microsoft Fax printer on your Desktop. Then, to fax a document, you can simply drag the document onto the Microsoft Fax icon. Windows 95, in turn, will start the Compose New Fax Wizard.

REQUESTING A FAX-ON-DEMAND MESSAGE

Today, many businesses use fax-on-demand marketing that lets a customer call the business' fax machine and request information on a specific product. To help you request such faxed-based information, Windows 95 provides a Request a Fax Wizard. To request a fax using the Wizard, perform these steps:

1. Select the Start menu Programs option and choose Accessories.

2. Select the Accessories menu Fax option and choose Request a Fax. Windows 95, in turn, will start the Request a Fax Wizard, shown in Figure 17.8.

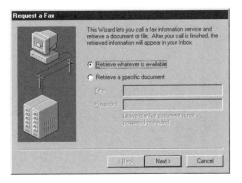

Figure 17.8 *The Request a Fax Wizard.*

3. Respond to the Wizard prompts to specify the fax number you want to call and the document number you desire.

CREATING A FAX COVER SHEET

If you send your faxes within Word for Windows, you can use the many different fax templates Word provides. If, instead, you use the Fax Wizard to send your faxes, you may want to create your own custom cover sheets. To help you create a custom fax-cover sheet, Windows 95 provides the Cover Page Editor. To start the Cover Page Editor, perform these steps:

1. Select the Start menu Programs option and choose Accessories.

2. Select the Accessories menu Fax option and choose Cover Page Editor. Windows 95, in turn, will start the Cover Page Editor, as shown in Figure 17.9.

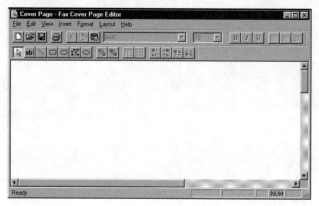

Figure 17.9 The Cover Page Editor.

The Cover Page Editor combines several tools you may recognize from the Paint and WordPad programs. Using these tools, you can build your own fax-cover sheets. To learn each tool's purpose, place the mouse pointer on top of the tool's button for a few seconds. The Cover Page Editor, in turn, will display a tool tip that describes the tool's purpose. If you want to use the Cover Page Editor to create your own cover sheet, the best way to get started is to examine a few existing cover sheets. Using the File menu Open option, open the cover sheets Windows 95 provides for your use. The cover-sheet files reside in the Windows folder and have the CPE extension (CPE for Cover Page Editor). For example, Figure 17.10 shows the Confidential cover sheet provided with the Cover Page Editor.

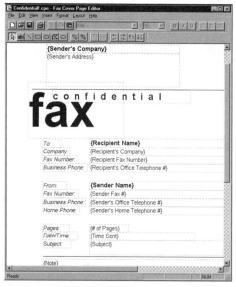

Figure 17.10 The Confidential cover sheet within the Cover Page Editor.

As you examine the existing cover sheets, pay close attention to how each sheet uses different text fields for names, phone, and fax numbers, and so on. For specifics on each Cover Page Editor tool, turn to the book *1001 Windows 95 Tips*, Jamsa Press, 1995.

Getting Started with Microsoft Exchange

To receive a fax using Windows 95, first you need to setup an inbox using Exchange. To help you get started, Windows 95 provides an Inbox Setup Wizard. To start the Wizard, double-click your mouse on the Inbox icon that appears on your Desktop. Windows 95, in turn, will display the Inbox Setup Wizard, as shown in Figure 17.11.

17: Using Exchange for Faxes and E-Mail

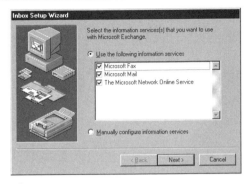

Figure 17.11 The Inbox Setup Wizard.

Within the dialog box's list of information services, select those services whose messages you want sent to your inbox. To continue your inbox setup, select Next.

Preparing to Use Microsoft Fax

If you select the Microsoft Fax service, the Inbox Setup Wizard will change its window to display information about your fax modem, as shown in Figure 17.12.

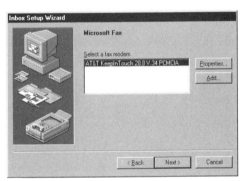

Figure 17.12 The Inbox Setup Wizard's fax modem settings dialog box.

Within the dialog box, click your mouse on the Properties dialog box. Windows 95, in turn, will display the Fax Modem Properties dialog box, as shown in Figure 17.13.

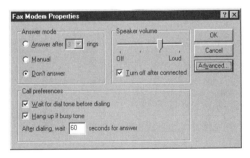

Figure 17.13 The Fax Modem Properties dialog box.

Using the Fax Modem Properties dialog box, you can specify how you want your fax modem to answer or place calls. Select the settings you desire and choose OK.

343

Within the Inbox Setup Wizard window, select Next. The Wizard, in turn, will change its window's contents to ask you how you want to handle incoming calls, as shown in Figure 17.14.

Figure 17.14 *The Inbox Setup Wizard's incoming-call prompt.*

If your PC has its own dedicated phone line, you may want Microsoft Fax to answer incoming calls. If Microsoft Fax answers the incoming fax call, it will display the Microsoft Fax Status dialog box within which you can watch the fax receival. Otherwise, if you select the manual answer mode, when an incoming fax arrives, Windows 95 will display the Receive Fax Now? dialog box as shown in Figure 17.15.

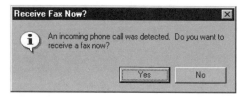

Figure 17.15 *The Receive Fax Now? dialog box.*

To receive an incoming fax, select the Yes option. Within the Wizard's dialog box, select the incoming-call option you desire and choose Next. The Inbox Setup Wizard will display a screen, similar to that shown in Figure 17.16, that prompts you for your name and fax number.

Figure 17.16 *The Inbox Setup Wizard's prompt for your name and fax number.*

Type in your name and fax number (the number you want to appear on your outgoing faxes) and choose Next.

PREPARING TO USE MICROSOFT MAIL

If you selected the Microsoft Mail service, the Inbox Setup Wizard will change its dialog box to prompt you for the location of your Microsoft Mail post-office, as shown in Figure 17.17.

17: Using Exchange for Faxes and E-Mail

Figure 17.17 The Inbox Setup Wizard's prompt for the location of your Microsoft Mail post-office.

Type in your post-office location and select Next. (You may need to ask your network administrator or Microsoft Mail administrator for your post-office information.) The Inbox Setup Wizard, in turn, will display a dialog box prompting you for your mailbox name and password, as shown in Figure 17.18.

Figure 17.18 The Inbox Setup Wizard prompt for your Mailbox name and password.

Again, you may need to get your mailbox name and password from your Microsoft Mail administrator. Type in your mailbox name and password and choose Next.

Preparing to Use Microsoft Network

If you selected the Microsoft Network service, the Inbox Setup Wizard will display a dialog box that tells you about MSN. Select Next. The Wizard will then display a dialog box asking you to specify the location of your personal address book, as shown in Figure 17.19.

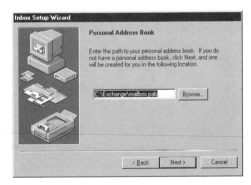

Figure 17.19 The Inbox Setup Wizard's prompt for the location of your personal address book.

345

Within your personal address book, you will store the names, fax numbers, and e-mail addresses of those users to whom you correspond on a regular basis. If you don't have a personal address book, the Wizard will create one for you. If you already have a personal address book, specify its location and select Next. If you don't have a personal address book, select Next to create one. The Inbox Setup Wizard, in turn, will display a dialog box asking you to specify the location of your personal folders, as shown in Figure 17.20.

Figure 17.20 *The Inbox Setup Wizard's prompt for the location of your personal folders.*

To better organize the messages and faxes you send and receive, Exchange places your messages within your own personal folders, whose contents will reside within your personal-folder files. As before, if you have a personal-folder file, specify the file's location and select Next. Otherwise, select Next, and the Wizard will create a file for you.

ADDING EXCHANGE TO THE STARTUP GROUP

After you specify your inbox settings, the Inbox Setup Wizard will display a dialog box asking you if you want to place Exchange in the Startup group. By placing Exchange within your Startup group, you direct Windows 95 to start Exchange automatically each time your system starts. Select the option you desire and choose Next. The Inbox Setup Wizard will display a dialog box telling you that you have successfully installed Exchange. Select Finish. You are now ready to use Exchange to receive e-mail messages and faxes.

STARTING EXCHANGE

As briefly discussed, Exchange is your universal inbox for faxes and e-mail. In other words, when you receive a fax, you will find the fax within Exchange. Likewise, when you receive e-mail, you will find it within Exchange. In addition, Exchange keeps a copy of each fax and e-mail message you send. To start Exchange, double-click your mouse on the Inbox icon. If you are using Microsoft Mail, Exchange will display a dialog box asking you for your mailbox and password. Next, Exchange will display its window, as shown in Figure 17.22.

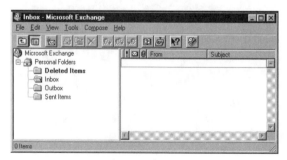

Figure 17.22 *The Microsoft Exchange window.*

Exchange organizes your messages using four primary folders, as described in Table 17.1.

17: Using Exchange for Faxes and E-Mail

Folder	Contents
Deleted Items	Messages you have recently deleted from another folder
Inbox	Mail messages and faxes you have received
Outbox	Mail messages and faxes you have sent, but Exchange has not yet delivered
Sent Items	Messages and faxes you have sent successfully

Table 17.1 Exchange organizes your messages using four primary folders.

Depending on your current folder, you may need to click your mouse on the Up-One Level toolbar button to display your four message folders, as shown in Figure 17.23.

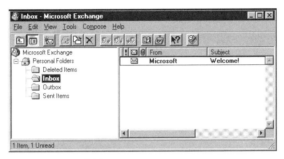

Figure 17.23 Exchange's four primary message folders.

From within the folder list, select the Inbox folder. Exchange, in turn, will display the list of mail messages and faxes you have received. If you examine your messages, you may find messages preceded by a sealed envelope icon, a paper clip icon, and so on. Table 17.2 briefly explains the icons Exchange uses to indicate your message's status.

Icon	Meaning
Sealed Envelope	A message you have not yet read
Paper clip	A message with an attached file
Circle with a red arrow	Exchange could not deliver the message
Down arrow	A low-priority message
Exclamation mark	A high-priority message

Table 17.2 The Exchange message icons.

To open a message, double-click your mouse on the message icon. Exchange, in turn, will display the message, as shown in Figure 17.24.

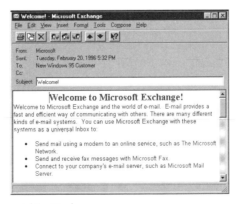

Figure 17.24 Reading a mail message within Exchange.

Exchange treats mail messages and faxes the same. If another user sends you a fax, Exchange will place the fax in your Inbox. To view the fax, simply double-click your mouse on the corresponding message within your message list. As you read a mail message or fax, you can use File menu options to save your message to a file, or to print a hardcopy of your message (or fax).

As you read a message within Exchange, you can use Compose menu options to reply to the sender, reply to everyone who received the message, or to forward your message to other users.

EXCHANGE USES EXPLORER-LIKE FOLDERS

Exchange, like My Computer, the Network Neighborhood, and the Recycle Bin, uses Explorer-like windows. As such, within your Exchange folders, you can create subfolders as well as move, copy, and delete messages. In addition, by right-clicking your mouse on a message and choosing the pop-up menu Properties option, you can view specifics about the message, as shown in Figure 17.25.

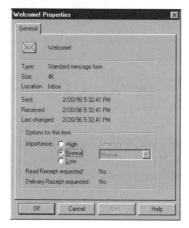

Figure 17.25 Displaying a message's properties.

SENDING A MAIL MESSAGE FROM WITHIN EXCHANGE

To send a mail message from within Exchange, select the Compose menu New Message option. Exchange, in turn, will display the New Message window, as shown in Figure 17.26.

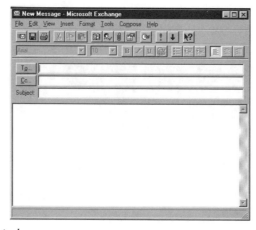

Figure 17.26 The New Message window.

17: Using Exchange for Faxes and E-Mail

The New Message window contains several of the tools you will find in WordPad. You can use these tools to change fonts, align text, and more. However, depending on your recipient's e-mail software, your message recipient may view your message with a standard font and minimal formatting.

Within the New Message window, select the To field and type the address of your recipient. If your recipient is in your personal address book, click your mouse on the To button and select the recipient from your address book. If you need to send your message to more than one user, that's OK. Exchange lets you specify multiple message recipients. To send your message to more than one user, simply include the address of each user you desire within the To field, separating the names with a semicolon.

Within the Subject field, type in a one-line statement that describes your message contents. Later, when your recipient views his or her message list, Exchange will display your subject text. Finally, within the message box, type your message text and then send your message.

Attaching a File to Your Message

As you compose your e-mail message, there may be times when you want to attach an existing file to your message. For example, you might want to send a user a copy of a Microsoft Word document or an Excel spreadsheet. To attach a file to your message, perform these steps:

1. As you prepare your message, select the Insert menu File option. Exchange, in turn, will display the Insert File dialog box.
2. Select the Insert as an Attachment option.
3. Within the File name field, type in the complete pathname of the file you want to insert.
4. Select OK.

When your message recipient receives the message, they can use the File menu Save As option to save the attached file to a folder on their disk.

Composing a Fax within Exchange

To send a fax from within Exchange, select the Compose menu New Fax option. Exchange, in turn, will start the Compose New Fax Wizard previously discussed.

Receiving Mail from Your Internet-Based Account

Depending on your Internet provider's software, you may be able to receive mail within Exchange that was sent to your Internet account. Unfortunately, the steps you must perform to configure Exchange to receive Internet mail differ from one provider to the next. To eliminate a considerable amount of trial and error, contact your provider's technical support and ask them to assist you in receiving your e-mail from within Exchange.

Learning More about Exchange

Exchange is a very powerful program. Although this chapter got you started with Exchange, you have barely broken the surface of Exchange's capabilities. For example, by using Exchange, you can encrypt messages, send your messages and faxes at a specific time, control your fax-redial properties, and more. For specifics on how you perform each of these options, turn to the book *1001 Windows 95 Tips*, Jamsa Press, 1995.

UNDERSTANDING AND USING YOUR ADDRESS BOOK

To make it easier for you to send messages, Exchange provides a personal address book within which you can record names, e-mail addresses, fax numbers, and more. When you send a fax or e-mail message to someone who is not currently in your personal address book, Exchange gives you the option to add the recipient. Examine the Compose New Fax dialog box, shown in Figure 17.27, and locate the Address Book button.

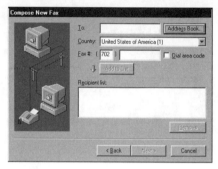

Figure 17.27 The Compose New Fax dialog box.

If you click your mouse on the Address Book button, Exchange will display the Address Book dialog box, as shown in Figure 17.28.

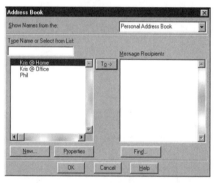

Figure 17.28 Your personal address book.

Using your personal address book, you can select recipients for your current fax or e-mail message. To select a recipient, click your mouse on the person or persons (hold down the CTRL key to select multiple recipients) you desire. Then, click your mouse on the To button. Exchange, in turn, will add the users to your Message Recipients list, as shown in Figure 17.29.

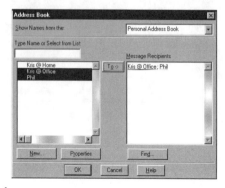

Figure 17.29 Selecting recipients for the current message.

17: Using Exchange for Faxes and E-Mail

In addition to letting you select message recipients, the Address Book dialog box lets you add a new entry to your personal address book. To add a new entry to your personal address book, perform these steps:

1. Within the Address Book dialog box, select the New button. Exchange, in turn, will display the New Entry dialog box, as shown in Figure 17.30.

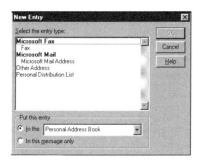

Figure 17.30 *The New Entry dialog box.*

2. Select the type of entry you want to add, such as a Fax, Microsoft Mail Address, and so on. To select an entry, click your mouse on the text that is not bold.

3. Choose OK. Depending on the entry type you selected, Exchange will display a dialog box that prompts you for the corresponding information. For example, if you select a Fax entry, Exchange will display the New Fax Properties dialog box, as shown in Figure 17.31.

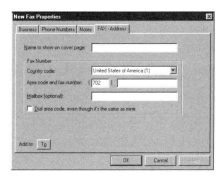

Figure 17.31 *The New Fax Properties dialog box.*

4. Type in the corresponding information and choose OK.

Take time now to click your mouse on each of the tabs that appear in the Properties dialog box for your new entry. You will find that you can store quite a bit of information about each person within your personal address book. For example, Figure 17.32 shows the Business tab for an address-book entry.

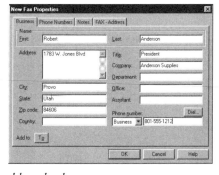

Figure 17.32 *The Business tab for an address-book entry.*

351

Managing Your Personal Address Book Entries

Over time, you will need to update address-book entries, add new entries, and delete entries you no longer use. To manage the entries in your personal address book better, select the Exchange Tools menu Address book entry. Exchange, in turn, will display the Address Book window, shown in Figure 17.33.

Figure 17.33 *The Exchange Address Book window.*

Adding a New Address-Book Entry

To add a new address-book entry using the Address Book window, perform these steps:

1. Select the File menu New Entry option. Exchange, in turn, will display the New Entry dialog box, previously shown in Figure 17.30.
2. Select the entry type you want to add and choose OK. Exchange will display a Properties dialog box that corresponds to the entry you select.
3. Within the Properties dialog box, type in the corresponding information and choose OK.

Deleting an Address-Book Entry

To delete an entry from your personal address book, perform these steps:

1. Within your personal address book entries, click your mouse on the entry you want to delete.
2. Select the File menu Delete option. Exchange, in turn, will display a dialog box confirming that you want to delete the entry.
3. Select Yes.

Updating an Address-Book Entry

To update an existing address-book entry, perform these steps:

1. Within your personal address book entries, click your mouse on the entry you want to change.
2. Select the File menu Properties option. Exchange, in turn, will display a dialog box for the entry, similar to that shown in Figure 17.34.
3. Within the Properties dialog box, change the fields as required. You may need to select one or more of the tabs that appear at the top of the dialog box to locate the fields.
4. Choose OK.

17: Using Exchange for Faxes and E-Mail

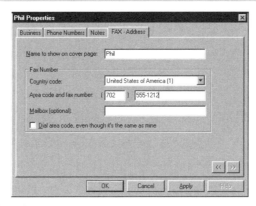

Figure 17.34 Properties of an address-book entry.

Using a Personal Distribution-List

As you send messages, you may find that you often send the same message to the same group of people. In such cases, you can create a personal distribution-list that contains each person's name. When you later need to send a message to the group, you simply use your distribution list as the message recipient. Exchange, in turn, will oversee the process of sending the message to each list member. For example, you might place the names of your sales staff into a distribution list called Sales. To send a memo to your sales staff, you simply address the memo to Sales.

To create a personal distribution-list, perform these steps:

1. Within the Address Book window, select New Entry.

2. Within the New Entry dialog box, select Personal Distribution List and choose OK. Exchange, in turn, will display the New Personal Distribution List Properties dialog box, as shown in Figure 17.35.

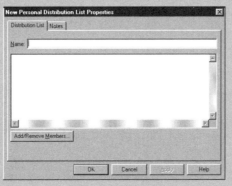

Figure 17.35 The New Personal Distribution List Properties dialog box.

3. Within the Name field, type in your desired distribution name list, such as Sales.

4. Select the Add/Remove member button. Exchange will display a dialog box that lists your personal-address-book entries. Select a member you want to add to the list and click your mouse on the Members button.

5. Repeat step 4 for each member you want to add to the list.

6. Choose OK. Within the New Personal Distribution List Properties dialog box, choose OK.

KEYS TO SUCCESS

The use of electronic mail and faxes has become a critical business component. In this chapter, you learned how to send and receive faxes and e-mail from within Windows 95. In Chapter 18, you will examine Windows 95 networking capabilities. Before you continue with Chapter 18, however, make sure you have learned the following key concepts:

- ✓ Exchange is your universal inbox. Using Exchange, you can receive e-mail messages and faxes in one location.

- ✓ If you use the Microsoft Network, you will send and receive your e-mail messages using Exchange.

- ✓ Depending on your Internet provider's software, you may be able to setup Exchange to receive your Internet mail.

- ✓ Using Exchange, you can receive faxes using Windows 95, view the fax contents on your screen, or print a copy of the fax as your needs require.

- ✓ Windows 95 lets you send a fax either by using Exchange, the Fax accessory, or by printing from within an application to Microsoft Fax, as opposed to a printer.

- ✓ Using the Fax Cover Page Editor, you can create custom fax-cover sheets.

- ✓ To help you track the people to whom you fax or e-mail on a regular basis, Windows 95 provides a personal address book.

Chapter 18
Windows 95 Networking Operations

If you work in an office with a local-area network, you may already use Microsoft Exchange, discussed in Chapter 17, to send and receive e-mail messages. In this chapter, you will learn how to share folders and printers with other users in your network. In addition, you will learn how to use dial-up networking to access your system from the road. Using dial-up networking, you connect to a server PC using your modem. After you are connected to the server, you have complete access to shared network files and printers. By the time you finish this chapter, you will understand the following key concepts:

- The 95 Network Neighborhood lists the computers and printers that make up your network.
- Within the Network Neighborhood, you double-click your mouse on a remote-computer's icon to display the computer's shared resources.
- Within a local area network, users share folders (and their files) and printers.
- Windows 95 provides ways you can protect your resources and control which network users can share them.
- Using Windows 95 dial-up networking, you can use a modem connection to access a computer (or a local-area network) as if your PC were part of the network.
- The Net Watcher accessory program lets you monitor your PC's network use.

SHARING RESOURCES ON A LOCAL-AREA NETWORK

Within a local-area network, users exchange information and share resources, such as folders and printers. In Chapter 17, "Using Exchange for Faxes and E-Mail," you learned to send and receive e-mail across your network. In this chapter, you will learn how to share resources. When you work within a local-area network, you don't have free access to everyone's files and printers. Instead, you only have access to items the other users have chosen to share. If you don't want other users to have access to any of your system resources, you simply don't share any.

GETTING AROUND YOUR NETWORK

The easiest way to find out what resources (folders and printers) are available for your use within the network is to double-click your mouse on your Desktop's Network Neighborhood icon. Windows 95, in turn, will open the network neighborhood folder. Within the Network Neighborhood folder, Windows 95 will display the other computers and printers that make up your network. To access another computer's shared resources, double-click your mouse on the computer's icon. Windows 95, in turn, will open a folder that contains the remote-computer's shared folders and printers, as shown in Figure 18.1.

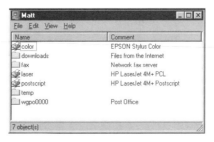

Figure 18.1 Shared folders and printers at a remote computer.

When you share a printer or folder, you can protect the object by using one of two types of protection:

- **Share-level access control** The remote-user requires you to specify a password to access the resource.
- **User-level access control** The remote-user specifies which users can access the resource.

To employ user-level access control, you must specify a server within your network that tracks all network users. Then, for each folder or printer you want to share, you select from the server's list those users who can access the resource. Because user-level access control is more complex, most users employ share-level access control, which requires other users to specify a password before they can access the resource.

To specify your system's access control (share- or user-level), select the Control Panel Network icon and choose the Access Control tab. Depending on the protection the remote user has selected, Windows 95 may prompt you to specify a password when you double-click your mouse on a shared device, as shown in Figure 18.2.

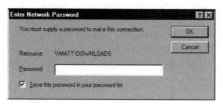

Figure 18.2 A Windows 95 password prompt for a shared resource.

Also, depending on how the remote-user has protected the object, you Windows 95 may limit you to read-only access to the object, which lets you view and copy, but not change the object's contents. Or, you may receive full access to the object, with which you can view, change, or even delete the object.

USING A REMOTE PRINTER

When you connect to a local-area network, you can use the printer that is connected to your PC, as well as printers that reside around the network. Just as users may protect their files and folders, users may also password-protect their printers. As such, if, you select a remote printer within a print-setup dialog box, Windows 95, in turn, may prompt you to type in a password to access the printer.

MAPPING TO A NETWORK DRIVE

As you have just learned, by clicking your mouse on shared folders, you can eventually access documents that reside on a remote computer. If you work with the same remote folder on a regular basis, you may find it more convenient to map the folder to a network drive.

When you map a folder to a network drive, you select an unused drive letter on your system, such as drive M:, and you map the remote folder to the drive. Then, whenever you want to access the folder's contents, you simply click your mouse on the corresponding drive icon—as if the drive physically existed on your PC.

To map a remote folder to a network drive, perform these steps:

1. Select the Start menu Programs option and choose Windows Explorer. Windows 95, in turn, will display the Explorer window, as shown in Figure 18.3.

18: WINDOWS 95 NETWORKING OPERATIONS

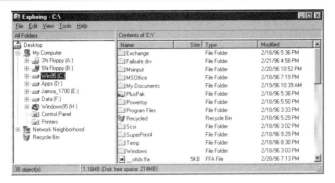

Figure 18.3 The Explorer window.

2. Select the Tools menu Map Network Drive option. The Explorer, in turn, will display the Map Network Drive dialog box, as shown in Figure 18.4.

Figure 18.4 The Map Network Drive dialog box.

3. Within the pull-down drives list, select the drive letter you want to map to the remote folder.

4. Within the Path field, type in the folder you want to access. To specify a folder name, you will type two backslashes (\\) and the remote-computer name, followed by the pathname, such as \\SALES\BUDGETS.

5. Select OK. The Explorer will add the mapped drive letter to your list of available disk drives.

If you want Windows 95 to map automatically, the remote folder to the drive each time you log into the network, select the Map Network Drive dialog box Reconnect at Logon checkbox.

DISCONNECTING FROM A MAPPED DRIVE

When you are done working with the files that reside within a remote folder, you may want to disconnect your mapped drive. To disconnect a mapped-network drive, perform these steps:

1. Select the Start menu Programs option and choose Windows Explorer. Windows 95, in turn, will start the Explorer.

2. Select the Tools menu Disconnect Network Drive option. Explorer, in turn, will display a dialog box, as shown in Figure 18.5, that lists your mapped drives.

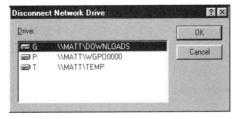

Figure 18.5 The Explorer's list of mapped-network drives.

3. Within the list of mapped drives, click on the drive you want to disconnect and choose OK.

357

ALLOWING REMOTE USERS TO ACCESS YOUR FOLDERS AND PRINTERS

To share your resources with remote users, you must first configure your system's network settings to support sharing. To enable your system to share resources, perform these steps:

1. Select the Start menu Settings option and choose Control Panel. Windows 95, in turn, will display the Control Panel window.

2. Double-click your mouse on the Network icon. Widows 95 will display the Network dialog box as shown in Figure 18.6.

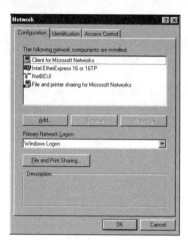

Figure 18.6 *The Network dialog box.*

3. Click your mouse on the File and Print Sharing button. Windows 95, in turn, will display the File and Print Sharing dialog box, as shown in Figure 18.7.

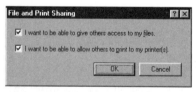

Figure 18.7 *The File and Print Sharing dialog box.*

4. Select the checkboxes to give remote users access to your files and printers. If, on the other hand, you want to turn off sharing, remove the checkboxes.

5. Select OK.

6. Within the Network dialog box, choose OK.

SHARING A FOLDER

To share a folder on your system, perform these steps:

1. Using the My Computer folder or Explorer, locate the folder you desire and click your mouse on the folder's icon.

2. Select the File menu Sharing option. Windows 95, in turn, will display the Sharing Properties dialog box for the folder, as shown in Figure 18.8.

18: WINDOWS 95 NETWORKING OPERATIONS

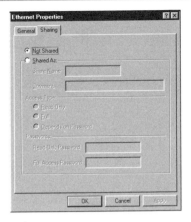

Figure 18.8 Setting a folder's sharing properties.

3. Within the Properties dialog box, select the sharing attributes you desire.

4. Choose OK.

If you don't specify a password, either for read-only or full access, any user on your network can access the folder. To protect your files better, you should restrict access to all the resources on your system as much as you can. In other words, only share those folders users truly need to access. Then, limit users who don't need to change the contents of files within the folder to read-only access. After you share a folder, Windows 95 will change the folder's icon to include a hand, as shown here, to indicate that the folder is shared:

TURNING OFF A FOLDER'S SHARED ACCESS

When remote users no longer need to access files within a folder, turn off the file's shared property. To turn off sharing for a folder, perform these steps:

1. Using the My Computer folder or Explorer, locate the folder you desire and click your mouse on the folder's icon.

2. Select the File menu Sharing option. Windows 95, in turn, will display the folder's sharing properties.

3. Select the Not shared button.

4. Choose OK.

SHARING A PRINTER

To share a printer that is connected to your PC, perform these steps:

1. Open the My Computer folder.

2. Within the My Computer folder, double-click your mouse on the Printers folder.

3. Within the Printers folder, click your mouse on the printer you desire.

4. Select the File menu Sharing option. Windows 95, in turn, will display the printer's sharing properties, as shown in Figure 18.9.

Success with Windows 95

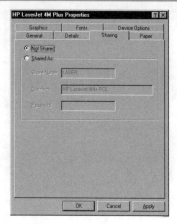

Figure 18.9 Setting a printer's sharing properties.

5. Select the Shared button and type in a name that describes your printer.

6. If you want remote users to specify a password before they can access your printer, select the Password field and type in the password you desire.

7. Choose OK.

Windows 95 will change the printer's icon to include a hand, as shown here, to indicate that the printer is shared:

Turning Off Printer Sharing

To disable sharing for a printer, perform these steps:

1. Open the My Computer folder.
2. Within the My Computer folder, double-click your mouse on the Printers folder.
3. Within the Printers folder, click your mouse on the printer you desire.
4. Select the File menu Sharing option. Windows 95, in turn, will display the printer's sharing properties, as shown in Figure 18.10.

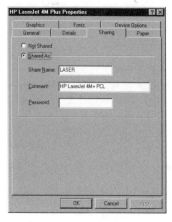

Figure 18.10 Setting a printer's sharing properties.

5. Select the Not Shared button.

6. Choose OK.

USING WINDOWS 95 DIAL-UP NETWORKING

Dial-up networking is one of Windows 95's most powerful networking features. Using your PC and a modem, you can connect to a network server running Windows NT, Novell Netware, and even Windows 95. Then, using your modem connection, you can access shared files and printers across the network.

By using dial-up networking, for example, you can access your PC at work from your home, a hotel, or even an airplane! To dial into a PC running Windows 95, you will need to install Windows 95 server software. You can get the server software within the Windows 95 Plus! Pack, which you can purchase at most computer stores.

After you install your server software, a remote computer can dial into the server and access its shared resources. In addition, if the server is part of a local-area network, you can access the network's shared resources as well! To dial into a network, perform these steps:

1. Select the Start menu Settings option and choose Control Panel. Windows 95, in turn, will display the Control Panel window.

2. Double-click your mouse on the Network icon. Windows 95, will display the Network dialog box.

3. If the list of network components does not include the Dial-Up adapter, select Add. Windows 95, in turn, will display the Select Network Component Type dialog box.

   3A. Select the Adapter option and choose Add. Windows 95 will display the Select Network adapters dialog box.

   3B. Scroll through the list of manufacturers and highlight Microsoft. Choose the Dial-Up Adapter and choose OK.

4. If your list of installed network components does not include NetBEUI and IPX/SPX, select Add. Windows 95, in turn, will display the Select Network Component Type dialog box.

   4A. Select Protocol and choose Add. Windows 95, in turn, will display the Select Network Protocol dialog box.

   4B. Within the list of manufacturers, highlight Microsoft. Click your mouse on the IPX/SPX option.

4C. Repeat steps 4A and 4B to add the NetBEUI protocol.

5. If your list of installed network components does not include the Client for Microsoft Networks (or a different client, depending on the server's network type), choose Add. Windows 95 will display the Select Network Component Type dialog box.

   5A. Select Client and choose Add. Windows 95, in turn, will display the Select Network Client dialog box.

   5B. Within the list of manufacturers, select Microsoft. Within the list of network clients, select the Client for Microsoft Networks (or Novell networks, depending on your server type). Choose OK.

6. Within the Network dialog box, choose OK. Windows 95 may restart your system to put your network changes into effect.

To connect your PC to the remote server, perform these steps:

1. Select the Start menu Programs option and choose Accessories.

2. Within the Accessories menu, choose Dial-Up Networking. Windows 95, in turn, will open the Dial-Up Networking folder.

3. Double-click your mouse on the Make New Connection icon. Windows 95, in turn, will start the Make New Connection Wizard, as shown in Figure 18.11.

Figure 18.11 *The Make New Connection Wizard.*

4. Within the dialog box, type in the name you want to use for this connection, such as Office Server. Select Next. Windows 95, in turn, will display a dialog box prompting you for the server's phone number, as shown in Figure 18.12.

Figure 18.12 *Specifying the remote-server's phone number.*

5. Type in the server's phone number and choose Next. The Wizard, in turn, will display a dialog box telling you that you have successfully created a new connection.

6. Select Finish.

Next, to ensure that your connection knows the type of software the remote server will use, perform these steps:

1. Within your Dial-Up Networking folder, right-click your mouse on your new-connection icon and choose Properties. Windows 95, in turn, will display the Properties dialog box, shown in Figure 18.13.

18: Windows 95 Networking Operations

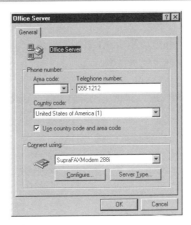

Figure 18.13 Viewing a connection's properties.

2. Select the Server Type button. Windows 95 will display the Server Type dialog box, as shown in Figure 18.14.

Figure 18.14 The Server Type dialog box.

3. Within the Type of Dial-Up Server pull-down list, select your server type. Choose OK.

4. Within the connection properties dialog box, choose OK.

You are now ready to connect to the remote server. Double-click your mouse on the connection icon to start your connection. To access the remote server, you may need to specify a password. If a password is required, you will need to get the password from the user who installed and configured the server software.

MONITORING YOUR PC'S NETWORK USE

If you let remote users share your folders and printers, each remote-user access will steal some of your PC's processing capabilities. In other words, each time a remote user accesses a file or printer that resides on your system, Windows 95 must stop and respond to the remote-user's request. Depending on the number of users or the number of requests your system receives, your system performance may begin to suffer. To help you monitor your system's use by remote users, Windows 95 provides the Net Watcher accessory. To start the Net Watcher program, perform these steps:

1. Select the Start menu Programs option and choose Accessories.

2. Within the Accessories menu, choose System Tools and select Net Watcher. Windows 95, in turn, will display the Net Watcher window, as shown in Figure 18.15.

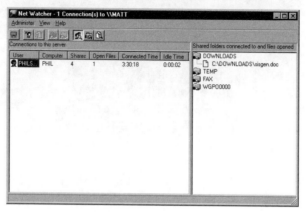

Figure 18.15 *The Net Watcher window.*

Within the Net Watcher window, you can determine which users are accessing your shared resources and which resources the users are using. In addition, by using the Administer menu, you can disconnect users from your system and control a folder's sharing. For more specifics on Net Watcher options, turn to the book *1001 Windows 95 Tips*, Jamsa Press, 1995.

KEYS TO SUCCESS

Windows 95 makes it very easy for you to share folders and printers within a local-area network. In addition, Windows 95 supports dial-up networking, which lets you connect to a PC using a modem connection. After you connect to the remote PC, you can access the remote-PC's shared resources as well as the shared resources that exist within the remote-PC's local-area network. In Chapter 19, you will learn how to use the Windows 95 Device Manager to set low-level hardware settings and to resolve hardware conflicts. Before you continue with Chapter 19, however, make sure you have learned the following key concepts:

- ✓ By traversing your Network Neighborhood folders, you can view the computers and printers that make up your network.

- ✓ Within the Network Neighborhood, you double-click your mouse on a computer icon to access that computer's shared resources.

- ✓ Depending on the protections the remote computer is using, you may have to type in a password before you can access a remote computer's shared folders or printers.

- ✓ Windows 95 lets you password-protect your shared resources, or control access based on a list of usernames.

- ✓ If you use a remote folder on a regular basis, you may find it convenient to map the folder to a drive letter. Later to use the folder's contents, you simply click your mouse on the corresponding drive letter.

- ✓ Using Windows 95 dial-up networking, you can use a modem connection to access a computer (or a local-area network) as if your PC were part of the network.

- ✓ The Net Watcher accessory program lets you monitor your PC's network use.

Chapter 19
Managing Low-Level Hardware Operations

Windows 95 provides many features that simplify the process of adding hardware to your system. To start, Windows 95 lets most devices you install resolve potential conflicts on their own. All you have to do is install the hardware card, which in turn, will communicate with the other cards in your system to determine which settings it should use. Second, by providing Wizards to walk you through common hardware installations, Windows 95 helps you ensure that you install the correct software for your card the first time. Lastly, using Control Panel entries, Windows 95 makes it easy for you to customize common hardware settings in minutes.

Unfortunately, even with all the hardware-support features Windows 95 provides, there may still be times when your hardware installation fails due to a device conflict. In this chapter, you will learn why such hardware conflicts occur, how you can use the Windows 95 Device Manager to detect them, and the steps you must take to resolve them. By the time you finish this chapter, you will understand the following key concepts:

- Hardware conflicts occur when two or more devices try to use the same settings, such as the same wire to communicate with the CPU.

- Depending on the conflicting devices, your system may not start, one or more of the devices may not work, or one device will work fine until you try to use a second device.

- Windows 95 supports plug-and-play hardware and software, which helps reduce hardware conflicts in your system.

- Using the Windows 95 Device Manager, you can detect hardware conflicts.

- Some hardware devices have settings you can use the Windows 95 Device Manager to specify.

UNDERSTANDING HOW HARDWARE CONFLICTS OCCUR

Within your PC, the central processing unit (CPU) controls all operations. The CPU executes the instructions that make up your program, as well as those that make up Windows 95. In addition, your CPU interacts with many of your hardware devices. For example, each time you move your mouse across your desk, the mouse interrupts the task the CPU is currently performing and asks the CPU to move your mouse pointer across the screen. You may, for example, have watched a user who has become so frustrated by how long an operation is taking to complete that they shake their mouse to move the hourglass pointer that appears on their screen. Each time the user moves the mouse, the mouse interrupts the CPU, which in turn stops doing the task for which the user is waiting, so that it can move the mouse pointer.

For a hardware device to interrupt the CPU in this way, the device needs a way to signal the CPU that it needs attention. We refer to that signal as an *interrupt request*. To send its interrupt request, the device generates an electronic signal, which travels down a wire that connects the device to the CPU. Each device in your system uses a different interrupt-request line.

For the CPU to know which device is interrupting it, each device must have its own wire on which it sends its interrupt request. When two devices use the same interrupt request line, a *hardware conflict* occurs. Table 19 lists the interrupt request lines (or IRQ lines, as the experts call them) for common devices.

Interrupt Line	Device
0	System timer
1	Keyboard
2	Provides access to interrupts 9 through 15
3	COM2
4	COM1
5	LPT2
6	Floppy disk
7	LPT1
8	Real-time clock
9	Redirected for IRQ 2 (Unused)
10	Unused
11	Unused
12	Unused
13	Math coprocessor
14	Hard disk
15	Unused

Table 19 Common interrupt-request line use.

Specifying a Device's Interrupt Request Line

In the past, when you installed a hardware device, such as a new modem, you had to manually select the card's interrupt request (IRQ) setting using DIP switches and jumpers that appear on the card itself. Before you installed your new card, you first had to determine which IRQ settings that other cards in your system were already using. By knowing the common IRQ settings listed in Table 19, you could start with the IRQ numbers marked Unused. Then, you could examine the cards your system contains to determine which of those IRQ settings other cards in your system are using. For example, if you had previously installed a sound card or a network adapter, that card would have used an IRQ. When you finally found an IRQ setting that was not in use, you could use that setting for your new card.

Plug-and-Play Simplifies the Installation Process

When you purchase hardware cards that support plug-and-play, you simplify the card's installation. In general, a plug-and-play card has a special built-in chip called the plug-and-play BIOS. When you install the card and power on your PC, the card's plug-and-play BIOS wakes up and tries to determine which settings it should use. To begin, the plug-and-play BIOS essentially shouts to the other plug-and-play devices, "Hey, I want to use IRQ 9. Is anyone using it?" If none of your other plug-and-play devices are using IRQ 9, your new card uses it. Otherwise, the card repeats its question using different IRQ numbers until it finds an available IRQ.

You may be thinking, "That sounds easy. All I need to do is buy plug-and-play hardware." In the future, your statement will be true. Today, however, the problem is that many of the cards in your system don't support plug-and-play. When your plug-and-play card asks if anyone is using IRQ 9, your two-year-old sound card (that doesn't use plug-and-play, but who is using IRQ 9) won't answer.

Sometimes, depending on the conflicting device, it may take you days to figure out that you have an IRQ conflict. For example, the first time you try your modem, your mouse might stop working. Or, each time you move your

20: MANAGING LOW-LEVEL HARDWARE OPERATIONS

mouse, your modem disconnects. Other times, however, as soon as you install your hardware card, your system simply won't start.

USING THE WINDOWS 95 DEVICE MANAGER TO TROUBLESHOOT HARDWARE CONFLICTS

To help you resolve hardware conflicts, Windows 95 provides the Device Manager. To start the Device Manager, perform these steps:

1. Select the Start menu Settings option and choose Control Panel. Windows 95, in turn, will open the Control Panel window.

2. Within the Control Panel, double-click your mouse on the System icon. Windows 95 will display the System Properties dialog box, as shown in Figure 19.1.

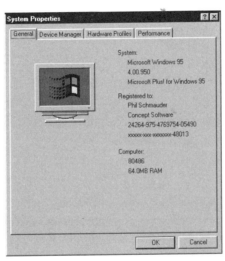

Figure 19.1 *The System Properties dialog box.*

3. Select the Device Manager tab. Windows 95 will display the Device Manager page, as shown in Figure 19.2.

Figure 19.2 *The Windows 95 Device Manager page.*

367

The Device Manager uses a tree-like structure to present your system devices. As you can see, the Device Manager precedes entries with a box that contains a small plus sign. If you click your mouse on the plus sign, the Device Manager will display the next level of devices. For example, if you click your mouse on the box that precedes the Disk drives entry, the Device Manager will expand the branch to display each of your disk-drive types, as shown in Figure 19.3.

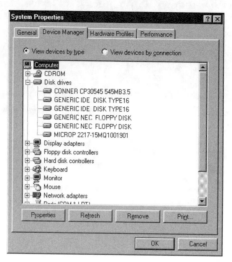

Figure 19.3 Using the Device Manager to display disk-drive types.

To collapse a branch of the Device Manager tree, click your mouse on the small minus sign that now appears within the box that precedes the branch entry.

Printing Your Device Settings

One of the best ways to understand your system's hardware settings is to print the settings from within the Device Manager. After you examine your system settings, store your printout in a safe location. Should you ever need to restore your settings, you can use your printout as your guide. To print your system settings from within the Device Manager, perform these steps:

1. Click your mouse on the Device Manager Print button. The Device Manager will display the Print dialog box, as shown in Figure 19.4.

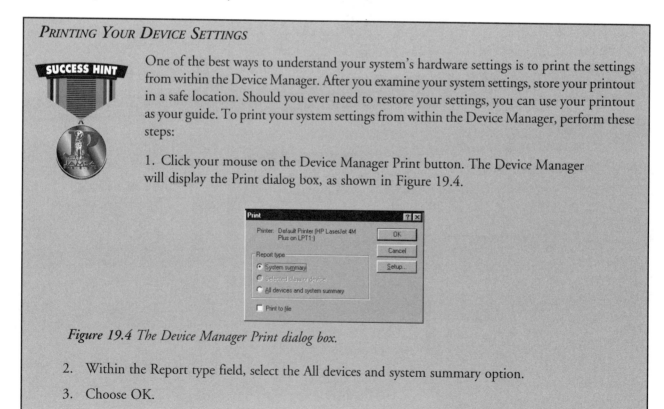

Figure 19.4 The Device Manager Print dialog box.

2. Within the Report type field, select the All devices and system summary option.
3. Choose OK.

20: Managing Low-Level Hardware Operations

Understanding Base Memory Addresses

When you install a new hardware device, you may have to specify a second setting in addition to the device's IRQ: the base memory address. In short, using the IRQ line, a device can interrupt the CPU, essentially saying, "Hey, I need you." Unfortunately, that's about all the device can use the IRQ line to do. When the CPU asks, "What now?", the device needs a way to respond. Your mouse, for example, needs to tell the CPU in which direction and how far the user has moved it.

To provide devices with a way to communicate with the CPU, most devices reserve a range of special memory addresses. When you install a device, you often need to tell Windows 95 where the device's memory starts—in other words, its *base address*. Just as each device must have its own IRQ setting, each device needs its own range of memory. If, for example, two devices had the same base-memory address, one device might overwrite the values a second device needs, causing a hardware conflict.

Using the Device Manager to Recognize Hardware Conflicts

When you install a hardware device, Windows 95 tries to determine the device's IRQ and base address. If Windows 95 realizes that the new device's settings conflict with another device, the Device Manager will display a red X on top of the device name that appears within the Device Manager hardware list, as shown in Figure 19.5.

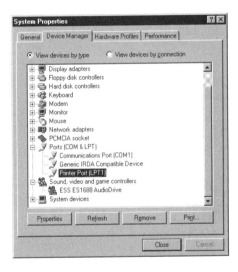

Figure 19.5 The Device Manager uses the red X (the ESS ES 1688 has an X) to inform you of hardware conflicts.

To resolve a hardware conflict for an older (non plug-and-play) device, you may need to remove the card and change jumper or DIP switch settings. Then, you must tell Windows 95 the new settings you have assigned to the card using the Device Manager, as discussed next.

Using the Device Manager to Specify New Device Settings

Using the Device Manager, you can display and change device settings. Depending on the corresponding device-driver software (the software which lets Windows 95 communicate with the device), the device settings you can change may differ.

To get a better feel for how you might change device settings, double-click your mouse on the Mouse entry within the Device Manager list. When the Device Manager expands the Mouse branch to display your mouse type, double-click on the icon that corresponds to your current mouse. The Device Manager, in turn, will display a Properties dialog box similar to the one shown in Figure 19.6.

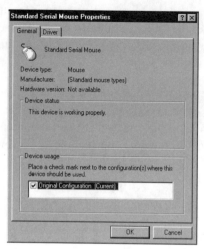

Figure 19.6 *The Mouse Properties dialog box.*

Within the Mouse Properties dialog box, you can display information about the mouse device driver, as well as the mouse hardware settings. For example, to display the mouse IRQ setting, select the Resources tab. The Device Manager will display the Resource page, as shown in Figure 19.7.

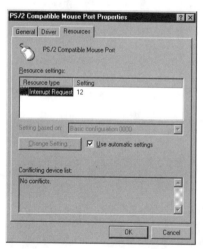

Figure 19.7 *The Mouse Properties Resources page.*

As you can see, the Resources page lists the mouse IRQ. For the devices that reserve a range of memory addresses, the Resources page will list the corresponding base (or starting address). Note that at the bottom of the Resources page, the Device Manager lists devices whose settings conflict with those of the mouse (which in this case is no devices). If the Device Manager recognizes a conflict, you can use this list to troubleshoot the error.

Note: *Depending on your mouse type, your Mouse Properties Resources page may not display an IRQ setting. For example, if you are using a serial mouse, you connect your mouse to a serial port, such as COM1 or COM2. In that case, your mouse IRQ corresponds to that of the serial port. Using the Device Manager, select the Properties for the corresponding serial port to learn the mouse IRQ.*

20: Managing Low-Level Hardware Operations

Changing Device Settings

To use the Device Manager to change a device setting, first click your mouse on the Use automatic settings checkbox that appears on the Resources page. When the box contains a check mark, Windows 95 will choose the device settings automatically. To manually override the Windows 95 settings, you must first remove the check mark. Next, click your mouse on the Change Setting button. Depending on your device type, Windows 95 will display a dialog box within which you can change settings. Some devices, however, do not have settings you can change using the Device Manager.

Note: Do not change device settings unless you thoroughly understand your change. An errant system setting may not only prevent a device from working, the setting may also prevent Windows 95 from starting. For more information on changing Windows 95 device settings, refer to the book **Rescued by Upgrading Your PC, Second Edition**, *Jamsa Press, 1996.*

Removing a Device

If you remove a device from your system, and the device still appears within the Device Manager list, you can use the Device Manager to remove the device from the list. Likewise, should you assign an errant value to a device setting within the Device Manager and you cannot get the device to work, you can remove the device and then reinstall the device software. To remove a device from your system, perform these steps:

1. Within the Device Manager list, expand the branch that contains the device you want to remove.
2. Click your mouse on the device and choose Remove. The Device Manager, in turn, will display a dialog box warning you that you are about to remove the device.
3. Choose OK.

If you immediately want Windows 95 to reinstall software support for the device (assuming you had removed the device due to a setting error), click your mouse on the Device Manager Refresh button. Windows 95, in turn, will examine your system for unknown devices and will install software for each device it finds.

Keys to Success

Newer hardware cards, such as modems and sound cards, support plug-and-play. This lets a card determine the settings other hardware in your PC use, so the card can use different settings. In this way, plug-and-play hardware is very easy to install and to get working. Unfortunately, many users still have older cards that don't support plug-and-play. In such cases, the user must determine the proper settings. Using the Windows 95 Device Manager, users can view the current system settings in order to find settings that are unused. Also, should a hardware conflict arise, the Device Manager may identify the conflict for the user, which reduces the user's trouble-shooting time. This chapter examined the Windows 95 Device Manager and how you use it to identify and resolve hardware conflicts. In Chapter 20, you will learn how Windows 95 supports MS-DOS-based programs. Before you continue with Chapter 20, however, make sure you have learned the following key concepts:

- ✓ When you install new hardware, you need to ensure your new hardware does not use settings that are in use for another device. If such conflicts arise, the hardware or your system may not work.
- ✓ Windows 95 supports plug-and-play hardware and software, which reduces hardware conflicts.
- ✓ Older hardware devices do not support plug-and-play.
- ✓ Using the Windows 95 Device Manager, you can view hardware settings and resolve hardware conflicts.
- ✓ Some hardware devices have settings you can change using the Device Manager.

Chapter 20
Windows 95 and DOS

If you have worked with Windows 3.1 in the past, you may know that before Windows 3.1 could run, your PC had to run a special program named DOS, your computer's *disk operating system*. As such, in the past, each time you turned on your computer, your PC automatically ran DOS. After DOS was running, you could start Windows 3.1. Windows 95 replaces DOS. As a result, now, when you turn on your computer, your PC starts Windows 95. In short, the DOS operating system no longer exists on your system. Instead, Windows 95 makes your system appear to support your older DOS-based programs. In fact, Windows 95 will even let you work from a DOS prompt. If, for example, you have one or more DOS-based video games you still play on a regular basis, relax. This chapter will show you how to run these programs using Windows 95. By the time you finish this chapter, you will understand the following key concepts:

- Windows 95 lets you run DOS-based programs and issue most DOS-based commands.

- Using Windows 95, you will run most DOS-based programs within a window that you can size or maximize to fill the entire screen.

- When a DOS-based program does not run within a window, you can direct Windows 95 to run the program using a special "DOS mode." Most DOS-based programs, even video games, will run successfully within DOS mode.

- To start your system, Windows 95 ignores most AUTOEXEC.BAT and CONFIG.SYS entries. In fact, the only entries Windows 95 may use are those that install real-mode (DOS-based) device drivers for which Windows 95 provides no counterpart.

- Windows 95 replaces the Windows 3.1 PIF Editor with program properties.

- Within a DOS-based window, you can cut and paste text to and from the clipboard.

- To access a system prompt, select the Start menu Programs option and choose MS-DOS prompt.

RUNNING A DOS-BASED PROGRAM

As you have learned, one of the fastest ways to run a program using Windows 95 is to use the Start menu. If you know the name and folder (directory) of the DOS program you want to run, click your mouse on the Start menu and choose Run. Windows 95, in turn, will display the Run dialog box as shown in Figure 20.1.

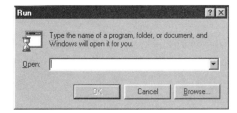

Figure 20.1 *The Run dialog box.*

Within the Open field, type in the name of the program you want to run. If the program resides in a directory you have specified in your command path (see the discussion of the PATH command that appears later in this chapter), Windows 95 will locate and run your program. If Windows 95 cannot locate the program, Windows 95 will display a dialog box similar to that shown in Figure 20.2 that tells you it could not locate the program.

Success with Windows 95

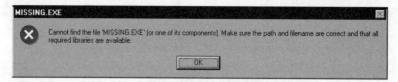

Figure 20.2 A dialog box that states Windows 95 could not locate a program file.

Should you encounter a "program not found" dialog box, click your mouse on the OK button and then use the Run dialog box Browse option to locate the program file on your disk.

Helping Windows 95 Locate Your Program Files

If Windows 95 cannot locate, on your disk, the program file that corresponds to the command you type within the Run dialog box, perform the following steps to help Windows 95 locate the file in the future:

1. Use the Run dialog box Browse button to search the folders on your disk for the file.

2. Next, when you later type the command within the Run dialog box, you can precede the command's name with the complete directory path (as discussed in Chapter 7), or you can edit your system's AUTOEXEC.BAT and add the directory to the PATH command.

For now, within the Run dialog box, type in the EDIT command to start the DOS-based file editor. Windows 95, in turn, will open a window within which it runs the EDIT program as shown in Figure 20.3.

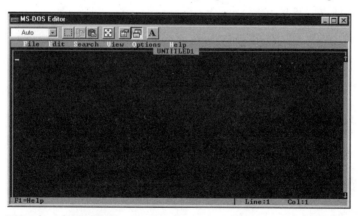

Figure 20.3 Running the DOS-based EDIT command within a window.

Windows 95 runs most DOS-based programs within a window. As such, you can maximize the window to full screen, minimize the window to a Taskbar icon, or incrementally size or move the window.

Closing a DOS-based Program Window

To close a DOS-based program window, simply exit the program you are running. Most programs, for example, will provide a quit or exit option. In the case of the EDIT command, for example, you can end the program by selecting the File menu Exit option. Depending on the DOS-based program you are running, you may be able to close the program by double-clicking your mouse on the program's Control menu button or by selecting the Control menu and choosing the Close option or by clicking your mouse on the window's Close button.

20: Windows 95 and DOS

> ### Use Alt-Esc to Expand a DOS-Based Program to Full Screen
>
>
> When you run a DOS-based program within a window, you can use the window's Maximize button to expand the window to full screen. However, depending on the program you are running, there may be times when you want to run the program *outside* of a window, using the entire screen. Computer games, for example, make extensive use of graphic images. In most cases, you will want to view these images full screen.
>
> To run a DOS-based program full screen, without a window, select the window and then press the Alt-Enter keyboard combination. The window that surrounds your program will disappear and your program's output will fill the entire screen. To restore the program's output back into a window, simply press the Alt-Enter keyboard combination a second time. In other words, Alt-Enter acts as a toggle. The first time you press Alt-Enter, you expand the program to full screen. The second time you press Alt-Enter, you collapse the program's output back into a window.

Accessing the DOS Command Line

Some kids never grow up, and I suppose some old-time DOS users (like me) will always want to access the DOS command-line prompt. Luckily, Windows 95 lets us "old-timers" open a window that displays a DOS prompt. To access a DOS prompt within a window, select the Start menu Run option. Windows 95, in turn, will display the Run dialog box. Within the Open field, type COMMAND as shown in Figure 20.4.

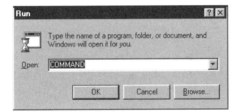

Figure 20.4 To open a window that contains a command-prompt, run COMMAND.

When you press Enter to run COMMAND, Windows 95 will display a window similar to the own shown in Figure 20.5 that contains a command prompt.

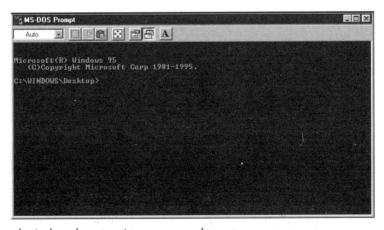

Figure 20.5 A DOS-based window that contains a command prompt.

Note: *In addition to accessing a command-line prompt by issuing COMMAND, you can select the Start menu Programs option and choose MS-DOS Prompt.*

From the command prompt, you can issue DOS-based commands. In addition, you can even start windows-based programs by typing the program's name at the prompt and pressing ENTER. For example, to run the Windows 95 Calculator program, type CALC at the command prompt and press ENTER. Windows 95, in turn, will open a window that contains the Calculator program. To close a window that contains a command prompt, double-click your mouse on the Control menu button, or type EXIT at the prompt and press ENTER.

STARTING PROGRAMS FROM A COMMAND PROMPT

Windows 95 lets you issue DOS commands, run DOS-based programs, and even start Windows-based programs from the DOS prompt. Using the START command from the DOS prompt (or from within a DOS batch file), you can better control how Windows 95 runs the program. For example, using the Start command, you can direct Windows 95 to run the program, initially displaying the program's window minimized as a Taskbar button. For more information on the START command, type START at the command prompt and press ENTER:

```
C:\> START   <Enter>
```

The START command, in turn, will display helpful information on your screen display.

WHERE WINDOWS 95 STORES YOUR DOS COMMANDS

In the past, users stored DOS commands in a directory on their hard disk named \DOS. Windows 95, however, places the commands within the directory \WINDOWS\COMMANDS. Because Windows 95 supports a new file system that uses long file names, you should use the new commands Windows 95 provides and not your older DOS commands. For a listing of the DOS commands Windows 95 supports, first use the CHDIR command to select the directory:

```
C:\> CHDIR \WINDOWS\COMMANDS   <Enter>
```

Next, use the DIR command to display a directory listing of the files:

```
C:\WINDOWS\COMMANDS> DIR   <Enter>
```

A QUICK WAY TO CHANGE DIRECTORIES WITHIN WINDOWS 95

If you have used the DOS change directory command CHDIR (abbreviated CD) command to change directories, you have very likely issued the following command to move up one level in the directory tree:

```
C:\WINDOWS> CD ..   <Enter>
```

In this case, the two dots (..) direct CHDIR to move up one level from the current subdirectory to its parent. Within Windows 95, you can use multiple dots with the CHDIR command to move up several directories in one command. For example, the following CHDIR command will move you up two directory levels:

```
C:\WINDOWS\COMMANDS> CD ...   <Enter>
```

Likewise, the following command uses four dots to move up three levels in the directory tree:

```
C:\WINDOWS\COMMANDS\INTERNET> CD ....   <Enter>
```

How Windows 95 Uses CONFIG.SYS and AUTOEXEC.BAT

If you have used DOS in the past, you may have frightening memories about each time you had to change entries within the AUTOEXEC.BAT or CONFIG.SYS system configuration files. As you may know, each time DOS started, it searched your disk's root directory for these two files.

The CONFIG.SYS file contained single line entries that told DOS to load device-driver software for specific hardware devices, the number of files DOS could open at one time, and how DOS was to configure itself in memory. The AUTOEXEC.BAT file, on the other hand, contained a list of commands you wanted DOS to automatically execute each time your system started. For example, most users placed a PROMPT command within AUTOEXEC.BAT that defined the appearance of the DOS command prompt. Also, users placed a PATH command within AUTOEXEC.BAT that told DOS which directories it should search to locate your program files.

Unlike DOS, Windows 95 does not need the CONFIG.SYS and AUTOEXEC.BAT files to start. In fact, if your root directory does not have these two files, Windows 95 will start using its own default settings. However, if your root directory has these two files, Windows 95 will examine each file's contents and may select specific entries.

For example, if your system has a unique hardware device for which you only have a DOS-based device driver, Windows 95 may install the corresponding real-mode device driver. Also, Windows 95 will use the command path you define using the PATH command within AUTOEXEC.BAT. Otherwise, the only time Windows 95 uses the CONFIG.SYS and AUTOEXEC.BAT is when you start Windows 95 in DOS mode (which this chapter discusses next) or when you run DOS-based programs.

Starting Your System in DOS Mode

As discussed, Windows 95 can run most of your DOS-based programs successfully within a window. However, if you have trouble running a particular program within a window (normally a computer game), you can restart Windows 95 in DOS mode. To start Windows 95 in DOS mode, first end all programs you have running. Next, you must shut down Windows 95 itself. To shut down Windows 95, select the Start menu Shut Down option. Windows 95, in turn, will display the Shut Down Windows dialog box as shown in Figure 20.6.

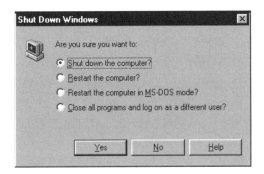

Figure 20.6 *The Shut Down Windows dialog box.*

Within the Shut Down Windows dialog box, select the Restart the Computer in MS-DOS Mode button and select Yes. Windows 95, in turn, will shut down and then restart, eventually displaying a DOS prompt. From this DOS prompt, you can run the program that you could not run within a window. After you are done using the program, you can restart Windows 95 by typing WIN at the DOS prompt and pressing ENTER.

If instead, you are done using your system, you can turn it off. Because your system is currently running in DOS mode (as opposed to a DOS-based window displaying a prompt), you can simply turn off your PC.

Understanding DOS Mode

If you run older DOS-based programs or video games, there may be times when your program won't run within a window. In such cases, you can shut down normal Windows 95 operations and restart Windows 95 in a special DOS mode. Within DOS mode, you no longer work from within a window. Rather, you work from a command-line prompt. Later to resume normal Windows 95 operations, you simply restart Windows 95 by typing WIN at the command line prompt. To select DOS mode, select the Start menu Shut Down option. When Windows 95 displays the Shut Down Windows dialog box, select the Restart the computer in MS-DOS mode option.

Starting Your System in DOS Mode

As you have just learned, when Windows 95 is running, you can use the Shut Down dialog box to restart your system in DOS mode. If your system is not running, you can power on your PC and select DOS mode before normal Windows 95 operations start. To select DOS mode when your system starts, press the F8 function key when your screen displays the following message:

```
Starting Windows 95 . . .
```

Windows 95, in turn, will display the following menu options on your screen:

```
Microsoft Windows 95 Startup Menu
=================================

     1. Normal
     2. Logged (/BOOTLOG.TXT)
     3. Safe mode
     4. Safe mode with network support
     5. Step-by-step confirmation
     6. Command prompt only
     7. Safe mode command prompt only
     8. Previous version of MS-DOS

Enter a choice: 1



F5=Safe mode  Shift+F5=Command prompt  Shift+F8=Step-by=step confirmation [N]
```

Table 20.1 briefly describes each Startup menu option. To direct Windows 95 to load and process your CONFIG.SYS and AUTOEXEC.BAT files before displaying the command-line prompt, select the Command prompt only option. If you want Windows 95 to bypass CONFIG.SYS. and AUTOEXEC.BAT, select the Safe mode command prompt only option. From the command prompt, you can run your DOS-based programs. When you are ready to resume normal Windows 95 operations, type WIN at the command prompt and press ENTER.

Understanding Safe Mode

As you install new hardware and software, there may be times that a change you make to your system prevents Windows 95 from running. In such cases, you can direct Windows 95 to start in a special "safe" mode. To start Windows 95 in a safe mode, press the F8 function key when Windows 95 displays the following message on your screen:

```
Starting Windows 95 . . .
```

Windows 95, in turn, will display a menu of startup options that lets you select how you want Windows 95 to start. Using these menu options, you can direct Windows 95 to bypass the processing of AUTOEXEC.BAT and

Start Menu Option	Purpose
Normal	Starts Windows 95 for normal operations
Logged	Starts Windows 95 logging startup information to the file BOOTLOG.TXT
Safe Mode	Lets you start Windows 95 with minimal hardware support so you can troubleshoot errors
Safe mode with network support	Same as Safe mode but Windows 95 loads network drivers
Step-by-step confirmation	Windows 95 prompts you for each CONFIG.SYS and AUTOEXEC.BAT entry to determine if you want Windows 95 to process the entry
Command prompt only	Windows 95 processes CONFIG.SYS and AUTOEXEC.BAT and then displays a command prompt
Safe mode command prompt only	Windows 95 bypasses CONFIG.SYS and AUTOEXEC.BAT displaying the command prompt

Table 20.1 Windows 95 Startup menu options.

CONFIG.SYS and to display only a command prompt. From the command prompt, you can edit the files whose entries are causing the conflict that prevents Windows 95 from running. After you make your changes, you can resume normal Windows 95 operations by rebooting your system.

USING THE DOS WINDOW TOOLBAR

If you examine the window that surrounds a DOS-based program, you should find a toolbar at the top of the window similar to the one shown in Figure 20.7.

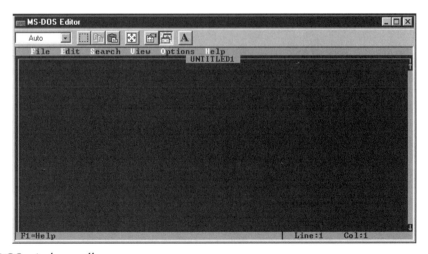

Figure 20.7 The DOS window toolbar.

If the toolbar does not appear in your current DOS-based window, right-click your mouse on the window's menu bar. Windows 95, in turn, will display a pop-up menu. Select the Toolbar menu option, placing a check mark before the option. The toolbar buttons let you perform cut-and-paste operations, expand the window's size to full screen, change fonts, and customize program settings. Table 20.2 briefly describes each toolbar button.

Success with Windows 95

Toolbar Button	Purpose
Auto	Lets you select the window's current font size from a pull-down list
	Lets you select text that you want to copy to the clipboard
	Copies selected text to the clipboard
	Pastes text from the clipboard into the current window
	Expands the current window's size to full screen
	Displays the program's Properties dialog box
	Enables and disables the program's background execution
A	Lets you change the current window's font

Table 20.2 Toolbar buttons for a DOS-based window.

The following sections discuss each of the toolbar buttons in detail.

Changing the Window's Font

If you have trouble reading text within a DOS-based window, you can use the toolbar's pull-down font-size list to increase or decrease the font size:

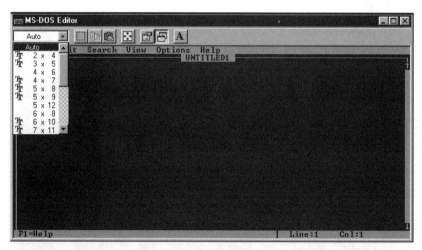

Take time now to experiment with different font sizes. If you select the Auto entry, Windows 95 selects the window's font size based on the window's current size.

By default, Windows 95 lets you use TrueType and bitmap fonts to display text within a DOS-based window. Most users will never have a need to change the font type settings. However, if for some reason you want to use TrueType fonts only or bitmap fonts only, click your mouse on the toolbar's font button. Windows 95, in turn, will display the Font sheet within the Properties dialog box as shown in Figure 20.8.

Within the Font sheet, choose the font type that you want Windows 95 to use within the window. You can also use the Font sheet to select a font size. As you make your font selections, the Font sheet will display a preview of how the font will later appear within the window. After you make the selections you desire, choose OK.

20: WINDOWS 95 AND DOS

Figure 20.8 *The Properties dialog box Font sheet.*

When you change the settings for a DOS-based window, Windows 95 records your settings. As such, the next time you run the program, the changes you make now will remain in effect. Also, the settings you change for one DOS-based program will not affect another program's window. As a result, you must change the settings for your DOS-based programs one program at a time.

PERFORMING CUT-AND-PASTE OPERATIONS

When you use Windows 95 to run two or more programs at the same time, there are times when you will want to copy data from one program to another. For example, if you have used a spreadsheet program to create a chart of your company sales, you might want to copy the chart into a report you are writing by using your word processor. To copy information from one program to another, you perform cut-and-paste operations using a Windows 95 special storage location called the clipboard.

To perform a cut-and-paste operation, you first select (highlight) the text or graphics that you want to copy from the first program. Then, you normally select an Edit menu Copy option (or Cut option if you are moving the item) to place a copy of the item on the Windows clipboard. Next, you start the program into which you want to place (paste) the item.

Using your mouse or keyboard arrow keys, you place the program's cursor at the location in your document at which you want to place the item. Normally, by selecting an Edit menu Paste option, you direct the program to copy the item from the clipboard into your document. Cut-and-paste operations get their name from the fact that they are similar to the steps you might perform using scissors and tape to place text or graphics within a printed document.

When you run a DOS-based program within a window, you can use the toolbar buttons to cut-and-paste text (not graphics). To copy text from a DOS-based window to the clipboard, click your mouse on the toolbar Mark button. Next, hold down your mouse select button and drag your mouse pointer over the text you want to select. As you drag your mouse over the text, Windows 95 will highlight your selected text in reverse video.

After you select the text you desire, click your mouse on the Toolbar Copy button. Windows 95 will place a copy of your text in the clipboard. You can now select the program that contains the document into which you want to paste the text. Using the second program's Edit menu Paste option, you can copy the text from the clipboard into your document. To paste text from the clipboard into a DOS-based program, position the cursor within the DOS-based program at the location at which you want to paste the clipboard text. Next, click you mouse on the toolbar Paste button.

SUCCESS WITH WINDOWS 95

HAVING A LITTLE CUT-AND-PASTE FUN

When you paste text into a DOS window, Windows 95 does not constrain you to pasting your text into a document. Instead, you can paste text to the command prompt. For example, using a Windows-based program such as the Notepad accessory, type the following text into a document and then copy the text to the clipboard:

```
CLS
ECHO Hello There
ECHO Goodbye!
```

Next, open a DOS-based window and position the cursor at the DOS prompt. Select the toolbar Paste option to copy the text into the DOS-based window. In this case, because you are pasting the text at the command-prompt, Windows 95 treats the text as commands and executes each of them.

UNDERSTANDING BACKGROUND PROCESSING

As you know, Windows 95 lets you run multiple programs at the same time. At any given time, however, Windows 95 considers only one program as active—the program that receives and responds to mouse and keyboard operations. Windows 95 refers to all other running programs as *background* programs. It's important that you understand that while programs are in the background (when they aren't the active program), the programs may still be running.

For example, assume that you have a program that monitors stock prices using a modem and your telephone lines. All day long the program watches for your stock prices to go up or down. If, for example, you work on a report using your word processor or chart other data using your spreadsheet, your stock market program will continue to run in the background, watching stock prices.

As you know, your computer only has one processing chip (its CPU or central processing unit). To let two or more programs run in the background in this way, Windows 95 lets the programs share the CPU. Because the exchange of the CPU happens so fast, each of the programs appears to be running at the same time as the others. Depending on the DOS-based program you are running, the program may not work if you try to run it as a background program.

As such, if you are running the program and need to switch to another program, click your mouse on the toolbar's Background button. Windows 95, in turn, will temporarily turn off the DOS-based program when the DOS-based program is not the active program. When you later select the program as the active program, Windows 95 will resume the program's processing.

To disable a DOS-based background program's execution, click your mouse on the toolbar Background button until the button appears depressed.

CONTROLLING PROGRAM PROPERTIES

If you used DOS-based programs under Windows 3.1, you probably used the PIF Editor to specify program settings. Windows 95 does not use the PIF Editor program. Instead, Windows 95 lets you specify program settings using the Properties dialog box. To view or change a program's properties, click your mouse on the program's toolbar Properties button. Windows 95, in turn, will display a properties dialog box similar to the one shown in Figure 20.9.

The following sections briefly examine each sheet within the Properties dialog box. For specifics on each option, refer to the book, *1001 Windows 95 Tips*, Jamsa Press, 1995.

Figure 20.9 The Properties dialog box.

WINDOWS 95 REPLACES THE PIF EDITOR WITH THE PROPERTIES DIALOG BOX

Under Windows 3.1, users ran a special program called the PIF Editor to assign settings to DOS-based programs. Such settings specified how the program could use memory, the video display, and which shortcut keys the program would support. The PIF Editor stored the program's settings in a special file that used the PIF extension. (PIF stands for Program Information File.) For example, assume you had a DOS-based budget program named BUDGET.EXE. The PIF Editor, in turn, would store the program's settings in the file BUDGET.PIF. Windows 95 replaces the PIF Editor with the Properties dialog box. Using the Properties dialog box, you can assign program settings which Windows 95, in turn, stores in a file with the PIF extension. To access a DOS-based program's Properties dialog box, click your mouse on the program's toolbar Properties button.

ACCESSING PROGRAM SETTINGS

When you click on the toolbar Properties button, Windows 95 will display the Properties dialog box Program sheet previously shown in Figure 20.9. Using the Program sheet, you can specify the title Windows 95 displays within the program's title bar, the command line that executes the program, and more. Table 20.3 describes the Program sheet fields.

Field	Purpose
Title	Contains the text that appears in the program's title bar
Cmd line	Specifies the directory path to the executable program file
Working	Specifies the directory within which the program runs—by default, Windows 95 uses the directory that contains the program
Batch file	Specifies the directory path to a DOS batch file that Windows 95 executes immediately before it runs the program
Shortcut Key	Specifies the shortcut key you can press to switch quickly to the program's window—to specify a shortcut key, select the field and then type a unique keyboard combination
Run	Specifies the window size within which Windows 95 runs the program
Close on Exit	Directs Windows 95 to close the program's window when you exit

Table 20.3 Fields within the Program sheet for a DOS-based program.

Controlling Advanced Program Settings

As discussed, most DOS-based programs will run within a window. If, however, you have problems running a DOS-based program within a window, you can use the Advanced Program Settings dialog box to customize the program further. To access these settings, click your mouse on the Program sheet's Advanced button. Windows 95, in turn, will display the Advanced Programs Settings dialog box as shown in Figure 20.10.

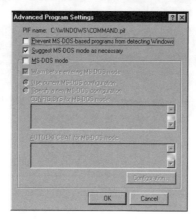

Figure 20.10 *The Advanced Program Settings dialog box.*

As they start, some DOS-based programs try to determine if Windows 95 is running. If the programs detect Windows 95, the programs may not run. Using a checkbox that appears in the Advanced Program Settings dialog box, you can prevent such programs from detecting Windows 95. In this way, you can trick the program into running within a window. When you execute DOS-based programs, Windows 95 can determine if the program would run better outside of a window and, if so, Windows 95 can suggest that you run this program only in DOS mode. Using the Suggest MS-DOS mode as required checkbox, you can direct Windows 95 to determine the best way to run the program.

Last, if you know the program must run in DOS mode, select the MS-DOS mode checkbox. The Advanced Program Settings dialog box, in turn, will make several additional settings available for your use. As you have learned, to run a program in DOS mode, you must close all open windows and shut down Windows 95 itself. When you specify that a program runs in DOS mode, Windows 95 will automatically initiate its shutdown process when you run the program. If you select the Warn before entering MS-DOS mode checkbox, Windows 95 will display a dialog box similar to the one shown in Figure 20.11 when you run the program.

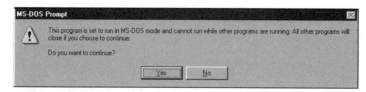

Figure 20.11 *Windows 95 warning for a DOS mode program.*

If you choose Yes, Windows 95 will shut down and restart in DOS mode. If you instead choose No, Windows 95 will cancel the program's execution. As you learned earlier is this chapter, the primary time Windows 95 uses the CONFIG.SYS and AUTOEXEC.BAT configuration files is when you start your system in DOS mode. If you select the Use current MS-DOS configuration button, Windows 95 will use your existing AUTOEXEC.BAT and CONFIG.SYS to configure DOS mode settings when you run this program. If you instead select the Specify a new configuration button, Windows 95 will highlight two text boxes within which you can select the CONFIG.SYS and AUTOEXEC.BAT entries you want to use specifically for this program.

FURTHER REFINING A PROGRAM'S CONFIGURATION

When you select the Specify a new MS-DOS configuration button, Windows 95 will activate the Configuration button. If you click your mouse on the configuration button, Windows 95 will display the Select MS-DOS Configuration Options dialog box as shown in Figure 20.12.

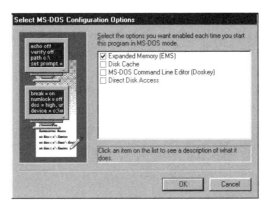

Figure 20.12 *The Select MS-DOS Configuration Options dialog box.*

The dialog box contains four checkboxes that let you quickly customize several AUTOEXEC.BAT and CONFIG.SYS settings. Table 20.4 briefly describes the purpose of each of these four checkboxes.

Checkbox	Purpose
Expanded Memory (EMS)	Loads the EMM386 device driver to support expanded and upper memory
DiskCache	Loads the SMARTDRV disk cache
MS-DOS Command Line Editor (Doskey)	Loads the DOSKEY memory-resident command line editor
Direct Disk Access	Lets DOS-based programs change low-level file system and disk data structures

Table 20.4 *The purpose of each advanced program configuration checkbox.*

As you select different boxes, Windows 95 will change the corresponding entries that appear within your CONFIG.SYS and AUTOEXEC.BAT files.

CONTROLLING PROGRAM FONTS

The Properties dialog box Font sheet lets you change the size and type of font Windows 95 uses to display text within this program's window. When you select the Font tab, Windows 95 displays the Font sheet previously shown in Figure 20.8. Follow the steps previously discussed to select a font size and then choose OK.

CONTROLLING A PROGRAM'S MEMORY USE

One of the more confusing aspects of DOS is the memory types your program can use. To specify a DOS-based program's memory requirements, select the Properties dialog box Memory tab. Windows 95, in turn, will display the Memory sheet shown in Figure 20.13.

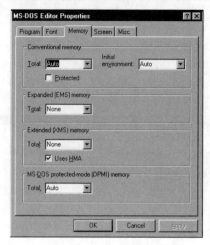

Figure 20.13 The Properties dialog box Memory sheet.

Each field labeled Total in the Memory sheet provides a pull-down list that lets you specify (in Kb) the amount of that memory type the program requires. In most cases, you will set each memory field to Auto.

The Initial Environment field lets you specify, in bytes, the initial size of the program's environment. As you may know, the operating system stores your system prompt setting and command path within the environment as well as other values you specify (normally from within AUTOEXEC.BAT) using the SET command. If a DOS-based program displays an "Out of environment space" error message, use this field to increase the program's environment size.

Controlling the Program's Screen Display

As you have learned, you can run DOS-based programs within a window or using the full screen. In addition, you can turn the display of toolbar buttons on or off. To control a DOS-based program's screen settings, select the Properties dialog box Screen tab. Windows 95, in turn, will display the Screen sheet as shown in Figure 20.14.

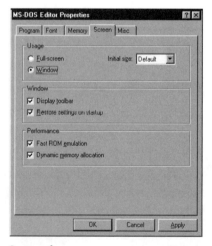

Figure 20.14 The Properties dialog box Screen sheet.

Table 20.5 briefly describes the Screen sheet's checkboxes.

Checkbox	Purpose
Full-screen	Directs Windows 95 to display the program's output full screen instead of within a window
Window	Directs Windows 95 to display the program's output within a window
Initial Size	Provides a pull-down menu that lets you select the number of lines in the program's screen display
Display toolbar	If selected, directs Windows 95 to display the toolbar buttons
Restore settings on startup	Restores the previous window settings when you end this program, in preparation for your next program
Fast ROM emulation	If selected, improves your system performance by directing Windows 95 to perform (emulate) the operations normally performed by slow ROM-based instructions—if you experience video errors, turn off this emulation
Dynamic memory allocation	If selected, directs Windows 95 to allocate video memory for the program only as needed, so more memory is available for other programs

Table 20.5 The purpose of Display sheet fields.

CONTROLLING OTHER PROGRAM SETTINGS

The Properties dialog box Misc sheet lets you control several other program settings such as the program's mouse support, background processing, and response to Windows 95 hot keys. When you select the Misc tab, Windows 95 will display the Misc sheet shown in Figure 20.15.

Figure 20.15 The Properties dialog box Misc sheet.

Table 20.6 briefly describes the Misc sheet fields.

Field	Purpose
Allow screen saver	If selected, allows Windows 95 to start a screen saver when this program is in the active window
Always suspend	If selected, prevents the program from processing in the background—the program will only run when it is the active window
Idle sensitivity	Controls how Windows 95 prioritizes this program's access to the CPU
Alt-Tab	If selected, lets you switch from this program to another by pressing the ALT-TAB keyboard combination
Alt-Esc	If selected, lets you switch from this program to other programs (cycling through the programs in the order you started them) by pressing the ALT-ESC keyboard combination
Ctrl-Esc	Selects the Windows 95 Start menu
PrtSc	If selected, lets you copy the screen image to the clipboard by pressing PrtSc; otherwise, Windows 95 prints the screen image
Alt-PrtSc	If selected, lets you copy the current window's contents to the clipboard
Alt-Enter	If selected, lets you toggle the program's output display between a window and the full screen
Alt-Space	If selected, lets you display the program's Control menu by pressing the ALT-SPACEBAR keyboard combination
QuickEdit	If selected, lets you select (highlight) text to copy to the clipboard without having to first click your mouse on the toolbar Mark button
Exclusive mode	If selected, the mouse will only respond within the program's window
Warn if still active	If selected, Windows 95 will display a warning message box if you try to close the window when this program is still active
Fast pasting	If selected, Windows 95 will perform fast-paste operations—if you experience errors pasting text into a DOS-based program, turn off fast-paste support

Table 20.6 Fields in the Properties dialog box Misc sheet.

Keys to Success

The Windows 95 developers went to great lengths to ensure that Windows 95 is compatible with your older Windows 3.1 and DOS programs. As you learned in this chapter, you will normally be able to run your DOS-based programs within a window. In those cases for which the program refuses to run within Windows 95, you can shut down your system and start it using a special DOS mode. Within DOS mode, even hard-to-run video games should run.

In Chapter 21, "Fine-Tuning Windows 95 Performance," you will learn ways you can monitor your system to detect bottlenecks that are decreasing your system performance. Before you continue with Chapter 21, however, make sure you have learned the following key concepts:

- ✓ Using Windows 95, you can run DOS-based programs and issue most DOS-based commands.
- ✓ Windows 95 lets you run most DOS-based programs within a window or full screen.
- ✓ If you run a DOS-based program within a window, you can incrementally size the window, maximize the window to fill the entire screen, or minimize the window to a Taskbar icon.
- ✓ Some DOS-based programs will not run within a window.
- ✓ If you can't run a DOS-based program within a window, direct Windows 95 to run the program using a special "DOS mode." Most DOS-based programs, even video games, will run successfully within DOS mode.
- ✓ In general, Windows 95 ignores most AUTOEXEC.BAT and CONFIG.SYS entries, using them primarily when you start your system in DOS mode.
- ✓ Windows 95 replaces the Windows 3.1 PIF Editor with program properties. However, Windows 95 still stores the program's settings within a PIF file.
- ✓ To access a program's settings, you use the Properties dialog box.
- ✓ Within a DOS-based window, you can cut and paste text to and from the clipboard.

Chapter 21
Improving Windows 95's Performance

As operating systems and applications programs become more powerful and easier to use, the trade-off is often performance. As you have learned, Windows 95 adds tremendous capabilities far beyond those of its predecessors. However, as they developed Windows 95, the Microsoft developers had to ensure that their new system consistently out-performed Windows 3.1. In most cases, they achieved this result. With Windows 3.1, users often combined third-party DOS-based memory-management software with Windows 3.1 INI settings to fine-tune their system performance. Under Windows 95, however, there are fewer ways for you to tweak the operating system. This chapter, however, examines some steps you can take to improve your system's performance, as well as techniques you can use to recognize bottlenecks that slow down your system. By the time you finish this chapter, you will understand the following key concepts:

- A bottleneck is an attribute that slows down your system performance, such as a slow disk drive or insufficient memory.

- Using the Windows 95 System Monitor, you can detect the cause of bottlenecks within your system.

- The System Monitor lets you monitor your system's Kernel operations, the file system, and its memory use.

- Using the System Monitor, you can create charts with which you detect potential bottlenecks.

- One of the most common causes of poor system performance is fragmented files. Fragmented files decrease your system performance because they require your system to perform more slow-disk operations.

- You can't prevent fragmented files, but you can correct them using the Windows 95 Disk Defragmenter program.

UNDERSTANDING SYSTEM BOTTLENECKS

When you set out to improve your system performance, you should start with the items that are slowing your system down—your system's bottlenecks. Think of your computer as consisting of raging rivers of flowing information. Some of the information flows to your disk, some to your computer's screen, some across the network, and some through a modem. Next, visualize a soda bottle. When you pour the soda into a glass, the soda must pass through the small opening at the top of the bottle. As the soda flows through the bottleneck, it slows down. When you seek ways to improve your system performance, you should try to eliminate bottlenecks. The most common places bottlenecks can occur within your system include:

- In the processor itself (the CPU)
- In the computer's electronic memory
- Within the video card
- Across a network
- Across a modem
- At your disk drives
- Within Windows 95 and your applications program

Understanding Hertz and Megahertz (MHz)

If you've shopped for a new computer, you've probably been overwhelmed by the wide variety of systems on the market. You can buy PCs with 60MHz (60 megahertz) Pentium chips, 100MHz chips, and even 200MHz chips. Most salespeople will tell you that more megahertz means more speed. They're right, and here's why.

Inside your computer's processor, the CPU, is a small clock that coordinates the computer's processing. A processor's speed tells you how many times per second the clock ticks. A processor whose clock ticks 1 million times per second has a speed of 1MHz. A 200MHz Pentium, therefore, is a processor whose clock ticks 200 million times per second! Each time the processor's clock ticks, the processor can perform one and sometimes two instructions! As you might guess, one of the easiest ways to improve your system's speed is to upgrade to a faster processor. As the price of computers continues to drop, those users who insist on top performance should plan to purchase a new PC every 18 months.

Measuring Your System Bottlenecks

As you work, there are going to be times when your system bottlenecks become obvious. For example, you may start to think (and correctly so) that your programs are taking longer to start this week than they did a few weeks ago. In such cases, files on your disk may have become fragmented, as will be discussed later in this chapter. Likewise, if you are continually sitting in front of your PC waiting for your modem to download information from the Internet, your modem may be a bottleneck.

At other times, however, your system bottlenecks may not be obvious. For such cases, Windows 95 provides the System Monitor program. Using the System Monitor, you can track your system's memory, processor, disk, and network use. To start the System Monitor, perform these steps:

1. Select the Start menu Programs option and choose Accessories.
2. Within the Accessories menu, choose the System Tools menu and choose System Monitor. Windows 95, in turn, will display the System Monitor, as shown in Figure 21.1.

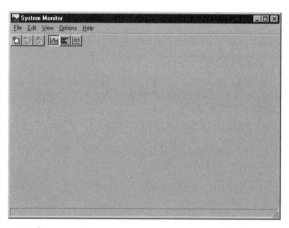

Figure 21.1 The System Monitor window.

Note: *If your system does not have the System Monitor, use the Control Panel Add/Remove Programs entry to install the System Monitor program from your Windows 95 CD-ROM or floppy disk.*

The System Monitor provides a window within which you monitor different system events. If you or another user has used the System Monitor on your system in the past, the System Monitor window may immediately display charts for different categories, such as the Windows 95 file system.

Within the System Monitor, you select the items you want to monitor. Within Windows 95 itself, you can monitor the file system, operating-system kernel (the key software within the operating system that Windows 95 uses to manage hardware and programs), and Windows 95 memory use. Depending on your network software, the items you can track using the System Monitor will differ. To monitor an item using the System Monitor, perform these steps:

1. Select the Edit menu Add Item option. The System Monitor, in turn, will display the Add Item dialog box, as shown in Figure 21.2.

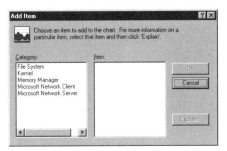

Figure 21.2 *The Add Item dialog box.*

2. Click your mouse on the category you desire. In this case, click your mouse on the File System category. The System Monitor will display a list of category items within the right-hand side of the Add Item dialog box, as shown in Figure 21.3.

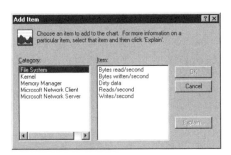

Figure 21.3 *Displaying category items you can monitor.*

3. Within the item list, you can select one item, or you can hold down your keyboard's CTRL key as you click your mouse to select multiple items.

4. Choose OK. The System Monitor will display charts for each item, as shown in Figure 21.4.

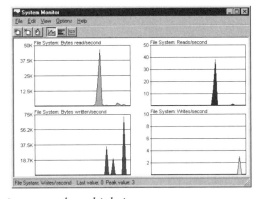

Figure 21.4 *Using the System Monitor to track multiple items.*

Note: *Within the Add Item dialog box, you can obtain information about an item (the item's purpose) by selecting the item and clicking your mouse on the Explain button. The System Monitor, in turn, will display a pop-up window that briefly describes the item.*

Removing an Item from Your Monitor List

Over time, you may find you no longer need to monitor a specific item. To remove an item from your monitor list, perform these steps:

1. Select the Edit menu Remove Item option. The System Monitor will display the Remove Item dialog box, as shown in Figure 21.5.

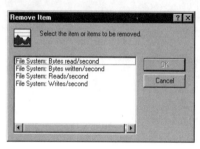

Figure 21.5 *The Remove Item dialog box.*

2. Within the item list, select the item you want to remove and choose OK.

Customizing a Monitored Item

If you use the System Monitor on a regular basis, you may eventually want to customize entries by using color codes or by changing the scale of the entry's chart. To customize a System Monitor entry, perform these steps:

1. Select the Edit menu Edit Item option. The System Monitor will display the Edit Item dialog box.
2. Within the item list, select the item you want to customize.
3. Choose OK. The System Monitor will display the Chart Options dialog box, as shown in Figure 21.6.

Figure 21.6 *The Chart Options dialog box.*

4. Using the Chart Options dialog box, select the item color and chart scale you desire.
5. Choose OK.

Note: *To access an item's Chart Options dialog box quickly, double-click your mouse on the item's chart within the System Monitor window.*

> ### Understanding the Numbers
>
>
>
> Because users have different processors, different amounts of memory, different disk-drive types, and different programs, it's difficult to give you a range of numbers within which the values of the items you are monitoring should fall. Instead, you need to get a feel for your system (where your numbers normally fall) and watch for symptoms. For example, rather than telling you that your system should always have 2Mb of free memory, a better guideline is to tell you that if your system slows down and you hear disk activity, check your system's free memory. If you have little free memory, you have two choices: run fewer programs at the same time or add more memory.

Changing the System Monitor's Chart Display

Depending on your preferences, the System Monitor lets you change the type of chart it displays. For example, Figure 21.7 displays system information using bar charts. Likewise, Figure 21.8 uses line charts to display similar information. Lastly, Figure 21.9 displays information using numbers only.

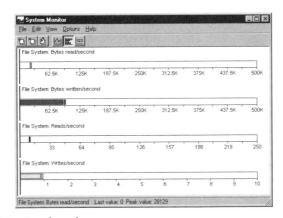

Figure 21.7 Displaying System Monitor bar charts.

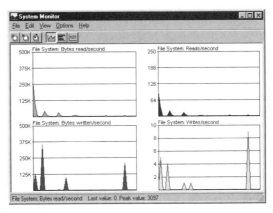

Figure 21.8 Displaying System Monitor line charts.

395

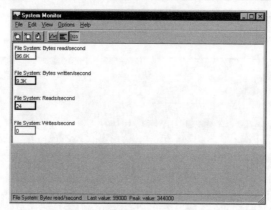

Figure 21.9 *Displaying System Monitor numeric values.*

To select the System Monitor chart type, select the View menu and choose the option that corresponds to the chart type you desire.

Customizing the System Monitor's Charting Interval

By default, the System Monitor checks your system every three seconds to obtain the information it charts. Because the System Monitor itself uses resources such as memory and kernel processor time, you probably don't want the System Monitor to examine your system more frequently. If, for example, you direct the System Monitor to examine your system every second, the System Monitor's processing will start to influence the data the system monitor charts. To change the System Monitor chart interval, perform these steps:

1. Select the Options menu and choose Chart. The System Monitor will display the Options dialog box, as shown in Figure 21.10.

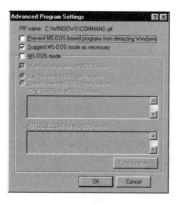

Figure 21.10 *The Options dialog box.*

2. Using your mouse, drag the slider left or right to decrease or increase the System Monitor's examination interval.

3. Choose OK.

Using the System Monitor Toolbar

To help you perform common operations quickly, the System Monitor provides a toolbar, whose buttons Table 21 defines. If your System Monitor window does not have a toolbar, select the View menu Toolbar option.

Button	Purpose
	Adds an item to the monitor's list
	Removes an item from the monitor's list
	Edits the item's chart display
	Displays line charts
	Displays bar charts
	Displays numeric charts

Table 21 The purpose of System Monitor toolbar buttons.

MONITORING A REMOTE COMPUTER

If you are responsible for managing the computers that reside within a local-area network, you can use the System Monitor to examine other computers within your network. To use the System Monitor to examine a remote computer, perform these steps:

1. Select the File menu Connect option. The System Monitor, in turn, will display the Connect dialog box, as shown in Figure 21.11.

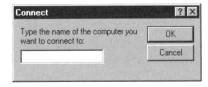

Figure 21.11 The Connect dialog box.

2. Type in the name of the remote computer you want to monitor.
3. Choose OK.

Remember, because the remote computer must monitor and send data across the network, your monitoring activity will influence the remote computer's data.

UNDERSTANDING THE WINDOWS 95 KERNEL

The Windows 95 operating system consists of three key parts: the user component, which manages the user interface (how users interact with the operating system); the graphical device interface (GDI), which manages the display of windows and their contents on the screen; and the kernel. The kernel is the core of the operating system. In other words, the kernel performs very low-level operations, such as managing memory and controlling hardware, as well as running and managing programs. Most of the operating system is built on top of the kernel. Because the kernel performs critical tasks, you can learn much about your system by monitoring kernel operations. The System Monitor lets you watch these kernel characteristics:

- The percentage of the time the processor is busy (in use)
- The number of system-wide threads
- The number of system-wide virtual machines

The processor's busy time lets you track how busy your processor really is. If, for example, your processor is busy much of the time, upgrading your processor will have a big impact on your system performance. On the other hand, if your processor has little to no busy time, you are getting your money's worth from your current processor, and you would not improve your system performance by upgrading to a faster processor. In the short term, if your processor is very busy, you may need to run fewer programs at one time. Related to the number of programs running in your system is your system's memory use. If you see high processor use and little free memory, Windows 95 may be spending considerable time trying to fit more programs into memory than your system has room for. In such cases, you need to add more memory to your system.

The System Monitor displays the busy time as a percentage. If you upgrade to a faster processor, you should see improved performance, and you should also see your processor's percentage of idle time decrease. The faster processor should require less time to get your work done, which will mean the processor will be busy less of the time. Think of a thread as the list of instructions your program executes. Under MS-DOS, programs have only one thread of execution. Windows 95 programs, however, can consist of one or more threads of execution. Using multiple threads of execution, a program can do two or more things at the same time. A word processor, for example, might use one thread of execution to process the keystrokes you type, a second to print your document while you work, and a third to check your document's spelling behind the scenes. Just as Windows 95 shares your processor among all the programs you run at the same time, Windows 95 also shares processing time among threads of execution. In this way, the word processor's three threads of execution appear to execute at the same time.

If your system slows down and you have only a few programs running, use the System Monitor to check the number of threads in your system. It's possible that one or more programs you are running is using multiple threads. The Windows 95 kernel manages each thread in your system. As the number of threads in your system increases, so, too, will your system kernel processor usage. Windows 95 uses virtual machines to trick programs into thinking each has the entire system to itself. Using virtual machines, Windows 95 gives each MS-DOS-based program the illusion it is running on a PC by itself—a PC with 640K of conventional memory, its own video memory and device drivers, and so on. Although Windows 95's use of virtual machines provides a powerful solution for MS-DOS-based programs, virtual machines can consume considerable system resources. As such, if your system slows, take note of the number of virtual machines you are using.

Understanding the Windows 95 File System

If you are familiar with MS-DOS and Windows 3.1, you may know that to improve performance, many users run a special disk-caching software called SMARTDRV.EXE. A disk cache improves your system performance by reducing the number of slow disk read-and-write operations your system must perform.

Although faster and faster disk drives continually appear on the marketplace, the disk's mechanical nature makes even the fastest disk slow in comparison to your PC's electronic counterparts, such as memory and the CPU. As such, to improve performance, the goal of a disk cache is to reduce slow disk operations. Here's how.

When Windows 95 creates a disk cache, it reserves a large section of your computer's fast electronic memory (RAM) to hold information that your programs read from and write to disk. When a program reads information from a file on disk, for example, the operating system reads not only the information the program requests, but also a little extra. The operating system places the data, and the little extra data, into the disk cache (the buffer) that resides in your computer's fast RAM. Later, should the program need more information from the disk file, the operating system checks to see if the cache already has the desired information in memory. If the cache contains the information, the operating system can immediately retrieve the information and give it to the program, without having to perform slow disk-read operations.

21: IMPROVING WINDOWS 95'S PERFORMANCE

Under Windows 3.1, you used a program called SMARTDRV.EXE to create a disk cache. With Windows 95, however, the disk cache is built in. In other words, you don't need a program such as SMARTDRV.EXE to create a cache with Windows 95. Instead, Windows 95 provides its own.

In addition to using a cache to reduce disk-read operations, Windows 95 also uses a cache to reduce disk-write operations. As you a have learned, a disk cache reduces read operations by allowing Windows 95 to read extra data from disk into memory each time it performs a read operation. Later, when the programs asks Windows 95 for more data from disk, Windows 95 may find the data in the cache, which eliminates its need to perform the slow disk read. For disk-write operations, on the other hand, Windows 95 uses the cache to consolidate data in memory that it needs to write to disk. In other words, when your programs writes information to a file, Windows 95 may not immediately record the data on disk. Instead, Windows 95 may hold the data (briefly) in its cache. Once Windows 95 accumulates sufficient data, it then writes (flushes) the cache to disk.

It's important you understand that it is because of the disk cache that you need to shutdown Windows 95 before you turn off your computer. For example, assume that you had just told your word processor to save your important memo to a file on disk. For your part, you feel comfortable that your data is saved as soon as your word processor returns from the Save dialog box. However, because Windows 95 is caching the data behind the scenes, your memo may not have been written to disk when you thought. As such, if you turn off your PC's power before Windows 95 flushes the cache to disk, the information the cache contained will be lost. It's important that you remember that disk caching improves your system performance significantly. As such, you want Windows 95 to use a cache. However, because Windows 95 uses the cache, you must ensure that you always shutdown Windows 95 before you power off your PC.

Unlike Windows 3.1, where you could specify the exact cache size you desired, Windows 95 gives you less control over your disk-cache size. To specify Windows 95 file-system settings, perform these steps:

1. Select the Start menu Settings option and choose Control Panel. Windows 95, in turn, will display the Control Panel window.

2. Double-click your mouse on the System icon. Windows 95 will open the System Properties dialog box.

3. Click your mouse on the Performance tab. Windows 95 will display the Performance page ,as shown in Figure 21.12.

Figure 21.12 *The System Properties Performance page.*

399

4. Click your mouse on the File System button. Windows 95 will display the File System Properties dialog box, as shown in Figure 21.13.

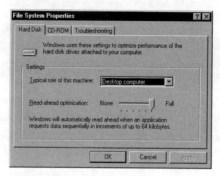

Figure 21.13 *The File System Properties dialog box.*

5. Open the Typical role of this machine pull-down list and select the option that best describes your computer.

6. Use the slide bar to specify how much extra data (in Kb) you want Windows 95 to read each time your program performs a disk-read operation. If you work with large files, such as a database program, select full optimization.

7. Choose OK.

Note: *If your system has a CD-ROM drive, you can use the File System Properties CD-ROM tab to specify your CD-ROM type and the CD-ROM cache size you desire.*

Using the System Monitor, you can examine the following file-system items:

- Bytes Read/Second — The number of bytes (in Kb) your system reads from disk per second

- Bytes Written/Second — The number of bytes (in Kb) your system writes to disk per second

- Dirty data — The amount of data (in Kb) that resides within the cache that your system must still write to disk

- Reads/Second — The number of disk-read requests your system performs per second

- Writes/Second — The number of disk-write requests your system performs per second

As the numbers on your File System charts increase, first determine if one program (such as a database) is performing a considerable number of disk operations. Also, if your system has limited free memory, the disk activity may be due to Windows 95 paging and swapping information (as discussed later in this chapter) between your disk and memory. If you determine that paging and swapping is the cause of your system's disk activity, you need to run fewer programs at the same time or install more memory. If you find that your programs simply perform a large number of file operations, you may improve your system performance by installing a faster disk drive or faster disk controller. If you have time, experiment with the size of the file-system read-ahead buffer and try to determine the setting that is best for you.

Understanding Windows 95 Memory Management

As you know, Windows 95 lets you run two or more programs at the same time. Before a program can run, the program must reside within your computer's random access memory (RAM). When you use Windows 95 to run multiple programs at the same time, Windows 95 loads each program into different locations in memory and ensures that one program does not interfere with another. Eventually, if you run a lot of programs at the same time, Windows 95 will run out of places to put the programs in memory. At that time, Windows 95 will swap one or more programs temporarily from memory to disk to make room for the new program. Should you click on the window of one of the programs Windows 95 has swapped to disk, Windows 95 will swap out a different program, giving it room to swap your selected program back into memory.

As you have learned, because your disk is a mechanical device, it is much slower than your computer's electronic components. When Windows 95 starts swapping programs in and out of memory, it performs many disk operations which significantly slow down your system. In fact, when you click on a window to select a program, you may experience a long delay and actually hear your disk drive as Windows 95 moves programs between your PC's memory and disk.

When Windows 95 starts swapping programs in this way, you will see the kernel-processing percentage increase, the number of disk read-and-write operations increase, and the amount of free memory decrease. Your solutions to swapping are to run fewer programs at the same time or to buy and install more memory. In fact, if you normally use Windows 95 to run several different programs at the same time, you should use at least 16Mb of RAM.

When Windows 95 swaps programs from memory to disk, Windows 95 places the programs it removes from memory into a *swap file* that resides on your disk. Using the System Monitor's Memory Manager items, you can view the swap file's current size and use. If you have used Windows 3.1 in the past, you may recall that Windows 3.1 let users define their system's swap file size and type (permanent or temporary). Although Windows 95 will let you use the Control Panel System entry to specify a Windows 95 swap file size, most users should let Windows 95 determine their system's swap file size for them.

As Windows 95-based programs increase their capabilities, they also increase their size. Rather than loading an entire program into memory, Windows 95 divides a program into fixed-sized pieces, called *pages*. When a program first runs, Windows 95 loads part of the program into RAM. For example, Windows 95 might load one-third of the program's pages into RAM, leaving two-thirds of the pages on disk. As the program executes, the program may need instructions or data that reside on a page that is not in memory. The program's attempt to access the missing page generates a *page fault*. When Windows 95 detects the page fault, Windows 95 loads the page from disk into memory. The process of loading pages into memory as the program needs them is *demand paging*. Over time, Windows 95 may determine that a program is not using some of its pages, and Windows 95 will move the pages from RAM to free up memory. Using the System Monitor, you can watch Windows 95 move pages in and out of memory.

Normally, Windows 95 will perform considerable paging when you first run a program. If you find that Windows 95 is constantly moving pages in and out of memory, first try shutting down one or two programs. If Windows 95's high rate of paging continues, end all your programs and restart your system. If, after you restart your system, the high rate of paging continues, you will need to add more memory to your system.

Figure 21.14 illustrates how the System Monitor will appear if you track all kernel, file system, and memory management items.

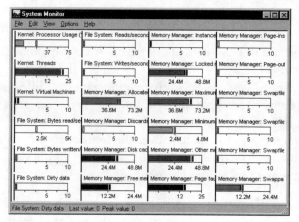

Figure 21.14 Monitoring all aspects of Windows 95.

Using the Resource Meter

As briefly discussed, Windows 95 consists of three key pieces, the kernel, the user component, and the graphics (GDI) component. For Windows 95 to perform well, each of these three items must have sufficient memory and other system resources. If any of these three components has insufficient resources, Windows 95 will slow down and may not be able run additional programs. Normally, when Windows 95 runs out of resources in this way, you should end the programs you are running and restart your system.

To help you monitor your system resources, Windows 95 provides the Resource Meter shown in Figure 21.15.

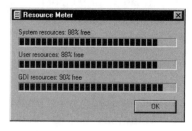

Figure 21.15 The Resource Meter.

As you can see, the Resource Meter tracks available resources for the three parts of Windows 95. To run the Resource Meter, perform these steps:

1. Select the Start menu Programs option and choose Accessories.
2. Within the Accessories menu, select the System Tools menu and choose Resource Meter.

Note: *If your system does not have the Resource Meter, use the Control Panel Add/Remove Programs entry to install the Resource Meter. You will need your Windows 95 CD-ROM or floppy disks.*

Defragment Your Disk on a Regular Basis

If, when you start a program, the program seems to take quite some time to load, files on your disk may have become fragmented. A fragmented file is a file whose contents do not reside in consecutive storage locations on your disk. Instead, the file's contents my be dispersed in storage locations spread across your disk. File fragmentation occurs naturally as you create, delete, and edit documents on your disk. The data that resides in a fragmented file is safe and you can fully access it. The problem with fragmented files is that they decrease your system's performance.

> *Running the Resource Meter Each Time You Start Windows 95*
>
>
> If you use the Resource Meter to monitor your system on a regular basis, you may want Windows 95 automatically to run the Resource Meter each time your system starts. To add the Resource Meter to the Startup folder that contains programs Windows 95 will run each time your system starts, perform these steps:
>
> 1. Using the Windows 95 Explorer, locate the file RSRCMTR.EXE in the Windows folder.
> 2. Click your mouse on the Resource Meter file and select the Edit menu Copy option.
> 3. Using the Explorer, open the \Windows\Start Menu\Programs\Startup folder.
> 4. Select the Edit menu Paste option to place a copy of the Resource Meter program into the folder.

For example, when Windows 95 reads a nonfragmented file (called a contiguous file) from your disk, Windows 95 can read consecutive storage locations on your disk as the disk spins past its read/write head. On the other hand, when Windows 95 reads a fragmented file, the disk must move its read/write head in and out to access the file-storage locations, which reside across the disk's surface. As you will recall, because disk operations are mechanical, they are much slower than the PC's electronic operations. To improve performance, you want to reduce slow disk operations. One way to reduce slow disk operations is to make sure your files are not fragmented.

In general, you can't prevent fragmented files from occurring. Instead, when you know (or suspect) that fragmented files exist, you can use the Windows 95 Disk Defragmenter program to correct the files. In short, the Disk Defragmenter examines your files and moves them, as necessary, so they reside in consecutive storage locations on your disk. Depending on the number of files you create, edit, and delete each day, how often you need to defragment your disk will vary. However, because the Disk Defragmenter program makes it easy and fast for you to defragment your disk, you should do so on a weekly basis. To use the Disk Defragmenter program to defragment your disk, perform these steps:

1. Select the Start menu Program option and choose Accessories.
2. Within the Accessories menu, select System Tools and choose Disk Defragmenter. Windows 95, in turn, will display the Select drive dialog box shown in Figure 21.16.

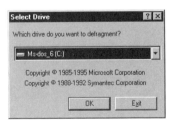

Figure 21.16 The Select Drive dialog box.

3. Within the pull-down drives list, select the disk drive you want to defragment.
4. Choose OK. The Disk Defragmenter, in turn, will display a dialog box telling you how much of your disk is fragmented.
5. Select Start. The Disk Defragmenter will defragment your disk. When the Disk Defragmenter is done, it will display a dialog box stating so and will then ask you if you want to exit the program.
6. Select Yes.

Note: Depending on your needs, the Disk Defragmenter supports options you can use to control how the Disk Defragmenter corrects the files and folders that reside on your disk. For more information on the Disk Defragmenter, turn to the book *1001 Windows 95 Tips,* Jamsa Press, 1995.

Keys to Success

As your programs become more powerful and more complex, they demand more system resources, such as a fast CPU and sufficient random access memory. In this chapter you learned how to use the System Monitor to help you detect potential bottlenecks within your system. Using the System Monitor, you can determine where your system is spending most of its processing time, and then you can upgrade that part of your system first. Over the past 21 chapters, you have learned a great deal about Windows 95. Before you continue on your journey, make sure you have learned the following key concepts:

- ✓ The Windows 95 System Monitor helps you detect bottlenecks within your system that decrease your system performance.

- ✓ The System Monitor lets you monitor your system's Kernel operations, the file system, and the Windows 95 memory use.

- ✓ Unlike Windows 3.1 which relied on the SMARTDRV program to perform disk caching, Windows 95 has built-in disk caching software in its file system.

- ✓ One of the most common causes of poor system performance is fragmented files. Fragmented files occur due to creating, deleting, and editing files. You cannot prevent fragmented files.

- ✓ When your files become fragmented, you will find that it takes Windows 95 longer to load them from disk than it may have in the past.

- ✓ To correct fragmented files, you should run the Disk Defragmenter program once a week.

INDEX

Accessibility Options component, description of the, 128
Accessories component, description of, 128
accessory programs
  Calculator
    performing simple arithmetic operations within, 247
    performing statistical operations within, 249-251
    using the scientific calculator within, 248-249
  Calendar
    cutting and pasting an appointment within, 261
    displaying appointments for a specific date, 262
    printing your appointments within, 261
    saving your appointments to a file within, 261
    setting alarms within, 262
    tracking your appointments within, 259-261
  Cardfile
    adding a card to your deck within, 256
    changing a card's contents within, 258
    controlling your card deck's display within, 258
    deleting a card from your deck within, 257
    moving through your card deck within, 257
    opening an existing card deck file within, 257
    printing your card deck within, 258
    saving your card deck to a file within, 257
    searching for a specific card within, 258-259
    using, 255-256
    using, to autodial, 259
  Character Map, 250-251
  Clipboard Viewer, 251-252
  Notepad
    creating a, document, 253
    creating a log file within, 254
    opening an existing, document, 253-254
    performing cut-and-paste operations in, 254
    searching your, document for text, 255
    using the, 252
    using, to edit ASCII files, 255
  Paint
    cutting or copying a, image to the clipboard, 268
    drawing simple illustrations within, 263-265
    printing your, image, 268
    saving screen captures within, 265
    saving your, image, 268
    using Clipart and photo images within, 266-267
  running, in Windows 95, 245-246
  WordPad
    controlling fonts within, 291-292
    controlling paragraph alignment within, 291
    customizing options within, 294-295
    ending your, session, 290
    identifying the, option, 1
    moving, text using a cut-and-paste operation, 294
    opening a, document from a file on disk, 290
    printing your, document, 290
    program, starting the, 25
    replacing, text within your document, 293-294
    saving your, document, 290
    searching your, document for specific text, 292-293
    typing within, 290
    using the, word processor, 289
active window, definition of, 54
Add New Hardware wizard, using the, 122-126
audio CD(s)
  adjusting volume for, 49
  controlling how the player uses your, play list, 200-201
  controlling, player preferences, 200
  customizing, 198
  defining the, track playback order, 199
  how the player keeps track of, understanding, 201
  naming an, track, 199
  playing, 49, 197
  recording information about, 198
  setting properties of, 50
  silencing, 51
  temporarily suspending autoplay for, 199
  working with multiple, tracks, 199
background patterns, selecting, 125-127
backup
  creating your own, set, 273-274
  files and folders, understanding the need for, 270
  file sets, 271-275
  full-disk, operation, performing a, 272-273
  operations, understanding, 271
  restoring, files, 275
  selecting your target device and saving your, 274-275
  using your, set, 275
Backup
  learning more about the, program, 276
  starting the, program, 271-272
Briefcase
  creating a, 236
  description of the, program, 130
  overriding the suggested update action, 239-240

splitting a document within, 240-241
understanding, 236
updating a selected file within, 238
updating documents within, 237-238
using the, 236-237
using, with a floppy disk, 241-242
button(s)
   Close, 4, 10, 29-30
   conversation, 80-81
   jump, 21, 80
   Maximize, 10, 28-29
   Minimize, 9, 28
   mouse, 105
   Online Registration, 4
   Open, 9-10
   Restore, 10
   Start, 2, 5-7
   Taskbar, 2, 7-8, 11
   title bar, 9-10, 28-30
   toolbar, 9-11, 28-29
   What's New, 5
Calculator
   performing simple arithmetic operations within, 247
   performing statistical operations within, 249-251
   understanding standard calculator buttons within, 247
   using the scientific calculator within, 248-249
Calendar
   cutting and pasting an appointment within, 261
   displaying appointments for a specific date within, 262
   printing your appointments within, 261
   saving your appointments to a file within, 261
   setting alarms within, 262
   tracking your appointments within, 259-261
Cardfile
   adding a card to your deck within, 256
   changing a card's contents within, 258
   controlling your card deck's display within, 258
   deleting a card from your deck within, 257
   moving through your card deck within, 257
   printing your card deck within, 258
   saving your card deck to a file within, 257
   searching for a specific card within, 258-259
   opening an existing card deck file within, 257
   using, 255-256
   using, to autodial, 259
CDs *see* audio CDs

Character Map, 250-251
check boxes, Taskbar, 58
Clipboard Viewer, 251-252
clock, Taskbar, using the, 86-88
Close button, description of the, 4, 10, 29-30
Communications component, description of the, 128
components
   choosing Windows 95, effectively, 133
   definition of, 130
   removing Windows 95, 133
Control menu, 27-28
Control Panel
   accessing the, 86
   exploring the, 83-85
   icon, viewing the, 148
   miscellaneous items on the, 147-148
   Password icon, 146
   tools, function of the, 85
conversation button, 80-81
customizing
   advanced system settings
      adding and removing programs, 127-128
      adding a screen saver, 93-95
      adding new hardware, 121-125
      calibrating a joystick, 137-139
      changing passwords, 144-145
      creating a startup disk, 133-134
      for international use, 146-147
      miscellaneous Control Panel items, 147-148
      removing a Windows 95 component, 133
      setting passwords, 143-144
      using ODBC, 139-143
      working with fonts, 134-137
   audio CDs
      adjusting volume for, 49
      playing, 49
      setting properties of, 50
      silencing, 51
   common hardware
      Control Panel, 83-86
      date-and-time, 86-87
      energy-saving features, 95-96
      keyboard, 102-104
      modem, 108-115
      mouse, 104-108
      password protection, 131

printer, 115-119
sounds, 119-120
time zone, 88-89
Desktop
appearance, 89-102
scaling fonts, 100-101
selecting a display adapter and monitor, 101-102
setting colors and Desktop area, 100
using an appearance scheme, 96-99
display, 89-93
international settings, 146-147
Start menu
adding a program by drag-and-drop, 62
adding a program to the, 59-60
adding sounds to the, 119-120
removing a program from the, 62-63
Taskbar
changing properties of the, 57
changing width of the, 56
volume control, adjusting, 48-49
date-and-time, setting and adjusting the, 86-88, 238
Desktop
changing display settings for the, 99
cleaning the, 36
customizing the
appearance, 89-102
scaling fonts, 100-101
selecting a display adapter and monitor, 101-102
setting colors and Desktop area, 100
using an appearance scheme, 96-99
description of the,
icons, 2
properties sheets, customizing, 42-45, 146
right-clicking on, to display pop-up menus, 40
dialog boxes,
recognizing Windows 95 and Windows 3.1, 163
working with, 42
Disk Tools component, description of the, 128
display, customizing the, 89-93
displaying a window full-screen, 8-9
docking bay, using a, 233-234
documents
shortcut icons for, 18-19
opening, 16
DOS and Windows 95
background processing, by controlling
fonts, 385

memory use, 385
screen display, 386
settings, 383-385, 387-388
properties, 382
CONFIG.SYS and AUTOEXEC.BAT within, 377
location of command storage, understanding, 376
DOS-based programs, running, 373-374
DOS-based program window, closing a, 374
DOS
command line, accessing the, 375-376
mode, starting your system within, 377-379
windows, 379-382
DriveSpace
compressing a disk, using, 281
compressing a floppy disk, 282
doubling your disk's storage capacity, 280
learning more about, 283
uncompressing a drive, using, 282-283
understanding host and compressed drives, 281-282
e-mail (electronic mail)
bulletin boards, 184-186
Categories
accessing Internet newsgroups, using, 188-190
browsing a folder hierarchy, using, 187
chats, online, 182-184
Favorite Places,
creating shortcuts to, 186
saving, 181
visiting a chat area, 182-184
Microsoft Mail
sending, messages, 180
understanding, 178-180
energy-saving features, 95-96
fax(es)
cover sheet, creating a, 341-352
customizing, settings, 338
drag-and-drop, 341
-on-demand message, requesting a, 341
Microsoft Fax, preparing to use, 343-344
receiving, 337, 342-343
retrying an unsuccessful, transmission, 340
sending, 337-341
file system, Windows 95 *see also* backup
browsing drives and directories within the, 155-157
browsing folders within the, 158
drive letters, 151
8.3 alias, 152, 155

extensions, 152
file icons, 157-158
long filenames, 154
naming drives, directories, and files, 150-151
pathnames in MS-DOS, 153-154
understanding the, 149-150
using, in MS-DOS and Windows 3.1, 155
using the toolbar in a folder window, 159-162
viewing the full MS-DOS names, 162
folders
browsing, 158
definition of, 14
opening, 16-17
starting programs from, 16
font(s)
installing a new, 136-137
viewing a, 135-136
working with, 134-135
hard disk, exploring your system's, 15
hardware
adding new, 121-122
Control Panel, exploring the, 83-85
installing, with a vendor-supplied disk, 126
system locks, 124
typical, additions, 123
understanding why Windows 95 needs to detect, 123
using the Add New Hardware wizard, 122
hardware operations, managing low-level
specifying a device's interrupt request line, 366
understanding base memory addresses, 365
understanding hardware conflicts, 366-367
using the Windows 95 Device Manager
to change device settings, 371
to print your device settings, 368
to recognize hardware conflicts, 369
to remove a device, 371
to specify new device settings, 369-370
to troubleshoot hardware conflicts, 367-368
Help
accessing, 66-67
button, 68-70
contents, browsing the, 69-70
conversation buttons, using the, 80
index, 21-23, 70-72
jump buttons, using the, 78-80
keywords, searching for, 22, 72-74

on the Help Topics sheet, 67-68
starting, from the Start menu, 67
topics
adding notes to, 76-77
browsing, 20-21
copying, 75-76
printing, 74-75
Topics sheet, 20-21
understanding, 19, 65-67
using in a program, 78
HyperTerminal
connecting to a remote computer, using, 285-287
downloading a file, using, 288
learning more about, 288
session, ending your, 288
icon(s)
file extension, 157-158
identifying types of, 17-18, 309
purpose of, 2
index, 21-23, 70-72
Internet (Net)
access provider(s)
connecting to, 223-224
costs, 215
information you must get from your, 217
addresses and hostnames, understanding, 217-218
connecting to the, using an online service, 214
description of the, 213-214
paying for connection to the, 214
TCP/IP networking
configuring your, settings, 220
establishing a, dial-up connection, 220-223
setting up Windows 95 to use, 218-220
World Wide Web (WWW) and the, 215-217
browsing "surfing" the, 228
understanding, homepages, 217
understanding, information retrieval, 217
understanding, site addresses, 216
viewing a, site's document, 215-216
Internet (Net)-based software in Windows 95
ftp
transferring files from a remote computer, 226-227
using to download a Web browser, 227
ping, testing a remote computer using, 224
Telnet, connecting to a remote computer, 225-226
interrupt request, definition of, 366

joystick, customizing a, 137-139
jump buttons
   definition of, 78-80
keyboard, controlling the, 102-104
keypress combinations, using the access menus, 41
keyword, searching for a, 22
Maximize button, 10, 28-29
memory management, understanding Windows 95, 401
menu(s)
   bar, 26
   Control, 27
   important facts about, 40-41
   Start, *see* Start menu
   Taskbar, 41
   types of
      pop-up, 12, 38-39
      pull-down, 38
      submenus, 38, 40
   using, with the keyboard, 41
Microsoft Exchange
   adding to the startup group, 346
   address-book
      managing your personal, entries, 352
      understanding and using your, 350-351
      using a personal distribution-list, 353
   component, description of the, 128
   composing a fax within, 349
   e-mail (electronic mail)
      attaching a file to your, message, 349
      receiving, from your Internet-based account, 349
      sending an, message from within, 348
   how, uses Explorer-like folders, 348
   learning more about, 349
   starting, 346-348
   fax(es)
      cover sheet, creating a, 341-342
      customizing, settings, 338
      drag-and-drop, 341
      -on-demand message, requesting a, 341
      Microsoft Fax, preparing to use, 343-344
      receiving, 337, 342-343
      retrying an unsuccessful, transmission, 340
      sending, 337-341
Microsoft Fax component, description of the, 129
Microsoft Network (MSN)
   browsing, 187
   component, description of the, 129, 167
   e-mail
      bulletin boards, using, 184-186
      Categories, 186-190
      chats, online, understanding, 182
      Favorite Places, 181-186
      sending, messages, 180
      understanding, 178-180
   fees, 173
   mechanics of using, 168-169
   signing up for, 169-173
   starting, 174
   using
      Help system, 177
      images, understanding how, draws, 175
      MSN Today, 174-176
MIDI, description of, 196
Minimize button, 9, 28
modem
   adding a new, 109-112
   customizing a, 108-115
   description of a, 108
   diagnostics, 114-115
   properties, 112-114
   setting up a, 108
   specifying a generic, 111-112
   understanding, speeds, 108
mouse
   buttons, managing the, 105
   clicking and double-clicking, 3, 12-14, 18
   customizing the, 104-105, 146
   moving and dragging, 3
   pointer, 106-108
   pressing and releasing, 3
   right button on the
      understanding the, 12-14
      using the, to identify an icon, 18
   using a, to drag-and-drop objects, 3
Microsoft Network component, 129
MS-DOS
   pathnames in, 153
   understanding directory names and filenames, 151-152
   viewing the full, names, 162
MSN Today, 174-176
Multilanguage Support component, 129

multimedia
  advanced, settings, 208-209
  audio CDs
    adjusting volume for, 49
    controlling, player preferences, 200
    customizing, 198
    defining the, track playback order, 199
    how the player keeps track of, understanding, 201
    naming an, track, 199
    playing, 49, 197
    recording information about, 198
    setting properties of, 50
    silencing, 51
    temporarily suspending autoplay, 199
    working with multiple tracks, 199
  controls, 205-206
  definition of, 191-192
  files, viewing information about, 210
  icon, 147
  sound
    controlling, file formats, 204-205
    editing a, file, 202-203
    recorder, using the, 201
    recording a new, 202
  understanding, 192
  volume controls, understanding, 197, 209
  Windows 95
    autoplay, 194
    media player, 194
    plug and play, 194
    sample AVI files, 193
    sound files, 195
    support, 193
Multimedia component, description of the, 129
Multimedia Properties sheet, using
  to control advanced multimedia settings, 208-209
  to control audio CD playback, 207
  to control audio devices, 206
  to control MIDI playback, 207-208
  to control video playback, 206
Multimedia component, description of the, 129
multiple programs, running, 32-33
multitasking, definition of, 32
My Computer
  arranging icons with, windows, 321
  changing the appearance of, 322
  controlling, windows, 320-321
  description of the, folder contents, 14
  icon, 5, 14
  learning more about, 319
  running programs from within, 321
network(s) *see also* notebook PC
  folders
    allowing remote users to use your, 358
    sharing, 358
    turning off shared access to, 359
  getting around your, 355-356
  local-area, sharing resources on a, 355
  mapping to a, drive, 356-357
  monitoring your PC's, use, 363-364
  printer
    allowing remote users to use your, 358
    sharing, 359-360
    turning off, sharing, 360
  using Windows 95 dial-up networking, 361-363
notebook PC
  connecting your, to your desktop PC, 231-236
  definition of, 230
  Briefcase
    creating a, 236
    keeping your date-and-time correct while using, 238
    overriding the suggested update action, 239
    splitting a document within, 240-241
    understanding, 236
    updating a selected file within, 238
    using, 236-237
    using documents within, 237-238
    using, with a floppy disk, 241-242
  networking
    learning a network computer's name, 233
    understanding, 231
    understanding shared folders, 233
    using a direct cable connection, 234-235
    using a docking bay, 233-234
  power management
    suspending your notebook PC, 243
    using Windows 95, 242-243
  using PCMCIA cards, 243-244
  using Windows 95 on your, 229-231
Notepad
  creating a, document, 253
  creating a log file within, 254

opening an existing, document, 253-254
performing cut-and-paste operations within, 254
searching your, document for text, 255
using the, 252
using, to edit ASCII files, 255
object-oriented environment, 13
ODBC (Open Database Connectivity Software)
adding data sources, 141
applications, preparing your system to use, 143
setting up and installing, drives, 140
understanding, 139
online Help
purpose of, 19, 65-67
using, in a program, 78
Online Registration, 4
online service(s) *see also* Microsoft Network (MSN)
description of, 168
fees, 173
mechanics of using, 168
signing up for, 169-173
Paint
cutting or copying a, image to the clipboard, 268
drawing simple illustrations within, 263-265
printing your, image, 268
saving screen captures within, 265
saving your, image, 268
using Clipart and photo images within, 266-267
parallel ports, understanding, 152
password(s)
changing your, 144
protection, 131
setting, 143-144
setting, user profile options, 145
specifying a new, 145
pathnames in MS-DOS, 153
performance *see* Windows 95 performance
Phone Dialer
changing a speed dial entry, using, 284
placing a call, using, 283-284
speed dialing, using, 283-284
understanding, properties, 285
pixels, understanding, 90
point-to-point protocol (PPP), 23
pop-up menus, 12, 39
printer
controlling a, 118-119

customizing a, 115-119
installing a, 115-117
working with a, 115
program(s)
adding and removing, 127-128
adding a, to the Start menu, 59-60
installing Windows 95, 128
running
multiple, 10
single, 7
using a shortcut, 18
starting
from folders, 16
from the Start menu, 5-6, 10-11, 31-33
from the Taskbar, 52
switching between, 11
by clicking on program windows, 38
by clicking on Taskbar buttons, 37-38, 54
by using the keyboard, 37-38
Properties sheets, customizing, 42-45, 146
providers *see* Internet access providers
pull-down menus, 38
Recycle Bin,
changing the appearance of the, 324
using the, 322-323
Registration, Online, 4
root directory, definition of, 151
ScanDisk
controlling, advanced options, 279
controlling, through test options, 279
performing a, standard test, 277-278
performing a, thorough test, 278-279
screen savers, 93-95
serial ports, understanding, 152
sheets
Help Topics, 20-21
in Windows 95, 20
Misc, 387-388
Properties, customizing, 42-45
shortcuts
to documents, 18-19
to programs, 18
using keypress combinations, 41
sounds, assigning system, 119-120
Start button, running programs from the, 5-14

Start menu
  accessing the
    with the keyboard, 41
    with the mouse, 6
  customizing the
    adding a program by drag-and-drop, 62
    adding a program to the, 59-60
    adding sounds to the, 119-120
    removing a program from the, 62-63
  Run option, 53-54
  selecting submenus from the, 40
  using the, 30-32
    to run multiple programs, 10-11, 32-33
    to run one program, 7
startup disk, creating a, 133
status bar, description of the, 27
submenus, 38-40
system settings, advanced, customizing
  adding and removing programs, 127-128
  adding a screen saver, 93-95
  adding new hardware, 121-125
  calibrating a joystick, 137-139
  changing passwords, 144-145
  creating a startup disk, 133-134
  for international use, 146-147
  miscellaneous Control Panel items, 147-148
  removing a Windows 95 component, 133
  setting passwords, 143-144
  using ODBC, 139-143
  working with fonts, 134-137
tape drives, 270
Taskbar
  adjusting date-and-time from the, 51-52
  buttons, 2, 7-8, 11
  changing location and size of the, 55
  changing properties of the, 57
  changing width of the, 56-57
  check boxes, 58
  clock, using the, 86-88
  customizing the, 47-49, 56-57
  finding and hiding the, 58-59
  moving the, 55
  parts of the, 47-48
  Properties sheet, 44-45
  purpose of the, 2, 7-8, 47
  speaker icon, 49
  starting programs from the, 52-53
  switching between programs from the, 11, 54
  volume control, 48-51
TCP/IP networking
  configuring your, settings, 220
  establishing a, dial-up connection, 220-223
  setting up Windows 95 to use, 218-220
time zone, setting the, 121-124
title bar
  buttons, 9, 28-30
  description of the, 26
toolbar
  buttons, 11, 27, 161
  description of the, 26
  using the, in a folder window, 159-162
volume controls, 49-51, 197
wallpaper, 91-92, 125-126, 128-129
Welcome window, 3-4
window(s)
  closing, 12
  description of a, 25-26
  displaying contents of a, full screen, 8-9
  maximizing, 10, 37
  minimizing, 9, 36
  moving, 12, 33-34
  piles, 34
  rearranging, 33, 35
  resizing, 12, 34
  restoring, 10
Windows 95
  components
    adding, 128-133
    choosing, effectively, 133
    definition of, 130
    list of, 133
    removing, 133
  Desktop
    changing display settings for the, 99
    cleaning the, 36
    customizing the, 96-102
  DOS and, understanding, 373
  ending a session in, 24
  file system
    browsing drives and directories within the, 155-157
    browsing folders within the, 158
    drive letters, 151

Index

8.3 alias, understanding the, 152, 155
extensions, understanding, 152
long filenames, 154
naming drives, directories, and files, 150-151
Open and Save As dialog boxes, 162-165
pathnames in MS-DOS, 153-154
understanding the, 149-150
using, in MS-DOS and Windows 3.1, 155, 163
using the toolbar in a folder window, 159
viewing folders within your system's hard drive, 155
viewing the full MS-DOS names, 162
international settings, 146-147
Internet (Net)-based software in
  ftp
    transferring files with, 226-227
    using to download a Web browser, 227
  ping, testing a remote computer using, 224
  Telnet, connecting to a remote computer, 225-226
installing, 1-2
memory management, controlling, 401
new features of, 5
performance, improving, 391
  customizing a monitored item, 396
  customizing the system monitor's chart interval, 396
  defragmenting your disk regularly, 402
  measuring your system bottlenecks, 392-393
  monitoring a remote computer, 397
  removing an item from your monitor list, 394
  understanding hertz and megahertz (MHz), 392
  understanding system bottlenecks, 391
  understanding the Windows 95 file system, 398-400
  understanding the Windows 95 kernel, 397-398
  using the Resource Meter, 402-403
  using the system monitor toolbar, 386-397
power management, 242-243
programs *see* accessory programs
Properties sheets, customizing, 42-45, 146
starting, 2-3
subcomponents, description of, 129
system tools, description of the, 269-270
  Backup *see also* backup
    learning more about the, program, 276
    starting the, program, 271-272
  DriveSpace
    compressing a disk, using, 281
    compressing a floppy disk, using, 282
    doubling your disk's storage capacity, using, 280
    learning more about, 283
    uncompressing a drive, using, 282-283
  HyperTerminal
    connecting to a remote computer, using, 285-287
    downloading a file, using, 288
    learning more about, 288
    session, ending your, 288
  Phone Dialer
    changing a speed dial entry, using, 284
    placing a call, using, 283-284
    speed dialing, using, 283-284
    understanding, properties, 285
  ScanDisk
    controlling, advanced options, 279
    controlling, through test options, 279
    performing a, standard test, 277-278
    performing a, thorough test, 278-279
  tape drives, 270
  windows *see* Windows 95 windows
Windows 95 Explorer
  display, changing the, 299-300
  documents, 300, 303-304
  file properties, understanding, 314-315
  files, 308-316
  files and folders, 302-308, 316
  filenames, icons for, 309
  file types, registering, within a program, 304-306
  folders, 300-301
  running programs within the, 308
  Send To option, understanding the, 313
  starting the, 297-299
  Toolbar, understanding the, 315-316
  windows, 310-312
Windows 95 Registry
  branch, exporting a, 333
  creating a, Editor shortcut, 328
  database, 329, 335-336
  entries, 327-328, 331-332
  exploiting the, 335
  file, importing a, 333-334
  understanding the, 325-327
  Windows 3.1 INI files and, 330
Windows 95 windows
  closing, 12

common characteristics of
  Close button, 4, 10
  Control menu, 1
  Maximize button, 10, 28-29
  Minimize button, 9, 28
  Restore button, 10
  Taskbar, 2, 7-8, 11
  title bar, 26, 28-30
displaying full screen, 8-9
exploring, 7-8
maximizing, 10, 28-29
minimizing, 9, 28
moving, 12, 33
resizing, 12, 34
Windows 3.1, 150-155
wizards, explanation of, 110
WordPad
  controlling fonts within, 291-292
  controlling paragraph alignment within, 291
  customizing options within, 294-295
  ending your, session, 290
  identifying the, option, 1
  moving, text using a cut-and-paste operation, 294
  opening a, document from a file on disk, 290
  printing your, document, 290
  program, starting, 25
  replacing, text within your document, 293-294
  saving your, document, 290
  searching your, document for specific text, 292-293
  typing within, 290
  using the, word processor, 289
work area, description of, 27
World Wide Web (WWW), 215-217
  browsing "surfing" the, 228
  homepages, 217
  information retrieval, 217
  site addresses, 216
  viewing a, site's document, 215-216